FreeBSD Handbook 2/2

A catalogue record for this book is available from the Hong Kong Public Libraries.

Published in Hong Kong by Samurai Media Limited.

Email: info@samuraimedia.org

ISBN 978-988-8381-14-2

FreeBSD Handbook

Revision: 47376
2015-09-06 by wblock.
Copyright © 1995, 1996, 1997, 1998, 1999, 2000, 2001, 2002, 2003, 2004, 2005, 2006, 2007, 2008, 2009, 2010, 2011, 2012, 2013, 2014, 2015 The FreeBSD Documentation Project

Abstract

Welcome to FreeBSD! This handbook covers the installation and day to day use of *FreeBSD 9.3-RELEASE* and *FreeBSD 10.2-RELEASE*. This manual is a *work in progress* and is the work of many individuals. As such, some sections may become dated and require updating. If you are interested in helping out with this project, send email to the FreeBSD documentation project mailing list. The latest version of this document is always available from the FreeBSD web site (previous versions of this handbook can be obtained from http://docs.Free-BSD.org/doc/). It may also be downloaded in a variety of formats and compression options from the FreeBSD FTP server or one of the numerous mirror sites. If you would prefer to have a hard copy of the handbook, you can purchase one at the FreeBSD Mall. You may also want to search the handbook.

Important

Table of Contents

List of Figures

List of Tables

List of Examples

Chapter 20. Other File Systems

Written by Tom Rhodes.

20.1. Synopsis

File systems are an integral part of any operating system. They allow users to upload and store files, provide access to data, and make hard drives useful. Different operating systems differ in their native file system. Traditionally, the native FreeBSD file system has been the Unix File System UFS which has been modernized as UFS2. Since FreeBSD 7.0, the Z File System (ZFS) is also available as a native file system. See Chapter 19, *The Z File System (ZFS)* for more information.

In addition to its native file systems, FreeBSD supports a multitude of other file systems so that data from other operating systems can be accessed locally, such as data stored on locally attached USB storage devices, flash drives, and hard disks. This includes support for the Linux® Extended File System (EXT) and the Reiser file system.

There are different levels of FreeBSD support for the various file systems. Some require a kernel module to be loaded and others may require a toolset to be installed. Some non-native file system support is full read-write while others are read-only.

After reading this chapter, you will know:

- The difference between native and supported file systems.

- Which file systems are supported by FreeBSD.

- How to enable, configure, access, and make use of non-native file systems.

Before reading this chapter, you should:

- Understand UNIX® and FreeBSD basics.

- Be familiar with the basics of kernel configuration and compilation.

- Feel comfortable installing software in FreeBSD.

- Have some familiarity with disks, storage, and device names in FreeBSD.

20.2. Linux® File Systems

FreeBSD provides built-in support for several Linux® file systems. This section demonstrates how to load support for and how to mount the supported Linux® file systems.

20.2.1. ext2

Kernel support for ext2 file systems has been available since FreeBSD 2.2. In FreeBSD 8.x and earlier, the code is licensed under the GPL. Since FreeBSD 9.0, the code has been rewritten and is now BSD licensed.

The ext2fs(5) driver allows the FreeBSD kernel to both read and write to ext2 file systems.

Note

This driver can also be used to access ext3 and ext4 file systems. However, ext3 journaling, extended attributes, and inodes greater than 128-bytes are not supported. Support for ext4 is read-only.

To access an ext file system, first load the kernel loadable module:

```
# kldload ext2fs
```

Then, mount the ext volume by specifying its FreeBSD partition name and an existing mount point. This example mounts /dev/ad1s1 on /mnt:

```
# mount -t ext2fs /dev/ad1s1 /mnt
```

20.2.2. ReiserFS

FreeBSD provides read-only support for The Reiser file system, ReiserFS.

To load the reiserfs(5) driver:

```
# kldload reiserfs
```

Then, to mount a ReiserFS volume located on /dev/ad1s1 :

```
# mount -t reiserfs /dev/ad1s1 /mnt
```

Chapter 21. Virtualization

Contributed by Murray Stokely.
bhyve section by Allan Jude.

21.1. Synopsis

Virtualization software allows multiple operating systems to run simultaneously on the same computer. Such software systems for PCs often involve a host operating system which runs the virtualization software and supports any number of guest operating systems.

After reading this chapter, you will know:

- The difference between a host operating system and a guest operating system.

- How to install FreeBSD on an Intel®-based Apple® Mac® computer.

- How to install FreeBSD on Microsoft® Windows® with Virtual PC.

- How to install FreeBSD as a guest in bhyve.

- How to tune a FreeBSD system for best performance under virtualization.

Before reading this chapter, you should:

- Understand the basics of UNIX® and FreeBSD.

- Know how to install FreeBSD.

- Know how to set up a network connection.

- Know how to install additional third-party software.

21.2. FreeBSD as a Guest on Parallels for Mac OS® X

Parallels Desktop for Mac® is a commercial software product available for Intel® based Apple® Mac® computers running Mac OS® 10.4.6 or higher. FreeBSD is a fully supported guest operating system. Once Parallels has been installed on Mac OS® X, the user must configure a virtual machine and then install the desired guest operating system.

21.2.1. Installing FreeBSD on Parallels/Mac OS® X

The first step in installing FreeBSD on Parallels is to create a new virtual machine for installing FreeBSD. Select FreeBSD as the Guest OS Type when prompted:

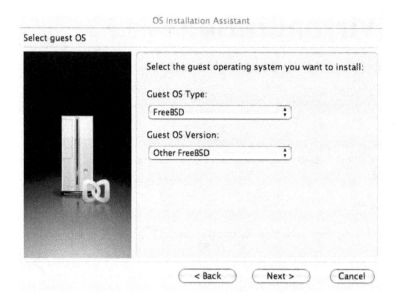

Choose a reasonable amount of disk and memory depending on the plans for this virtual FreeBSD instance. 4GB of disk space and 512MB of RAM work well for most uses of FreeBSD under Parallels:

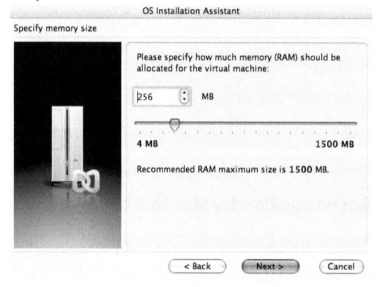

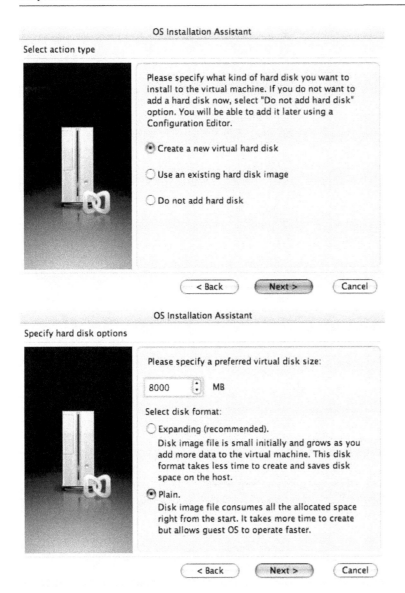

OS Installation Assistant

Select action type

Please specify what kind of hard disk you want to install to the virtual machine. If you do not want to add a hard disk now, select "Do not add hard disk" option. You will be able to add it later using a Configuration Editor.

⦿ Create a new virtual hard disk

◯ Use an existing hard disk image

◯ Do not add hard disk

(< Back) (Next >) (Cancel)

OS Installation Assistant

Specify hard disk options

Please specify a preferred virtual disk size:

[8000 ⦿] MB

Select disk format:

◯ Expanding (recommended).
   Disk image file is small initially and grows as you add more data to the virtual machine. This disk format takes less time to create and saves disk space on the host.

⦿ Plain.
   Disk image file consumes all the allocated space right from the start. It takes more time to create but allows guest OS to operate faster.

(< Back) (Next >) (Cancel)

OS Installation Assistant

Select an image file

Please specify a location of the hard disk image file:

;/murray/Library/Parallels/otherbsd/otherbsd.hdd [...]

[< Back]   [Next >]   [Cancel]

Select the type of networking and a network interface:

OS Installation Assistant

Select a type of networking

Please specify what kind of networking you want to add to the virtual machine:

⦿ Bridged Ethernet.
Use this option if you need to connect your virtual machine to Local or Wide Area Network.

○ Host-only Networking.
Use this option if you want to create private network shared with the host.

○ Shared Networking.
Use this option if you need to provide Network Address Translation feature to your virtual machine.

○ Networking is not required.

[< Back]   [Next >]   [Cancel]

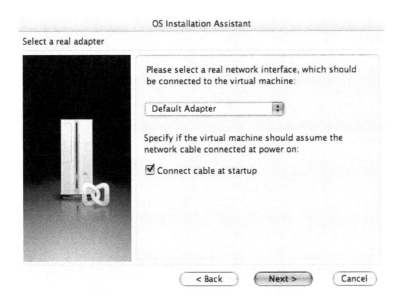

Save and finish the configuration:

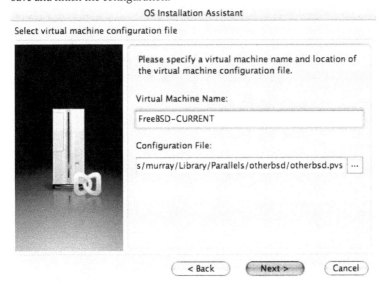

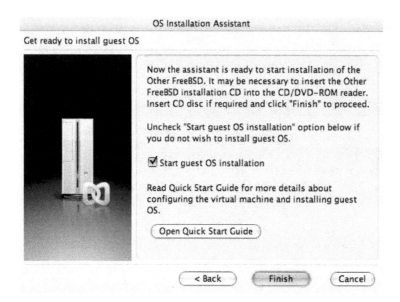

After the FreeBSD virtual machine has been created, FreeBSD can be installed on it. This is best done with an official FreeBSD CD/DVD or with an ISO image downloaded from an official FTP site. Copy the appropriate ISO image to the local Mac® filesystem or insert a CD/DVD in the Mac®'s CD-ROM drive. Click on the disc icon in the bottom right corner of the FreeBSD Parallels window. This will bring up a window that can be used to associate the CD-ROM drive in the virtual machine with the ISO file on disk or with the real CD-ROM drive.

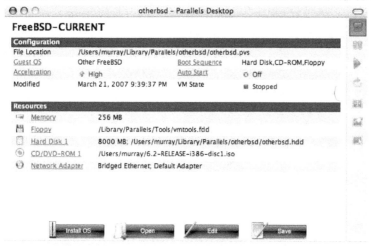

Once this association with the CD-ROM source has been made, reboot the FreeBSD virtual machine by clicking the reboot icon. Parallels will reboot with a special BIOS that first checks if there is a CD-ROM.

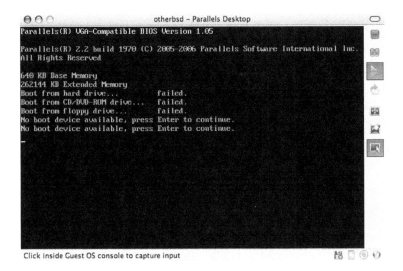

In this case it will find the FreeBSD installation media and begin a normal FreeBSD installation. Perform the installation, but do not attempt to configure Xorg at this time.

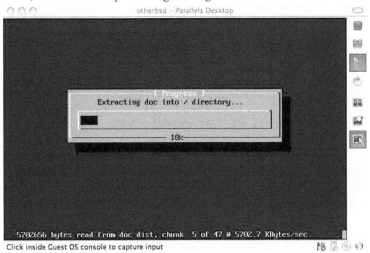

When the installation is finished, reboot into the newly installed FreeBSD virtual machine.

21.2.2. Configuring FreeBSD on Parallels

After FreeBSD has been successfully installed on Mac OS® X with Parallels, there are a number of configuration steps that can be taken to optimize the system for virtualized operation.

1. Set Boot Loader Variables

    The most important step is to reduce the `kern.hz` tunable to reduce the CPU utilization of FreeBSD under the Parallels environment. This is accomplished by adding the following line to `/boot/loader.conf` :

    ```
    kern.hz=100
    ```

    Without this setting, an idle FreeBSD Parallels guest will use roughly 15% of the CPU of a single processor iMac®. After this change the usage will be closer to 5%.

2. Create a New Kernel Configuration File

    All of the SCSI, FireWire, and USB device drivers can be removed from a custom kernel configuration file. Parallels provides a virtual network adapter used by the ed(4) driver, so all network devices except for ed(4) and miibus(4) can be removed from the kernel.

3. Configure Networking

    The most basic networking setup uses DHCP to connect the virtual machine to the same local area network as the host Mac®. This can be accomplished by adding `ifconfig_ed0="DHCP"` to `/etc/rc.conf` . More advanced networking setups are described in Chapter 30, *Advanced Networking*.

21.3. FreeBSD as a Guest on Virtual PC for Windows®

Virtual PC for Windows® is a Microsoft® software product available for free download. See this website for the system requirements. Once Virtual PC has been installed on Microsoft® Windows®, the user can configure a virtual machine and then install the desired guest operating system.

21.3.1. Installing FreeBSD on Virtual PC

The first step in installing FreeBSD on Virtual PC is to create a new virtual machine for installing FreeBSD. Select Create a virtual machine when prompted:

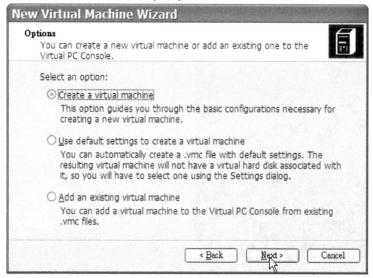

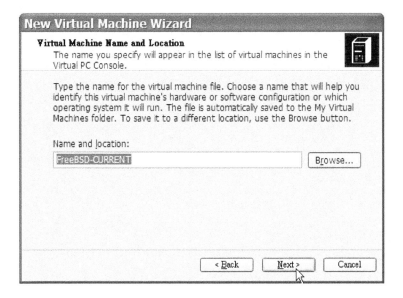

Select Other as the Operating system when prompted:

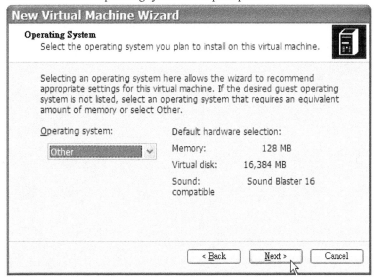

Then, choose a reasonable amount of disk and memory depending on the plans for this virtual FreeBSD instance. 4GB of disk space and 512MB of RAM work well for most uses of FreeBSD under Virtual PC:

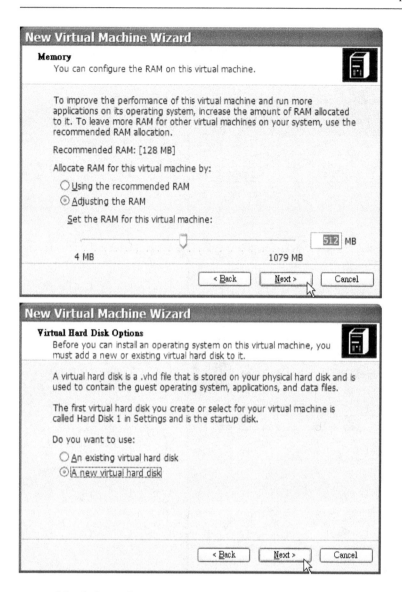

Save and finish the configuration:

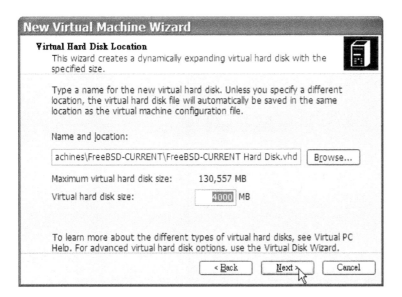

Select the FreeBSD virtual machine and click Settings, then set the type of networking and a network interface:

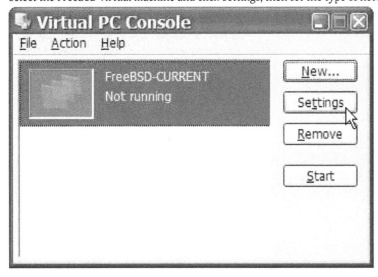

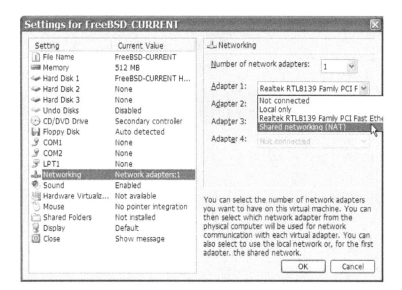

After the FreeBSD virtual machine has been created, FreeBSD can be installed on it. This is best done with an official FreeBSD CD/DVD or with an ISO image downloaded from an official FTP site. Copy the appropriate ISO image to the local Windows® filesystem or insert a CD/DVD in the CD drive, then double click on the FreeBSD virtual machine to boot. Then, click CD and choose Capture ISO Image... on the Virtual PC window. This will bring up a window where the CD-ROM drive in the virtual machine can be associated with an ISO file on disk or with the real CD-ROM drive.

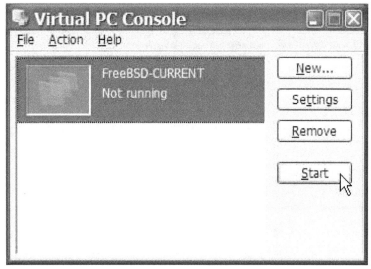

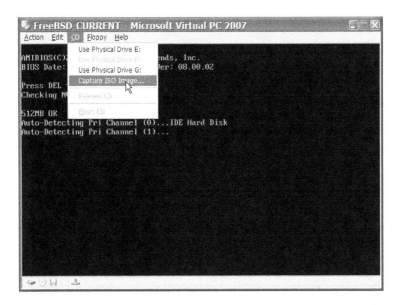

Once this association with the CD-ROM source has been made, reboot the FreeBSD virtual machine by clicking Action and Reset. Virtual PC will reboot with a special BIOS that first checks for a CD-ROM.

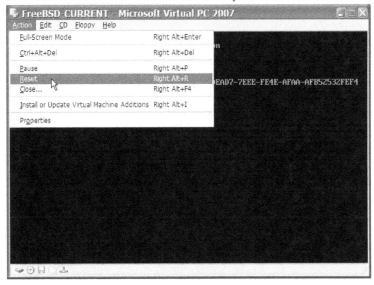

In this case it will find the FreeBSD installation media and begin a normal FreeBSD installation. Continue with the installation, but do not attempt to configure Xorg at this time.

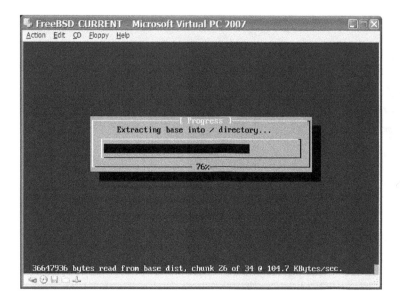

When the installation is finished, remember to eject the CD/DVD or release the ISO image. Finally, reboot into the newly installed FreeBSD virtual machine.

21.3.2. Configuring FreeBSD on Virtual PC

After FreeBSD has been successfully installed on Microsoft® Windows® with Virtual PC, there are a number of configuration steps that can be taken to optimize the system for virtualized operation.

1. Set Boot Loader Variables

    The most important step is to reduce the `kern.hz` tunable to reduce the CPU utilization of FreeBSD under the Virtual PC environment. This is accomplished by adding the following line to `/boot/loader.conf` :

    ```
    kern.hz=100
    ```

    Without this setting, an idle FreeBSD Virtual PC guest OS will use roughly 40% of the CPU of a single processor computer. After this change, the usage will be closer to 3%.

2.   Create a New Kernel Configuration File

All of the SCSI, FireWire, and USB device drivers can be removed from a custom kernel configuration file. Virtual PC provides a virtual network adapter used by the de(4) driver, so all network devices except for de(4) and miibus(4) can be removed from the kernel.

3.   Configure Networking

The most basic networking setup uses DHCP to connect the virtual machine to the same local area network as the Microsoft® Windows® host. This can be accomplished by adding `ifconfig_de0="DHCP"` to `/etc/rc.conf` . More advanced networking setups are described in Chapter 30, *Advanced Networking*.

21.4. FreeBSD as a Guest on VMware Fusion for Mac OS®

VMware Fusion for Mac® is a commercial software product available for Intel® based Apple® Mac® computers running Mac OS® 10.4.9 or higher. FreeBSD is a fully supported guest operating system. Once VMware Fusion has been installed on Mac OS® X, the user can configure a virtual machine and then install the desired guest operating system.

21.4.1. Installing FreeBSD on VMware Fusion

The first step is to start VMware Fusion which will load the Virtual Machine Library. Click New to create the virtual machine:

This will load the New Virtual Machine Assistant. Click Continue to proceed:

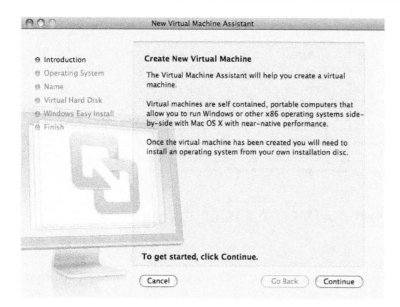

Select Other as the Operating System and either FreeBSD or FreeBSD 64-bit, as the Version when prompted:

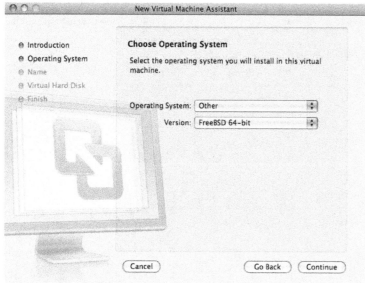

Choose the name of the virtual machine and the directory where it should be saved:

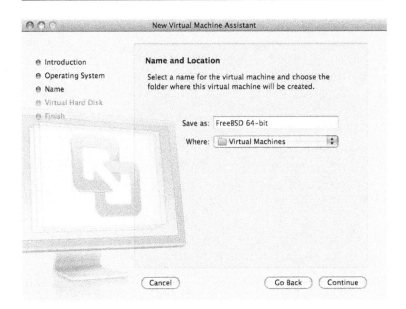

Choose the size of the Virtual Hard Disk for the virtual machine:

Choose the method to install the virtual machine, either from an ISO image or from a CD/DVD:

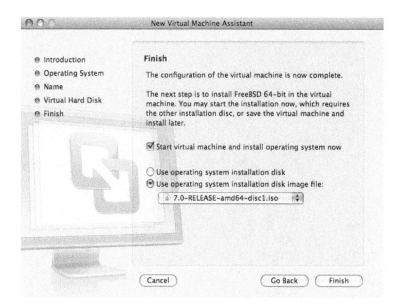

Click Finish and the virtual machine will boot:

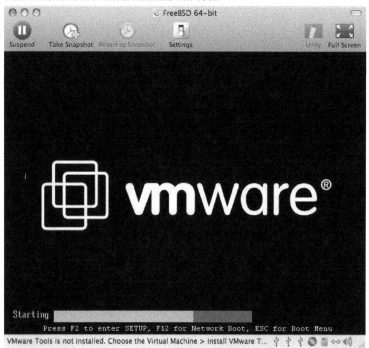

Install FreeBSD as usual:

Once the install is complete, the settings of the virtual machine can be modified, such as memory usage:

Note

The System Hardware settings of the virtual machine cannot be modified while the virtual machine is running.

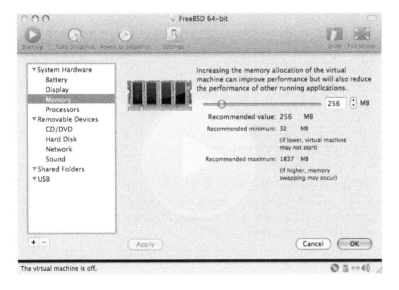

The number of CPUs the virtual machine will have access to:

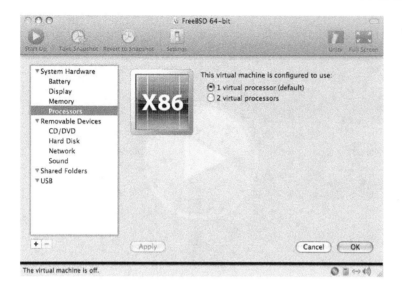

The status of the CD-ROM device. Normally the CD/DVD/ISO is disconnected from the virtual machine when it is no longer needed.

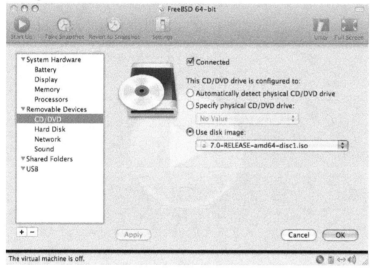

The last thing to change is how the virtual machine will connect to the network. To allow connections to the virtual machine from other machines besides the host, choose Connect directly to the physical network (Bridged). Otherwise, Share the host's internet connection (NAT) is preferred so that the virtual machine can have access to the Internet, but the network cannot access the virtual machine.

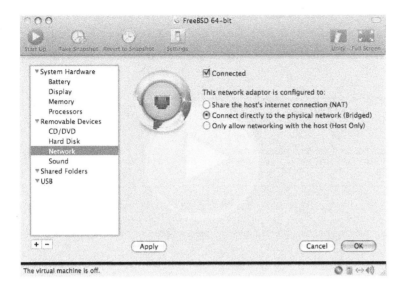

After modifying the settings, boot the newly installed FreeBSD virtual machine.

21.4.2. Configuring FreeBSD on VMware Fusion

After FreeBSD has been successfully installed on Mac OS® X with VMware Fusion, there are a number of configuration steps that can be taken to optimize the system for virtualized operation.

1. Set Boot Loader Variables

    The most important step is to reduce the `kern.hz` tunable to reduce the CPU utilization of FreeBSD under the VMware Fusion environment. This is accomplished by adding the following line to `/boot/loader.conf` :

    ```
    kern.hz=100
    ```

    Without this setting, an idle FreeBSD VMware Fusion guest will use roughly 15% of the CPU of a single processor iMac®. After this change, the usage will be closer to 5%.

2. Create a New Kernel Configuration File

    All of the FireWire, and USB device drivers can be removed from a custom kernel configuration file. VMware Fusion provides a virtual network adapter used by the em(4) driver, so all network devices except for em(4) can be removed from the kernel.

3. Configure Networking

    The most basic networking setup uses DHCP to connect the virtual machine to the same local area network as the host Mac®. This can be accomplished by adding `ifconfig_em0="DHCP"` to `/etc/rc.conf` . More advanced networking setups are described in Chapter 30, *Advanced Networking*.

21.5. VirtualBox™ Guest Additions on a FreeBSD Guest

FreeBSD works well as a guest in VirtualBox™. The virtualization software is available for most common operating systems, including FreeBSD itself.

The VirtualBox™ guest additions provide support for:

*   Clipboard sharing.

*   Mouse pointer integration.

- Host time synchronization.

- Window scaling.

- Seamless mode.

 Note

These commands are run in the FreeBSD guest.

First, install the emulators/virtualbox-ose-additions package or port in the FreeBSD guest. This will install the port:

```
# cd /usr/ports/emulators/virtualbox-ose-additions && make install clean
```

Add these lines to /etc/rc.conf :

```
vboxguest_enable="YES"
vboxservice_enable="YES"
```

If ntpd(8) or ntpdate(8) is used, disable host time synchronization:

```
vboxservice_flags="--disable-timesync"
```

Xorg will automatically recognize the vboxvideo driver. It can also be manually entered in /etc/X11/xorg.conf :

```
Section "Device"
 Identifier "Card0"
 Driver "vboxvideo"
 VendorName "InnoTek Systemberatung GmbH"
 BoardName "VirtualBox Graphics Adapter"
EndSection
```

To use the vboxmouse driver, adjust the mouse section in /etc/X11/xorg.conf :

```
Section "InputDevice"
 Identifier "Mouse0"
 Driver "vboxmouse"
EndSection
```

HAL users should create the following /usr/local/etc/hal/fdi/policy/90-vboxguest.fdi   or copy it from /usr/local/share/hal/fdi/policy/10osvendor/90-vboxguest.fdi :

```
<?xml version="1.0" encoding="utf-8"?>
<!--
# Sun VirtualBox
# Hal driver description for the vboxmouse driver
# $Id: chapter.xml,v 1.33 2012-03-17 04:53:52 eadler Exp $

Copyright (C) 2008-2009 Sun Microsystems, Inc.

This file is part of VirtualBox Open Source Edition (OSE, as
available from http://www.virtualbox.org. This file is free software;
you can redistribute it and/or modify it under the terms of the GNU
General Public License (GPL) as published by the Free Software
Foundation, in version 2 as it comes in the "COPYING" file of the
VirtualBox OSE distribution. VirtualBox OSE is distributed in the
hope that it will be useful, but WITHOUT ANY WARRANTY of any kind.

Please contact Sun Microsystems, Inc., 4150 Network Circle, Santa
Clara, CA 95054 USA or visit http://www.sun.com if you need
additional information or have any questions.
```

```
-->
<deviceinfo version="0.2">
  <device>
    <match key="info.subsystem" string="pci">
      <match key="info.product" string="VirtualBox guest Service">
        <append key="info.capabilities" type="strlist">input</append>
 <append key="info.capabilities" type="strlist">input.mouse</append>
        <merge key="input.x11_driver" type="string">vboxmouse</merge>
 <merge key="input.device" type="string">/dev/vboxguest</merge>
      </match>
    </match>
  </device>
</deviceinfo>
```

21.6. FreeBSD as a Host with VirtualBox

VirtualBox™ is an actively developed, complete virtualization package, that is available for most operating systems including Windows®, Mac OS®, Linux® and FreeBSD. It is equally capable of running Windows® or UNIX®-like guests. It is released as open source software, but with closed-source components available in a separate extension pack. These components include support for USB 2.0 devices. More information may be found on the "Downloads" page of the VirtualBox™ wiki. Currently, these extensions are not available for FreeBSD.

21.6.1. Installing VirtualBox™

VirtualBox™ is available as a FreeBSD package or port in emulators/virtualbox-ose. The port can be installed using these commands:

```
# cd /usr/ports/emulators/virtualbox-ose
# make install clean
```

One useful option in the port's configuration menu is the GuestAdditions suite of programs. These provide a number of useful features in guest operating systems, like mouse pointer integration (allowing the mouse to be shared between host and guest without the need to press a special keyboard shortcut to switch) and faster video rendering, especially in Windows® guests. The guest additions are available in the Devices menu, after the installation of the guest is finished.

A few configuration changes are needed before VirtualBox™ is started for the first time. The port installs a kernel module in /boot/modules which must be loaded into the running kernel:

```
# kldload vboxdrv
```

To ensure the module is always loaded after a reboot, add this line to /boot/loader.conf :

```
vboxdrv_load="YES"
```

To use the kernel modules that allow bridged or host-only networking, add this line to /etc/rc.conf and reboot the computer:

```
vboxnet_enable="YES"
```

The vboxusers group is created during installation of VirtualBox™. All users that need access to VirtualBox™ will have to be added as members of this group. pw can be used to add new members:

```
# pw groupmod vboxusers -m yourusername
```

The default permissions for /dev/vboxnetctl are restrictive and need to be changed for bridged networking:

```
# chown root:vboxusers /dev/vboxnetctl
# chmod 0660 /dev/vboxnetctl
```

To make this permissions change permanent, add these lines to /etc/devfs.conf:

```
own     vboxnetctl root:vboxusers
perm    vboxnetctl 0660
```

To launch VirtualBox™, type from a Xorg session:

```
% VirtualBox
```

For more information on configuring and using VirtualBox™, refer to the official website. For FreeBSD-specific information and troubleshooting instructions, refer to the relevant page in the FreeBSD wiki.

21.6.2. VirtualBox™ USB Support

In order to be able to read and write to USB devices, users need to be members of operator:

```
# pw groupmod operator -m jerry
```

Then, add the following to /etc/devfs.rules, or create this file if it does not exist yet:

```
[system=10]
add path 'usb/*' mode 0660 group operator
```

To load these new rules, add the following to /etc/rc.conf :

```
devfs_system_ruleset="system"
```

Then, restart devfs:

```
# service devfs restart
```

USB can now be enabled in the guest operating system. USB devices should be visible in the VirtualBox™ preferences.

21.6.3. VirtualBox™ Host DVD/CD Access

Access to the host DVD/CD drives from guests is achieved through the sharing of the physical drives. Within VirtualBox™, this is set up from the Storage window in the Settings of the virtual machine. If needed, create an empty IDE CD/DVD device first. Then choose the Host Drive from the popup menu for the virtual CD/DVD drive selection. A checkbox labeled Passthrough will appear. This allows the virtual machine to use the hardware directly. For example, audio CDs or the burner will only function if this option is selected.

HAL needs to run for VirtualBox™ DVD/CD functions to work, so enable it in /etc/rc.conf and start it if it is not already running:

```
hald_enable="YES"
```

```
# service hald start
```

In order for users to be able to use VirtualBox™ DVD/CD functions, they need access to /dev/xpt0 , /dev/cd N, and /dev/pass N. This is usually achieved by making the user a member of operator. Permissions to these devices have to be corrected by adding these lines to /etc/devfs.conf :

```
perm cd* 0660
perm xpt0 0660
perm pass* 0660
```

```
# service devfs restart
```

21.7. FreeBSD as a Host with bhyve

Starting with FreeBSD 10.0-RELEASE, the bhyve BSD-licensed hypervisor is part of the base system. This hypervisor supports a number of guests, including FreeBSD, OpenBSD, and many Linux® distributions. Currently, bhyve only supports a serial console and does not emulate a graphical console. As a legacy-free hypervisor, it relies on the virtualization offload features of newer CPUs, instead of translating instructions and manually managing memory mappings.

Due to the design of bhyve, it requires a computer with a newer processor that supports Intel® Extended Page Tables (EPT) or AMD® Rapid Virtualization Indexing (RVI), also known as Nested Page Tables (NPT). In addition, to host Linux® guests, or FreeBSD guests with more than one vCPU, VMX unrestricted mode support (UG) is also required. Most newer processors, specifically the Intel® Core™ i3/i5/i7 and Intel® Xeon™ E3/E5/E7, support these features. UG support was introduced with Intel's Westmere micro-architecture. For a complete list of Intel® processors that support EPT, refer to http://ark.intel.com/search/advanced?s=t&ExtendedPageTables=true. RVI is found on the third generation and later of the AMD Opteron™ (Barcelona) processors. The easiest way to tell if a processor will support bhyve is to run dmesg or look in /var/run/dmesg.boot for the POPCNT processor feature flag on the Features2 line and EPT and UG on the VT-x line.

21.7.1. Preparing the Host

The first step to creating a virtual machine in bhyve is configuring the host system. First, load the bhyve kernel module:

```
# kldload vmm
```

Then, create a tap interface for the network device in the virtual machine to attach to. In order for the network device to participate in the network, also create a bridge interface containing the tap interface and the physical interface as members. In this example, the physical interface is *igb0*:

```
# ifconfig tap0 create
# sysctl net.link.tap.up_on_open=1
net.link.tap.up_on_open: 0 -> 1
# ifconfig bridge0 create
# ifconfig bridge0 addm igb0 addm tap0
# ifconfig bridge0 up
```

21.7.2. Creating a FreeBSD Guest

Create a file to use as the virtual disk for the guest machine. Specify the size and name of the virtual disk:

```
# truncate -s 16G guest.img
```

Download an installation image of FreeBSD to install:

```
# fetch ftp://ftp.freebsd.org/pub/FreeBSD/releases/ISO-IMAGES/10.2/FreeBSD-10.2-RELEASE-
amd64-bootonly.iso
FreeBSD-10.2-RELEASE-amd64-bootonly.iso          100% of  230 MB  570 kBps 06m17s
```

FreeBSD comes with an example script for running a virtual machine in bhyve. The script will start the virtual machine and run it in a loop, so it will automatically restart if it crashes. The script takes a number of options to control the configuration of the machine: -c controls the number of virtual CPUs, -m limits the amount of memory available to the guest, -t defines which tap device to use, -d indicates which disk image to use, -i tells bhyve to boot from the CD image instead of the disk, and -I defines which CD image to use. The last parameter is the name of the virtual machine, used to track the running machines. This example starts the virtual machine in installation mode:

```
# sh /usr/share/examples/bhyve/vmrun.sh -c   4 -m 1024M -t tap0 -d guest.img -i -
I FreeBSD-10.0-RELEASE-amd64-bootonly.iso     guestname
```

The virtual machine will boot and start the installer. After installing a system in the virtual machine, when the system asks about dropping in to a shell at the end of the installation, choose Yes. A small change needs to be made to make the system start with a serial console. Edit /etc/ttys and replace the existing ttyu0 line with:

```
ttyu0   "/usr/libexec/getty 3wire"   xterm  on secure
```

Note

Beginning with FreeBSD 9.3-RELEASE and 10.1-RELEASE the console is configured automatically.

Reboot the virtual machine. While rebooting the virtual machine causes bhyve to exit, the vmrun.sh script runs bhyve in a loop and will automatically restart it. When this happens, choose the reboot option from the boot loader menu in order to escape the loop. Now the guest can be started from the virtual disk:

```
# sh /usr/share/examples/bhyve/vmrun.sh -c  4 -m 1024M -t tap0 -d guest.img guestname
```

21.7.3. Creating a Linux® Guest

In order to boot operating systems other than FreeBSD, the sysutils/grub2-bhyve port must be first installed.

Next, create a file to use as the virtual disk for the guest machine:

```
# truncate -s 16G linux.img
```

Starting a virtual machine with bhyve is a two step process. First a kernel must be loaded, then the guest can be started. The Linux® kernel is loaded with sysutils/grub2-bhyve. Create a device.map that grub will use to map the virtual devices to the files on the host system:

```
(hd0) ./linux.img
(cd0) ./somelinux.iso
```

Use sysutils/grub2-bhyve to load the Linux® kernel from the ISO image:

```
# grub-bhyve -m device.map -r cd0 -M  1024M linuxguest
```

This will start grub. If the installation CD contains a grub.cfg, a menu will be displayed. If not, the vmlinuz and initrd files must be located and loaded manually:

```
grub> ls
(hd0) (cd0) (cd0,msdos1) (host)
grub> ls (cd0)/isolinux
boot.cat boot.msg grub.conf initrd.img isolinux.bin isolinux.cfg memtest
splash.jpg TRANS.TBL vesamenu.c32 vmlinuz
grub> linux (cd0)/isolinux/vmlinuz
grub> initrd (cd0)/isolinux/initrd.img
grub> boot
```

Now that the Linux® kernel is loaded, the guest can be started:

```
# bhyve -A -H -P -s 0:0,hostbridge -s 1:0,lpc -s 2:0,virtio-net,  tap1 -s 3:0,virtio-blk, ./
linux.img \
   -s 4:0,ahci-cd, ./somelinux.iso  -l com1,stdio -c 4 -m 1024M linuxguest
```

The system will boot and start the installer. After installing a system in the virtual machine, reboot the virtual machine. This will cause bhyve to exit. The instance of the virtual machine needs to be destroyed before it can be started again:

```
# bhyvectl --destroy --vm= linuxguest
```

Now the guest can be started directly from the virtual disk. Load the kernel:

```
# grub-bhyve -m device.map -r hd0,msdos1 -M  1024M linuxguest
grub> ls
(hd0) (hd0,msdos2) (hd0,msdos1) (cd0) (cd0,msdos1) (host)
```

```
(lvm/VolGroup-lv_swap) (lvm/VolGroup-lv_root)
grub> ls (hd0,msdos1)/
lost+found/ grub/ efi/ System.map-2.6.32-431.el6.x86_64 config-2.6.32-431.el6.x
86_64 symvers-2.6.32-431.el6.x86_64.gz vmlinuz-2.6.32-431.el6.x86_64
initramfs-2.6.32-431.el6.x86_64.img
grub> linux (hd0,msdos1)/vmlinuz-2.6.32-431.el6.x86_64 root=/dev/mapper/VolGroup-lv_root
grub> initrd (hd0,msdos1)/initramfs-2.6.32-431.el6.x86_64.img
grub> boot
```

Boot the virtual machine:

```
# bhyve -A -H -P -s 0:0,hostbridge -s 1:0,lpc -s 2:0,virtio-net,  tap1 \
    -s 3:0,virtio-blk, ./linux.img -l com1,stdio -c 4 -m 1024M linuxguest
```

Linux® will now boot in the virtual machine and eventually present you with the login prompt. Login and use the virtual machine. When you are finished, reboot the virtual machine to exit bhyve. Destroy the virtual machine instance:

```
# bhyvectl --destroy --vm= linuxguest
```

21.7.4. Using ZFS with bhyve Guests

If ZFS is available on the host machine, using ZFS volumes instead of disk image files can provide significant performance benefits for the guest VMs. A ZFS volume can be created by:

```
# zfs create -V 16G -o volmode=dev  zroot/linuxdisk0
```

When starting the VM, specify the ZFS volume as the disk drive:

```
# bhyve -A -H -P -s 0:0,hostbridge -s 1:0,lpc -s 2:0,virtio-net,  tap1 -s3:0,virtio-blk, /dev/
zvol/zroot/linuxdisk0 \
    -l com1,stdio -c 4 -m 1024M linuxguest
```

21.7.5. Virtual Machine Consoles

It is advantageous to wrap the bhyve console in a session management tool such as sysutils/tmux or sysutils/screen in order to detach and reattach to the console. It is also possible to have the console of bhyve be a null modem device that can be accessed with cu. To do this, load the nmdm kernel module and replace -l com1,stdio with -l com1,/dev/nmdm0A. The /dev/nmdm devices are created automatically as needed, where each is a pair, corresponding to the two ends of the null modem cable (/dev/nmdm1A and /dev/nmdm1B). See nmdm(4) for more information.

```
# kldload nmdm
# bhyve -A -H -P -s 0:0,hostbridge -s 1:0,lpc -s 2:0,virtio-net,  tap1 -s 3:0,virtio-blk, ./
linux.img \
    -l com1,/dev/nmdm0A -c 4 -m 1024M linuxguest
# cu -l /dev/nmdm0B -s 9600
Connected

Ubuntu 13.10 handbook ttyS0

handbook login:
```

21.7.6. Managing Virtual Machines

A device node is created in /dev/vmm for each virtual machine. This allows the administrator to easily see a list of the running virtual machines:

```
# ls -al /dev/vmm
total 1
dr-xr-xr-x   2 root   wheel    512 Mar 17 12:19 ./
dr-xr-xr-x  14 root   wheel    512 Mar 17 06:38 ../
crw-------   1 root   wheel  0x1a2 Mar 17 12:20 guestname
crw-------   1 root   wheel  0x19f Mar 17 12:19 linuxguest
```

```
crw-------   1 root  wheel  0x1a1 Mar 17 12:19 otherguest
```

A specified virtual machine can be destroyed using `bhyvectl`:

```
# bhyvectl --destroy --vm=guestname
```

21.7.7. Persistent Configuration

In order to configure the system to start bhyve guests at boot time, add the following entries to in the following files:

1. **/etc/sysctl.conf**

   ```
   net.link.tap.up_on_open=1
   ```

2. **/boot/loader.conf**

   ```
   vmm_load="YES"
   nmdm_load="YES"
   if_bridge_load="YES"
   if_tap_load="YES"
   ```

3. **/etc/rc.conf**

   ```
   cloned_interfaces="bridge0 tap0"
   ifconfig_bridge0="addm igb0 addm tap0"
   ```

Chapter 22. Localization - i18n/L10n Usage and Setup

Contributed by Andrey Chernov.
Rewritten by Michael C. Wu.

22.1. Synopsis

FreeBSD is a distributed project with users and contributors located all over the world. As such, FreeBSD supports localization into many languages, allowing users to view, input, or process data in non-English languages. One can choose from most of the major languages, including, but not limited to: Chinese, German, Japanese, Korean, French, Russian, and Vietnamese.

The term internationalization has been shortened to i18n, which represents the number of letters between the first and the last letters of `internationalization`. L10n uses the same naming scheme, but from `localization`. The i18n/L10n methods, protocols, and applications allow users to use languages of their choice.

This chapter discusses the internationalization and localization features of FreeBSD. After reading this chapter, you will know:

- How locale names are constructed.

- How to set the locale for a login shell.

- How to configure the console for non-English languages.

- How to configure Xorg for different languages.

- How to find i18n-compliant applications.

- Where to find more information for configuring specific languages.

Before reading this chapter, you should:

- Know how to install additional third-party applications.

22.2. Using Localization

Localization settings are based on three components: the language code, country code, and encoding. Locale names are constructed from these parts as follows:

```
LanguageCode _CountryCode .Encoding
```

The *LanguageCode* and *CountryCode* are used to determine the country and the specific language variation. Table 22.1, "Common Language and Country Codes" provides some examples of *LanguageCode_CountryCode*:

Table 22.1. Common Language and Country Codes

LanguageCode_Country Code	Description
en_US	English, United States
ru_RU	Russian, Russia
zh_TW	Traditional Chinese, Taiwan

A complete listing of available locales can be found by typing:

```
% locale -a | more
```

To determine the current locale setting:

```
% locale
```

Language specific character sets, such as ISO8859-1, ISO8859-15, KOI8-R, and CP437, are described in multibyte(3). The active list of character sets can be found at the IANA Registry.

Some languages, such as Chinese or Japanese, cannot be represented using ASCII characters and require an extended language encoding using either wide or multibyte characters. Examples of wide or multibyte encodings include EUC and Big5. Older applications may mistake these encodings for control characters while newer applications usually recognize these characters. Depending on the implementation, users may be required to compile an application with wide or multibyte character support, or to configure it correctly.

Note

FreeBSD uses Xorg-compatible locale encodings.

The rest of this section describes the various methods for configuring the locale on a FreeBSD system. The next section will discuss the considerations for finding and compiling applications with i18n support.

22.2.1. Setting Locale for Login Shell

Locale settings are configured either in a user's ~/.login_conf or in the startup file of the user's shell: ~/.profile, ~/.bashrc, or ~/.cshrc.

Two environment variables should be set:

• LANG, which sets the locale

• MM_CHARSET, which sets the MIME character set used by applications

In addition to the user's shell configuration, these variables should also be set for specific application configuration and Xorg configuration.

Two methods are available for making the needed variable assignments: the login class method, which is the recommended method, and the startup file method. The next two sections demonstrate how to use both methods.

22.2.1.1. Login Classes Method

This first method is the recommended method as it assigns the required environment variables for locale name and MIME character sets for every possible shell. This setup can either be performed by each user or it can be configured for all users by the superuser.

This minimal example sets both variables for Latin-1 encoding in the .login_conf of an individual user's home directory:

```
me:\
 :charset=ISO-8859-1:\
 :lang=de_DE.ISO8859-1:
```

Here is an example of a user's ~/.login_conf that sets the variables for Traditional Chinese in BIG-5 encoding. More variables are needed because some applications do not correctly respect locale variables for Chinese, Japanese, and Korean:

```
#Users who do not wish to use monetary units or time formats
#of Taiwan can manually change each variable
me:\
  :lang=zh_TW.Big5:\
  :setenv=LC_ALL=zh_TW.Big5,LC_COLLATE=zh_TW.Big5,LC_CTYPE=zh_TW.Big5,LC_MESSAGES=zh_TW.↵
Big5,LC_MONETARY=zh_TW.Big5,LC_NUMERIC=zh_TW.Big5,LC_TIME=zh_TW.Big5:\
  :charset=big5:\
  :xmodifiers="@im=gcin": #Set gcin as the XIM Input Server
```

Alternately, the superuser can configure all users of the system for localization. The following variables in /etc/login.conf are used to set the locale and MIME character set:

```
language_name |Account Type Description :\
  :charset=MIME_charset :\
  :lang=locale_name :\
  :tc=default:
```

So, the previous Latin-1 example would look like this:

```
german|German Users Accounts:\
  :charset=ISO-8859-1:\
  :lang=de_DE.ISO8859-1:\
  :tc=default:
```

See login.conf(5) for more details about these variables.

Whenever /etc/login.conf is edited, remember to execute the following command to update the capability database:

```
# cap_mkdb /etc/login.conf
```

22.2.1.1.1. Utilities Which Change Login Classes

In addition to manually editing /etc/login.conf, several utilities are available for setting the locale for newly created users.

When using vipw to add new users, specify the *language* to set the locale:

```
user:password:1111:11:language :0:0:User Name:/home/user:/bin/sh
```

When using adduser to add new users, the default language can be pre-configured for all new users or specified for an individual user.

If all new users use the same language, set defaultclass=*language* in /etc/adduser.conf.

To override this setting when creating a user, either input the required locale at this prompt:

```
Enter login class: default []:
```

or specify the locale to set when invoking adduser:

```
# adduser -class  language
```

If pw is used to add new users, specify the locale as follows:

```
# pw useradd user_name  -L language
```

22.2.1.2. Shell Startup File Method

This second method is not recommended as each shell that is used requires manual configuration, where each shell has a different configuration file and differing syntax. As an example, to set the German language for the sh shell, these lines could be added to ~/.profile to set the shell for that user only. These lines could also be added to /etc/profile or /usr/share/skel/dot.profile to set that shell for all users:

```
LANG=de_DE.ISO8859-1; export LANG
MM_CHARSET =ISO-8859-1; export MM_CHARSET
```

However, the name of the configuration file and the syntax used differs for the csh shell. These are the equivalent settings for ~/.csh.login, /etc/csh.login, or /usr/share/skel/dot.login :

```
setenv LANG de_DE.ISO8859-1
setenv MM_CHARSET ISO-8859-1
```

To complicate matters, the syntax needed to configure Xorg in ~/.xinitrc also depends upon the shell. The first example is for the sh shell and the second is for the csh shell:

```
LANG=de_DE.ISO8859-1; export LANG
```

```
setenv LANG de_DE.ISO8859-1
```

22.2.2. Console Setup

Several localized fonts are available for the console. To see a listing of available fonts, type ls /usr/share/syscons/fonts . To configure the console font, specify the *font_name* , without the .fnt suffix, in /etc/rc.conf :

```
font8x16=font_name
font8x14=font_name
font8x8=font_name
```

The keymap and screenmap can be set by adding the following to /etc/rc.conf :

```
scrnmap=screenmap_name
keymap=keymap_name
keychange="fkey_number sequence "
```

To see the list of available screenmaps, type ls /usr/share/syscons/scrnmaps . Do not include the .scm suffix when specifying *screenmap_name*. A screenmap with a corresponding mapped font is usually needed as a workaround for expanding bit 8 to bit 9 on a VGA adapter's font character matrix so that letters are moved out of the pseudographics area if the screen font uses a bit 8 column.

To see the list of available keymaps, type ls /usr/share/syscons/keymaps . When specifying the *keymap_name* , do not include the .kbd suffix. To test keymaps without rebooting, use kbdmap(1).

The keychange entry is usually needed to program function keys to match the selected terminal type because function key sequences cannot be defined in the keymap.

Next, set the correct console terminal type in /etc/ttys for all virtual terminal entries. Table 22.2, "Defined Terminal Types for Character Sets" summarizes the available terminal types.:

Table 22.2. Defined Terminal Types for Character Sets

Character Set	Terminal Type
ISO8859-1 or ISO8859-15	cons25l1
ISO8859-2	cons25l2
ISO8859-7	cons25l7
KOI8-R	cons25r
KOI8-U	cons25u
CP437 (VGA default)	cons25
US-ASCII	cons25w

For languages with wide or multibyte characters, install a console for that language from the FreeBSD Ports Collection. The available ports are summarized in Table 22.3, "Available Console from Ports Collection". Once installed, refer to the port's `pkg-message` or man pages for configuration and usage instructions.

Table 22.3. Available Console from Ports Collection

Language	Port Location
Traditional Chinese (BIG-5)	chinese/big5con
Chinese/Japanese/Korean	chinese/cce
Chinese/Japanese/Korean	chinese/zhcon
Japanese	chinese/kon2
Japanese	japanese/kon2-14dot
Japanese	japanese/kon2-16dot

If moused is enabled in `/etc/rc.conf`, additional configuration may be required. By default, the mouse cursor of the syscons(4) driver occupies the `0xd0-0xd3` range in the character set. If the language uses this range, move the cursor's range by adding the following line to `/etc/rc.conf`:

```
mousechar_start=3
```

22.2.3. Xorg Setup

Chapter 5, *The X Window System* describes how to install and configure Xorg. When configuring Xorg for localization, additional fonts and input methods are available from the FreeBSD Ports Collection. Application specific i18n settings such as fonts and menus can be tuned in `~/.Xresources` and should allow users to view their selected language in graphical application menus.

The X Input Method (XIM) protocol is an Xorg standard for inputting non-English characters. Table 22.4, "Available Input Methods" summarizes the input method applications which are available in the FreeBSD Ports Collection. Additional Fcitx and Uim applications are also available.

Table 22.4. Available Input Methods

Language	Input Method
Chinese	chinese/gcin
Chinese	chinese/ibus-chewing
Chinese	chinese/ibus-pinyin
Chinese	chinese/oxim
Chinese	chinese/scim-fcitx
Chinese	chinese/scim-pinyin
Chinese	chinese/scim-tables
Japanese	japanese/ibus-anthy
Japanese	japanese/ibus-mozc
Japanese	japanese/ibus-skk
Japanese	japanese/im-ja
Japanese	japanese/kinput2
Japanese	japanese/scim-anthy
Japanese	japanese/scim-canna
Japanese	japanese/scim-honoka

Language	Input Method
Japanese	japanese/scim-honoka-plugin-romkan
Japanese	japanese/scim-honoka-plugin-wnn
Japanese	japanese/scim-prime
Japanese	japanese/scim-skk
Japanese	japanese/scim-tables
Japanese	japanese/scim-tomoe
Japanese	japanese/scim-uim
Japanese	japanese/skkinput
Japanese	japanese/skkinput3
Japanese	japanese/uim-anthy
Korean	korean/ibus-hangul
Korean	korean/imhangul
Korean	korean/nabi
Korean	korean/scim-hangul
Korean	korean/scim-tables
Vietnamese	vietnamese/xvnkb
Vietnamese	vietnamese/x-unikey

22.3. Finding i18n Applications

i18n applications are programmed using i18n kits under libraries. These allow developers to write a simple file and translate displayed menus and texts to each language.

The FreeBSD Ports Collection contains many applications with built-in support for wide or multibyte characters for several languages. Such applications include i18n in their names for easy identification. However, they do not always support the language needed.

Some applications can be compiled with the specific charset. This is usually done in the port's Makefile or by passing a value to configure. Refer to the i18n documentation in the respective FreeBSD port's source for more information on how to determine the needed configure value or the port's Makefile to determine which compile options to use when building the port.

22.4. Locale Configuration for Specific Languages

This section provides configuration examples for localizing a FreeBSD system for the Russian language. It then provides some additional resources for localizing other languages.

22.4.1. Russian Language (KOI8-R Encoding)

Originally contributed by Andrey Chernov.

This section shows the specific settings needed to localize a FreeBSD system for the Russian language. Refer to Using Localization for a more complete description of each type of setting.

To set this locale for the login shell, add the following lines to each user's ~/.login_conf:

```
me:My Account:\
  :charset=KOI8-R:\
```

```
:lang=ru_RU.KOI8-R:
```

To configure the console, add the following lines to /etc/rc.conf :

```
keymap="ru.koi8-r"
scrnmap="koi8-r2cp866"
font8x16="cp866b-8x16"
font8x14="cp866-8x14"
font8x8="cp866-8x8"
mousechar_start=3
```

For each ttyv entry in /etc/ttys , use cons25r as the terminal type.

To configure printing, a special output filter is needed to convert from KOI8-R to CP866 since most printers with Russian characters come with hardware code page CP866. FreeBSD includes a default filter for this purpose, /usr/libexec/lpr/ru/koi2alt . To use this filter, add this entry to /etc/printcap:

```
lp|Russian local line printer:\
 :sh:of=/usr/libexec/lpr/ru/koi2alt:\
 :lp=/dev/lpt0:sd=/var/spool/output/lpd:lf=/var/log/lpd-errs:
```

Refer to printcap(5) for a more detailed explanation.

To configure support for Russian filenames in mounted MS-DOS® file systems, include -L and the locale name when adding an entry to /etc/fstab :

```
/dev/ad0s2      /dos/c  msdos   rw,-Lru_RU.KOI8-R 0 0
```

Refer to mount_msdosfs(8) for more details.

To configure Russian fonts for Xorg, install the x11-fonts/xorg-fonts-cyrillic package. Then, check the "Files" section in /etc/X11/xorg.conf . The following line must be added *before* any other FontPath entries:

```
FontPath    "/usr/local/lib/X11/fonts/cyrillic"
```

Additional Cyrillic fonts are available in the Ports Collection.

To activate a Russian keyboard, add the following to the "Keyboard" section of /etc/xorg.conf :

```
Option "XkbLayout"   "us,ru"
Option "XkbOptions"  "grp:toggle"
```

Make sure that XkbDisable is commented out in that file.

For grp:toggle use Right Alt, for grp:ctrl_shift_toggle use Ctrl+Shift. For grp:caps_toggle use CapsLock. The old CapsLock function is still available in LAT mode only using Shift+CapsLock. grp:caps_toggle does not work in Xorg for some unknown reason.

If the keyboard has "Windows®" keys, and some non-alphabetical keys are mapped incorrectly, add the following line to /etc/xorg.conf :

```
Option "XkbVariant" ",winkeys"
```

Note

The Russian XKB keyboard may not work with non-localized applications. Minimally localized applications should call a XtSetLanguageProc (NULL, NULL, NULL); function early in the program.

See `http://koi8.pp.ru/xwin.html` for more instructions on localizing Xorg applications. For more general information about KOI8-R encoding, refer to `http://koi8.pp.ru/` .

22.4.2. Additional Language-Specific Resources

This section lists some additional resources for configuring other locales.

Traditional Chinese for Taiwan
> The FreeBSD-Taiwan Project has a Chinese HOWTO for FreeBSD at `http://netlab.cse.yzu.edu.tw/~statue/freebsd/zh-tut/` .

German Language Localization for All ISO 8859-1 Languages
> A tutorial on using umlauts on FreeBSD is available in German at `http://user.cs.tu-berlin.de/~eserte/FreeBSD/doc/umlaute/umlaute.html` .

Greek Language Localization
> A complete article on Greek support in FreeBSD is available here, in Greek only, as part of the official FreeBSD Greek documentation.

Japanese and Korean Language Localization
> For Japanese, refer to `http://www.jp.FreeBSD.org/` , and for Korean, refer to `http://www.kr.FreeBSD.org/` .

Non-English FreeBSD Documentation
> Some FreeBSD contributors have translated parts of the FreeBSD documentation to other languages. They are available through links on the FreeBSD web site or in `/usr/share/doc` .

Chapter 23. Updating and Upgrading FreeBSD

Restructured, reorganized, and parts updated by Jim Mock.
Original work by Jordan Hubbard, Poul-Henning Kamp, John Polstra and Nik Clayton.

23.1. Synopsis

FreeBSD is under constant development between releases. Some people prefer to use the officially released versions, while others prefer to keep in sync with the latest developments. However, even official releases are often updated with security and other critical fixes. Regardless of the version used, FreeBSD provides all the necessary tools to keep the system updated, and allows for easy upgrades between versions. This chapter describes how to track the development system and the basic tools for keeping a FreeBSD system up-to-date.

After reading this chapter, you will know:

- How to keep a FreeBSD system up-to-date with freebsd-update, Subversion, or CTM.

- How to compare the state of an installed system against a known pristine copy.

- How to keep the installed documentation up-to-date with Subversion or documentation ports.

- The difference between the two development branches: FreeBSD-STABLE and FreeBSD-CURRENT.

- How to rebuild and reinstall the entire base system.

Before reading this chapter, you should:

- Properly set up the network connection (Chapter 30, *Advanced Networking*).

- Know how to install additional third-party software (Chapter 4, *Installing Applications: Packages and Ports*).

Note

Throughout this chapter, svn is used to obtain and update FreeBSD sources. To use it, first install the devel/subversion port or package.

23.2. FreeBSD Update

Written by Tom Rhodes.
Based on notes provided by Colin Percival.

Applying security patches in a timely manner and upgrading to a newer release of an operating system are important aspects of ongoing system administration. FreeBSD includes a utility called freebsd-update which can be used to perform both these tasks.

This utility supports binary security and errata updates to FreeBSD, without the need to manually compile and install the patch or a new kernel. Binary updates are available for all architectures and releases currently supported by the security team. The list of supported releases and their estimated end-of-life dates are listed at http://www.FreeBSD.org/security/.

This utility also supports operating system upgrades to minor point releases as well as upgrades to another release branch. Before upgrading to a new release, review its release announcement as it contains important information pertinent to the release. Release announcements are available from `http://www.FreeBSD.org/releases/` .

 Note

If a `crontab` utilizing the features of freebsd-update(8) exists, it must be disabled before upgrading the operating system.

This section describes the configuration file used by `freebsd-update`, demonstrates how to apply a security patch and how to upgrade to a minor or major operating system release, and discusses some of the considerations when upgrading the operating system.

23.2.1. The Configuration File

The default configuration file for `freebsd-update` works as-is. Some users may wish to tweak the default configuration in `/etc/freebsd-update.conf`, allowing better control of the process. The comments in this file explain the available options, but the following may require a bit more explanation:

```
# Components of the base system which should be kept updated.
Components world kernel
```

This parameter controls which parts of FreeBSD will be kept up-to-date. The default is to update the entire base system and the kernel. Individual components can instead be specified, such as `src/base` or `src/sys`. However, the best option is to leave this at the default as changing it to include specific items requires every needed item to be listed. Over time, this could have disastrous consequences as source code and binaries may become out of sync.

```
# Paths which start with anything matching an entry in an IgnorePaths
# statement will be ignored.
IgnorePaths /boot/kernel/linker.hints
```

To leave specified directories, such as `/bin` or `/sbin`, untouched during the update process, add their paths to this statement. This option may be used to prevent `freebsd-update` from overwriting local modifications.

```
# Paths which start with anything matching an entry in an UpdateIfUnmodified
# statement will only be updated if the contents of the file have not been
# modified by the user (unless changes are merged; see below).
UpdateIfUnmodified /etc/ /var/ /root/ /.cshrc /.profile
```

This option will only update unmodified configuration files in the specified directories. Any changes made by the user will prevent the automatic updating of these files. There is another option, `KeepModifiedMetadata`, which will instruct `freebsd-update` to save the changes during the merge.

```
# When upgrading to a new FreeBSD release, files which match MergeChanges
# will have any local changes merged into the version from the new release.
MergeChanges /etc/ /var/named/etc/ /boot/device.hints
```

List of directories with configuration files that `freebsd-update` should attempt to merge. The file merge process is a series of diff(1) patches similar to mergemaster(8), but with fewer options. Merges are either accepted, open an editor, or cause `freebsd-update` to abort. When in doubt, backup `/etc` and just accept the merges. See Section 23.6.4, "Merging Configuration Files" for more information about `mergemaster`.

```
# Directory in which to store downloaded updates and temporary
# files used by FreeBSD Update.
# WorkDir /var/db/freebsd-update
```

This directory is where all patches and temporary files are placed. In cases where the user is doing a version upgrade, this location should have at least a gigabyte of disk space available.

```
# When upgrading between releases, should the list of Components be
# read strictly (StrictComponents yes) or merely as a list of components
# which *might* be installed of which FreeBSD Update should figure out
# which actually are installed and upgrade those (StrictComponents no)?
# StrictComponents no
```

When this option is set to `yes`, `freebsd-update` will assume that the `Components` list is complete and will not attempt to make changes outside of the list. Effectively, `freebsd-update` will attempt to update every file which belongs to the `Components` list.

23.2.2. Applying Security Patches

The process of applying FreeBSD security patches has been simplified, allowing an administrator to keep a system fully patched using `freebsd-update`. More information about FreeBSD security advisories can be found in Section 13.11, "FreeBSD Security Advisories".

FreeBSD security patches may be downloaded and installed using the following commands. The first command will determine if any outstanding patches are available, and if so, will list the files that will be modifed if the patches are applied. The second command will apply the patches.

```
# freebsd-update fetch
# freebsd-update install
```

If the update applies any kernel patches, the system will need a reboot in order to boot into the patched kernel. If the patch was applied to any running binaries, the affected applications should be restarted so that the patched version of the binary is used.

The system can be configured to automatically check for updates once every day by adding this entry to `/etc/crontab`:

```
@daily                                  root    freebsd-update cron
```

If patches exist, they will automatically be downloaded but will not be applied. The `root` user will be sent an email so that the patches may be reviewed and manually installed with `freebsd-update install`.

If anything goes wrong, `freebsd-update` has the ability to roll back the last set of changes with the following command:

```
# freebsd-update rollback
Uninstalling updates... done.
```

Again, the system should be restarted if the kernel or any kernel modules were modified and any affected binaries should be restarted.

Only the `GENERIC` kernel can be automatically updated by `freebsd-update`. If a custom kernel is installed, it will have to be rebuilt and reinstalled after `freebsd-update` finishes installing the updates. However, `freebsd-update` will detect and update the `GENERIC` kernel if `/boot/GENERIC` exists, even if it is not the current running kernel of the system.

Note

Always keep a copy of the `GENERIC` kernel in `/boot/GENERIC`. It will be helpful in diagnosing a variety of problems and in performing version upgrades. Refer to Section 23.2.3.1, "Custom Kernels with FreeBSD 9.X and Later" for instructions on how to get a copy of the `GENERIC` kernel.

Unless the default configuration in /etc/freebsd-update.conf has been changed, freebsd-update will install the updated kernel sources along with the rest of the updates. Rebuilding and reinstalling a new custom kernel can then be performed in the usual way.

The updates distributed by freebsd-update do not always involve the kernel. It is not necessary to rebuild a custom kernel if the kernel sources have not been modified by freebsd-update install. However, freebsd-update will always update /usr/src/sys/conf/newvers.sh . The current patch level, as indicated by the -p number reported by uname -r, is obtained from this file. Rebuilding a custom kernel, even if nothing else changed, allows uname to accurately report the current patch level of the system. This is particularly helpful when maintaining multiple systems, as it allows for a quick assessment of the updates installed in each one.

23.2.3. Performing Major and Minor Version Upgrades

Upgrades from one minor version of FreeBSD to another, like from FreeBSD 9.0 to FreeBSD 9.1, are called *minor version* upgrades. *Major version* upgrades occur when FreeBSD is upgraded from one major version to another, like from FreeBSD 9.X to FreeBSD 10.X. Both types of upgrades can be performed by providing freebsd-update with a release version target.

Note

If the system is running a custom kernel, make sure that a copy of the GENERIC kernel exists in /boot/GENERIC before starting the upgrade. Refer to Section 23.2.3.1, "Custom Kernels with FreeBSD 9.X and Later" for instructions on how to get a copy of the GENERIC kernel.

The following command, when run on a FreeBSD 9.0 system, will upgrade it to FreeBSD 9.1:

```
# freebsd-update -r 9.1-RELEASE upgrade
```

After the command has been received, freebsd-update will evaluate the configuration file and current system in an attempt to gather the information necessary to perform the upgrade. A screen listing will display which components have and have not been detected. For example:

```
Looking up update.FreeBSD.org mirrors... 1 mirrors found.
Fetching metadata signature for 9.0-RELEASE from update1.FreeBSD.org... done.
Fetching metadata index... done.
Inspecting system... done.

The following components of FreeBSD seem to be installed:
kernel/smp src/base src/bin src/contrib src/crypto src/etc src/games
src/gnu src/include src/krb5 src/lib src/libexec src/release src/rescue
src/sbin src/secure src/share src/sys src/tools src/ubin src/usbin
world/base world/info world/lib32 world/manpages

The following components of FreeBSD do not seem to be installed:
kernel/generic world/catpages world/dict world/doc world/games
world/proflibs

Does this look reasonable (y/n)? y
```

At this point, freebsd-update will attempt to download all files required for the upgrade. In some cases, the user may be prompted with questions regarding what to install or how to proceed.

When using a custom kernel, the above step will produce a warning similar to the following:

```
WARNING: This system is running a "MYKERNEL " kernel, which is not a
kernel configuration distributed as part of FreeBSD 9.0-RELEASE.
This kernel will not be updated: you MUST update the kernel manually
before running "/usr/sbin/freebsd-update install"
```

This warning may be safely ignored at this point. The updated GENERIC kernel will be used as an intermediate step in the upgrade process.

Once all the patches have been downloaded to the local system, they will be applied. This process may take a while, depending on the speed and workload of the machine. Configuration files will then be merged. The merging process requires some user intervention as a file may be merged or an editor may appear on screen for a manual merge. The results of every successful merge will be shown to the user as the process continues. A failed or ignored merge will cause the process to abort. Users may wish to make a backup of /etc and manually merge important files, such as master.passwd or group at a later time.

Note

The system is not being altered yet as all patching and merging is happening in another directory. Once all patches have been applied successfully, all configuration files have been merged and it seems the process will go smoothly, the changes can be committed to disk by the user using the following command:

```
# freebsd-update install
```

The kernel and kernel modules will be patched first. If the system is running with a custom kernel, use nextboot(8) to set the kernel for the next boot to the updated /boot/GENERIC :

```
# nextboot -k GENERIC
```

Warning

Before rebooting with the GENERIC kernel, make sure it contains all the drivers required for the system to boot properly and connect to the network, if the machine being updated is accessed remotely. In particular, if the running custom kernel contains built-in functionality usually provided by kernel modules, make sure to temporarily load these modules into the GENERIC kernel using the /boot/loader.conf facility. It is recommended to disable non-essential services as well as any disk and network mounts until the upgrade process is complete.

The machine should now be restarted with the updated kernel:

```
# shutdown -r now
```

Once the system has come back online, restart freebsd-update using the following command. Since the state of the process has been saved, freebsd-update will not start from the beginning, but will instead move on to the next phase and remove all old shared libraries and object files.

```
# freebsd-update install
```

Note

Depending upon whether any library version numbers were bumped, there may only be two install phases instead of three.

The upgrade is now complete. If this was a major version upgrade, reinstall all ports and packages as described in Section 23.2.3.2, "Upgrading Packages After a Major Version Upgrade".

23.2.3.1. Custom Kernels with FreeBSD 9.X and Later

Before using `freebsd-update`, ensure that a copy of the GENERIC kernel exists in `/boot/GENERIC`. If a custom kernel has only been built once, the kernel in `/boot/kernel.old` is the GENERIC kernel. Simply rename this directory to `/boot/kernel`.

If a custom kernel has been built more than once or if it is unknown how many times the custom kernel has been built, obtain a copy of the GENERIC kernel that matches the current version of the operating system. If physical access to the system is available, a copy of the GENERIC kernel can be installed from the installation media:

```
# mount /cdrom
# cd /cdrom/usr/freebsd-dist
# tar -C/ -xvf kernel.txz boot/kernel/kernel
```

Alternately, the GENERIC kernel may be rebuilt and installed from source:

```
# cd /usr/src
# make kernel __MAKE_CONF=/dev/null SRCCONF=/dev/null
```

For this kernel to be identified as the GENERIC kernel by `freebsd-update`, the GENERIC configuration file must not have been modified in any way. It is also suggested that the kernel is built without any other special options.

Rebooting into the GENERIC kernel is not required as `freebsd-update` only needs `/boot/GENERIC` to exist.

23.2.3.2. Upgrading Packages After a Major Version Upgrade

Generally, installed applications will continue to work without problems after minor version upgrades. Major versions use different Application Binary Interfaces (ABIs), which will break most third-party applications. After a major version upgrade, all installed packages and ports need to be upgraded. Packages can be upgraded using `pkg upgrade`. To upgrade installed ports, use a utility such as ports-mgmt/portmaster.

A forced upgrade of all installed packages will replace the packages with fresh versions from the repository even if the version number has not increased. This is required because of the ABI version change when upgrading between major versions of FreeBSD. The forced upgrade can be accomplished by performing:

```
# pkg-static upgrade -f
```

A rebuild of all installed applications can be accomplished with this command:

```
# portmaster -af
```

This command will display the configuration screens for each application that has configurable options and wait for the user to interact with those screens. To prevent this behavior, and use only the default options, include -G in the above command.

Once the software upgrades are complete, finish the upgrade process with a final call to `freebsd-update` in order to tie up all the loose ends in the upgrade process:

```
# freebsd-update install
```

If the GENERIC kernel was temporarily used, this is the time to build and install a new custom kernel using the instructions in Chapter 8, *Configuring the FreeBSD Kernel*.

Reboot the machine into the new FreeBSD version. The upgrade process is now complete.

23.2.4. System State Comparison

The state of the installed FreeBSD version against a known good copy can be tested using `freebsd-update IDS`. This command evaluates the current version of system utilities, libraries, and configuration files and can be used as a built-in Intrusion Detection System (IDS).

Warning

This command is not a replacement for a real IDS such as security/snort. As `freebsd-update` stores data on disk, the possibility of tampering is evident. While this possibility may be reduced using `kern.securelevel` and by storing the `freebsd-update` data on a read-only file system when not in use, a better solution would be to compare the system against a secure disk, such as a DVD or securely stored external USB disk device. An alternative method for providing IDS functionality using a built-in utility is described in Section 13.2.6, "Binary Verification"

To begin the comparison, specify the output file to save the results to:

```
# freebsd-update IDS >> outfile.ids
```

The system will now be inspected and a lengthy listing of files, along with the SHA256 hash values for both the known value in the release and the current installation, will be sent to the specified output file.

The entries in the listing are extremely long, but the output format may be easily parsed. For instance, to obtain a list of all files which differ from those in the release, issue the following command:

```
# cat outfile.ids | awk '{ print $1 }' | more
/etc/master.passwd
/etc/motd
/etc/passwd
/etc/pf.conf
```

This sample output has been truncated as many more files exist. Some files have natural modifications. For example, `/etc/passwd` will be modified if users have been added to the system. Kernel modules may differ as `freebsd-update` may have updated them. To exclude specific files or directories, add them to the `IDSIgnorePaths` option in `/etc/freebsd-update.conf`.

23.3. Updating the Documentation Set

Documentation is an integral part of the FreeBSD operating system. While an up-to-date version of the FreeBSD documentation is always available on the FreeBSD web site (http://www.freebsd.org/doc/), it can be handy to have an up-to-date, local copy of the FreeBSD website, handbooks, FAQ, and articles.

This section describes how to use either source or the FreeBSD Ports Collection to keep a local copy of the FreeBSD documentation up-to-date.

For information on editing and submitting corrections to the documentation, refer to the FreeBSD Documentation Project Primer for New Contributors (http://www.freebsd.org/doc/en_US.ISO8859-1/books/fdp-primer/).

23.3.1. Updating Documentation from Source

Rebuilding the FreeBSD documentation from source requires a collection of tools which are not part of the FreeBSD base system. The required tools, including svn, can be installed from the textproc/docproj package or port developed by the FreeBSD Documentation Project.

Once installed, use svn to fetch a clean copy of the documentation source. Replace *https://svn0.us-west.FreeBSD.org* with the address of the closest geographic mirror from Section A.4.6, "Subversion Mirror Sites":

```
# svn checkout https://svn0.us-west.FreeBSD.org /doc/head /usr/doc
```

The initial download of the documentation sources may take a while. Let it run until it completes.

Future updates of the documentation sources may be fetched by running:

```
# svn update /usr/doc
```

Once an up-to-date snapshot of the documentation sources has been fetched to /usr/doc , everything is ready for an update of the installed documentation.

A full update of all available languages may be performed by typing:

```
# cd /usr/doc
# make install clean
```

If an update of only a specific language is desired, make can be invoked in a language-specific subdirectory of /usr/doc :

```
# cd /usr/doc/en_US.ISO8859-1
# make install clean
```

An alternative way of updating the documentation is to run this command from /usr/doc or the desired language-specific subdirectory:

```
# make update
```

The output formats that will be installed may be specified by setting FORMATS:

```
# cd /usr/doc
# make FORMATS='html html-split' install clean
```

Several options are available to ease the process of updating only parts of the documentation, or the build of specific translations. These options can be set either as system-wide options in /etc/make.conf , or as command-line options passed to make.

The options include:

DOC_LANG
> The list of languages and encodings to build and install, such as en_US.ISO8859-1 for English documentation.

FORMATS
> A single format or a list of output formats to be built. Currently, html, html-split , txt, ps, and pdf are supported.

DOCDIR
> Where to install the documentation. It defaults to /usr/share/doc .

For more make variables supported as system-wide options in FreeBSD, refer to make.conf(5).

23.3.2. Updating Documentation from Ports

Based on the work of Marc Fonvieille.

The previous section presented a method for updating the FreeBSD documentation from sources. This section describes an alternative method which uses the Ports Collection and makes it possible to:

- Install pre-built packages of the documentation, without having to locally build anything or install the documentation toolchain.

- Build the documentation sources through the ports framework, making the checkout and build steps a bit easier.

This method of updating the FreeBSD documentation is supported by a set of documentation ports and packages which are updated by the Documentation Engineering Team <doceng@FreeBSD.org> on a monthly basis. These are listed in the FreeBSD Ports Collection, under the docs category (http://www.freshports.org/docs/).

Organization of the documentation ports is as follows:

- The misc/freebsd-doc-en package or port installs all of the English documentation.

- The misc/freebsd-doc-all meta-package or port installs all documentation in all available languages.

- There is a package and port for each translation, such as misc/freebsd-doc-hu for the Hungarian documentation.

When binary packages are used, the FreeBSD documentation will be installed in all available formats for the given language. For example, the following command will install the latest package of the Hungarian documentation:

```
# pkg install hu-freebsd-doc
```

Note

Packages use a format that differs from the corresponding port's name: *lang*-freebsd-doc, where *lang* is the short format of the language code, such as hu for Hungarian, or zh_cn for Simplified Chinese.

To specify the format of the documentation, build the port instead of installing the package. For example, to build and install the English documentation:

```
# cd /usr/ports/misc/freebsd-doc-en
# make install clean
```

The port provides a configuration menu where the format to build and install can be specified. By default, split HTML, similar to the format used on http://www.FreeBSD.org , and PDF are selected.

Alternately, several make options can be specified when building a documentation port, including:

WITH_HTML
  Builds the HTML format with a single HTML file per document. The formatted documentation is saved to a file called article.html, or book.html .

WITH_PDF
  The formatted documentation is saved to a file called article.pdf or book.pdf .

DOCBASE
  Specifies where to install the documentation. It defaults to /usr/local/share/doc/freebsd .

This example uses variables to install the Hungarian documentation as a PDF in the specified directory:

```
# cd /usr/ports/misc/freebsd-doc-hu
# make -DWITH_PDF DOCBASE=share/doc/freebsd/hu install clean
```

Documentation packages or ports can be updated using the instructions in Chapter 4, *Installing Applications: Packages and Ports*. For example, the following command updates the installed Hungarian documentation using ports-mgmt/portmaster by using packages only:

```
# portmaster -PP hu-freebsd-doc
```

23.4. Tracking a Development Branch

FreeBSD has two development branches: FreeBSD-CURRENT and FreeBSD-STABLE.

This section provides an explanation of each branch and its intended audience, as well as how to keep a system up-to-date with each respective branch.

23.4.1. Using FreeBSD-CURRENT

FreeBSD-CURRENT is the "bleeding edge" of FreeBSD development and FreeBSD-CURRENT users are expected to have a high degree of technical skill. Less technical users who wish to track a development branch should track FreeBSD-STABLE instead.

FreeBSD-CURRENT is the very latest source code for FreeBSD and includes works in progress, experimental changes, and transitional mechanisms that might or might not be present in the next official release. While many FreeBSD developers compile the FreeBSD-CURRENT source code daily, there are short periods of time when the source may not be buildable. These problems are resolved as quickly as possible, but whether or not FreeBSD-CURRENT brings disaster or new functionality can be a matter of when the source code was synced.

FreeBSD-CURRENT is made available for three primary interest groups:

1. Members of the FreeBSD community who are actively working on some part of the source tree.

2. Members of the FreeBSD community who are active testers. They are willing to spend time solving problems, making topical suggestions on changes and the general direction of FreeBSD, and submitting patches.

3. Users who wish to keep an eye on things, use the current source for reference purposes, or make the occasional comment or code contribution.

FreeBSD-CURRENT should *not* be considered a fast-track to getting new features before the next release as pre-release features are not yet fully tested and most likely contain bugs. It is not a quick way of getting bug fixes as any given commit is just as likely to introduce new bugs as to fix existing ones. FreeBSD-CURRENT is not in any way "officially supported".

To track FreeBSD-CURRENT:

1. Join the freebsd-current and the svn-src-head lists. This is *essential* in order to see the comments that people are making about the current state of the system and to receive important bulletins about the current state of FreeBSD-CURRENT.

   The svn-src-head list records the commit log entry for each change as it is made, along with any pertinent information on possible side effects.

   To join these lists, go to http://lists.FreeBSD.org/mailman/listinfo, click on the list to subscribe to, and follow the instructions. In order to track changes to the whole source tree, not just the changes to FreeBSD-CURRENT, subscribe to the svn-src-all list.

2. Synchronize with the FreeBSD-CURRENT sources. Typically, svn is used to check out the -CURRENT code from the **head** branch of one of the Subversion mirror sites listed in Section A.4.6, "Subversion Mirror Sites".

   Users with very slow or limited Internet connectivity can instead use CTM as described in Section A.3, "Using CTM", but it is not as reliable as svn and svn is the recommended method for synchronizing source.

3. Due to the size of the repository, some users choose to only synchronize the sections of source that interest them or which they are contributing patches to. However, users that plan to compile the operating system from source must download *all* of FreeBSD-CURRENT, not just selected portions.

   Before compiling FreeBSD-CURRENT , read `/usr/src/Makefile` very carefully and follow the instructions in Section 23.6, "Rebuilding World". Read the FreeBSD-CURRENT mailing list and `/usr/src/UPDATING` to stay up-to-date on other bootstrapping procedures that sometimes become necessary on the road to the next release.

4. Be active! FreeBSD-CURRENT users are encouraged to submit their suggestions for enhancements or bug fixes. Suggestions with accompanying code are always welcome.

23.4.2. Using FreeBSD-STABLE

FreeBSD-STABLE is the development branch from which major releases are made. Changes go into this branch at a slower pace and with the general assumption that they have first been tested in FreeBSD-CURRENT. This is *still* a development branch and, at any given time, the sources for FreeBSD-STABLE may or may not be suitable for general use. It is simply another engineering development track, not a resource for end-users. Users who do not have the resources to perform testing should instead run the most recent release of FreeBSD.

Those interested in tracking or contributing to the FreeBSD development process, especially as it relates to the next release of FreeBSD, should consider following FreeBSD-STABLE.

While the FreeBSD-STABLE branch should compile and run at all times, this cannot be guaranteed. Since more people run FreeBSD-STABLE than FreeBSD-CURRENT, it is inevitable that bugs and corner cases will sometimes be found in FreeBSD-STABLE that were not apparent in FreeBSD-CURRENT. For this reason, one should not blindly track FreeBSD-STABLE. It is particularly important *not* to update any production servers to FreeBSD-STABLE without thoroughly testing the code in a development or testing environment.

To track FreeBSD-STABLE:

1. Join the freebsd-stable list in order to stay informed of build dependencies that may appear in FreeBSD-STABLE or any other issues requiring special attention. Developers will also make announcements in this mailing list when they are contemplating some controversial fix or update, giving the users a chance to respond if they have any issues to raise concerning the proposed change.

   Join the relevant svn list for the branch being tracked. For example, users tracking the 9-STABLE branch should join the svn-src-stable-9 list. This list records the commit log entry for each change as it is made, along with any pertinent information on possible side effects.

   To join these lists, go to http://lists.FreeBSD.org/mailman/listinfo, click on the list to subscribe to, and follow the instructions. In order to track changes for the whole source tree, subscribe to svn-src-all.

2. To install a new FreeBSD-STABLE system, install the most recent FreeBSD-STABLE release from the FreeBSD mirror sites or use a monthly snapshot built from FreeBSD-STABLE. Refer to www.freebsd.org/snapshots for more information about snapshots.

   To compile or upgrade to an existing FreeBSD system to FreeBSD-STABLE, use svn to check out the source for the desired branch. Branch names, such as **stable/9**, are listed at www.freebsd.org/releng. CTM (Section A.3, "Using CTM") can be used if a reliable Internet connection is not available.

3. Before compiling or upgrading to FreeBSD-STABLE , read **/usr/src/Makefile** carefully and follow the instructions in Section 23.6, "Rebuilding World". Read FreeBSD-STABLE mailing list and **/usr/src/UPDATING** to keep up-to-date on other bootstrapping procedures that sometimes become necessary on the road to the next release.

23.5. Synchronizing Source

There are various methods for staying up-to-date with the FreeBSD sources. This section compares the primary services, Subversion and CTM.

Warning

While it is possible to update only parts of the source tree, the only supported update procedure is to update the entire tree and recompile all the programs that run in user space, such as those in **/bin** and **/sbin**, and kernel sources. Updating only part of the source tree, only the kernel, or only the userland programs will often result in problems ranging from compile errors to kernel panics or data corruption.

Subversion uses the *pull* model of updating sources. The user, or a **cron** script, invokes the **svn** program which updates the local version of the source. Subversion is the preferred method for updating local source trees as updates are up-to-the-minute and the user controls when updates are downloaded. It is easy to restrict updates to specific files or directories and the requested updates are generated on the fly by the server. How to synchronize source using Subversion is described in Section A.4, "Using Subversion".

CTM does not interactively compare the local sources with those on the master archive or otherwise pull them across. Instead, a script which identifies changes in files since its previous run is executed several times a day on the master CTM machine. Any detected changes are compressed, stamped with a sequence-number, and encoded for transmission over email in printable ASCII only. Once downloaded, these *deltas* can be run through ctm.rmail which will automatically decode, verify, and apply the changes to the user's copy of the sources. This process is more efficient than Subversion and places less strain on server resources since it is a *push*, rather than a *pull*, model. Instructions for using CTM to synchronize source can be found at Section A.3, "Using CTM".

If a user inadvertently wipes out portions of the local archive, Subversion will detect and rebuild the damaged portions. CTM will not, and if a user deletes some portion of the source tree and does not have a backup, they will have to start from scratch from the most recent *base delta* and rebuild it all with CTM.

23.6. Rebuilding World

Once the local source tree is synchronized against a particular version of FreeBSD such as FreeBSD-STABLE or FreeBSD-CURRENT, the source tree can be used to rebuild the system. This process is known as rebuilding world.

Before rebuilding world, be sure to perform the following tasks:

Procedure 23.1. Perform These Tasks *Before* Building World

1. Backup all important data to another system or removable media, verify the integrity of the backup, and have a bootable installation media at hand. It cannot be stressed enough how important it is to make a backup of the system *before* rebuilding the system. While rebuilding world is an easy task, there will inevitably be times when mistakes in the source tree render the system unbootable. You will probably never have to use the backup, but it is better to be safe than sorry!

2.
   Review the recent freebsd-stable or freebsd-current entries, depending upon the branch being tracked. Be aware of any known problems and which systems are affected. If a known issue affects the version of synchronized code, wait for an "all clear" announcement to be posted stating that the problem has been solved. Resynchronize the sources to ensure that the local version of source has the needed fix.

3. Read /usr/src/UPDATING for any extra steps necessary for that version of the source. This file contains important information about potential problems and may specify the order to run certain commands. Many upgrades require specific additional steps such as renaming or deleting specific files prior to installing the new world. These will be listed at the end of this file where the currently recommended upgrade sequence is explicitly spelled out. If UPDATING contradicts any steps in this chapter, the instructions in UPDATING take precedence and should be followed.

Do Not Use make world

Some older documentation recommends using make world. However, that command skips some important steps and should only be used by experts. For almost all circumstances make world is the wrong thing to do, and the procedure described here should be used instead.

23.6.1. Overview of Process

The build world process assumes an upgrade from an older FreeBSD version using the source of a newer version that was obtained using the instructions in Section 23.5, "Synchronizing Source".

In FreeBSD, the term "world" includes the kernel, core system binaries, libraries, programming files, and built-in compiler. The order in which these components are built and installed is important.

For example, the old compiler might have a bug and not be able to compile the new kernel. Since the new kernel should be built with the new compiler, the new compiler must be built, but not necessarily installed, before the new kernel is built.

The new world might rely on new kernel features, so the new kernel must be installed before the new world is installed. The old world might not run correctly on the new kernel, so the new world must be installed immediately upon installing the new kernel.

Some configuration changes must be made before the new world is installed, but others might break the old world. Hence, two different configuration upgrade steps are used. For the most part, the update process only replaces or adds files and existing old files are not deleted. Since this can cause problems, /usr/src/UPDATING will indicate if any files need to be manually deleted and at which step to do so.

These concerns have led to the recommended upgrade sequence described in the following procedure.

Note

It is a good idea to save the output from running make to a file. If something goes wrong, a copy of the error message can be posted to one of the FreeBSD mailing lists.

The easiest way to do this is to use script with a parameter that specifies the name of the file to save all output to. Do not save the output to /tmp as this directory may be cleared at next reboot. A better place to save the file is /var/tmp. Run this command immediately before rebuilding the world, and then type **exit** when the process has finished:

```
# script /var/tmp/mw.out
Script started, output file is /var/tmp/mw.out
```

Procedure 23.2. Overview of Build World Process

The commands used in the build world process should be run in the order specified here. This section summarizes the function of each command.

1. If the build world process has previously been run on this system, a copy of the previous build may still exist in /usr/obj. To speed up the new build world process, and possibly save some dependency headaches, remove this directory if it already exists:

    ```
    # chflags -R noschg /usr/obj/*
    # rm -rf /usr/obj
    ```

2. Compile the new compiler and a few related tools, then use the new compiler to compile the rest of the new world. The result is saved to /usr/obj.

    ```
    # cd /usr/src
    # make buildworld
    ```

3. Use the new compiler residing in /usr/obj to build the new kernel, in order to protect against compiler-kernel mismatches. This is necessary, as certain memory structures may have changed, and programs like ps and top will fail to work if the kernel and source code versions are not the same.

    ```
    # make buildkernel
    ```

4. Install the new kernel and kernel modules, making it possible to boot with the newly updated kernel. If kern.securelevel has been raised above 1 *and* noschg or similar flags have been set on the kernel binary, drop

the system into single-user mode first. Otherwise, this command can be run from multi-user mode without problems. See init(8) for details about `kern.securelevel` and chflags(1) for details about the various file flags.

```
# make installkernel
```

5. Drop the system into single-user mode in order to minimize problems from updating any binaries that are already running. It also minimizes any problems from running the old world on a new kernel.

```
# shutdown now
```

Once in single-user mode, run these commands if the system is formatted with UFS:

```
# mount -u /
# mount -a -t ufs
# swapon -a
```

If the system is instead formatted with ZFS, run these two commands. This example assumes a zpool name of `zroot`:

```
# zfs set readonly=off zroot
# zfs mount -a
```

6. Optional: If a keyboard mapping other than the default US English is desired, it can be changed with kbdmap(1):

```
# kbdmap
```

7. Then, for either file system, if the CMOS clock is set to local time (this is true if the output of date(1) does not show the correct time and zone), run:

```
# adjkerntz -i
```

8. Remaking the world will not update certain directories, such as `/etc`, `/var` and `/usr`, with new or changed configuration files. The next step is to perform some initial configuration file updates to `/etc` in preparation for the new world. The following command compares only those files that are essential for the success of `installworld`. For instance, this step may add new groups, system accounts, or startup scripts which have been added to FreeBSD since the last update. This is necessary so that the `installworld` step will be able to use any new system accounts, groups, and scripts. Refer to Section 23.6.4, "Merging Configuration Files" for more detailed instructions about this command:

```
# mergemaster -p
```

9. Install the new world and system binaries from `/usr/obj` .

```
# cd /usr/src
# make installworld
```

10. Update any remaining configuration files.

```
# mergemaster -iF
```

11. Delete any obsolete files. This is important as they may cause problems if left on the disk.

```
# make delete-old
```

12. A full reboot is now needed to load the new kernel and new world with the new configuration files.

```
# reboot
```

13. Make sure that all installed ports have first been rebuilt before old libraries are removed using the instructions in Section 4.5.3, "Upgrading Ports". When finished, remove any obsolete libraries to avoid conflicts with newer ones. For a more detailed description of this step, refer to Section 23.6.5, "Deleting Obsolete Files and Libraries".

```
# make delete-old-libs
```

If the system can have a window of down-time, consider compiling the system in single-user mode instead of compiling the system in multi-user mode, and then dropping into single-user mode for the installation. Reinstalling the system touches a lot of important system files, all the standard system binaries, libraries, and include files. Changing these on a running system, particularly one with active users, is asking for trouble.

23.6.2. Configuration Files

This build world process uses several configuration files.

The Makefile located in /usr/src describes how the programs that comprise FreeBSD should be built and the order in which they should be built.

The options available to make are described in make.conf(5) and some common examples are included in /usr/share/examples/etc/make.conf . Any options which are added to /etc/make.conf will control the how make runs and builds programs. These options take effect every time make is used, including compiling applications from the Ports Collection, compiling custom C programs, or building the FreeBSD operating system. Changes to some settings can have far-reaching and potentially surprising effects. Read the comments in both locations and keep in mind that the defaults have been chosen for a combination of performance and safety.

How the operating system is built from source code is controlled by /etc/src.conf. Unlike /etc/make.conf , the contents of /etc/src.conf only take effect when the FreeBSD operating system itself is being built. Descriptions of the many options available for this file are shown in src.conf(5). Be cautious about disabling seemingly unneeded kernel modules and build options. Sometimes there are unexpected or subtle interactions.

23.6.3. Variables and Targets

The general format for using make is as follows:

```
# make -x -DVARIABLE target
```

In this example, -x is an option passed to make. Refer to make(1) for examples of the available options.

To pass a variable, specify the variable name with -DVARIABLE . The behavior of the Makefile is controlled by variables. These can either be set in /etc/make.conf or they can be specified when using make. For example, this variable specifies that profiled libraries should not be built:

```
# make -DNO_PROFILE target
```

It corresponds with this setting in /etc/make.conf :

```
NO_PROFILE=    true    #    Avoid compiling profiled libraries
```

The target tells make what to do and the Makefile defines the available targets. Some targets are used by the build process to break out the steps necessary to rebuild the system into a number of sub-steps.

Having separate options is useful for two reasons. First, it allows for a build that does not affect any components of a running system. Because of this, buildworld can be safely run on a machine running in multi-user mode. It is still recommended that installworld be run in part in single-user mode, though.

Secondly, it allows NFS mounts to be used to upgrade multiple machines on a network, as described in Section 23.7, "Tracking for Multiple Machines".

It is possible to specify -j which will cause make to spawn several simultaneous processes. Since much of the compiling process is I/O-bound rather than CPU-bound, this is useful on both single CPU and multi-CPU machines.

On a single-CPU machine, run the following command to have up to 4 processes running at any one time. Empirical evidence posted to the mailing lists shows this generally gives the best performance benefit.

```
# make -j4 buildworld
```

On a multi-CPU machine, try values between 6 and 10 to see how they speed things up.

 Note

If any variables were specified to make buildworld, specify the same variables to make installworld. However, -j must *never* be used with installworld.

For example, if this command was used:

```
# make -DNO_PROFILE buildworld
```

Install the results with:

```
# make -DNO_PROFILE installworld
```

Otherwise, the second command will try to install profiled libraries that were not built during the make buildworld phase.

23.6.4. Merging Configuration Files

Contributed by Tom Rhodes.

FreeBSD provides the mergemaster(8) Bourne script to aid in determining the differences between the configuration files in /etc, and the configuration files in /usr/src/etc . This is the recommended solution for keeping the system configuration files up to date with those located in the source tree.

Before using mergemaster, it is recommended to first copy the existing /etc somewhere safe. Include -R which does a recursive copy and -p which preserves times and the ownerships on files:

```
# cp -Rp /etc /etc.old
```

When run, mergemaster builds a temporary root environment, from / down, and populates it with various system configuration files. Those files are then compared to the ones currently installed in the system. Files that differ will be shown in diff(1) format, with the + sign representing added or modified lines, and - representing lines that will be either removed completely or replaced with a new file. Refer to diff(1) for more information about how file differences are shown.

Next, mergemaster will display each file that differs, and present options to: delete the new file, referred to as the temporary file, install the temporary file in its unmodified state, merge the temporary file with the currently installed file, or view the results again.

Choosing to delete the temporary file will tell mergemaster to keep the current file unchanged and to delete the new version. This option is not recommended. To get help at any time, type ? at the mergemaster prompt. If the user chooses to skip a file, it will be presented again after all other files have been dealt with.

Choosing to install the unmodified temporary file will replace the current file with the new one. For most unmodified files, this is the best option.

Choosing to merge the file will present a text editor, and the contents of both files. The files can be merged by reviewing both files side by side on the screen, and choosing parts from both to create a finished product. When the files are compared side by side, l selects the left contents and r selects contents from the right. The final output will be a file consisting of both parts, which can then be installed. This option is customarily used for files where settings have been modified by the user.

Choosing to view the results again will redisplay the file differences.

After `mergemaster` is done with the system files, it will prompt for other options. It may prompt to rebuild the password file and will finish up with an option to remove left-over temporary files.

23.6.5. Deleting Obsolete Files and Libraries

Based on notes provided by Anton Shterenlikht.

As a part of the FreeBSD development lifecycle, files and their contents occasionally become obsolete. This may be because functionality is implemented elsewhere, the version number of the library has changed, or it was removed from the system entirely. These obsoleted files, libraries, and directories should be removed when updating the system. This ensures that the system is not cluttered with old files which take up unnecessary space on the storage and backup media. Additionally, if the old library has a security or stability issue, the system should be updated to the newer library to keep it safe and to prevent crashes caused by the old library. Files, directories, and libraries which are considered obsolete are listed in `/usr/src/ObsoleteFiles.inc` . The following instructions should be used to remove obsolete files during the system upgrade process.

After the `make installworld` and the subsequent `mergemaster` have finished successfully, check for obsolete files and libraries:

```
# cd /usr/src
# make check-old
```

If any obsolete files are found, they can be deleted using the following command:

```
# make delete-old
```

A prompt is displayed before deleting each obsolete file. To skip the prompt and let the system remove these files automatically, use `BATCH_DELETE_OLD_FILES` :

```
# make -DBATCH_DELETE_OLD_FILES delete-old
```

The same goal can be achieved by piping these commands through **yes**:

```
# yes|make delete-old
```

 Warning

Deleting obsolete files will break applications that still depend on those obsolete files. This is especially true for old libraries. In most cases, the programs, ports, or libraries that used the old library need to be recompiled before `make delete-old-libs` is executed.

Utilities for checking shared library dependencies include sysutils/libchk and sysutils/bsdadminscripts.

Obsolete shared libraries can conflict with newer libraries, causing messages like these:

```
/usr/bin/ld: warning: libz.so.4, needed by /usr/local/lib/libtiff.so, may conflict with ↺
libz.so.5
/usr/bin/ld: warning: librpcsvc.so.4, needed by /usr/local/lib/libXext.so, may conflict ↺
with librpcsvc.so.5
```

To solve these problems, determine which port installed the library:

```
# pkg which /usr/local/lib/libtiff.so
  /usr/local/lib/libtiff.so was installed by package tiff-3.9.4
# pkg which /usr/local/lib/libXext.so
  /usr/local/lib/libXext.so was installed by package libXext-1.1.1,1
```

Then deinstall, rebuild, and reinstall the port. To automate this process, ports-mgmt/portmaster can be used. After all ports are rebuilt and no longer use the old libraries, delete the old libraries using the following command:

```
# make delete-old-libs
```

If something goes wrong, it is easy to rebuild a particular piece of the system. For example, if /etc/magic was accidentally deleted as part of the upgrade or merge of /etc, file will stop working. To fix this, run:

```
# cd /usr/src/usr.bin/file
# make all install
```

23.6.6. Common Questions

Do I need to re-make the world for every change?
It depends upon the nature of the change. For example, if svn only shows the following files as being updated:

```
src/games/cribbage/instr.c
src/games/sail/pl_main.c
src/release/sysinstall/config.c
src/release/sysinstall/media.c
src/share/mk/bsd.port.mk
```

it probably is not worth rebuilding the entire world. Instead, go into the appropriate sub-directories and run make all install. But if something major changes, such as src/lib/libc/stdlib , consider rebuilding world.

Some users rebuild world every fortnight and let changes accumulate over that fortnight. Others only re-make those things that have changed and are careful to spot all the dependencies. It all depends on how often a user wants to upgrade and whether they are tracking FreeBSD-STABLE or FreeBSD-CURRENT.

What would cause a compile to fail with lots of signal 11 (or other signal number) errors?
This normally indicates a hardware problem. Building world is an effective way to stress test hardware, especially memory. A sure indicator of a hardware issue is when make is restarted and it dies at a different point in the process.

To resolve this error, swap out the components in the machine, starting with RAM, to determine which component is failing.

Can /usr/obj be removed when finished?
This directory contains all the object files that were produced during the compilation phase. Normally, one of the first steps in the make buildworld process is to remove this directory and start afresh. Keeping /usr/obj around when finished makes little sense, and its removal frees up a approximately 2GB of disk space.

Can interrupted builds be resumed?
This depends on how far into the process the problem occurs. In general, make buildworld builds new copies of essential tools and the system libraries. These tools and libraries are then installed, used to rebuild themselves, and are installed again. The rest of the system is then rebuilt with the new system tools.

During the last stage, it is fairly safe to run these commands as they will not undo the work of the previous make buildworld:

```
# cd /usr/src
# make -DNO_CLEAN all
```

If this message appears:

```
--------------------------------------------------------------------
Building everything..
--------------------------------------------------------------------
```

in the make buildworld output, it is probably fairly safe to do so.

If that message is not displayed, it is always better to be safe than sorry and to restart the build from scratch.

Is it possible to speed up making the world?

Several actions can speed up the build world process. For example, the entire process can be run from single-user mode. However, this will prevent users from having access to the system until the process is complete.

Careful file system design or the use of ZFS datasets can make a difference. Consider putting /usr/src and /usr/obj on separate file systems. If possible, place the file systems on separate disks on separate disk controllers. When mounting /usr/src, use noatime which prevents the file system from recording the file access time. If /usr/src is not on its own file system, consider remounting /usr with noatime.

The file system holding /usr/obj can be mounted or remounted with async so that disk writes happen asynchronously. The write completes immediately, and the data is written to the disk a few seconds later. This allows writes to be clustered together, and can provide a dramatic performance boost.

Warning

Keep in mind that this option makes the file system more fragile. With this option, there is an increased chance that, should power fail, the file system will be in an unrecoverable state when the machine restarts.

If /usr/obj is the only directory on this file system, this is not a problem. If you have other, valuable data on the same file system, ensure that there are verified backups before enabling this option.

Turn off profiling by setting "NO_PROFILE=true" in /etc/make.conf .

Pass -j*n* to make(1) to run multiple processes in parallel. This usually helps on both single- and multi-processor machines.

What if something goes wrong?

First, make absolutely sure that the environment has no extraneous cruft from earlier builds:

```
# chflags -R noschg /usr/obj/usr
# rm -rf /usr/obj/usr
# cd /usr/src
# make cleandir
# make cleandir
```

Yes, make cleandir really should be run twice.

Then, restart the whole process, starting with make buildworld.

If problems persist, send the error and the output of uname -a to FreeBSD general questions mailing list. Be prepared to answer other questions about the setup!

23.7. Tracking for Multiple Machines

Contributed by Mike Meyer.

When multiple machines need to track the same source tree, it is a waste of disk space, network bandwidth, and CPU cycles to have each system download the sources and rebuild everything. The solution is to have one machine do most of the work, while the rest of the machines mount that work via NFS. This section outlines a method of doing so. For more information about using NFS, refer to Section 28.3, "Network File System (NFS)".

First, identify a set of machines which will run the same set of binaries, known as a *build set*. Each machine can have a custom kernel, but will run the same userland binaries. From that set, choose a machine to be the *build machine* that the world and kernel are built on. Ideally, this is a fast machine that has sufficient spare CPU to run `make buildworld` and `make buildkernel`.

Select a machine to be the *test machine*, which will test software updates before they are put into production. This *must* be a machine that can afford to be down for an extended period of time. It can be the build machine, but need not be.

All the machines in this build set need to mount `/usr/obj` and `/usr/src` from the build machine via NFS. For multiple build sets, `/usr/src` should be on one build machine, and NFS mounted on the rest.

Ensure that `/etc/make.conf` and `/etc/src.conf` on all the machines in the build set agree with the build machine. That means that the build machine must build all the parts of the base system that any machine in the build set is going to install. Also, each build machine should have its kernel name set with `KERNCONF` in `/etc/make.conf`, and the build machine should list them all in its `KERNCONF`, listing its own kernel first. The build machine must have the kernel configuration files for each machine in its `/usr/src/sys/ arch /conf`.

On the build machine, build the kernel and world as described in Section 23.6, "Rebuilding World", but do not install anything on the build machine. Instead, install the built kernel on the test machine. On the test machine, mount `/usr/src` and `/usr/obj` via NFS. Then, run `shutdown now` to go to single-user mode in order to install the new kernel and world and run `mergemaster` as usual. When done, reboot to return to normal multi-user operations.

After verifying that everything on the test machine is working properly, use the same procedure to install the new software on each of the other machines in the build set.

The same methodology can be used for the ports tree. The first step is to share `/usr/ports` via NFS to all the machines in the build set. To configure `/etc/make.conf` to share distfiles, set `DISTDIR` to a common shared directory that is writable by whichever user `root` is mapped to by the NFS mount. Each machine should set `WRKDIRPREFIX` to a local build directory, if ports are to be built locally. Alternately, if the build system is to build and distribute packages to the machines in the build set, set `PACKAGES` on the build system to a directory similar to `DISTDIR`.

Chapter 24. DTrace

Written by Tom Rhodes.

24.1. Synopsis

DTrace, also known as Dynamic Tracing, was developed by Sun™ as a tool for locating performance bottlenecks in production and pre-production systems. In addition to diagnosing performance problems, DTrace can be used to help investigate and debug unexpected behavior in both the FreeBSD kernel and in userland programs.

DTrace is a remarkable profiling tool, with an impressive array of features for diagnosing system issues. It may also be used to run pre-written scripts to take advantage of its capabilities. Users can author their own utilities using the DTrace D Language, allowing them to customize their profiling based on specific needs.

The FreeBSD implementation provides full support for kernel DTrace and experimental support for userland DTrace. Userland DTrace allows users to perform function boundary tracing for userland programs using the pid provider, and to insert static probes into userland programs for later tracing. Some ports, such as databases/postgres-server and lang/php56 have a DTrace option to enable static probes. FreeBSD 10.0-RELEASE has reasonably good userland DTrace support, but it is not considered production ready. In particular, it is possible to crash traced programs.

The official guide to DTrace is maintained by the Illumos project at DTrace Guide .

After reading this chapter, you will know:

- What DTrace is and what features it provides.

- Differences between the Solaris™ DTrace implementation and the one provided by FreeBSD.

- How to enable and use DTrace on FreeBSD.

Before reading this chapter, you should:

- Understand UNIX® and FreeBSD basics (Chapter 3, *UNIX Basics*).

- Have some familiarity with security and how it pertains to FreeBSD (Chapter 13, *Security*).

24.2. Implementation Differences

While the DTrace in FreeBSD is similar to that found in Solaris™, differences do exist. The primary difference is that in FreeBSD, DTrace is implemented as a set of kernel modules and DTrace can not be used until the modules are loaded. To load all of the necessary modules:

```
# kldload dtraceall
```

Beginning with FreeBSD 10.0-RELEASE, the modules are automatically loaded when dtrace is run.

FreeBSD uses the DDB_CTF kernel option to enable support for loading CTF data from kernel modules and the kernel itself. CTF is the Solaris™ Compact C Type Format which encapsulates a reduced form of debugging information similar to DWARF and the venerable stabs. CTF data is added to binaries by the ctfconvert and ctfmerge build tools. The ctfconvert utility parses DWARF ELF debug sections created by the compiler and ctfmerge merges CTF ELF sections from objects into either executables or shared libraries.

Some different providers exist for FreeBSD than for Solaris™. Most notable is the dtmalloc provider, which allows tracing malloc() by type in the FreeBSD kernel. Some of the providers found in Solaris™, such as cpc and mib, are not present in FreeBSD. These may appear in future versions of FreeBSD. Moreover, some of the providers available in both operating systems are not compatible, in the sense that their probes have different argument types. Thus, D scripts written on Solaris™ may or may not work unmodified on FreeBSD, and vice versa.

Due to security differences, only `root` may use DTrace on FreeBSD. Solaris™ has a few low level security checks which do not yet exist in FreeBSD. As such, the `/dev/dtrace/dtrace` is strictly limited to `root`.

DTrace falls under the Common Development and Distribution License (CDDL) license. To view this license on FreeBSD, see `/usr/src/cddl/contrib/opensolaris/OPENSOLARIS.LICENSE` or view it online at `http://opensource.org/licenses/CDDL-1.0`. While a FreeBSD kernel with DTrace support is BSD licensed, the CDDL is used when the modules are distributed in binary form or the binaries are loaded.

24.3. Enabling DTrace Support

In FreeBSD 9.2 and 10.0, DTrace support is built into the `GENERIC` kernel. Users of earlier versions of FreeBSD or who prefer to statically compile in DTrace support should add the following lines to a custom kernel configuration file and recompile the kernel using the instructions in Chapter 8, *Configuring the FreeBSD Kernel*:

```
options        KDTRACE_HOOKS
options        DDB_CTF
makeoptions DEBUG=-g
makeoptions WITH_CTF=1
```

Users of the AMD64 architecture should also add this line:

```
options        KDTRACE_FRAME
```

This option provides support for FBT. While DTrace will work without this option, there will be limited support for function boundary tracing.

Once the FreeBSD system has rebooted into the new kernel, or the DTrace kernel modules have been loaded using `kldload dtraceall`, the system will need support for the Korn shell as the DTrace Toolkit has several utilities written in `ksh`. Make sure that the shells/ksh93 package or port is installed. It is also possible to run these tools under shells/pdksh or shells/mksh.

Finally, install the current DTrace Toolkit, a collection of ready-made scripts for collecting system information. There are scripts to check open files, memory, CPU usage, and a lot more. FreeBSD 10 installs a few of these scripts into `/usr/share/dtrace`. On other FreeBSD versions, or to install the full DTrace Toolkit, use the sysutils/DTrace-Toolkit package or port.

Note

The scripts found in `/usr/share/dtrace` have been specifically ported to FreeBSD. Not all of the scripts found in the DTrace Toolkit will work as-is on FreeBSD and some scripts may require some effort in order for them to work on FreeBSD.

The DTrace Toolkit includes many scripts in the special language of DTrace. This language is called the D language and it is very similar to C++. An in depth discussion of the language is beyond the scope of this document. It is extensively discussed at `http://wikis.oracle.com/display/DTrace/Documentation`.

24.4. Using DTrace

DTrace scripts consist of a list of one or more *probes*, or instrumentation points, where each probe is associated with an action. Whenever the condition for a probe is met, the associated action is executed. For example, an action may occur when a file is opened, a process is started, or a line of code is executed. The action might be to log some information or to modify context variables. The reading and writing of context variables allows probes to share information and to cooperatively analyze the correlation of different events.

To view all probes, the administrator can execute the following command:

```
# dtrace -l | more
```

Each probe has an ID, a PROVIDER (dtrace or fbt), a MODULE, and a FUNCTION NAME. Refer to dtrace(1) for more information about this command.

The examples in this section provide an overview of how to use two of the fully supported scripts from the DTrace Toolkit: the hotkernel and procsystime scripts.

The hotkernel script is designed to identify which function is using the most kernel time. It will produce output similar to the following:

```
# cd /usr/share/dtrace/toolkit
# ./hotkernel
Sampling... Hit Ctrl-C to end.
```

As instructed, use the Ctrl+C key combination to stop the process. Upon termination, the script will display a list of kernel functions and timing information, sorting the output in increasing order of time:

```
kernel`_thread_lock_flags              2    0.0%
0xc1097063                             2    0.0%
kernel`sched_userret                   2    0.0%
kernel`kern_select                     2    0.0%
kernel`generic_copyin                  3    0.0%
kernel`mtx_assert                      3    0.0%
kernel`vm_fault                        3    0.0%
kernel`sopoll_generic                  3    0.0%
kernel`fixup_filename                  4    0.0%
kernel`_isitmyx                        4    0.0%
kernel`find_instance                   4    0.0%
kernel`_mtx_unlock_flags               5    0.0%
kernel`syscall                         5    0.0%
kernel`DELAY                           5    0.0%
0xc108a253                             6    0.0%
kernel`witness_lock                    7    0.0%
kernel`read_aux_data_no_wait           7    0.0%
kernel`Xint0x80_syscall                7    0.0%
kernel`witness_checkorder              7    0.0%
kernel`sse2_pagezero                   8    0.0%
kernel`strncmp                         9    0.0%
kernel`spinlock_exit                   10   0.0%
kernel`_mtx_lock_flags                 11   0.0%
kernel`witness_unlock                  15   0.0%
kernel`sched_idletd                    137  0.3%
0xc10981a5                             42139 99.3%
```

This script will also work with kernel modules. To use this feature, run the script with -m:

```
# ./hotkernel -m
Sampling... Hit Ctrl-C to end.
^C
MODULE                              COUNT   PCNT
0xc107882e                            1    0.0%
0xc10e6aa4                            1    0.0%
0xc1076983                            1    0.0%
0xc109708a                            1    0.0%
0xc1075a5d                            1    0.0%
0xc1077325                            1    0.0%
0xc108a245                            1    0.0%
0xc107730d                            1    0.0%
0xc1097063                            2    0.0%
```

```
0xc108a253                                        73   0.0%
kernel                                           874   0.4%
0xc10981a5                                    213781  99.6%
```

The procsystime script captures and prints the system call time usage for a given process ID (PID) or process name. In the following example, a new instance of /bin/csh was spawned. Then, procsystime was executed and remained waiting while a few commands were typed on the other incarnation of csh. These are the results of this test:

```
# ./procsystime -n csh
Tracing... Hit Ctrl-C to end...
^C

Elapsed Times for processes csh,

          SYSCALL         TIME (ns)
           getpid              6131
         sigreturn            8121
            close            19127
            fcntl            19959
              dup            26955
           setpgid           28070
             stat            31899
         setitimer           40938
            wait4            62717
         sigaction           67372
        sigprocmask         119091
       gettimeofday         183710
            write           263242
           execve           492547
            ioctl           770073
            vfork          3258923
        sigsuspend         6985124
             read       3988049784
```

As shown, the read() system call used the most time in nanoseconds while the getpid() system call used the least amount of time.

Part IV. Network Communication

FreeBSD is one of the most widely deployed operating systems for high performance network servers. The chapters in this part cover:

- Serial communication

- PPP and PPP over Ethernet

- Electronic Mail

- Running Network Servers

- Firewalls

- Other Advanced Networking Topics

These chapters are designed to be read when you need the information. You do not have to read them in any particular order, nor do you need to read all of them before you can begin using FreeBSD in a network environment.

Table of Contents

Chapter 25. Serial Communications

25.1. Synopsis

UNIX® has always had support for serial communications as the very first UNIX® machines relied on serial lines for user input and output. Things have changed a lot from the days when the average terminal consisted of a 10-character-per-second serial printer and a keyboard. This chapter covers some of the ways serial communications can be used on FreeBSD.

After reading this chapter, you will know:

- How to connect terminals to a FreeBSD system.

- How to use a modem to dial out to remote hosts.

- How to allow remote users to login to a FreeBSD system with a modem.

- How to boot a FreeBSD system from a serial console.

Before reading this chapter, you should:

- Know how to configure and install a custom kernel.

- Understand FreeBSD permissions and processes.

- Have access to the technical manual for the serial hardware to be used with FreeBSD.

25.2. Serial Terminology and Hardware

The following terms are often used in serial communications:

bps
> Bits per Second (bps) is the rate at which data is transmitted.

DTE
> Data Terminal Equipment (DTE) is one of two endpoints in a serial communication. An example would be a computer.

DCE
> Data Communications Equipment (DTE) is the other endpoint in a serial communication. Typically, it is a modem or serial terminal.

RS-232
> The original standard which defined hardware serial communications. It has since been renamed to TIA-232.

When referring to communication data rates, this section does not use the term *baud*. Baud refers to the number of electrical state transitions made in a period of time, while bps is the correct term to use.

To connect a serial terminal to a FreeBSD system, a serial port on the computer and the proper cable to connect to the serial device are needed. Users who are already familiar with serial hardware and cabling can safely skip this section.

25.2.1. Serial Cables and Ports

There are several different kinds of serial cables. The two most common types are null-modem cables and standard RS-232 cables. The documentation for the hardware should describe the type of cable required.

These two types of cables differ in how the wires are connected to the connector. Each wire represents a signal, with the defined signals summarized in Table 25.1, "RS-232C Signal Names". A standard serial cable passes all of the RS-232C signals straight through. For example, the "Transmitted Data" pin on one end of the cable goes to the "Transmitted Data" pin on the other end. This is the type of cable used to connect a modem to the FreeBSD system, and is also appropriate for some terminals.

A null-modem cable switches the "Transmitted Data" pin of the connector on one end with the "Received Data" pin on the other end. The connector can be either a DB-25 or a DB-9.

A null-modem cable can be constructed using the pin connections summarized in Table 25.2, "DB-25 to DB-25 Null-Modem Cable", Table 25.3, "DB-9 to DB-9 Null-Modem Cable", and Table 25.4, "DB-9 to DB-25 Null-Modem Cable". While the standard calls for a straight-through pin 1 to pin 1 "Protective Ground" line, it is often omitted. Some terminals work using only pins 2, 3, and 7, while others require different configurations. When in doubt, refer to the documentation for the hardware.

Table 25.1. RS-232C Signal Names

Acronyms	Names
RD	Received Data
TD	Transmitted Data
DTR	Data Terminal Ready
DSR	Data Set Ready
DCD	Data Carrier Detect
SG	Signal Ground
RTS	Request to Send
CTS	Clear to Send

Table 25.2. DB-25 to DB-25 Null-Modem Cable

Signal	Pin #		Pin #	Signal
SG	7	connects to	7	SG
TD	2	connects to	3	RD
RD	3	connects to	2	TD
RTS	4	connects to	5	CTS
CTS	5	connects to	4	RTS
DTR	20	connects to	6	DSR
DTR	20	connects to	8	DCD
DSR	6	connects to	20	DTR
DCD	8	connects to	20	DTR

Table 25.3. DB-9 to DB-9 Null-Modem Cable

Signal	Pin #		Pin #	Signal
RD	2	connects to	3	TD
TD	3	connects to	2	RD
DTR	4	connects to	6	DSR
DTR	4	connects to	1	DCD
SG	5	connects to	5	SG
DSR	6	connects to	4	DTR

Signal	Pin #		Pin #	Signal
DCD	1	connects to	4	DTR
RTS	7	connects to	8	CTS
CTS	8	connects to	7	RTS

Table 25.4. DB-9 to DB-25 Null-Modem Cable

Signal	Pin #		Pin #	Signal
RD	2	connects to	2	TD
TD	3	connects to	3	RD
DTR	4	connects to	6	DSR
DTR	4	connects to	8	DCD
SG	5	connects to	7	SG
DSR	6	connects to	20	DTR
DCD	1	connects to	20	DTR
RTS	7	connects to	5	CTS
CTS	8	connects to	4	RTS

Note

When one pin at one end connects to a pair of pins at the other end, it is usually implemented with one short wire between the pair of pins in their connector and a long wire to the other single pin.

Serial ports are the devices through which data is transferred between the FreeBSD host computer and the terminal. Several kinds of serial ports exist. Before purchasing or constructing a cable, make sure it will fit the ports on the terminal and on the FreeBSD system.

Most terminals have DB-25 ports. Personal computers may have DB-25 or DB-9 ports. A multiport serial card may have RJ-12 or RJ-45/ ports. See the documentation that accompanied the hardware for specifications on the kind of port or visually verify the type of port.

In FreeBSD, each serial port is accessed through an entry in /dev. There are two different kinds of entries:

- Call-in ports are named /dev/ttyu N where N is the port number, starting from zero. If a terminal is connected to the first serial port (COM1), use /dev/ttyu0 to refer to the terminal. If the terminal is on the second serial port (COM2), use /dev/ttyu1 , and so forth. Generally, the call-in port is used for terminals. Call-in ports require that the serial line assert the "Data Carrier Detect" signal to work correctly.

- Call-out ports are named /dev/cuau N on FreeBSD versions 10.x and higher and /dev/cuad N on FreeBSD versions 9.x and lower. Call-out ports are usually not used for terminals, but are used for modems. The call-out port can be used if the serial cable or the terminal does not support the "Data Carrier Detect" signal.

FreeBSD also provides initialization devices (/dev/ttyu N.init and /dev/cuau N.init or /dev/cuad N.init) and locking devices (/dev/ttyu N.lock and /dev/cuau N.lock or /dev/cuad N.lock). The initialization devices are used to initialize communications port parameters each time a port is opened, such as crtscts for modems which use RTS/CTS signaling for flow control. The locking devices are used to lock flags on ports to prevent users or programs changing certain parameters. Refer to termios(4), sio(4), and stty(1) for information on terminal settings, locking and initializing devices, and setting terminal options, respectively.

25.2.2. Serial Port Configuration

By default, FreeBSD supports four serial ports which are commonly known as COM1, COM2, COM3, and COM4. FreeBSD also supports dumb multi-port serial interface cards, such as the BocaBoard 1008 and 2016, as well as more intelligent multi-port cards such as those made by Digiboard. However, the default kernel only looks for the standard COM ports.

To see if the system recognizes the serial ports, look for system boot messages that start with uart:

```
# grep uart /var/run/dmesg.boot
```

If the system does not recognize all of the needed serial ports, additional entries can be added to /boot/device.hints. This file already contains hint.uart.0.* entries for COM1 and hint.uart.1.* entries for COM2. When adding a port entry for COM3 use 0x3E8, and for COM4 use 0x2E8. Common IRQ addresses are 5 for COM3 and 9 for COM4.

To determine the default set of terminal I/O settings used by the port, specify its device name. This example determines the settings for the call-in port on COM2:

```
# stty -a -f /dev/ ttyu1
```

System-wide initialization of serial devices is controlled by /etc/rc.d/serial . This file affects the default settings of serial devices. To change the settings for a device, use stty. By default, the changed settings are in effect until the device is closed and when the device is reopened, it goes back to the default set. To permanently change the default set, open and adjust the settings of the initialization device. For example, to turn on CLOCAL mode, 8 bit communication, and XON/XOFF flow control for ttyu5, type:

```
# stty -f /dev/ttyu5.init clocal cs8 ixon ixoff
```

To prevent certain settings from being changed by an application, make adjustments to the locking device. For example, to lock the speed of ttyu5 to 57600 bps, type:

```
# stty -f /dev/ttyu5.lock 57600
```

Now, any application that opens ttyu5 and tries to change the speed of the port will be stuck with 57600 bps.

25.3. Terminals

Contributed by Sean Kelly.

Terminals provide a convenient and low-cost way to access a FreeBSD system when not at the computer's console or on a connected network. This section describes how to use terminals with FreeBSD.

The original UNIX® systems did not have consoles. Instead, users logged in and ran programs through terminals that were connected to the computer's serial ports.

The ability to establish a login session on a serial port still exists in nearly every UNIX®-like operating system today, including FreeBSD. By using a terminal attached to an unused serial port, a user can log in and run any text program that can normally be run on the console or in an xterm window.

Many terminals can be attached to a FreeBSD system. An older spare computer can be used as a terminal wired into a more powerful computer running FreeBSD. This can turn what might otherwise be a single-user computer into a powerful multiple-user system.

FreeBSD supports three types of terminals:

Dumb terminals

Dumb terminals are specialized hardware that connect to computers over serial lines. They are called "dumb" because they have only enough computational power to display, send, and receive text. No programs can be run on these devices. Instead, dumb terminals connect to a computer that runs the needed programs.

There are hundreds of kinds of dumb terminals made by many manufacturers, and just about any kind will work with FreeBSD. Some high-end terminals can even display graphics, but only certain software packages can take advantage of these advanced features.

Dumb terminals are popular in work environments where workers do not need access to graphical applications.

Computers Acting as Terminals

Since a dumb terminal has just enough ability to display, send, and receive text, any spare computer can be a dumb terminal. All that is needed is the proper cable and some *terminal emulation* software to run on the computer.

This configuration can be useful. For example, if one user is busy working at the FreeBSD system's console, another user can do some text-only work at the same time from a less powerful personal computer hooked up as a terminal to the FreeBSD system.

There are at least two utilities in the base-system of FreeBSD that can be used to work through a serial connection: cu(1) and tip(1).

For example, to connect from a client system that runs FreeBSD to the serial connection of another system:

```
# cu -l serial-port-device
```

Replace *serial-port-device* with the device name of the connected serial port. These device files are called /dev/cuau *N* on FreeBSD versions 10.x and higher and /dev/cuad *N* on FreeBSD versions 9.x and lower. In either case, *N* is the serial port number, starting from zero. This means that COM1 is /dev/cuau0 or /dev/cuad0 in FreeBSD.

Additional programs are available through the Ports Collection, such as comms/minicom.

X Terminals

X terminals are the most sophisticated kind of terminal available. Instead of connecting to a serial port, they usually connect to a network like Ethernet. Instead of being relegated to text-only applications, they can display any Xorg application.

This chapter does not cover the setup, configuration, or use of X terminals.

25.3.1. Terminal Configuration

This section describes how to configure a FreeBSD system to enable a login session on a serial terminal. It assumes that the system recognizes the serial port to which the terminal is connected and that the terminal is connected with the correct cable.

In FreeBSD, init reads /etc/ttys and starts a getty process on the available terminals. The getty process is responsible for reading a login name and starting the login program. The ports on the FreeBSD system which allow logins are listed in /etc/ttys . For example, the first virtual console, ttyv0, has an entry in this file, allowing logins on the console. This file also contains entries for the other virtual consoles, serial ports, and pseudo-ttys. For a hardwired terminal, the serial port's /dev entry is listed without the /dev part. For example, /dev/ttyv0 is listed as ttyv0.

The default /etc/ttys configures support for the first four serial ports, ttyu0 through ttyu3:

```
ttyu0    "/usr/libexec/getty std.9600"    dialup  off secure
ttyu1    "/usr/libexec/getty std.9600"    dialup  off secure
ttyu2    "/usr/libexec/getty std.9600"    dialup  off secure
ttyu3    "/usr/libexec/getty std.9600"    dialup  off secure
```

When attaching a terminal to one of those ports, modify the default entry to set the required speed and terminal type, to turn the device on and, if needed, to change the port's secure setting. If the terminal is connected to another port, add an entry for the port.

Example 25.1, "Configuring Terminal Entries" configures two terminals in /etc/ttys . The first entry configures a Wyse-50 connected to COM2. The second entry configures an old computer running Procomm terminal software emulating a VT-100 terminal. The computer is connected to the sixth serial port on a multi-port serial card.

Example 25.1. Configuring Terminal Entries

```
ttyu1❶  "/usr/libexec/getty std.38400"❷  wy50❸  on❹  insecure❺
ttyu5  "/usr/libexec/getty std.19200"  vt100  on insecure
```

❶　The first field specifies the device name of the serial terminal.

❷　The second field tells **getty** to initialize and open the line, set the line speed, prompt for a user name, and then execute the **login** program. The optional *getty type* configures characteristics on the terminal line, like bps rate and parity. The available getty types are listed in /etc/gettytab . In almost all cases, the getty types that start with **std** will work for hardwired terminals as these entries ignore parity. There is a **std** entry for each bps rate from 110 to 115200. Refer to gettytab(5) for more information.

When setting the getty type, make sure to match the communications settings used by the terminal. For this example, the Wyse-50 uses no parity and connects at 38400 bps. The computer uses no parity and connects at 19200 bps.

❸　The third field is the type of terminal. For dial-up ports, **unknown** or **dialup** is typically used since users may dial up with practically any type of terminal or software. Since the terminal type does not change for hardwired terminals, a real terminal type from /etc/termcap can be specified. For this example, the Wyse-50 uses the real terminal type while the computer running Procomm is set to emulate a VT-100.

❹　The fourth field specifies if the port should be enabled. To enable logins on this port, this field must be set to **on**.

❺　The final field is used to specify whether the port is secure. Marking a port as **secure** means that it is trusted enough to allow **root** to login from that port. Insecure ports do not allow **root** logins. On an insecure port, users must login from unprivileged accounts and then use **su** or a similar mechanism to gain superuser privileges, as described in Section 3.3.1.3, "The Superuser Account". For security reasons, it is recommended to change this setting to **insecure**.

After making any changes to /etc/ttys , send a SIGHUP (hangup) signal to the **init** process to force it to re-read its configuration file:

```
# kill -HUP 1
```

Since **init** is always the first process run on a system, it always has a process ID of 1.

If everything is set up correctly, all cables are in place, and the terminals are powered up, a **getty** process should now be running on each terminal and login prompts should be available on each terminal.

25.3.2. Troubleshooting the Connection

Even with the most meticulous attention to detail, something could still go wrong while setting up a terminal. Here is a list of common symptoms and some suggested fixes.

If no login prompt appears, make sure the terminal is plugged in and powered up. If it is a personal computer acting as a terminal, make sure it is running terminal emulation software on the correct serial port.

Make sure the cable is connected firmly to both the terminal and the FreeBSD computer. Make sure it is the right kind of cable.

Make sure the terminal and FreeBSD agree on the bps rate and parity settings. For a video display terminal, make sure the contrast and brightness controls are turned up. If it is a printing terminal, make sure paper and ink are in good supply.

Use `ps` to make sure that a `getty` process is running and serving the terminal. For example, the following listing shows that a `getty` is running on the second serial port, `ttyu1`, and is using the `std.38400` entry in `/etc/gettytab`:

```
# ps -axww|grep ttyu
22189  d1  Is+   0:00.03 /usr/libexec/getty std.38400 ttyu1
```

If no `getty` process is running, make sure the port is enabled in `/etc/ttys`. Remember to run `kill -HUP 1` after modifying `/etc/ttys`.

If the `getty` process is running but the terminal still does not display a login prompt, or if it displays a prompt but will not accept typed input, the terminal or cable may not support hardware handshaking. Try changing the entry in `/etc/ttys` from `std.38400` to `3wire.38400`, then run `kill -HUP 1` after modifying `/etc/ttys`. The `3wire` entry is similar to `std`, but ignores hardware handshaking. The baud rate may need to be reduced or software flow control enabled when using `3wire` to prevent buffer overflows.

If garbage appears instead of a login prompt, make sure the terminal and FreeBSD agree on the bps rate and parity settings. Check the `getty` processes to make sure the correct *getty* type is in use. If not, edit `/etc/ttys` and run `kill -HUP 1`.

If characters appear doubled and the password appears when typed, switch the terminal, or the terminal emulation software, from "half duplex" or "local echo" to "full duplex."

25.4. Dial-in Service

Contributed by Guy Helmer.
Additions by Sean Kelly.

Configuring a FreeBSD system for dial-in service is similar to configuring terminals, except that modems are used instead of terminal devices. FreeBSD supports both external and internal modems.

External modems are more convenient because they often can be configured via parameters stored in non-volatile RAM and they usually provide lighted indicators that display the state of important RS-232 signals, indicating whether the modem is operating properly.

Internal modems usually lack non-volatile RAM, so their configuration may be limited to setting DIP switches. If the internal modem has any signal indicator lights, they are difficult to view when the system's cover is in place.

When using an external modem, a proper cable is needed. A standard RS-232C serial cable should suffice.

FreeBSD needs the RTS and CTS signals for flow control at speeds above 2400 bps, the CD signal to detect when a call has been answered or the line has been hung up, and the DTR signal to reset the modem after a session is complete. Some cables are wired without all of the needed signals, so if a login session does not go away when the line hangs up, there may be a problem with the cable. Refer to Section 25.2.1, "Serial Cables and Ports" for more information about these signals.

Like other UNIX®-like operating systems, FreeBSD uses the hardware signals to find out when a call has been answered or a line has been hung up and to hangup and reset the modem after a call. FreeBSD avoids sending commands to the modem or watching for status reports from the modem.

FreeBSD supports the NS8250, NS16450, NS16550, and NS16550A-based RS-232C (CCITT V.24) communications interfaces. The 8250 and 16450 devices have single-character buffers. The 16550 device provides a 16-character buffer, which allows for better system performance. Bugs in plain 16550 devices prevent the use of the 16-character buffer, so use 16550A devices if possible. Because single-character-buffer devices require more work by the operating system than the 16-character-buffer devices, 16550A-based serial interface cards are preferred. If the system has many active serial ports or will have a heavy load, 16550A-based cards are better for low-error-rate communications.

The rest of this section demonstrates how to configure a modem to receive incoming connections, how to communicate with the modem, and offers some troubleshooting tips.

25.4.1. Modem Configuration

As with terminals, init spawns a getty process for each configured serial port used for dial-in connections. When a user dials the modem's line and the modems connect, the "Carrier Detect" signal is reported by the modem. The kernel notices that the carrier has been detected and instructs getty to open the port and display a login: prompt at the specified initial line speed. In a typical configuration, if garbage characters are received, usually due to the modem's connection speed being different than the configured speed, getty tries adjusting the line speeds until it receives reasonable characters. After the user enters their login name, getty executes login, which completes the login process by asking for the user's password and then starting the user's shell.

There are two schools of thought regarding dial-up modems. One configuration method is to set the modems and systems so that no matter at what speed a remote user dials in, the dial-in RS-232 interface runs at a locked speed. The benefit of this configuration is that the remote user always sees a system login prompt immediately. The downside is that the system does not know what a user's true data rate is, so full-screen programs like Emacs will not adjust their screen-painting methods to make their response better for slower connections.

The second method is to configure the RS-232 interface to vary its speed based on the remote user's connection speed. Because getty does not understand any particular modem's connection speed reporting, it gives a login: message at an initial speed and watches the characters that come back in response. If the user sees junk, they should press Enter until they see a recognizable prompt. If the data rates do not match, getty sees anything the user types as junk, tries the next speed, and gives the login: prompt again. This procedure normally only takes a keystroke or two before the user sees a good prompt. This login sequence does not look as clean as the locked-speed method, but a user on a low-speed connection should receive better interactive response from full-screen programs.

When locking a modem's data communications rate at a particular speed, no changes to /etc/gettytab should be needed. However, for a matching-speed configuration, additional entries may be required in order to define the speeds to use for the modem. This example configures a 14.4 Kbps modem with a top interface speed of 19.2 Kbps using 8-bit, no parity connections. It configures getty to start the communications rate for a V.32bis connection at 19.2 Kbps, then cycles through 9600 bps, 2400 bps, 1200 bps, 300 bps, and back to 19.2 Kbps. Communications rate cycling is implemented with the nx= (next table) capability. Each line uses a tc= (table continuation) entry to pick up the rest of the settings for a particular data rate.

```
#
# Additions for a V.32bis Modem
#
um|V300|High Speed Modem at 300,8-bit:\
        :nx=V19200:tc=std.300:
un|V1200|High Speed Modem at 1200,8-bit:\
        :nx=V300:tc=std.1200:
uo|V2400|High Speed Modem at 2400,8-bit:\
        :nx=V1200:tc=std.2400:
up|V9600|High Speed Modem at 9600,8-bit:\
        :nx=V2400:tc=std.9600:
uq|V19200|High Speed Modem at 19200,8-bit:\
        :nx=V9600:tc=std.19200:
```

For a 28.8 Kbps modem, or to take advantage of compression on a 14.4 Kbps modem, use a higher communications rate, as seen in this example:

```
#
# Additions for a V.32bis or V.34 Modem
# Starting at 57.6 Kbps
#
vm|VH300|Very High Speed Modem at 300,8-bit:\
```

```
        :nx=VH57600:tc=std.300:
vn|VH1200|Very High Speed Modem at 1200,8-bit:\
        :nx=VH300:tc=std.1200:
vo|VH2400|Very High Speed Modem at 2400,8-bit:\
        :nx=VH1200:tc=std.2400:
vp|VH9600|Very High Speed Modem at 9600,8-bit:\
        :nx=VH2400:tc=std.9600:
vq|VH57600|Very High Speed Modem at 57600,8-bit:\
        :nx=VH9600:tc=std.57600:
```

For a slow CPU or a heavily loaded system without 16550A-based serial ports, this configuration may produce sio "silo" errors at 57.6 Kbps.

The configuration of /etc/ttys is similar to Example 25.1, "Configuring Terminal Entries", but a different argument is passed to getty and dialup is used for the terminal type. Replace *xxx* with the process init will run on the device:

```
ttyu0   "/usr/libexec/getty xxx"   dialup on
```

The dialup terminal type can be changed. For example, setting vt102 as the default terminal type allows users to use VT102 emulation on their remote systems.

For a locked-speed configuration, specify the speed with a valid type listed in /etc/gettytab. This example is for a modem whose port speed is locked at 19.2 Kbps:

```
ttyu0   "/usr/libexec/getty std.19200"   dialup on
```

In a matching-speed configuration, the entry needs to reference the appropriate beginning "auto-baud" entry in /etc/gettytab. To continue the example for a matching-speed modem that starts at 19.2 Kbps, use this entry:

```
ttyu0   "/usr/libexec/getty V19200"   dialup on
```

After editing /etc/ttys , wait until the modem is properly configured and connected before signaling init:

```
# kill -HUP 1
```

High-speed modems, like V.32, V.32bis, and V.34 modems, use hardware (RTS/CTS) flow control. Use stty to set the hardware flow control flag for the modem port. This example sets the crtscts flag on COM2's dial-in and dial-out initialization devices:

```
# stty -f /dev/ttyu1.init crtscts
# stty -f /dev/cuau1.init crtscts
```

25.4.2. Troubleshooting

This section provides a few tips for troubleshooting a dial-up modem that will not connect to a FreeBSD system.

Hook up the modem to the FreeBSD system and boot the system. If the modem has status indication lights, watch to see whether the modem's DTR indicator lights when the login: prompt appears on the system's console. If it lights up, that should mean that FreeBSD has started a getty process on the appropriate communications port and is waiting for the modem to accept a call.

If the DTR indicator does not light, login to the FreeBSD system through the console and type ps ax to see if FreeBSD is running a getty process on the correct port:

```
  114 ??  I      0:00.10 /usr/libexec/getty V19200 ttyu0
```

If the second column contains a d0 instead of a ?? and the modem has not accepted a call yet, this means that getty has completed its open on the communications port. This could indicate a problem with the cabling or a misconfigured modem because getty should not be able to open the communications port until the carrier detect signal has been asserted by the modem.

If no `getty` processes are waiting to open the port, double-check that the entry for the port is correct in `/etc/ttys`. Also, check `/var/log/messages` to see if there are any log messages from `init` or `getty`.

Next, try dialing into the system. Be sure to use 8 bits, no parity, and 1 stop bit on the remote system. If a prompt does not appear right away, or the prompt shows garbage, try pressing Enter about once per second. If there is still no `login:` prompt, try sending a BREAK. When using a high-speed modem, try dialing again after locking the dialing modem's interface speed.

If there is still no `login:` prompt, check `/etc/gettytab` again and double-check that:

- The initial capability name specified in the entry in `/etc/ttys` matches the name of a capability in `/etc/gettytab`.

- Each `nx=` entry matches another `gettytab` capability name.

- Each `tc=` entry matches another `gettytab` capability name.

If the modem on the FreeBSD system will not answer, make sure that the modem is configured to answer the phone when DTR is asserted. If the modem seems to be configured correctly, verify that the DTR line is asserted by checking the modem's indicator lights.

If it still does not work, try sending an email to the FreeBSD general questions mailing list describing the modem and the problem.

25.5. Dial-out Service

The following are tips for getting the host to connect over the modem to another computer. This is appropriate for establishing a terminal session with a remote host.

This kind of connection can be helpful to get a file on the Internet if there are problems using PPP. If PPP is not working, use the terminal session to FTP the needed file. Then use zmodem to transfer it to the machine.

25.5.1. Using a Stock Hayes Modem

A generic Hayes dialer is built into `tip`. Use `at=hayes` in `/etc/remote`.

The Hayes driver is not smart enough to recognize some of the advanced features of newer modems messages like BUSY, NO DIALTONE, or CONNECT 115200. Turn those messages off when using `tip` with ATX0&W.

The dial timeout for `tip` is 60 seconds. The modem should use something less, or else `tip` will think there is a communication problem. Try ATS7=45&W.

25.5.2. Using AT Commands

Create a "direct" entry in `/etc/remote`. For example, if the modem is hooked up to the first serial port, `/dev/cuau0`, use the following line:

```
cuau0:dv=/dev/cuau0:br#19200:pa=none
```

Use the highest bps rate the modem supports in the `br` capability. Then, type `tip cuau0` to connect to the modem.

Or, use `cu` as `root` with the following command:

```
# cu -lline -sspeed
```

line is the serial port, such as /dev/cuau0, and *speed* is the speed, such as 57600. When finished entering the AT commands, type ~. to exit.

25.5.3. The @ Sign Does Not Work

The @ sign in the phone number capability tells tip to look in /etc/phones for a phone number. But, the @ sign is also a special character in capability files like /etc/remote, so it needs to be escaped with a backslash:

```
pn=\@
```

25.5.4. Dialing from the Command Line

Put a "generic" entry in /etc/remote. For example:

```
tip115200|Dial any phone number at 115200 bps:\
        :dv=/dev/cuau0:br#115200:at=hayes:pa=none:du:
tip57600|Dial any phone number at 57600 bps:\
        :dv=/dev/cuau0:br#57600:at=hayes:pa=none:du:
```

This should now work:

```
# tip -115200 5551234
```

Users who prefer cu over tip, can use a generic cu entry:

```
cu115200|Use cu to dial any number at 115200bps:\
        :dv=/dev/cuau1:br#57600:at=hayes:pa=none:du:
```

and type:

```
# cu 5551234 -s 115200
```

25.5.5. Setting the bps Rate

Put in an entry for tip1200 or cu1200, but go ahead and use whatever bps rate is appropriate with the br capability. tip thinks a good default is 1200 bps which is why it looks for a tip1200 entry. 1200 bps does not have to be used, though.

25.5.6. Accessing a Number of Hosts Through a Terminal Server

Rather than waiting until connected and typing CONNECT *host* each time, use tip's cm capability. For example, these entries in /etc/remote will let you type tip pain or tip muffin to connect to the hosts pain or muffin, and tip deep13 to connect to the terminal server.

```
pain|pain.deep13.com|Forrester's machine:\
        :cm=CONNECT pain\n:tc=deep13:
muffin|muffin.deep13.com|Frank's machine:\
        :cm=CONNECT muffin\n:tc=deep13:
deep13:Gizmonics Institute terminal server:\
        :dv=/dev/cuau2:br#38400:at=hayes:du:pa=none:pn=5551234:
```

25.5.7. Using More Than One Line with tip

This is often a problem where a university has several modem lines and several thousand students trying to use them.

Make an entry in /etc/remote and use @ for the pn capability:

```
big-university:\
        :pn=\@:tc=dialout
dialout:\
        :dv=/dev/cuau3:br#9600:at=courier:du:pa=none:
```

Then, list the phone numbers in /etc/phones :

```
big-university 5551111
```

```
big-university 5551112
big-university 5551113
big-university 5551114
```

tip will try each number in the listed order, then give up. To keep retrying, run tip in a while loop.

25.5.8. Using the Force Character

Ctrl+P is the default "force" character, used to tell tip that the next character is literal data. The force character can be set to any other character with the ~s escape, which means "set a variable."

Type ~sforce=*single-char* followed by a newline. *single-char* is any single character. If *single-char* is left out, then the force character is the null character, which is accessed by typing Ctrl+2 or Ctrl+Space. A pretty good value for *single-char* is Shift+Ctrl+6, which is only used on some terminal servers.

To change the force character, specify the following in ~/.tiprc:

```
force=single-char
```

25.5.9. Upper Case Characters

This happens when Ctrl+A is pressed, which is tip's "raise character", specially designed for people with broken caps-lock keys. Use ~s to set raisechar to something reasonable. It can be set to be the same as the force character, if neither feature is used.

Here is a sample ~/.tiprc for Emacs users who need to type Ctrl+2 and Ctrl+A:

```
force=^^
raisechar=^^
```

The ^^ is Shift+Ctrl+6.

25.5.10. File Transfers with tip

When talking to another UNIX®-like operating system, files can be sent and received using ~p (put) and ~t (take). These commands run cat and echo on the remote system to accept and send files. The syntax is:

~p local-file [remote-file]

~t remote-file [local-file]

There is no error checking, so another protocol, like zmodem, should probably be used.

25.5.11. Using zmodem with tip?

To receive files, start the sending program on the remote end. Then, type ~C rz to begin receiving them locally.

To send files, start the receiving program on the remote end. Then, type ~C sz *files* to send them to the remote system.

25.6. Setting Up the Serial Console

Contributed by Kazutaka YOKOTA.
Based on a document by Bill Paul.

FreeBSD has the ability to boot a system with a dumb terminal on a serial port as a console. This configuration is useful for system administrators who wish to install FreeBSD on machines that have no keyboard or monitor attached, and developers who want to debug the kernel or device drivers.

As described in Chapter 12, *The FreeBSD Booting Process*, FreeBSD employs a three stage bootstrap. The first two stages are in the boot block code which is stored at the beginning of the FreeBSD slice on the boot disk. The boot block then loads and runs the boot loader as the third stage code.

In order to set up booting from a serial console, the boot block code, the boot loader code, and the kernel need to be configured.

25.6.1. Quick Serial Console Configuration

This section provides a fast overview of setting up the serial console. This procedure can be used when the dumb terminal is connected to COM1.

Procedure 25.1. Configuring a Serial Console on COM1

1. Connect the serial cable to COM1 and the controlling terminal.

2. To configure boot messages to display on the serial console, issue the following command as the superuser:

    ```
    # echo 'console="comconsole"' >> /boot/loader.conf
    ```

3. Edit /etc/ttys and change off to on and dialup to vt100 for the ttyu0 entry. Otherwise, a password will not be required to connect via the serial console, resulting in a potential security hole.

4. Reboot the system to see if the changes took effect.

If a different configuration is required, see the next section for a more in-depth configuration explanation.

25.6.2. In-Depth Serial Console Configuration

This section provides a more detailed explanation of the steps needed to setup a serial console in FreeBSD.

Procedure 25.2. Configuring a Serial Console

1. Prepare a serial cable.

    Use either a null-modem cable or a standard serial cable and a null-modem adapter. See Section 25.2.1, "Serial Cables and Ports" for a discussion on serial cables.

2. Unplug the keyboard.

    Many systems probe for the keyboard during the Power-On Self-Test (POST) and will generate an error if the keyboard is not detected. Some machines will refuse to boot until the keyboard is plugged in.

    If the computer complains about the error, but boots anyway, no further configuration is needed.

    If the computer refuses to boot without a keyboard attached, configure the BIOS so that it ignores this error. Consult the motherboard's manual for details on how to do this.

    ### Tip

    Try setting the keyboard to "Not installed" in the BIOS. This setting tells the BIOS not to probe for a keyboard at power-on so it should not complain if the keyboard is absent. If that option is not present in the BIOS, look for an "Halt on Error" option instead. Setting this to "All but Keyboard" or to "No Errors" will have the same effect.

    If the system has a PS/2® mouse, unplug it as well. PS/2® mice share some hardware with the keyboard and leaving the mouse plugged in can fool the keyboard probe into thinking the keyboard is still there.

Note

While most systems will boot without a keyboard, quite a few will not boot without a graphics adapter. Some systems can be configured to boot with no graphics adapter by changing the "graphics adapter" setting in the BIOS configuration to "Not installed". Other systems do not support this option and will refuse to boot if there is no display hardware in the system. With these machines, leave some kind of graphics card plugged in, even if it is just a junky mono board. A monitor does not need to be attached.

3. Plug a dumb terminal, an old computer with a modem program, or the serial port on another UNIX® box into the serial port.

4. Add the appropriate `hint.sio.*` entries to `/boot/device.hints` for the serial port. Some multi-port cards also require kernel configuration options. Refer to sio(4) for the required options and device hints for each supported serial port.

5. Create `boot.config` in the root directory of the **a** partition on the boot drive.

   This file instructs the boot block code how to boot the system. In order to activate the serial console, one or more of the following options are needed. When using multiple options, include them all on the same line:

   -h

   Toggles between the internal and serial consoles. Use this to switch console devices. For instance, to boot from the internal (video) console, use -h to direct the boot loader and the kernel to use the serial port as its console device. Alternatively, to boot from the serial port, use -h to tell the boot loader and the kernel to use the video display as the console instead.

   -D

   Toggles between the single and dual console configurations. In the single configuration, the console will be either the internal console (video display) or the serial port, depending on the state of -h. In the dual console configuration, both the video display and the serial port will become the console at the same time, regardless of the state of -h. However, the dual console configuration takes effect only while the boot block is running. Once the boot loader gets control, the console specified by -h becomes the only console.

   -P

   Makes the boot block probe the keyboard. If no keyboard is found, the -D and -h options are automatically set.

Note

Due to space constraints in the current version of the boot blocks, -P is capable of detecting extended keyboards only. Keyboards with less than 101 keys and without F11 and F12 keys may not be detected. Keyboards on some laptops may not be properly found because of this limitation. If this is the case, do not use -P.

Use either -P to select the console automatically or -h to activate the serial console. Refer to boot(8) and boot.config(5) for more details.

The options, except for -P, are passed to the boot loader. The boot loader will determine whether the internal video or the serial port should become the console by examining the state of -h. This means that if -D is specified but -h is not specified in /boot.config, the serial port can be used as the console only during the boot block as the boot loader will use the internal video display as the console.

6. Boot the machine.

When FreeBSD starts, the boot blocks echo the contents of /boot.config to the console. For example:

```
/boot.config: -P
Keyboard: no
```

The second line appears only if -P is in /boot.config and indicates the presence or absence of the keyboard. These messages go to either the serial or internal console, or both, depending on the option in /boot.config:

Options	Message goes to
none	internal console
-h	serial console
-D	serial and internal consoles
-Dh	serial and internal consoles
-P, keyboard present	internal console
-P, keyboard absent	serial console

After the message, there will be a small pause before the boot blocks continue loading the boot loader and before any further messages are printed to the console. Under normal circumstances, there is no need to interrupt the boot blocks, but one can do so in order to make sure things are set up correctly.

Press any key, other than Enter, at the console to interrupt the boot process. The boot blocks will then prompt for further action:

```
>> FreeBSD/i386 BOOT
Default: 0:ad(0,a)/boot/loader
boot:
```

Verify that the above message appears on either the serial or internal console, or both, according to the options in /boot.config. If the message appears in the correct console, press Enter to continue the boot process.

If there is no prompt on the serial terminal, something is wrong with the settings. Enter -h then Enter or Return to tell the boot block (and then the boot loader and the kernel) to choose the serial port for the console. Once the system is up, go back and check what went wrong.

During the third stage of the boot process, one can still switch between the internal console and the serial console by setting appropriate environment variables in the boot loader. See loader(8) for more information.

Note

This line in /boot/loader.conf or /boot/loader.conf.local configures the boot loader and the kernel to send their boot messages to the serial console, regardless of the options in /boot.config:

```
console="comconsole"
```

That line should be the first line of /boot/loader.conf so that boot messages are displayed on the serial console as early as possible.

If that line does not exist, or if it is set to console="vidconsole", the boot loader and the kernel will use whichever console is indicated by -h in the boot block. See loader.conf(5) for more information.

> At the moment, the boot loader has no option equivalent to -P in the boot block, and there is no provision to automatically select the internal console and the serial console based on the presence of the keyboard.

Tip

While it is not required, it is possible to provide a login prompt over the serial line. To configure this, edit the entry for the serial port in /etc/ttys using the instructions in Section 25.3.1, "Terminal Configuration". If the speed of the serial port has been changed, change std.9600 to match the new setting.

25.6.3. Setting a Faster Serial Port Speed

By default, the serial port settings are 9600 baud, 8 bits, no parity, and 1 stop bit. To change the default console speed, use one of the following options:

- Edit /etc/make.conf and set BOOT_COMCONSOLE_SPEED to the new console speed. Then, recompile and install the boot blocks and the boot loader:

```
# cd /sys/boot
# make clean
# make
# make install
```

If the serial console is configured in some other way than by booting with -h, or if the serial console used by the kernel is different from the one used by the boot blocks, add the following option, with the desired speed, to a custom kernel configuration file and compile a new kernel:

```
options CONSPEED=19200
```

- Add the -S19200 boot option to /boot.config, replacing 19200 with the speed to use.

- Add the following options to /boot/loader.conf. Replace 115200 with the speed to use.

```
boot_multicons="YES"
boot_serial="YES"
comconsole_speed="115200"
console="comconsole,vidconsole"
```

25.6.4. Entering the DDB Debugger from the Serial Line

To configure the ability to drop into the kernel debugger from the serial console, add the following options to a custom kernel configuration file and compile the kernel using the instructions in Chapter 8, *Configuring the FreeBSD Kernel*. Note that while this is useful for remote diagnostics, it is also dangerous if a spurious BREAK is generated on the serial port. Refer to ddb(4) and ddb(8) for more information about the kernel debugger.

```
options BREAK_TO_DEBUGGER
options DDB
```

Chapter 26. PPP

26.1. Synopsis

FreeBSD supports the Point-to-Point (PPP) protocol which can be used to establish a network or Internet connection using a dial-up modem. This chapter describes how to configure modem-based communication services in FreeBSD.

After reading this chapter, you will know:

- How to configure, use, and troubleshoot a PPP connection.

- How to set up PPP over Ethernet (PPPoE).

- How to set up PPP over ATM (PPPoA).

Before reading this chapter, you should:

- Be familiar with basic network terminology.

- Understand the basics and purpose of a dial-up connection and PPP.

26.2. Configuring PPP

FreeBSD provides built-in support for managing dial-up PPP connections using ppp(8). The default FreeBSD kernel provides support for tun which is used to interact with a modem hardware. Configuration is performed by editing at least one configuration file, and configuration files containing examples are provided. Finally, ppp is used to start and manage connections.

In order to use a PPP connection, the following items are needed:

- A dial-up account with an Internet Service Provider (ISP).

- A dial-up modem.

- The dial-up number for the ISP.

- The login name and password assigned by the ISP.

- The IP address of one or more DNS servers. Normally, the ISP provides these addresses. If it did not, FreeBSD can be configured to use DNS negotiation.

If any of the required information is missing, contact the ISP.

The following information may be supplied by the ISP, but is not necessary:

- The IP address of the default gateway. If this information is unknown, the ISP will automatically provide the correct value during connection setup. When configuring PPP on FreeBSD, this address is referred to as HISADDR.

- The subnet mask. If the ISP has not provided one, 255.255.255.255 will be used in the ppp(8) configuration file.

-
  If the ISP has assigned a static IP address and hostname, it should be input into the configuration file. Otherwise, this information will be automatically provided during connection setup.

The rest of this section demonstrates how to configure FreeBSD for common PPP connection scenarios. The required configuration file is /etc/ppp/ppp.conf and additional files and examples are available in /usr/share/examples/ppp/.

Note

Throughout this section, many of the file examples display line numbers. These line numbers have been added to make it easier to follow the discussion and are not meant to be placed in the actual file.

When editing a configuration file, proper indentation is important. Lines that end in a : start in the first column (beginning of the line) while all other lines should be indented as shown using spaces or tabs.

26.2.1. Basic Configuration

In order to configure a PPP connection, first edit /etc/ppp/ppp.conf with the dial-in information for the ISP. This file is described as follows:

```
1    default:
2      set log Phase Chat LCP IPCP CCP tun command
3      ident user-ppp VERSION
4      set device /dev/cuau0
5      set speed 115200
6      set dial "ABORT BUSY ABORT NO\\sCARRIER TIMEOUT 5 \
7              \"\" AT OK-AT-OK ATE1Q0 OK \\dATDT\\T TIMEOUT 40 CONNECT"
8      set timeout 180
9      enable dns
10
11   provider:
12      set phone "(123) 456 7890"
13      set authname foo
14      set authkey bar
15      set timeout 300
16      set ifaddr x.x.x.x/0 y.y.y.y/0 255.255.255.255 0.0.0.0
17      add default HISADDR
```

Line 1:
> Identifies the default entry. Commands in this entry (lines 2 through 9) are executed automatically when ppp is run.

Line 2:
> Enables verbose logging parameters for testing the connection. Once the configuration is working satisfactorily, this line should be reduced to:

```
set log phase tun
```

Line 3:
> Displays the version of ppp(8) to the PPP software running on the other side of the connection.

Line 4:
> Identifies the device to which the modem is connected, where COM1 is /dev/cuau0 and COM2 is /dev/cuau1.

Line 5:
> Sets the connection speed. If 115200 does not work on an older modem, try 38400 instead.

Lines 6 & 7:
> The dial string written as an expect-send syntax. Refer to chat(8) for more information.

Note that this command continues onto the next line for readability. Any command in `ppp.conf` may do this if the last character on the line is \.

Line 8:
> Sets the idle timeout for the link in seconds.

Line 9:
> Instructs the peer to confirm the DNS settings. If the local network is running its own DNS server, this line should be commented out, by adding a # at the beginning of the line, or removed.

Line 10:
> A blank line for readability. Blank lines are ignored by ppp(8).

Line 11:
> Identifies an entry called `provider`. This could be changed to the name of the ISP so that `load ISP` can be used to start the connection.

Line 12:
> Use the phone number for the ISP. Multiple phone numbers may be specified using the colon (:) or pipe character (|) as a separator. To rotate through the numbers, use a colon. To always attempt to dial the first number first and only use the other numbers if the first number fails, use the pipe character. Always enclose the entire set of phone numbers between quotation marks (") to prevent dialing failures.

Lines 13 & 14:
> Use the user name and password for the ISP.

Line 15:
> Sets the default idle timeout in seconds for the connection. In this example, the connection will be closed automatically after 300 seconds of inactivity. To prevent a timeout, set this value to zero.

Line 16:
> Sets the interface addresses. The values used depend upon whether a static IP address has been obtained from the ISP or if it instead negotiates a dynamic IP address during connection.
>
> If the ISP has allocated a static IP address and default gateway, replace *x.x.x.x* with the static IP address and replace *y.y.y.y* with the IP address of the default gateway. If the ISP has only provided a static IP address without a gateway address, replace *y.y.y.y* with `10.0.0.2/0`.
>
> If the IP address changes whenever a connection is made, change this line to the following value. This tells ppp(8) to use the IP Configuration Protocol (IPCP) to negotiate a dynamic IP address:
>
> ```
> set ifaddr 10.0.0.1/0 10.0.0.2/0 255.255.255.255 0.0.0.0
> ```

Line 17:
> Keep this line as-is as it adds a default route to the gateway. The `HISADDR` will automatically be replaced with the gateway address specified on line 16. It is important that this line appears after line 16.

Depending upon whether ppp(8) is started manually or automatically, a `/etc/ppp/ppp.linkup` may also need to be created which contains the following lines. This file is required when running `ppp` in `-auto` mode. This file is used after the connection has been established. At this point, the IP address will have been assigned and it is now be possible to add the routing table entries. When creating this file, make sure that *provider* matches the value demonstrated in line 11 of `ppp.conf`.

```
provider:
    add default HISADDR
```

This file is also needed when the default gateway address is "guessed" in a static IP address configuration. In this case, remove line 17 from `ppp.conf` and create `/etc/ppp/ppp.linkup` with the above two lines. More examples for this file can be found in `/usr/share/examples/ppp/`.

By default, ppp must be run as root. To change this default, add the account of the user who should run ppp to the network group in /etc/group .

Then, give the user access to one or more entries in /etc/ppp/ppp.conf with allow. For example, to give fred and mary permission to only the provider: entry, add this line to the provider: section:

```
allow users fred mary
```

To give the specified users access to all entries, put that line in the default section instead.

26.2.2. Advanced Configuration

It is possible to configure PPP to supply DNS and NetBIOS nameserver addresses on demand.

To enable these extensions with PPP version 1.x, the following lines might be added to the relevant section of /etc/ppp/ppp.conf .

```
enable msext
set ns 203.14.100.1 203.14.100.2
set nbns 203.14.100.5
```

And for PPP version 2 and above:

```
accept dns
set dns 203.14.100.1 203.14.100.2
set nbns 203.14.100.5
```

This will tell the clients the primary and secondary name server addresses, and a NetBIOS nameserver host.

In version 2 and above, if the set dns line is omitted, PPP will use the values found in /etc/resolv.conf .

26.2.2.1. PAP and CHAP Authentication

Some ISPs set their system up so that the authentication part of the connection is done using either of the PAP or CHAP authentication mechanisms. If this is the case, the ISP will not give a login: prompt at connection, but will start talking PPP immediately.

PAP is less secure than CHAP, but security is not normally an issue here as passwords, although being sent as plain text with PAP, are being transmitted down a serial line only. There is not much room for crackers to "eavesdrop".

The following alterations must be made:

```
13      set authname MyUserName
14      set authkey MyPassword
15      set login
```

Line 13:
>   This line specifies the PAP/CHAP user name. Insert the correct value for MyUserName.

Line 14:
>   This line specifies the PAP/CHAP password. Insert the correct value for MyPassword. You may want to add an additional line, such as:

```
16      accept PAP
```

or

```
16      accept CHAP
```

to make it obvious that this is the intention, but PAP and CHAP are both accepted by default.

Line 15:

The ISP will not normally require a login to the server when using PAP or CHAP. Therefore, disable the "set login" string.

26.2.2.2. Using PPP Network Address Translation Capability

PPP has ability to use internal NAT without kernel diverting capabilities. This functionality may be enabled by the following line in /etc/ppp/ppp.conf :

```
nat enable yes
```

Alternatively, NAT may be enabled by command-line option -nat. There is also /etc/rc.conf knob named ppp_nat, which is enabled by default.

When using this feature, it may be useful to include the following /etc/ppp/ppp.conf options to enable incoming connections forwarding:

```
nat port tcp 10.0.0.2:ftp ftp
nat port tcp 10.0.0.2:http http
```

or do not trust the outside at all

```
nat deny_incoming yes
```

26.2.3. Final System Configuration

While ppp is now configured, some edits still need to be made to /etc/rc.conf .

Working from the top down in this file, make sure the hostname= line is set:

```
hostname="foo.example.com"
```

If the ISP has supplied a static IP address and name, use this name as the host name.

Look for the network_interfaces variable. To configure the system to dial the ISP on demand, make sure the tun0 device is added to the list, otherwise remove it.

```
network_interfaces="lo0 tun0"
ifconfig_tun0=
```

> ### Note
>
> The ifconfig_tun0 variable should be empty, and a file called /etc/start_if.tun0 should be created. This file should contain the line:
>
> ```
> ppp -auto mysystem
> ```
>
> This script is executed at network configuration time, starting the ppp daemon in automatic mode. If this machine acts as a gateway, consider including -alias. Refer to the manual page for further details.

Make sure that the router program is set to NO with the following line in /etc/rc.conf :

```
router_enable="NO"
```

It is important that the routed daemon is not started, as routed tends to delete the default routing table entries created by ppp.

It is probably a good idea to ensure that the `sendmail_flags` line does not include the `-q` option, otherwise **send-mail** will attempt to do a network lookup every now and then, possibly causing your machine to dial out. You may try:

```
sendmail_flags="-bd"
```

The downside is that `sendmail` is forced to re-examine the mail queue whenever the ppp link. To automate this, include `!bg` in `ppp.linkup`:

```
1    provider:
2       delete ALL
3       add 0 0 HISADDR
4       !bg sendmail -bd -q30m
```

An alternative is to set up a "dfilter" to block SMTP traffic. Refer to the sample files for further details.

26.2.4. Using ppp

All that is left is to reboot the machine. After rebooting, either type:

```
# ppp
```

and then `dial provider` to start the PPP session, or, to configure ppp to establish sessions automatically when there is outbound traffic and `start_if.tun0` does not exist, type:

```
# ppp -auto provider
```

It is possible to talk to the ppp program while it is running in the background, but only if a suitable diagnostic port has been set up. To do this, add the following line to the configuration:

```
set server /var/run/ppp-tun%d DiagnosticPassword 0177
```

This will tell PPP to listen to the specified UNIX® domain socket, asking clients for the specified password before allowing access. The `%d` in the name is replaced with the `tun` device number that is in use.

Once a socket has been set up, the pppctl(8) program may be used in scripts that wish to manipulate the running program.

26.2.5. Configuring Dial-in Services

Section 25.4, "Dial-in Service" provides a good description on enabling dial-up services using getty(8).

An alternative to **getty** is comms/mgetty+sendfax port), a smarter version of **getty** designed with dial-up lines in mind.

The advantages of using mgetty is that it actively *talks* to modems, meaning if port is turned off in /etc/ttys then the modem will not answer the phone.

Later versions of mgetty (from 0.99beta onwards) also support the automatic detection of PPP streams, allowing clients scriptless access to the server.

Refer to http://mgetty.greenie.net/doc/mgetty_toc.html for more information on mgetty.

By default the comms/mgetty+sendfax port comes with the AUTO_PPP option enabled allowing mgetty to detect the LCP phase of PPP connections and automatically spawn off a ppp shell. However, since the default login/password sequence does not occur it is necessary to authenticate users using either PAP or CHAP.

This section assumes the user has successfully compiled, and installed the comms/mgetty+sendfax port on his system.

486

Ensure that `/usr/local/etc/mgetty+sendfax/login.config` has the following:

```
/AutoPPP/ -        - /etc/ppp/ppp-pap-dialup
```

This tells `mgetty` to run `ppp-pap-dialup` for detected PPP connections.

Create an executable file called `/etc/ppp/ppp-pap-dialup` containing the following:

```
#!/bin/sh
exec /usr/sbin/ppp -direct pap$IDENT
```

For each dial-up line enabled in `/etc/ttys`, create a corresponding entry in `/etc/ppp/ppp.conf`. This will happily co-exist with the definitions we created above.

```
pap:
    enable pap
    set ifaddr 203.14.100.1 203.14.100.20-203.14.100.40
    enable proxy
```

Each user logging in with this method will need to have a username/password in `/etc/ppp/ppp.secret`, or alternatively add the following option to authenticate users via PAP from `/etc/passwd`.

```
enable passwdauth
```

To assign some users a static IP number, specify the number as the third argument in `/etc/ppp/ppp.secret`. See `/usr/share/examples/ppp/ppp.secret.sample` for examples.

26.3. Troubleshooting PPP Connections

This section covers a few issues which may arise when using PPP over a modem connection. Some ISPs present the `ssword` prompt while others present `password`. If the `ppp` script is not written accordingly, the login attempt will fail. The most common way to debug `ppp` connections is by connecting manually as described in this section.

26.3.1. Check the Device Nodes

When using a custom kernel, make sure to include the following line in the kernel configuration file:

```
device    uart
```

The `uart` device is already included in the `GENERIC` kernel, so no additional steps are necessary in this case. Just check the `dmesg` output for the modem device with:

```
# dmesg | grep uart
```

This should display some pertinent output about the `uart` devices. These are the COM ports we need. If the modem acts like a standard serial port, it should be listed on `uart1`, or `COM2`. If so, a kernel rebuild is not required. When matching up, if the modem is on `uart1`, the modem device would be `/dev/cuau1`.

26.3.2. Connecting Manually

Connecting to the Internet by manually controlling `ppp` is quick, easy, and a great way to debug a connection or just get information on how the ISP treats `ppp` client connections. Lets start PPP from the command line. Note that in all of our examples we will use *example* as the hostname of the machine running PPP. To start `ppp`:

```
# ppp
```

```
ppp ON example> set device /dev/cuau1
```

This second command sets the modem device to `cuau1`.

```
ppp ON example> set speed 115200
```

This sets the connection speed to 115,200 kbps.

```
ppp ON example> enable dns
```

This tells ppp to configure the resolver and add the nameserver lines to /etc/resolv.conf. If ppp cannot determine the hostname, it can manually be set later.

```
ppp ON example> term
```

This switches to "terminal" mode in order to manually control the modem.

```
deflink: Entering terminal mode on /dev/cuau1
type '~h' for help
```

```
at
OK
atdt 123456789
```

Use at to initialize the modem, then use atdt and the number for the ISP to begin the dial in process.

```
CONNECT
```

Confirmation of the connection, if we are going to have any connection problems, unrelated to hardware, here is where we will attempt to resolve them.

```
ISP Login:myusername
```

At this prompt, return the prompt with the username that was provided by the ISP.

```
ISP Pass:mypassword
```

At this prompt, reply with the password that was provided by the ISP. Just like logging into FreeBSD, the password will not echo.

```
Shell or PPP:ppp
```

Depending on the ISP, this prompt might not appear. If it does, it is asking whether to use a shell on the provider or to start ppp. In this example, ppp was selected in order to establish an Internet connection.

```
Ppp ON example>
```

Notice that in this example the first p has been capitalized. This shows that we have successfully connected to the ISP.

```
PPp ON example>
```

We have successfully authenticated with our ISP and are waiting for the assigned IP address.

```
PPP ON example>
```

We have made an agreement on an IP address and successfully completed our connection.

```
PPP ON example>add default HISADDR
```

Here we add our default route, we need to do this before we can talk to the outside world as currently the only established connection is with the peer. If this fails due to existing routes, put a bang character ! in front of the add. Alternatively, set this before making the actual connection and it will negotiate a new route accordingly.

If everything went good we should now have an active connection to the Internet, which could be thrown into the background using CTRL+z If PPP returns to ppp then the connection has bee lost. This is good to know because it shows the connection status. Capital P's represent a connection to the ISP and lowercase p's show that the connection has been lost.

26.3.3. Debugging

If a connection cannot be established, turn hardware flow CTS/RTS to off using `set ctsrts off`. This is mainly the case when connected to some PPP-capable terminal servers, where PPP hangs when it tries to write data to the communication link, and waits for a Clear To Send (CTS) signal which may never come. When using this option, include `set accmap` as it may be required to defeat hardware dependent on passing certain characters from end to end, most of the time XON/XOFF. Refer to ppp(8) for more information on this option and how it is used.

An older modem may need `set parity even`. Parity is set at none be default, but is used for error checkingm with a large increase in traffic, on older modems.

PPP may not return to the command mode, which is usually a negotiation error where the ISP is waiting for negotiating to begin. At this point, using ~p will force ppp to start sending the configuration information.

If a login prompt never appears, PAP or CHAP authentication is most likely required. To use PAP or CHAP, add the following options to PPP before going into terminal mode:

```
ppp ON example> set authname myusername
```

Where *myusername* should be replaced with the username that was assigned by the ISP.

```
ppp ON example> set authkey mypassword
```

Where *mypassword* should be replaced with the password that was assigned by the ISP.

If a connection is established, but cannot seem to find any domain name, try to ping(8) an IP address. If there is 100 percent (100%) packet loss, it is likely that a default route was not assigned. Double check that `add default HISADDR` was set during the connection. If a connection can be made to a remote IP address, it is possible that a resolver address has not been added to `/etc/resolv.conf`. This file should look like:

```
domain example.com
nameserver x.x.x.x
nameserver y.y.y.y
```

Where `x.x.x.x` and `y.y.y.y` should be replaced with the IP address of the ISP's DNS servers.

To configure syslog(3) to provide logging for the PPP connection, make sure this line exists in `/etc/syslog.conf`:

```
!ppp
*.*      /var/log/ppp.log
```

26.4. Using PPP over Ethernet (PPPoE)

This section describes how to set up PPP over Ethernet (PPPoE).

Here is an example of a working `ppp.conf`:

```
default:
  set log Phase tun command # you can add more detailed logging if you wish
  set ifaddr 10.0.0.1/0 10.0.0.2/0

name_of_service_provider:
  set device PPPoE:xl1 # replace xl1 with your Ethernet device
  set authname YOURLOGINNAME
  set authkey YOURPASSWORD
  set dial
  set login
  add default HISADDR
```

As `root`, run:

```
# ppp -ddial name_of_service_provider
```

Add the following to /etc/rc.conf :

```
ppp_enable="YES"
ppp_mode="ddial"
ppp_nat="YES" # if you want to enable nat for your local network, otherwise NO
ppp_profile="name_of_service_provider"
```

26.4.1. Using a PPPoE Service Tag

Sometimes it will be necessary to use a service tag to establish the connection. Service tags are used to distinguish between different PPPoE servers attached to a given network.

Any required service tag information should be in the documentation provided by the ISP.

As a last resort, one could try installing the net/rr-pppoe package or port. Bear in mind however, this may de-program your modem and render it useless, so think twice before doing it. Simply install the program shipped with the modem. Then, access the System menu from the program. The name of the profile should be listed there. It is usually *ISP*.

The profile name (service tag) will be used in the PPPoE configuration entry in ppp.conf as the provider part for set device. Refer to ppp(8) for full details. It should look like this:

```
set device PPPoE:xl1:ISP
```

Do not forget to change *xl1* to the proper device for the Ethernet card.

Do not forget to change *ISP* to the profile.

For additional information, refer to Cheaper Broadband with FreeBSD on DSL by Renaud Waldura.

26.4.2. PPPoE with a 3Com® HomeConnect® ADSL Modem Dual Link

This modem does not follow the PPPoE specification defined in RFC 2516.

In order to make FreeBSD capable of communicating with this device, a sysctl must be set. This can be done automatically at boot time by updating /etc/sysctl.conf :

```
net.graph.nonstandard_pppoe=1
```

or can be done immediately with the command:

```
# sysctl net.graph.nonstandard_pppoe=1
```

Unfortunately, because this is a system-wide setting, it is not possible to talk to a normal PPPoE client or server and a 3Com® HomeConnect® ADSL Modem at the same time.

26.5. Using PPP over ATM (PPPoA)

The following describes how to set up PPP over ATM (PPPoA). PPPoA is a popular choice among European DSL providers.

26.5.1. Using mpd

The mpd application can be used to connect to a variety of services, in particular PPTP services. It can be installed using the net/mpd5 package or port. Many ADSL modems require that a PPTP tunnel is created between the modem and computer.

Once installed, configure mpd to suit the provider's settings. The port places a set of sample configuration files which are well documented in /usr/local/etc/mpd/ . A complete guide to configure mpd is available in HTML format in /usr/ports/share/doc/mpd/ . Here is a sample configuration for connecting to an ADSL service with mpd. The configuration is spread over two files, first the mpd.conf :

Note

This example mpd.conf only works with mpd 4.x.

```
default:
    load adsl

adsl:
    new -i ng0 adsl adsl
    set bundle authname username ❶
    set bundle password password ❷
    set bundle disable multilink

    set link no pap acfcomp protocomp
    set link disable chap
    set link accept chap
    set link keep-alive 30 10

    set ipcp no vjcomp
    set ipcp ranges 0.0.0.0/0 0.0.0.0/0

    set iface route default
    set iface disable on-demand
    set iface enable proxy-arp
    set iface idle 0

    open
```

❶ The username used to authenticate with your ISP.
❷ The password used to authenticate with your ISP.

Information about the link, or links, to establish is found in mpd.links . An example mpd.links to accompany the above example is given beneath:

```
adsl:
    set link type pptp
    set pptp mode active
    set pptp enable originate outcall
    set pptp self 10.0.0.1 ❶
    set pptp peer 10.0.0.138 ❷
```

❶ The IP address of FreeBSD computer running mpd.
❷ The IP address of the ADSL modem. The Alcatel SpeedTouch™ Home defaults to 10.0.0.138 .

It is possible to initialize the connection easily by issuing the following command as root:

```
# mpd -b adsl
```

To view the status of the connection:

```
% ifconfig ng0
ng0: flags=88d1<UP,POINTOPOINT,RUNNING,NOARP,SIMPLEX,MULTICAST> mtu 1500
        inet 216.136.204.117 --> 204.152.186.171 netmask 0xffffffff
```

Using mpd is the recommended way to connect to an ADSL service with FreeBSD.

26.5.2. Using pptpclient

It is also possible to use FreeBSD to connect to other PPPoA services using net/pptpclient.

To use net/pptpclient to connect to a DSL service, install the port or package, then edit /etc/ppp/ppp.conf . An example section of ppp.conf is given below. For further information on ppp.conf options consult ppp(8).

```
adsl:
  set log phase chat lcp ipcp ccp tun command
  set timeout 0
  enable dns
  set authname username ❶
  set authkey password ❷
  set ifaddr 0 0
  add default HISADDR
```

❶   The username for the DSL provider.
❷   The password for your account.

Warning

Since the account's password is added to ppp.conf in plain text form, make sure nobody can read the contents of this file:

```
# chown root:wheel /etc/ppp/ppp.conf
# chmod 600 /etc/ppp/ppp.conf
```

This will open a tunnel for a PPP session to the DSL router. Ethernet DSL modems have a preconfigured LAN IP address to connect to. In the case of the Alcatel SpeedTouch™ Home, this address is 10.0.0.138 . The router's documentation should list the address the device uses. To open the tunnel and start a PPP session:

```
# pptp address adsl
```

Tip

If an ampersand ("&") is added to the end of this command, pptp will return the prompt.

A tun virtual tunnel device will be created for interaction between the pptp and ppp processes. Once the prompt is returned, or the pptp process has confirmed a connection, examine the tunnel:

```
% ifconfig tun0
tun0: flags=8051<UP,POINTOPOINT,RUNNING,MULTICAST> mtu 1500
      inet 216.136.204.21 --> 204.152.186.171 netmask 0xffffff00
  Opened by PID 918
```

If the connection fails, check the configuration of the router, which is usually accessible using a web browser. Also, examine the output of pptp and the contents of the log file, /var/log/ppp.log for clues.

Chapter 27. Electronic Mail

Original work by Bill Lloyd.
Rewritten by Jim Mock.

27.1. Synopsis

"Electronic Mail", better known as email, is one of the most widely used forms of communication today. This chapter provides a basic introduction to running a mail server on FreeBSD, as well as an introduction to sending and receiving email using FreeBSD. For more complete coverage of this subject, refer to the books listed in Appendix B, *Bibliography*.

After reading this chapter, you will know:

• Which software components are involved in sending and receiving electronic mail.

• Where basic Sendmail configuration files are located in FreeBSD.

• The difference between remote and local mailboxes.

• How to block spammers from illegally using a mail server as a relay.

• How to install and configure an alternate Mail Transfer Agent, replacing Sendmail.

• How to troubleshoot common mail server problems.

• How to set up the system to send mail only.

• How to use mail with a dialup connection.

• How to configure SMTP authentication for added security.

• How to install and use a Mail User Agent, such as mutt, to send and receive email.

• How to download mail from a remote POP or IMAP server.

• How to automatically apply filters and rules to incoming email.

Before reading this chapter, you should:

• Properly set up a network connection (Chapter 30, *Advanced Networking*).

• Properly set up the DNS information for a mail host (Chapter 28, *Network Servers*).

• Know how to install additional third-party software (Chapter 4, *Installing Applications: Packages and Ports*).

27.2. Mail Components

There are five major parts involved in an email exchange: the Mail User Agent (MUA), the Mail Transfer Agent (MTA), a mail host, a remote or local mailbox, and DNS. This section provides an overview of these components.

Mail User Agent (MUA)

The Mail User Agent (MUA) is an application which is used to compose, send, and receive emails. This application can be a command line program, such as the built-in `mail` utility or a third-party application from the Ports Collection, such as mutt, alpine, or elm. Dozens of graphical programs are also available in the Ports Collection, including Claws Mail, Evolution, and Thunderbird. Some organizations provide a web mail program which can be accessed through a web browser. More information about installing and using a MUA on FreeBSD can be found in Section 27.10, "Mail User Agents".

Mail Transfer Agent (MTA)

The Mail Transfer Agent (MTA) is responsible for receiving incoming mail and delivering outgoing mail. Free-BSD ships with Sendmail as the default MTA, but it also supports numerous other mail server daemons, including Exim, Postfix, and qmail. Sendmail configuration is described in Section 27.3, "Sendmail Configuration Files". If another MTA is installed using the Ports Collection, refer to its post-installation message for Free-BSD-specific configuration details and the application's website for more general configuration instructions.

Mail Host and Mailboxes

The mail host is a server that is responsible for delivering and receiving mail for a host or a network. The mail host collects all mail sent to the domain and stores it either in the default mbox or the alternative Maildir format, depending on the configuration. Once mail has been stored, it may either be read locally using a MUA or remotely accessed and collected using protocols such as POP or IMAP. If mail is read locally, a POP or IMAP server does not need to be installed.

To access mailboxes remotely, a POP or IMAP server is required as these protocols allow users to connect to their mailboxes from remote locations. IMAP offers several advantages over POP. These include the ability to store a copy of messages on a remote server after they are downloaded and concurrent updates. IMAP can be useful over low-speed links as it allows users to fetch the structure of messages without downloading them. It can also perform tasks such as searching on the server in order to minimize data transfer between clients and servers.

Several POP and IMAP servers are available in the Ports Collection. These include mail/qpopper, mail/imap-uw, mail/courier-imap, and mail/dovecot2.

Warning

It should be noted that both POP and IMAP transmit information, including username and password credentials, in clear-text. To secure the transmission of information across these protocols, consider tunneling sessions over ssh(1) (Section 13.8.1.2, "SSH Tunneling") or using SSL (Section 13.6, "OpenSSL").

Domain Name System (DNS)

The Domain Name System (DNS) and its daemon named play a large role in the delivery of email. In order to deliver mail from one site to another, the MTA will look up the remote site in DNS to determine which host will receive mail for the destination. This process also occurs when mail is sent from a remote host to the MTA.

In addition to mapping hostnames to IP addresses, DNS is responsible for storing information specific to mail delivery, known as Mail eXchanger MX records. The MX record specifies which hosts will receive mail for a particular domain.

To view the MX records for a domain, specify the type of record. Refer to host(1), for more details about this command:

```
% host -t mx FreeBSD.org
FreeBSD.org mail is handled by 10 mx1.FreeBSD.org
```

Refer to Section 28.7, "Domain Name System (DNS)" for more information about DNS and its configuration.

27.3. Sendmail Configuration Files

Contributed by Christopher Shumway.

Sendmail is the default MTA installed with FreeBSD. It accepts mail from MUAs and delivers it to the appropriate mail host, as defined by its configuration. Sendmail can also accept network connections and deliver mail to local mailboxes or to another program.

The configuration files for Sendmail are located in /etc/mail . This section describes these files in more detail.

/etc/mail/access

This access database file defines which hosts or IP addresses have access to the local mail server and what kind of access they have. Hosts listed as OK, which is the default option, are allowed to send mail to this host as long as the mail's final destination is the local machine. Hosts listed as REJECT are rejected for all mail connections. Hosts listed as RELAY are allowed to send mail for any destination using this mail server. Hosts listed as ERROR will have their mail returned with the specified mail error. If a host is listed as SKIP, Sendmail will abort the current search for this entry without accepting or rejecting the mail. Hosts listed as QUARANTINE will have their messages held and will receive the specified text as the reason for the hold.

Examples of using these options for both IPv4 and IPv6 addresses can be found in the FreeBSD sample configuration, /etc/mail/access.sample :

```
# $FreeBSD: head/en_US.ISO8859-1/books/handbook/mail/chapter.xml 47505 2015-10-05 ↺
13:05:43Z dru $
#
# Mail relay access control list.  Default is to reject mail unless the
# destination is local, or listed in /etc/mail/local-host-names
#
## Examples (commented out for safety)
#From:cyberspammer.com           ERROR:"550 We don't accept mail from spammers"
#From:okay.cyberspammer.com      OK
#Connect:sendmail.org            RELAY
#To:sendmail.org                 RELAY
#Connect:128.32                  RELAY
#Connect:128.32.2               SKIP
#Connect:IPv6:1:2:3:4:5:6:7      RELAY
#Connect:suspicious.example.com QUARANTINE:Mail from suspicious host
#Connect:[127.0.0.3]             OK
#Connect:[IPv6:1:2:3:4:5:6:7:8] OK
```

To configure the access database, use the format shown in the sample to make entries in /etc/mail/access , but do not put a comment symbol (#) in front of the entries. Create an entry for each host or network whose access should be configured. Mail senders that match the left side of the table are affected by the action on the right side of the table.

Whenever this file is updated, update its database and restart Sendmail:

```
# makemap hash /etc/mail/access < /etc/mail/access
# service sendmail restart
```

/etc/mail/aliases

This database file contains a list of virtual mailboxes that are expanded to users, files, programs, or other aliases. Here are a few entries to illustrate the file format:

```
root: localuser
ftp-bugs: joe,eric,paul
bit.bucket:  /dev/null
procmail: "|/usr/local/bin/procmail"
```

The mailbox name on the left side of the colon is expanded to the target(s) on the right. The first entry expands the root mailbox to the localuser mailbox, which is then looked up in the /etc/mail/aliases database. If no match is found, the message is delivered to localuser. The second entry shows a mail list. Mail to ftp-bugs is expanded to the three local mailboxes joe, eric, and paul. A remote mailbox could be specified as *user@example.com*. The third entry shows how to write mail to a file, in this case /dev/null . The last entry demonstrates how to send mail to a program, /usr/local/bin/procmail , through á UNIX® pipe. Refer to aliases(5) for more information about the format of this file.

Whenever this file is updated, run `newaliases` to update and initialize the aliases database.

/etc/mail/sendmail.cf

This is the master configuration file for Sendmail. It controls the overall behavior of Sendmail, including everything from rewriting email addresses to printing rejection messages to remote mail servers. Accordingly, this configuration file is quite complex. Fortunately, this file rarely needs to be changed for standard mail servers.

The master Sendmail configuration file can be built from m4(1) macros that define the features and behavior of Sendmail. Refer to `/usr/src/contrib/sendmail/cf/README` for some of the details.

Whenever changes to this file are made, Sendmail needs to be restarted for the changes to take effect.

/etc/mail/virtusertable

This database file maps mail addresses for virtual domains and users to real mailboxes. These mailboxes can be local, remote, aliases defined in `/etc/mail/aliases`, or files. This allows multiple virtual domains to be hosted on one machine.

FreeBSD provides a sample configuration file in `/etc/mail/virtusertable.sample` to further demonstrate its format. The following example demonstrates how to create custom entries using that format:

```
root@example.com               root
postmaster@example.com         postmaster@noc.example.net
@example.com                   joe
```

This file is processed in a first match order. When an email address matches the address on the left, it is mapped to the local mailbox listed on the right. The format of the first entry in this example maps a specific email address to a local mailbox, whereas the format of the second entry maps a specific email address to a remote mailbox. Finally, any email address from `example.com` which has not matched any of the previous entries will match the last mapping and be sent to the local mailbox `joe`. When creating custom entries, use this format and add them to `/etc/mail/virtusertable`. Whenever this file is edited, update its database and restart Sendmail:

```
# makemap hash /etc/mail/virtusertable < /etc/mail/virtusertable
# service sendmail restart
```

/etc/mail/relay-domains

In a default FreeBSD installation, Sendmail is configured to only send mail from the host it is running on. For example, if a POP server is available, users will be able to check mail from remote locations but they will not be able to send outgoing emails from outside locations. Typically, a few moments after the attempt, an email will be sent from `MAILER-DAEMON` with a 5.7 Relaying Denied message.

The most straightforward solution is to add the ISP's FQDN to `/etc/mail/relay-domains`. If multiple addresses are needed, add them one per line:

```
your.isp.example.com
other.isp.example.net
users-isp.example.org
www.example.org
```

After creating or editing this file, restart Sendmail with `service sendmail restart`.

Now any mail sent through the system by any host in this list, provided the user has an account on the system, will succeed. This allows users to send mail from the system remotely without opening the system up to relaying SPAM from the Internet.

27.4. Changing the Mail Transfer Agent

Written by Andrew Boothman.

Information taken from emails written by Gregory Neil Shapiro.

FreeBSD comes with Sendmail already installed as the MTA which is in charge of outgoing and incoming mail. However, the system administrator can change the system's MTA. A wide choice of alternative MTAs is available from the `mail` category of the FreeBSD Ports Collection.

Once a new MTA is installed, configure and test the new software before replacing Sendmail. Refer to the documentation of the new MTA for information on how to configure the software.

Once the new MTA is working, use the instructions in this section to disable Sendmail and configure FreeBSD to use the replacement MTA.

27.4.1. Disable Sendmail

 Warning

If Sendmail's outgoing mail service is disabled, it is important that it is replaced with an alternative mail delivery system. Otherwise, system functions such as periodic(8) will be unable to deliver their results by email. Many parts of the system expect a functional MTA. If applications continue to use Sendmail's binaries to try to send email after they are disabled, mail could go into an inactive Sendmail queue and never be delivered.

In order to completely disable Sendmail, add or edit the following lines in `/etc/rc.conf` :

```
sendmail_enable="NO"
sendmail_submit_enable="NO"
sendmail_outbound_enable="NO"
sendmail_msp_queue_enable="NO"
```

To only disable Sendmail's incoming mail service, use only this entry in `/etc/rc.conf` :

```
sendmail_enable="NO"
```

More information on Sendmail's startup options is available in rc.sendmail(8).

27.4.2. Replace the Default MTA

When a new MTA is installed using the Ports Collection, its startup script is also installed and startup instructions are mentioned in its package message. Before starting the new MTA, stop the running Sendmail processes. This example stops all of these services, then starts the Postfix service:

```
# service sendmail stop
# service postfix start
```

To start the replacement MTA at system boot, add its configuration line to `/etc/rc.conf` . This entry enables the Postfix MTA:

```
postfix_enable="YES"
```

Some extra configuration is needed as Sendmail is so ubiquitous that some software assumes it is already installed and configured. Check `/etc/periodic.conf` and make sure that these values are set to NO. If this file does not exist, create it with these entries:

```
daily_clean_hoststat_enable="NO"
daily_status_mail_rejects_enable="NO"
daily_status_include_submit_mailq="NO"
daily_submit_queuerun="NO"
```

Some alternative MTAs provide their own compatible implementations of the Sendmail command-line interface in order to facilitate using them as drop-in replacements for Sendmail. However, some MUAs may try to execute standard Sendmail binaries instead of the new MTA's binaries. FreeBSD uses /etc/mail/mailer.conf to map the expected Sendmail binaries to the location of the new binaries. More information about this mapping can be found in mailwrapper(8).

The default /etc/mail/mailer.conf looks like this:

```
# $FreeBSD: head/en_US.ISO8859-1/books/handbook/mail/chapter.xml 47505 2015-10-05 ↺
13:05:43Z dru $
#
# Execute the "real" sendmail program, named /usr/libexec/sendmail/sendmail
#
sendmail        /usr/libexec/sendmail/sendmail
send-mail       /usr/libexec/sendmail/sendmail
mailq           /usr/libexec/sendmail/sendmail
newaliases      /usr/libexec/sendmail/sendmail
hoststat        /usr/libexec/sendmail/sendmail
purgestat       /usr/libexec/sendmail/sendmail
```

When any of the commands listed on the left are run, the system actually executes the associated command shown on the right. This system makes it easy to change what binaries are executed when these default binaries are invoked.

Some MTAs, when installed using the Ports Collection, will prompt to update this file for the new binaries. For example, Postfix will update the file like this:

```
#
# Execute the Postfix sendmail program, named /usr/local/sbin/sendmail
#
sendmail        /usr/local/sbin/sendmail
send-mail       /usr/local/sbin/sendmail
mailq           /usr/local/sbin/sendmail
newaliases      /usr/local/sbin/sendmail
```

If the installation of the MTA does not automatically update /etc/mail/mailer.conf , edit this file in a text editor so that it points to the new binaries. This example points to the binaries installed by mail/ssmtp:

```
sendmail        /usr/local/sbin/ssmtp
send-mail       /usr/local/sbin/ssmtp
mailq           /usr/libexec/sendmail/sendmail
newaliases      /usr/libexec/sendmail/sendmail
hoststat        /usr/libexec/sendmail/sendmail
purgestat       /usr/libexec/sendmail/sendmail
```

Once everything is configured, it is recommended to reboot the system. Rebooting provides the opportunity to ensure that the system is correctly configured to start the new MTA automatically on boot.

27.5. Troubleshooting

Q: Why do I have to use the FQDN for hosts on my site?

A: The host may actually be in a different domain. For example, in order for a host in foo.bar.edu to reach a host called mumble in the bar.edu domain, refer to it by the Fully-Qualified Domain Name FQDN, mumble.bar.edu, instead of just mumble.

This is because the version of BIND which ships with FreeBSD no longer provides default abbreviations for non-FQDNs other than the local domain. An unqualified host such as mumble must either be found as mumble.foo.bar.edu, or it will be searched for in the root domain.

In older versions of BIND, the search continued across `mumble.bar.edu`, and `mumble.edu`. RFC 1535 details why this is considered bad practice or even a security hole.

As a good workaround, place the line:

```
search foo.bar.edu bar.edu
```

instead of the previous:

```
domain foo.bar.edu
```

into `/etc/resolv.conf`. However, make sure that the search order does not go beyond the "boundary between local and public administration", as RFC 1535 calls it.

Q: How can I run a mail server on a dial-up PPP host?

A: Connect to a FreeBSD mail gateway on the LAN. The PPP connection is non-dedicated.

One way to do this is to get a full-time Internet server to provide secondary MX services for the domain. In this example, the domain is `example.com` and the ISP has configured `example.net` to provide secondary MX services to the domain:

```
example.com.          MX      10      example.com.
                      MX      20      example.net.
```

Only one host should be specified as the final recipient. For Sendmail, add `Cw example.com` in `/etc/mail/sendmail.cf` on `example.com`.

When the sending MTA attempts to deliver mail, it will try to connect to the system, `example.com`, over the PPP link. This will time out if the destination is offline. The MTA will automatically deliver it to the secondary MX site at the Internet Service Provider (ISP), `example.net`. The secondary MX site will periodically try to connect to the primary MX host, `example.com`.

Use something like this as a login script:

```
#!/bin/sh
# Put me in /usr/local/bin/pppmyisp
( sleep 60 -; /usr/sbin/sendmail -q ) &
/usr/sbin/ppp -direct pppmyisp
```

When creating a separate login script for users, instead use `sendmail -qRexample.com` in the script above. This will force all mail in the queue for `example.com` to be processed immediately.

A further refinement of the situation can be seen from this example from the FreeBSD Internet service provider's mailing list:

```
> we provide the secondary MX for a customer. The customer connects to
> our services several times a day automatically to get the mails to
> his primary MX (We do not call his site when a mail for his domains
> arrived). Our sendmail sends the mailqueue every 30 minutes. At the
> moment he has to stay 30 minutes online to be sure that all mail is
> gone to the primary MX.
>
> Is there a command that would initiate sendmail to send all the mails
> now? The user has not root-privileges on our machine of course.

In the "privacy flags" section of sendmail.cf, there is a
definition Opgoaway,restrictqrun

Remove restrictqrun to allow non-root users to start the queue processing.
You might also like to rearrange the MXs. We are the 1st MX for our
customers like this, and we have defined:
```

```
# If we are the best MX for a host, try directly instead of generating
# local config error.
OwTrue

That way a remote site will deliver straight to you, without trying
the customer connection.  You then send to your customer.  Only works for
"hosts", so you need to get your customer to name their mail
machine "customer.com" as well as
"hostname.customer.com" in the DNS.  Just put an A record in
the DNS for "customer.com".
```

27.6. Advanced Topics

This section covers more involved topics such as mail configuration and setting up mail for an entire domain.

27.6.1. Basic Configuration

Out of the box, one can send email to external hosts as long as /etc/resolv.conf is configured or the network has access to a configured DNS server. To have email delivered to the MTA on the FreeBSD host, do one of the following:

• Run a DNS server for the domain.

• Get mail delivered directly to the FQDN for the machine.

In order to have mail delivered directly to a host, it must have a permanent static IP address, not a dynamic IP address. If the system is behind a firewall, it must be configured to allow SMTP traffic. To receive mail directly at a host, one of these two must be configured:

• Make sure that the lowest-numbered MX record in DNS points to the host's static IP address.

• Make sure there is no MX entry in the DNS for the host.

Either of the above will allow mail to be received directly at the host.

Try this:

```
# hostname
example.FreeBSD.org
# host example.FreeBSD.org
example.FreeBSD.org has address 204.216.27.XX
```

In this example, mail sent directly to <yourlogin@example.FreeBSD.org> should work without problems, assuming Sendmail is running correctly on example.FreeBSD.org.

For this example:

```
# host example.FreeBSD.org
example.FreeBSD.org has address 204.216.27.XX
example.FreeBSD.org mail is handled (pri=10) by nevdull.FreeBSD.org
```

All mail sent to example.FreeBSD.org will be collected on hub under the same username instead of being sent directly to your host.

The above information is handled by the DNS server. The DNS record that carries mail routing information is the MX entry. If no MX record exists, mail will be delivered directly to the host by way of its IP address.

The MX entry for freefall.FreeBSD.org at one time looked like this:

```
freefall  MX 30 mail.crl.net
freefall  MX 40 agora.rdrop.com
```

```
freefall  MX 10 freefall.FreeBSD.org
freefall  MX 20 who.cdrom.com
```

`freefall` had many MX entries. The lowest MX number is the host that receives mail directly, if available. If it is not accessible for some reason, the next lower-numbered host will accept messages temporarily, and pass it along when a lower-numbered host becomes available.

Alternate MX sites should have separate Internet connections in order to be most useful. Your ISP can provide this service.

27.6.2. Mail for a Domain

When configuring a MTA for a network, any mail sent to hosts in its domain should be diverted to the MTA so that users can receive their mail on the master mail server.

To make life easiest, a user account with the same *username* should exist on both the MTA and the system with the MUA. Use adduser(8) to create the user accounts.

The MTA must be the designated mail exchanger for each workstation on the network. This is done in theDNS configuration with an MX record:

```
example.FreeBSD.org A 204.216.27.XX  ; Workstation
   MX 10 nevdull.FreeBSD.org ; Mailhost
```

This will redirect mail for the workstation to the MTA no matter where the A record points. The mail is sent to the MX host.

This must be configured on a DNS server. If the network does not run its own DNS server, talk to the ISP or DNS provider.

The following is an example of virtual email hosting. Consider a customer with the domain `customer1.org`, where all the mail for `customer1.org` should be sent to `mail.myhost.com`. The DNS entry should look like this:

```
customer1.org  MX 10 mail.myhost.com
```

An `A>` record is *not* needed for `customer1.org` in order to only handle email for that domain. However, running `ping` against `customer1.org` will not work unless an `A` record exists for it.

Tell the MTA which domains and/or hostnames it should accept mail for. Either of the following will work for Sendmail:

- Add the hosts to `/etc/mail/local-host-names` when using the `FEATURE(use_cw_file)`.

- Add a `Cwyour.host.com` line to `/etc/sendmail.cf`.

27.7. Setting Up to Send Only

Contributed by Bill Moran.

There are many instances where one may only want to send mail through a relay. Some examples are:

- The computer is a desktop machine that needs to use programs such as send-pr(1), using the ISP's mail relay.

- The computer is a server that does not handle mail locally, but needs to pass off all mail to a relay for processing.

While any MTA is capable of filling this particular niche, it can be difficult to properly configure a full-featured MTA just to handle offloading mail. Programs such as Sendmail and Postfix are overkill for this use.

Additionally, a typical Internet access service agreement may forbid one from running a "mail server".

The easiest way to fulfill those needs is to install the mail/ssmtp port:

```
# cd /usr/ports/mail/ssmtp
# make install replace clean
```

Once installed, mail/ssmtp can be configured with /usr/local/etc/ssmtp/ssmtp.conf :

```
root=yourrealemail@example.com
mailhub=mail.example.com
rewriteDomain=example.com
hostname=_HOSTNAME_
```

Use the real email address for root. Enter the ISP's outgoing mail relay in place of mail.example.com. Some ISPs call this the "outgoing mail server" or "SMTP server").

Make sure to disable Sendmail, including the outgoing mail service. See Section 27.4.1, "Disable Sendmail" for details.

mail/ssmtp has some other options available. Refer to the examples in /usr/local/etc/ssmtp or the manual page of ssmtp for more information.

Setting up ssmtp in this manner allows any software on the computer that needs to send mail to function properly, while not violating the ISP's usage policy or allowing the computer to be hijacked for spamming.

27.8. Using Mail with a Dialup Connection

When using a static IP address, one should not need to adjust the default configuration. Set the hostname to the assigned Internet name and Sendmail will do the rest.

When using a dynamically assigned IP address and a dialup PPP connection to the Internet, one usually has a mailbox on the ISP's mail server. In this example, the ISP's domain is example.net, the user name is user, the hostname is bsd.home, and the ISP has allowed relay.example.net as a mail relay.

In order to retrieve mail from the ISP's mailbox, install a retrieval agent from the Ports Collection. mail/fetchmail is a good choice as it supports many different protocols. Usually, the ISP will provide POP. When using user PPP, email can be automatically fetched when an Internet connection is established with the following entry in /etc/ppp/ppp.linkup:

```
MYADDR:
 !bg su user -c fetchmail
```

When using Sendmail to deliver mail to non-local accounts, configure Sendmail to process the mail queue as soon as the Internet connection is established. To do this, add this line after the above fetchmail entry in /etc/ppp/ppp.linkup:

```
 !bg su user -c "sendmail -q"
```

In this example, there is an account for user on bsd.home. In the home directory of user on bsd.home, create a .fetchmailrc which contains this line:

```
poll example.net protocol pop3 fetchall pass MySecret
```

This file should not be readable by anyone except user as it contains the password MySecret.

In order to send mail with the correct from: header, configure Sendmail to use <user@example.net> rather than <user@bsd.home> and to send all mail via relay.example.net, allowing quicker mail transmission.

The following .mc should suffice:

```
VERSIONID(`bsd.home.mc version 1.0')
OSTYPE(bsd4.4)dnl
FEATURE(nouucp)dnl
```

```
MAILER(local)dnl
MAILER(smtp)dnl
Cwlocalhost
Cwbsd.home
MASQUERADE_AS(`example.net')dnl
FEATURE(allmasquerade)dnl
FEATURE(masquerade_envelope)dnl
FEATURE(nocanonify)dnl
FEATURE(nodns)dnl
define(`SMART_HOST', `relay.example.net')
Dmbsd.home
define(`confDOMAIN_NAME',`bsd.home')dnl
define(`confDELIVERY_MODE',`deferred')dnl
```

Refer to the previous section for details of how to convert this file into the `sendmail.cf` format. Do not forget to restart Sendmail after updating `sendmail.cf`.

27.9. SMTP Authentication

Written by James Gorham.

Configuring SMTP authentication on the MTA provides a number of benefits. SMTP authentication adds a layer of security to Sendmail, and provides mobile users who switch hosts the ability to use the same MTA without the need to reconfigure their mail client's settings each time.

1. Install security/cyrus-sasl2 from the Ports Collection. This port supports a number of compile-time options. For the SMTP authentication method demonstrated in this example, make sure that LOGIN is not disabled.

2. After installing security/cyrus-sasl2, edit `/usr/local/lib/sasl2/Sendmail.conf` , or create it if it does not exist, and add the following line:

```
pwcheck_method: saslauthd
```

3. Next, install security/cyrus-sasl2-saslauthd and add the following line to `/etc/rc.conf` :

```
saslauthd_enable="YES"
```

Finally, start the saslauthd daemon:

```
# service saslauthd start
```

This daemon serves as a broker for Sendmail to authenticate against the FreeBSD passwd(5) database. This saves the trouble of creating a new set of usernames and passwords for each user that needs to use SMTP authentication, and keeps the login and mail password the same.

4. Next, edit `/etc/make.conf` and add the following lines:

```
SENDMAIL_CFLAGS=-I/usr/local/include/sasl -DSASL
SENDMAIL_LDFLAGS=-L/usr/local/lib
SENDMAIL_LDADD=-lsasl2
```

These lines provide Sendmail the proper configuration options for linking to cyrus-sasl2 at compile time. Make sure that cyrus-sasl2 has been installed before recompiling Sendmail.

5. Recompile Sendmail by executing the following commands:

```
# cd /usr/src/lib/libsmutil
# make cleandir && make obj && make
# cd /usr/src/lib/libsm
# make cleandir && make obj && make
# cd /usr/src/usr.sbin/sendmail
# make cleandir && make obj && make && make install
```

This compile should not have any problems if /usr/src has not changed extensively and the shared libraries it needs are available.

6. After Sendmail has been compiled and reinstalled, edit /etc/mail/freebsd.mc or the local .mc. Many administrators choose to use the output from hostname(1) as the name of .mc for uniqueness. Add these lines:

```
dnl set SASL options
TRUST_AUTH_MECH(`GSSAPI DIGEST-MD5 CRAM-MD5 LOGIN')dnl
define(`confAUTH_MECHANISMS', `GSSAPI DIGEST-MD5 CRAM-MD5 LOGIN')dnl
```

These options configure the different methods available to Sendmail for authenticating users. To use a method other than pwcheck, refer to the Sendmail documentation.

7. Finally, run make(1) while in /etc/mail. That will run the new .mc and create a .cf named either freebsd.cf or the name used for the local .mc. Then, run make install restart, which will copy the file to sendmail.cf, and properly restart Sendmail. For more information about this process, refer to /etc/mail/Makefile.

To test the configuration, use a MUA to send a test message. For further investigation, set the LogLevel of Sendmail to 13 and watch /var/log/maillog for any errors.

For more information, refer to SMTP authentication.

27.10. Mail User Agents

Contributed by Marc Silver.

A MUA is an application that is used to send and receive email. As email "evolves" and becomes more complex, MUAs are becoming increasingly powerful and provide users increased functionality and flexibility. The mail category of the FreeBSD Ports Collection contains numerous MUAs. These include graphical email clients such as Evolution or Balsa and console based clients such as mutt or alpine.

27.10.1. mail

mail(1) is the default MUA installed with FreeBSD. It is a console based MUA that offers the basic functionality required to send and receive text-based email. It provides limited attachment support and can only access local mailboxes.

Although mail does not natively support interaction with POP or IMAP servers, these mailboxes may be downloaded to a local mbox using an application such as fetchmail.

In order to send and receive email, run mail:

```
% mail
```

The contents of the user's mailbox in /var/mail are automatically read by mail. Should the mailbox be empty, the utility exits with a message indicating that no mail could be found. If mail exists, the application interface starts, and a list of messages will be displayed. Messages are automatically numbered, as can be seen in the following example:

```
Mail version 8.1 6/6/93.  Type ? for help.
"/var/mail/marcs": 3 messages 3 new
>N  1 root@localhost       Mon Mar  8 14:05   14/510    "test"
 N  2 root@localhost       Mon Mar  8 14:05   14/509    "user account"
 N  3 root@localhost       Mon Mar  8 14:05   14/509    "sample"
```

Messages can now be read by typing t followed by the message number. This example reads the first email:

```
& t 1
Message 1:
```

```
From root@localhost  Mon Mar  8 14:05:52 2004
X-Original-To: marcs@localhost
Delivered-To: marcs@localhost
To: marcs@localhost
Subject: test
Date: Mon,  8 Mar 2004 14:05:52 +0200 (SAST)
From: root@localhost (Charlie Root)

This is a test message, please reply if you receive it.
```

As seen in this example, the message will be displayed with full headers. To display the list of messages again, press h.

If the email requires a reply, press either R or r mail keys. R instructs mail to reply only to the sender of the email, while r replies to all other recipients of the message. These commands can be suffixed with the mail number of the message to reply to. After typing the response, the end of the message should be marked by a single . on its own line. An example can be seen below:

```
& R 1
To: root@localhost
Subject: Re: test

Thank you, I did get your email.
.
EOT
```

In order to send a new email, press m, followed by the recipient email address. Multiple recipients may be specified by separating each address with the , delimiter. The subject of the message may then be entered, followed by the message contents. The end of the message should be specified by putting a single . on its own line.

```
& mail root@localhost
Subject: I mastered mail

Now I can send and receive email using mail ... :)
.
EOT
```

While using mail, press ? to display help at any time. Refer to mail(1) for more help on how to use mail.

Note

mail(1) was not designed to handle attachments and thus deals with them poorly. Newer MUAs handle attachments in a more intelligent way. Users who prefer to use mail may find the converters/mpack port to be of considerable use.

27.10.2. mutt

mutt is a powerful MUA, with many features, including:

- The ability to thread messages.

- PGP support for digital signing and encryption of email.

- MIME support.

- Maildir support.

- Highly customizable.

Refer to http://www.mutt.org for more information on mutt.

mutt may be installed using the mail/mutt port. After the port has been installed, mutt can be started by issuing the following command:

```
% mutt
```

mutt will automatically read and display the contents of the user mailbox in /var/mail . If no mails are found, mutt will wait for commands from the user. The example below shows mutt displaying a list of messages:

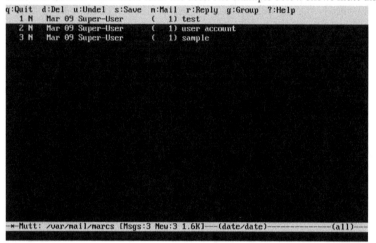

```
q:Quit  d:Del  u:Undel  s:Save  m:Mail  r:Reply  g:Group  ?:Help
   1 N    Mar 09 Super-User    (   1) test
   2 N    Mar 09 Super-User    (   1) user account
   3 N    Mar 09 Super-User    (   1) sample
```

```
-*-Mutt: /var/mail/marcs [Msgs:3 New:3 1.6K]---(date/date)-------------(all)---
```

To read an email, select it using the cursor keys and press Enter. An example of mutt displaying email can be seen below:

```
i:Exit  -:PrevPg  <Space>:NextPg  v:View Attachm.  d:Del  r:Reply  j:Next ?:Help
X-Original-To: marcs@localhost
Delivered-To: marcs@localhost
To: marcs@localhost
Subject: test
Date: Tue,  9 Mar 2004 10:28:36 +0200 (SAST)
From: Super-User <root@localhost>

This is a test message, please reply if you receieve it.
```

```
-N  -  1/1: Super-User              test                         -- (all)
```

Similar to mail(1), mutt can be used to reply only to the sender of the message as well as to all recipients. To reply only to the sender of the email, press r. To send a group reply to the original sender as well as all the message recipients, press g.

Note

By default, mutt uses the vi(1) editor for creating and replying to emails. Each user can customize this by creating or editing the .muttrc in their home directory and setting the editor variable or by setting the EDITOR environment variable. Refer to http://www.mutt.org/ for more information about configuring mutt.

To compose a new mail message, press m. After a valid subject has been given, mutt will start vi(1) so the email can be written. Once the contents of the email are complete, save and quit from **vi**. mutt will resume, displaying a summary screen of the mail that is to be delivered. In order to send the mail, press y. An example of the summary screen can be seen below:

```
y:Send  q:Abort  t:To  c:CC  s:Subj  a:Attach file  d:Descrip  ?:Help
     From: Marc Silver <marcs@localhost>
       To: Super-User <root@localhost>
       Cc:
      Bcc:
  Subject: Re: test
 Reply-To:
      Fcc:
 Security: Clear


-- Attachments
-  I      1 /tmp/mutt-bsd-c0hobscQ              [text/plain, 7bit, us-ascii, 1.1K]









-- Mutt: Compose  [Approx. msg size: 1.1K    Atts: 1]---------------------------
```

mutt contains extensive help which can be accessed from most of the menus by pressing ?. The top line also displays the keyboard shortcuts where appropriate.

27.10.3. alpine

alpine is aimed at a beginner user, but also includes some advanced features.

Warning

alpine has had several remote vulnerabilities discovered in the past, which allowed remote attackers to execute arbitrary code as users on the local system, by the action of sending a specially-prepared email. While *known* problems have been fixed, alpine code is written in an insecure style and the FreeBSD Security Officer believes there are likely to be other undiscovered vulnerabilities. Users install alpine at their own risk.

The current version of alpine may be installed using the mail/alpine port. Once the port has installed, alpine can be started by issuing the following command:

```
% alpine
```

The first time alpine runs, it displays a greeting page with a brief introduction, as well as a request from the alpine development team to send an anonymous email message allowing them to judge how many users are using their client. To send this anonymous message, press Enter. Alternatively, press E to exit the greeting without sending an anonymous message. An example of the greeting page is shown below:

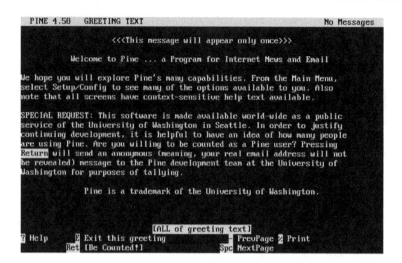

The main menu is then presented, which can be navigated using the cursor keys. This main menu provides short-cuts for the composing new mails, browsing mail directories, and administering address book entries. Below the main menu, relevant keyboard shortcuts to perform functions specific to the task at hand are shown.

The default directory opened by alpine is inbox. To view the message index, press I, or select the MESSAGE INDEX option shown below:

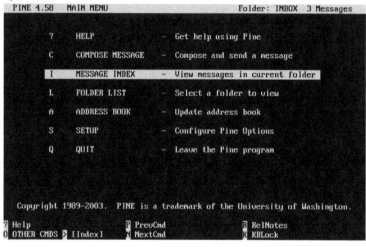

The message index shows messages in the current directory and can be navigated by using the cursor keys. High-lighted messages can be read by pressing Enter.

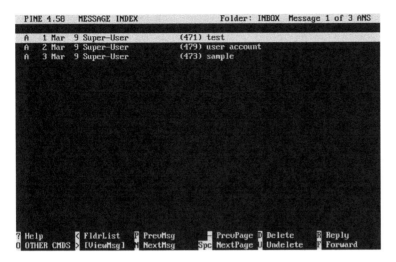

In the screenshot below, a sample message is displayed by alpine. Contextual keyboard shortcuts are displayed at the bottom of the screen. An example of one of a shortcut is r, which tells the MUA to reply to the current message being displayed.

Replying to an email in alpine is done using the pico editor, which is installed by default with alpine. pico makes it easy to navigate the message and is easier for novice users to use than vi(1) or mail(1). Once the reply is complete, the message can be sent by pressing Ctrl+X. alpine will ask for confirmation before sending the message.

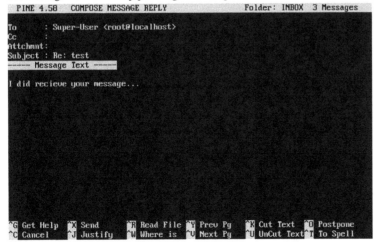

alpine can be customized using the SETUP option from the main menu. Consult `http://www.washington.edu/alpine/` for more information.

27.11. Using fetchmail

Contributed by Marc Silver.

fetchmail is a full-featured IMAP and POP client. It allows users to automatically download mail from remote IMAP and POP servers and save it into local mailboxes where it can be accessed more easily. fetchmail can be installed using the mail/fetchmail port, and offers various features, including:

• Support for the POP3, APOP, KPOP, IMAP, ETRN and ODMR protocols.

• Ability to forward mail using SMTP, which allows filtering, forwarding, and aliasing to function normally.

• May be run in daemon mode to check periodically for new messages.

• Can retrieve multiple mailboxes and forward them, based on configuration, to different local users.

This section explains some of the basic features of fetchmail. This utility requires a `.fetchmailrc` configuration in the user's home directory in order to run correctly. This file includes server information as well as login credentials. Due to the sensitive nature of the contents of this file, it is advisable to make it readable only by the user, with the following command:

```
% chmod 600 .fetchmailrc
```

The following `.fetchmailrc` serves as an example for downloading a single user mailbox using POP. It tells fetchmail to connect to `example.com` using a username of `joesoap` and a password of `XXX`. This example assumes that the user `joesoap` exists on the local system.

```
poll example.com protocol pop3 username "joesoap" password "XXX"
```

The next example connects to multiple POP and IMAP servers and redirects to different local usernames where applicable:

```
poll example.com proto pop3:
user "joesoap", with password "XXX", is "jsoap" here;
user "andrea", with password "XXXX";
poll example2.net proto imap:
user "john", with password "XXXXX", is "myth" here;
```

fetchmail can be run in daemon mode by running it with `-d`, followed by the interval (in seconds) that fetchmail should poll servers listed in `.fetchmailrc`. The following example configures fetchmail to poll every 600 seconds:

```
% fetchmail -d 600
```

More information on fetchmail can be found at `http://www.fetchmail.info/`.

27.12. Using procmail

Contributed by Marc Silver.

procmail is a powerful application used to filter incoming mail. It allows users to define "rules" which can be matched to incoming mails to perform specific functions or to reroute mail to alternative mailboxes or email addresses. procmail can be installed using the mail/procmail port. Once installed, it can be directly integrated into most MTAs. Consult the MTA documentation for more information. Alternatively, procmail can be integrated by adding the following line to a `.forward` in the home directory of the user:

```
"|exec /usr/local/bin/procmail || exit 75"
```

The following section displays some basic procmail rules, as well as brief descriptions of what they do. Rules must be inserted into a .procmailrc, which must reside in the user's home directory.

The majority of these rules can be found in procmailex(5).

To forward all mail from <user@example.com> to an external address of <goodmail@example2.com>:

```
:0
* ^From.*user@example.com
! goodmail@example2.com
```

To forward all mails shorter than 1000 bytes to an external address of <goodmail@example2.com>:

```
:0
* < 1000
! goodmail@example2.com
```

To send all mail sent to <alternate@example.com> to a mailbox called **alternate**:

```
:0
* ^TOalternate@example.com
alternate
```

To send all mail with a subject of "Spam" to /dev/null :

```
:0
^Subject:.*Spam
/dev/null
```

A useful recipe that parses incoming FreeBSD.org mailing lists and places each list in its own mailbox:

```
:0
* ^Sender:.owner-freebsd-\/[^@]+@FreeBSD.ORG
{
 LISTNAME=${MATCH}
 :0
 * LISTNAME??^\/[^@]+
 FreeBSD-${MATCH}
}
```

Chapter 28. Network Servers

28.1. Synopsis

This chapter covers some of the more frequently used network services on UNIX® systems. This includes installing, configuring, testing, and maintaining many different types of network services. Example configuration files are included throughout this chapter for reference.

By the end of this chapter, readers will know:

- How to manage the inetd daemon.

- How to set up the Network File System (NFS).

- How to set up the Network Information Server (NIS) for centralizing and sharing user accounts.

- How to set FreeBSD up to act as an LDAP server or client

- How to set up automatic network settings using DHCP.

- How to set up a Domain Name Server (DNS).

- How to set up the Apache HTTP Server.

- How to set up a File Transfer Protocol (FTP) server.

- How to set up a file and print server for Windows® clients using Samba.

- How to synchronize the time and date, and set up a time server using the Network Time Protocol (NTP).

- How to set up iSCSI.

This chapter assumes a basic knowledge of:

- /etc/rc scripts.

- Network terminology.

- Installation of additional third-party software (Chapter 4, *Installing Applications: Packages and Ports*).

28.2. The inetd Super-Server

The inetd(8) daemon is sometimes referred to as a Super-Server because it manages connections for many services. Instead of starting multiple applications, only the inetd service needs to be started. When a connection is received for a service that is managed by inetd, it determines which program the connection is destined for, spawns a process for that program, and delegates the program a socket. Using inetd for services that are not heavily used can reduce system load, when compared to running each daemon individually in stand-alone mode.

Primarily, inetd is used to spawn other daemons, but several trivial protocols are handled internally, such as chargen, auth, time, echo, discard, and daytime.

This section covers the basics of configuring inetd.

28.2.1. Configuration File

Configuration of inetd is done by editing /etc/inetd.conf. Each line of this configuration file represents an application which can be started by inetd. By default, every line starts with a comment (#), meaning that inetd is not listening for any applications. To configure inetd to listen for an application's connections, remove the # at the beginning of the line for that application.

After saving your edits, configure inetd to start at system boot by editing /etc/rc.conf :

```
inetd_enable="YES"
```

To start inetd now, so that it listens for the service you configured, type:

```
# service inetd start
```

Once inetd is started, it needs to be notified whenever a modification is made to /etc/inetd.conf :

Example 28.1. Reloading the inetd Configuration File

```
# service inetd reload
```

Typically, the default entry for an application does not need to be edited beyond removing the #. In some situations, it may be appropriate to edit the default entry.

As an example, this is the default entry for ftpd(8) over IPv4:

```
ftp     stream  tcp     nowait  root    /usr/libexec/ftpd       ftpd -l
```

The seven columns in an entry are as follows:

```
service-name
socket-type
protocol
{wait|nowait}[/max-child[/max-connections-per-ip-per-minute[/max-child-per-ip]]]
user[:group][/login-class]
server-program
server-program-arguments
```

where:

service-name
    The service name of the daemon to start. It must correspond to a service listed in /etc/services . This determines which port inetd listens on for incoming connections to that service. When using a custom service, it must first be added to /etc/services .

socket-type
    Either stream, dgram, raw, or seqpacket. Use stream for TCP connections and dgram for UDP services.

protocol
    Use one of the following protocol names:

Protocol Name	Explanation
tcp or tcp4	TCP IPv4
udp or udp4	UDP IPv4
tcp6	TCP IPv6
udp6	UDP IPv6
tcp46	Both TCP IPv4 and IPv6
udp46	Both UDP IPv4 and IPv6

514

{wait|nowait}[/max-child[/max-connections-per-ip-per-minute[/max-child-per-ip]]]

In this field, `wait` or `nowait` must be specified. `max-child`, `max-connections-per-ip-per-minute` and `max-child-per-ip` are optional.

`wait|nowait` indicates whether or not the service is able to handle its own socket. `dgram` socket types must use `wait` while `stream` daemons, which are usually multi-threaded, should use `nowait`. `wait` usually hands off multiple sockets to a single daemon, while `nowait` spawns a child daemon for each new socket.

The maximum number of child daemons inetd may spawn is set by `max-child`. For example, to limit ten instances of the daemon, place a `/10` after `nowait`. Specifying `/0` allows an unlimited number of children.

`max-connections-per-ip-per-minute` limits the number of connections from any particular IP address per minute. Once the limit is reached, further connections from this IP address will be dropped until the end of the minute. For example, a value of `/10` would limit any particular IP address to ten connection attempts per minute. `max-child-per-ip` limits the number of child processes that can be started on behalf on any single IP address at any moment. These options can limit excessive resource consumption and help to prevent Denial of Service attacks.

An example can be seen in the default settings for fingerd(8):

```
finger stream  tcp     nowait/3/10 nobody /usr/libexec/fingerd fingerd -k -s
```

user
: The username the daemon will run as. Daemons typically run as `root`, `daemon`, or `nobody`.

server-program
: The full path to the daemon. If the daemon is a service provided by inetd internally, use `internal`.

server-program-arguments
: Used to specify any command arguments to be passed to the daemon on invocation. If the daemon is an internal service, use `internal`.

28.2.2. Command-Line Options

Like most server daemons, inetd has a number of options that can be used to modify its behaviour. By default, inetd is started with `-wW -C 60`. These options enable TCP wrappers for all services, including internal services, and prevent any IP address from requesting any service more than 60 times per minute.

To change the default options which are passed to inetd, add an entry for `inetd_flags` in `/etc/rc.conf`. If inetd is already running, restart it with `service inetd restart`.

The available rate limiting options are:

-c maximum
: Specify the default maximum number of simultaneous invocations of each service, where the default is unlimited. May be overridden on a per-service basis by using `max-child` in `/etc/inetd.conf`.

-C rate
: Specify the default maximum number of times a service can be invoked from a single IP address per minute. May be overridden on a per-service basis by using `max-connections-per-ip-per-minute` in `/etc/inetd.conf`.

-R rate
: Specify the maximum number of times a service can be invoked in one minute, where the default is `256`. A rate of `0` allows an unlimited number.

-s maximum
: Specify the maximum number of times a service can be invoked from a single IP address at any one time, where the default is unlimited. May be overridden on a per-service basis by using `max-child-per-ip` in `/etc/inetd.conf`.

515

Additional options are available. Refer to inetd(8) for the full list of options.

28.2.3. Security Considerations

Many of the daemons which can be managed by inetd are not security-conscious. Some daemons, such as fingerd, can provide information that may be useful to an attacker. Only enable the services which are needed and monitor the system for excessive connection attempts. `max-connections-per-ip-per-minute` , `max-child` and `max-child-per-ip` can be used to limit such attacks.

By default, TCP wrappers is enabled. Consult hosts_access(5) for more information on placing TCP restrictions on various inetd invoked daemons.

28.3. Network File System (NFS)

Reorganized and enhanced by Tom Rhodes.
Written by Bill Swingle.

FreeBSD supports the Network File System (NFS), which allows a server to share directories and files with clients over a network. With NFS, users and programs can access files on remote systems as if they were stored locally.

NFS has many practical uses. Some of the more common uses include:

- Data that would otherwise be duplicated on each client can be kept in a single location and accessed by clients on the network.

- Several clients may need access to the `/usr/ports/distfiles` directory. Sharing that directory allows for quick access to the source files without having to download them to each client.

- On large networks, it is often more convenient to configure a central NFS server on which all user home directories are stored. Users can log into a client anywhere on the network and have access to their home directories.

- Administration of NFS exports is simplified. For example, there is only one file system where security or backup policies must be set.

- Removable media storage devices can be used by other machines on the network. This reduces the number of devices throughout the network and provides a centralized location to manage their security. It is often more convenient to install software on multiple machines from a centralized installation media.

NFS consists of a server and one or more clients. The client remotely accesses the data that is stored on the server machine. In order for this to function properly, a few processes have to be configured and running.

These daemons must be running on the server:

Daemon	Description
nfsd	The NFS daemon which services requests from NFS clients.
mountd	The NFS mount daemon which carries out requests received from nfsd.
rpcbind	This daemon allows NFS clients to discover which port the NFS server is using.

Running nfsiod(8) on the client can improve performance, but is not required.

28.3.1. Configuring the Server

The file systems which the NFS server will share are specified in `/etc/exports` . Each line in this file specifies a file system to be exported, which clients have access to that file system, and any access options. When adding entries to this file, each exported file system, its properties, and allowed hosts must occur on a single line. If no clients are listed in the entry, then any client on the network can mount that file system.

The following /etc/exports entries demonstrate how to export file systems. The examples can be modified to match the file systems and client names on the reader's network. There are many options that can be used in this file, but only a few will be mentioned here. See exports(5) for the full list of options.

This example shows how to export /cdrom to three hosts named *alpha*, *bravo*, and *charlie*:

```
/cdrom -ro alpha bravo charlie
```

The -ro flag makes the file system read-only, preventing clients from making any changes to the exported file system. This example assumes that the host names are either in DNS or in /etc/hosts . Refer to hosts(5) if the network does not have a DNS server.

The next example exports /home to three clients by IP address. This can be useful for networks without DNS or /etc/hosts entries. The -alldirs flag allows subdirectories to be mount points. In other words, it will not automatically mount the subdirectories, but will permit the client to mount the directories that are required as needed.

```
/home  -alldirs  10.0.0.2 10.0.0.3 10.0.0.4
```

This next example exports /a so that two clients from different domains may access that file system. The -maproot=root allows root on the remote system to write data on the exported file system as root. If -maproot=root is not specified, the client's root user will be mapped to the server's nobody account and will be subject to the access limitations defined for nobody.

```
/a -maproot=root  host.example.com box.example.org
```

A client can only be specified once per file system. For example, if /usr is a single file system, these entries would be invalid as both entries specify the same host:

```
# Invalid when /usr is one file system
/usr/src   client
/usr/ports client
```

The correct format for this situation is to use one entry:

```
/usr/src /usr/ports  client
```

The following is an example of a valid export list, where /usr and /exports are local file systems:

```
# Export src and ports to client01 and client02, but only
# client01 has root privileges on it
/usr/src /usr/ports -maproot=root    client01
/usr/src /usr/ports             client02
# The client machines have root and can mount anywhere
# on /exports. Anyone in the world can mount /exports/obj read-only
/exports -alldirs -maproot=root      client01 client02
/exports/obj -ro
```

To enable the processes required by the NFS server at boot time, add these options to /etc/rc.conf :

```
rpcbind_enable="YES"
nfs_server_enable="YES"
mountd_flags="-r"
```

The server can be started now by running this command:

```
# service nfsd start
```

Whenever the NFS server is started, mountd also starts automatically. However, mountd only reads /etc/exports when it is started. To make subsequent /etc/exports edits take effect immediately, force mountd to reread it:

```
# service mountd reload
```

28.3.2. Configuring the Client

To enable NFS clients, set this option in each client's /etc/rc.conf :

```
nfs_client_enable="YES"
```

Then, run this command on each NFS client:

```
# service nfsclient start
```

The client now has everything it needs to mount a remote file system. In these examples, the server's name is server and the client's name is client. To mount /home on server to the /mnt mount point on client:

```
# mount server:/home /mnt
```

The files and directories in /home will now be available on client, in the /mnt directory.

To mount a remote file system each time the client boots, add it to /etc/fstab :

```
server:/home /mnt nfs rw 0 0
```

Refer to fstab(5) for a description of all available options.

28.3.3. Locking

Some applications require file locking to operate correctly. To enable locking, add these lines to /etc/rc.conf on both the client and server:

```
rpc_lockd_enable="YES"
rpc_statd_enable="YES"
```

Then start the applications:

```
# service lockd start
# service statd start
```

If locking is not required on the server, the NFS client can be configured to lock locally by including -L when running mount. Refer to mount_nfs(8) for further details.

28.3.4. Automating Mounts with amd(8)

Contributed by Wylie Stilwell.
Rewritten by Chern Lee.

The automatic mounter daemon, amd, automatically mounts a remote file system whenever a file or directory within that file system is accessed. File systems that are inactive for a period of time will be automatically unmounted by amd.

This daemon provides an alternative to modifying /etc/fstab to list every client. It operates by attaching itself as an NFS server to the /host and /net directories. When a file is accessed within one of these directories, amd looks up the corresponding remote mount and automatically mounts it. /net is used to mount an exported file system from an IP address while /host is used to mount an export from a remote hostname. For instance, an attempt to access a file within /host/foobar/usr would tell amd to mount the /usr export on the host foobar.

Example 28.2. Mounting an Export with amd

In this example, showmount -e shows the exported file systems that can be mounted from the NFS server, foobar:

```
% showmount -e foobar
Exports list on foobar:
```

```
/usr                        10.10.10.0
/a                          10.10.10.0
% cd /host/foobar/usr
```

The output from showmount shows /usr as an export. When changing directories to /host/foobar/usr , amd intercepts the request and attempts to resolve the hostname foobar. If successful, amd automatically mounts the desired export.

To enable amd at boot time, add this line to /etc/rc.conf :

```
amd_enable="YES"
```

To start amd now:

```
# service amd start
```

Custom flags can be passed to amd from the amd_flags environment variable. By default, amd_flags is set to:

```
amd_flags="-a /.amd_mnt -l syslog /host /etc/amd.map /net /etc/amd.map"
```

The default options with which exports are mounted are defined in /etc/amd.map . Some of the more advanced features of amd are defined in /etc/amd.conf .

Consult amd(8) and amd.conf(5) for more information.

28.3.5. Automating Mounts with autofs(5)

 Note

The autofs(5) automount facility is supported starting with FreeBSD 10.1-RELEASE. To use the automounter functionality in older versions of FreeBSD, use amd(8) instead. This chapter only describes the autofs(5) automounter.

The autofs(5) facility is a common name for several components that, together, allow for automatic mounting of remote and local filesystems whenever a file or directory within that file system is accessed. It consists of the kernel component, autofs(5), and several userspace applications: automount(8), automountd(8) and autounmountd(8). It serves as an alternative for amd(8) from previous FreeBSD releases. Amd is still provided for backward compatibility purposes, as the two use different map format; the one used by autofs is the same as with other SVR4 automounters, such as the ones in Solaris, MacOS X, and Linux.

The autofs(5) virtual filesystem is mounted on specified mountpoints by automount(8), usually invoked during boot.

Whenever a process attempts to access file within the autofs(5) mountpoint, the kernel will notify automountd(8) daemon and pause the triggering process. The automountd(8) daemon will handle kernel requests by finding the proper map and mounting the filesystem according to it, then signal the kernel to release blocked process. The autounmountd(8) daemon automatically unmounts automounted filesystems after some time, unless they are still being used.

The primary autofs configuration file is /etc/auto_master . It assigns individual maps to top-level mounts. For an explanation of auto_master and the map syntax, refer to auto_master(5).

There is a special automounter map mounted on /net. When a file is accessed within this directory, autofs(5) looks up the corresponding remote mount and automatically mounts it. For instance, an attempt to access a file within /net/foobar/usr would tell automountd(8) to mount the /usr export from the host foobar.

Example 28.3. Mounting an Export with autofs(5)

In this example, showmount -e shows the exported file systems that can be mounted from the NFS server, foobar:

```
% showmount -e foobar
Exports list on foobar:
/usr                        10.10.10.0
/a                          10.10.10.0
% cd /net/foobar/usr
```

The output from showmount shows /usr as an export. When changing directories to /host/foobar/usr , automountd(8) intercepts the request and attempts to resolve the hostname foobar. If successful, automountd(8) automatically mounts the source export.

To enable autofs(5) at boot time, add this line to /etc/rc.conf :

```
autofs_enable="YES"
```

Then autofs(5) can be started by running:

```
# service automount start
# service automountd start
# service autounmountd start
```

The autofs(5) map format is the same as in other operating systems, it might be desirable to consult information from other operating systems, such as the Mac OS X document.

Consult the automount(8), automountd(8), autounmountd(8), and auto_master(5) manual pages for more information.

28.4. Network Information System (NIS)

Network Information System (NIS) is designed to centralize administration of UNIX®-like systems such as Solaris™, HP-UX, AIX®, Linux, NetBSD, OpenBSD, and FreeBSD. NIS was originally known as Yellow Pages but the name was changed due to trademark issues. This is the reason why NIS commands begin with yp.

NIS is a Remote Procedure Call (RPC)-based client/server system that allows a group of machines within an NIS domain to share a common set of configuration files. This permits a system administrator to set up NIS client systems with only minimal configuration data and to add, remove, or modify configuration data from a single location.

FreeBSD uses version 2 of the NIS protocol.

28.4.1. NIS Terms and Processes

Table 28.1 summarizes the terms and important processes used by NIS:

Table 28.1. NIS Terminology

Term	Description
NIS domain name	NIS servers and clients share an NIS domain name. Typically, this name does not have anything to do with DNS.

Term	Description
rpcbind(8)	This service enables RPC and must be running in order to run an NIS server or act as an NIS client.
ypbind(8)	This service binds an NIS client to its NIS server. It will take the NIS domain name and use RPC to connect to the server. It is the core of client/server communication in an NIS environment. If this service is not running on a client machine, it will not be able to access the NIS server.
ypserv(8)	This is the process for the NIS server. If this service stops running, the server will no longer be able to respond to NIS requests so hopefully, there is a slave server to take over. Some non-FreeBSD clients will not try to reconnect using a slave server and the ypbind process may need to be restarted on these clients.
rpc.yppasswdd(8)	This process only runs on NIS master servers. This daemon allows NIS clients to change their NIS passwords. If this daemon is not running, users will have to login to the NIS master server and change their passwords there.

28.4.2. Machine Types

There are three types of hosts in an NIS environment:

- NIS master server

  This server acts as a central repository for host configuration information and maintains the authoritative copy of the files used by all of the NIS clients. The passwd, group, and other various files used by NIS clients are stored on the master server. While it is possible for one machine to be an NIS master server for more than one NIS domain, this type of configuration will not be covered in this chapter as it assumes a relatively small-scale NIS environment.

- NIS slave servers

  NIS slave servers maintain copies of the NIS master's data files in order to provide redundancy. Slave servers also help to balance the load of the master server as NIS clients always attach to the NIS server which responds first.

- NIS clients

  NIS clients authenticate against the NIS server during log on.

Information in many files can be shared using NIS. The master.passwd, group, and hosts files are commonly shared via NIS. Whenever a process on a client needs information that would normally be found in these files locally, it makes a query to the NIS server that it is bound to instead.

28.4.3. Planning Considerations

This section describes a sample NIS environment which consists of 15 FreeBSD machines with no centralized point of administration. Each machine has its own /etc/passwd and /etc/master.passwd. These files are kept in sync with each other only through manual intervention. Currently, when a user is added to the lab, the process must be repeated on all 15 machines.

The configuration of the lab will be as follows:

Machine name	IP address	Machine role
ellington	10.0.0.2	NIS master
coltrane	10.0.0.3	NIS slave
basie	10.0.0.4	Faculty workstation

Machine name	IP address	Machine role
bird	10.0.0.5	Client machine
cli[1-11]	10.0.0.[6-17]	Other client machines

If this is the first time an NIS scheme is being developed, it should be thoroughly planned ahead of time. Regardless of network size, several decisions need to be made as part of the planning process.

28.4.3.1. Choosing a NIS Domain Name

When a client broadcasts its requests for info, it includes the name of the NIS domain that it is part of. This is how multiple servers on one network can tell which server should answer which request. Think of the NIS domain name as the name for a group of hosts.

Some organizations choose to use their Internet domain name for their NIS domain name. This is not recommended as it can cause confusion when trying to debug network problems. The NIS domain name should be unique within the network and it is helpful if it describes the group of machines it represents. For example, the Art department at Acme Inc. might be in the "acme-art" NIS domain. This example will use the domain name test-domain.

However, some non-FreeBSD operating systems require the NIS domain name to be the same as the Internet domain name. If one or more machines on the network have this restriction, the Internet domain name *must* be used as the NIS domain name.

28.4.3.2. Physical Server Requirements

There are several things to keep in mind when choosing a machine to use as a NIS server. Since NIS clients depend upon the availability of the server, choose a machine that is not rebooted frequently. The NIS server should ideally be a stand alone machine whose sole purpose is to be an NIS server. If the network is not heavily used, it is acceptable to put the NIS server on a machine running other services. However, if the NIS server becomes unavailable, it will adversely affect all NIS clients.

28.4.4. Configuring the NIS Master Server

The canonical copies of all NIS files are stored on the master server. The databases used to store the information are called NIS maps. In FreeBSD, these maps are stored in /var/yp/[domainname] where [domainname] is the name of the NIS domain. Since multiple domains are supported, it is possible to have several directories, one for each domain. Each domain will have its own independent set of maps.

NIS master and slave servers handle all NIS requests through ypserv(8). This daemon is responsible for receiving incoming requests from NIS clients, translating the requested domain and map name to a path to the corresponding database file, and transmitting data from the database back to the client.

Setting up a master NIS server can be relatively straight forward, depending on environmental needs. Since FreeBSD provides built-in NIS support, it only needs to be enabled by adding the following lines to /etc/rc.conf :

```
nisdomainname="test-domain" ❶
nis_server_enable="YES"  ❷
nis_yppasswdd_enable="YES" ❸
```

❶ This line sets the NIS domain name to test-domain.
❷ This automates the start up of the NIS server processes when the system boots.
❸ This enables the rpc.yppasswdd(8) daemon so that users can change their NIS password from a client machine.

Care must be taken in a multi-server domain where the server machines are also NIS clients. It is generally a good idea to force the servers to bind to themselves rather than allowing them to broadcast bind requests and possibly become bound to each other. Strange failure modes can result if one server goes down and others are dependent upon it. Eventually, all the clients will time out and attempt to bind to other servers, but the delay involved can be considerable and the failure mode is still present since the servers might bind to each other all over again.

A server that is also a client can be forced to bind to a particular server by adding these additional lines to /etc/rc.conf:

```
nis_client_enable="YES" # run client stuff as well
nis_client_flags="-S NIS domain,server"
```

After saving the edits, type /etc/netstart to restart the network and apply the values defined in /etc/rc.conf. Before initializing the NIS maps, start ypserv(8):

```
# service ypserv start
```

28.4.4.1. Initializing the NIS Maps

NIS maps are generated from the configuration files in /etc on the NIS master, with one exception: /etc/master.passwd. This is to prevent the propagation of passwords to all the servers in the NIS domain. Therefore, before the NIS maps are initialized, configure the primary password files:

```
# cp /etc/master.passwd /var/yp/master.passwd
# cd /var/yp
# vi master.passwd
```

It is advisable to remove all entries for system accounts as well as any user accounts that do not need to be propagated to the NIS clients, such as the root and any other administrative accounts.

> Note
>
> Ensure that the /var/yp/master.passwd is neither group or world readable by setting its permissions to 600.

After completing this task, initialize the NIS maps. FreeBSD includes the ypinit(8) script to do this. When generating maps for the master server, include -m and specify the NIS domain name:

```
ellington# ypinit -m test-domain
Server Type: MASTER Domain: test-domain
Creating an YP server will require that you answer a few questions.
Questions will all be asked at the beginning of the procedure.
Do you want this procedure to quit on non-fatal errors? [y/n: n] n
Ok, please remember to go back and redo manually whatever fails.
If not, something might not work.
At this point, we have to construct a list of this domains YP servers.
rod.darktech.org is already known as master server.
Please continue to add any slave servers, one per line. When you are
done with the list, type a <control D>.
master server   : ellington
next host to add: coltrane
next host to add: ^D
The current list of NIS servers looks like this:
ellington
coltrane
Is this correct?  [y/n: y] y

[..output from map generation..-]

NIS Map update completed.
ellington has been setup as an YP master server without any errors.
```

This will create /var/yp/Makefile from /var/yp/Makefile.dist. By default, this file assumes that the environment has a single NIS server with only FreeBSD clients. Since test-domain has a slave server, edit this line in /var/yp/Makefile so that it begins with a comment (#):

```
NOPUSH = "True"
```

28.4.4.2. Adding New Users

Every time a new user is created, the user account must be added to the master NIS server and the NIS maps rebuilt. Until this occurs, the new user will not be able to login anywhere except on the NIS master. For example, to add the new user jsmith to the test-domain domain, run these commands on the master server:

```
# pw useradd jsmith
# cd /var/yp
# make test-domain
```

The user could also be added using adduser jsmith instead of pw useradd smith.

28.4.5. Setting up a NIS Slave Server

To set up an NIS slave server, log on to the slave server and edit /etc/rc.conf as for the master server. Do not generate any NIS maps, as these already exist on the master server. When running ypinit on the slave server, use -s (for slave) instead of -m (for master). This option requires the name of the NIS master in addition to the domain name, as seen in this example:

```
coltrane# ypinit -s ellington test-domain

Server Type: SLAVE Domain: test-domain Master: ellington

Creating an YP server will require that you answer a few questions.
Questions will all be asked at the beginning of the procedure.

Do you want this procedure to quit on non-fatal errors? [y/n: n]  n

Ok, please remember to go back and redo manually whatever fails.
If not, something might not work.
There will be no further questions. The remainder of the procedure
should take a few minutes, to copy the databases from ellington.
Transferring netgroup...
ypxfr: Exiting: Map successfully transferred
Transferring netgroup.byuser...
ypxfr: Exiting: Map successfully transferred
Transferring netgroup.byhost...
ypxfr: Exiting: Map successfully transferred
Transferring master.passwd.byuid...
ypxfr: Exiting: Map successfully transferred
Transferring passwd.byuid...
ypxfr: Exiting: Map successfully transferred
Transferring passwd.byname...
ypxfr: Exiting: Map successfully transferred
Transferring group.bygid...
ypxfr: Exiting: Map successfully transferred
Transferring group.byname...
ypxfr: Exiting: Map successfully transferred
Transferring services.byname...
ypxfr: Exiting: Map successfully transferred
Transferring rpc.bynumber...
ypxfr: Exiting: Map successfully transferred
Transferring rpc.byname...
ypxfr: Exiting: Map successfully transferred
Transferring protocols.byname...
ypxfr: Exiting: Map successfully transferred
Transferring master.passwd.byname...
ypxfr: Exiting: Map successfully transferred
Transferring networks.byname...
ypxfr: Exiting: Map successfully transferred
Transferring networks.byaddr...
ypxfr: Exiting: Map successfully transferred
```

```
Transferring netid.byname...
ypxfr: Exiting: Map successfully transferred
Transferring hosts.byaddr...
ypxfr: Exiting: Map successfully transferred
Transferring protocols.bynumber...
ypxfr: Exiting: Map successfully transferred
Transferring ypservers...
ypxfr: Exiting: Map successfully transferred
Transferring hosts.byname...
ypxfr: Exiting: Map successfully transferred

coltrane has been setup as an YP slave server without any errors.
Remember to update map ypservers on ellington.
```

This will generate a directory on the slave server called `/var/yp/test-domain` which contains copies of the NIS master server's maps. Adding these `/etc/crontab` entries on each slave server will force the slaves to sync their maps with the maps on the master server:

```
20      *       *       *       *       root    /usr/libexec/ypxfr passwd.byname
21      *       *       *       *       root    /usr/libexec/ypxfr passwd.byuid
```

These entries are not mandatory because the master server automatically attempts to push any map changes to its slaves. However, since clients may depend upon the slave server to provide correct password information, it is recommended to force frequent password map updates. This is especially important on busy networks where map updates might not always complete.

To finish the configuration, run `/etc/netstart` on the slave server in order to start the NIS services.

28.4.6. Setting Up an NIS Client

An NIS client binds to an NIS server using ypbind(8). This daemon broadcasts RPC requests on the local network. These requests specify the domain name configured on the client. If an NIS server in the same domain receives one of the broadcasts, it will respond to ypbind, which will record the server's address. If there are several servers available, the client will use the address of the first server to respond and will direct all of its NIS requests to that server. The client will automatically ping the server on a regular basis to make sure it is still available. If it fails to receive a reply within a reasonable amount of time, ypbind will mark the domain as unbound and begin broadcasting again in the hopes of locating another server.

To configure a FreeBSD machine to be an NIS client:

1. Edit `/etc/rc.conf` and add the following lines in order to set the NIS domain name and start ypbind(8) during network startup:

    ```
    nisdomainname="test-domain"
    nis_client_enable="YES"
    ```

2. To import all possible password entries from the NIS server, use `vipw` to remove all user accounts except one from `/etc/master.passwd`. When removing the accounts, keep in mind that at least one local account should remain and this account should be a member of `wheel`. If there is a problem with NIS, this local account can be used to log in remotely, become the superuser, and fix the problem. Before saving the edits, add the following line to the end of the file:

    ```
    +:::::::::
    ```

    This line configures the client to provide anyone with a valid account in the NIS server's password maps an account on the client. There are many ways to configure the NIS client by modifying this line. One method is described in Section 28.4.8, "Using Netgroups". For more detailed reading, refer to the book `Managing NFS and NIS`, published by O'Reilly Media.

3. To import all possible group entries from the NIS server, add this line to `/etc/group`:

    ```
    +:*::
    ```

To start the NIS client immediately, execute the following commands as the superuser:

```
# /etc/netstart
# service ypbind start
```

After completing these steps, running `ypcat passwd` on the client should show the server's `passwd` map.

28.4.7. NIS Security

Since RPC is a broadcast-based service, any system running ypbind within the same domain can retrieve the contents of the NIS maps. To prevent unauthorized transactions, ypserv(8) supports a feature called "securenets" which can be used to restrict access to a given set of hosts. By default, this information is stored in `/var/yp/securenets`, unless ypserv(8) is started with `-p` and an alternate path. This file contains entries that consist of a network specification and a network mask separated by white space. Lines starting with # are considered to be comments. A sample `securenets` might look like this:

```
# allow connections from local host -- mandatory
127.0.0.1      255.255.255.255
# allow connections from any host
# on the 192.168.128.0 network
192.168.128.0 255.255.255.0
# allow connections from any host
# between 10.0.0.0 to 10.0.15.255
# this includes the machines in the testlab
10.0.0.0       255.255.240.0
```

If ypserv(8) receives a request from an address that matches one of these rules, it will process the request normally. If the address fails to match a rule, the request will be ignored and a warning message will be logged. If the `securenets` does not exist, `ypserv` will allow connections from any host.

Section 13.4, "TCP Wrapper" is an alternate mechanism for providing access control instead of `securenets`. While either access control mechanism adds some security, they are both vulnerable to "IP spoofing" attacks. All NIS-related traffic should be blocked at the firewall.

Servers using `securenets` may fail to serve legitimate NIS clients with archaic TCP/IP implementations. Some of these implementations set all host bits to zero when doing broadcasts or fail to observe the subnet mask when calculating the broadcast address. While some of these problems can be fixed by changing the client configuration, other problems may force the retirement of these client systems or the abandonment of `securenets`.

The use of TCP Wrapper increases the latency of the NIS server. The additional delay may be long enough to cause timeouts in client programs, especially in busy networks with slow NIS servers. If one or more clients suffer from latency, convert those clients into NIS slave servers and force them to bind to themselves.

28.4.7.1. Barring Some Users

In this example, the `basie` system is a faculty workstation within the NIS domain. The `passwd` map on the master NIS server contains accounts for both faculty and students. This section demonstrates how to allow faculty logins on this system while refusing student logins.

To prevent specified users from logging on to a system, even if they are present in the NIS database, use `vipw` to add *-username* with the correct number of colons towards the end of `/etc/master.passwd` on the client, where *username* is the username of a user to bar from logging in. The line with the blocked user must be before the + line that allows NIS users. In this example, `bill` is barred from logging on to `basie`:

```
basie# cat /etc/master.passwd
root:[password]:0:0::0:0:The super-user:/root:/bin/csh
toor:[password]:0:0::0:0:The other super-user:/root:/bin/sh
daemon:*:1:1::0:0:Owner of many system processes:/root:/sbin/nologin
operator:*:2:5::0:0:System &:/:/sbin/nologin
bin:*:3:7::0:0:Binaries Commands and Source,,,:/:/sbin/nologin
tty:*:4:65533::0:0:Tty Sandbox:/:/sbin/nologin
kmem:*:5:65533::0:0:KMem Sandbox:/:/sbin/nologin
```

```
games:*:7:13::0:0:Games pseudo-user:/usr/games:/sbin/nologin
news:*:8:8::0:0:News Subsystem:/:/sbin/nologin
man:*:9:9::0:0:Mister Man Pages:/usr/share/man:/sbin/nologin
bind:*:53:53::0:0:Bind Sandbox:/:/sbin/nologin
uucp:*:66:66::0:0:UUCP pseudo-user:/var/spool/uucppublic:/usr/libexec/uucp/uucico
xten:*:67:67::0:0:X-10 daemon:/usr/local/xten:/sbin/nologin
pop:*:68:6::0:0:Post Office Owner:/nonexistent:/sbin/nologin
nobody:*:65534:65534::0:0:Unprivileged user:/nonexistent:/sbin/nologin
-bill:::::::::
+:::::::::::

basie#
```

28.4.8. Using Netgroups

Barring specified users from logging on to individual systems becomes unscaleable on larger networks and quickly loses the main benefit of NIS: *centralized* administration.

Netgroups were developed to handle large, complex networks with hundreds of users and machines. Their use is comparable to UNIX® groups, where the main difference is the lack of a numeric ID and the ability to define a netgroup by including both user accounts and other netgroups.

To expand on the example used in this chapter, the NIS domain will be extended to add the users and systems shown in Tables 28.2 and 28.3:

Table 28.2. Additional Users

User Name(s)	Description
alpha, beta	IT department employees
charlie, delta	IT department apprentices
echo, foxtrott, golf, ...	employees
able, baker, ...	interns

Table 28.3. Additional Systems

Machine Name(s)	Description
war, death, famine, pollution	Only IT employees are allowed to log onto these servers.
pride, greed, envy, wrath, lust, sloth	All members of the IT department are allowed to login onto these servers.
one, two, three, four, ...	Ordinary workstations used by employees.
trashcan	A very old machine without any critical data. Even interns are allowed to use this system.

When using netgroups to configure this scenario, each user is assigned to one or more netgroups and logins are then allowed or forbidden for all members of the netgroup. When adding a new machine, login restrictions must be defined for all netgroups. When a new user is added, the account must be added to one or more netgroups. If the NIS setup is planned carefully, only one central configuration file needs modification to grant or deny access to machines.

The first step is the initialization of the NIS netgroup map. In FreeBSD, this map is not created by default. On the NIS master server, use an editor to create a map named /var/yp/netgroup .

This example creates four netgroups to represent IT employees, IT apprentices, employees, and interns:

```
IT_EMP   (,alpha,test-domain)      (,beta,test-domain)
IT_APP   (,charlie,test-domain)    (,delta,test-domain)
USERS    (,echo,test-domain)       (,foxtrott,test-domain) \
```

```
        (,golf,test-domain)
INTERNS (,able,test-domain)        (,baker,test-domain)
```

Each entry configures a netgroup. The first column in an entry is the name of the netgroup. Each set of brackets represents either a group of one or more users or the name of another netgroup. When specifying a user, the three comma-delimited fields inside each group represent:

1. The name of the host(s) where the other fields representing the user are valid. If a hostname is not specified, the entry is valid on all hosts.

2. The name of the account that belongs to this netgroup.

3. The NIS domain for the account. Accounts may be imported from other NIS domains into a netgroup.

If a group contains multiple users, separate each user with whitespace. Additionally, each field may contain wildcards. See netgroup(5) for details.

Netgroup names longer than 8 characters should not be used. The names are case sensitive and using capital letters for netgroup names is an easy way to distinguish between user, machine and netgroup names.

Some non-FreeBSD NIS clients cannot handle netgroups containing more than 15 entries. This limit may be circumvented by creating several sub-netgroups with 15 users or fewer and a real netgroup consisting of the sub-netgroups, as seen in this example:

```
BIGGRP1  (,joe1,domain)  (,joe2,domain)  (,joe3,domain) [...-]
BIGGRP2  (,joe16,domain)  (,joe17,domain) [...-]
BIGGRP3  (,joe31,domain)  (,joe32,domain)
BIGGROUP  BIGGRP1 BIGGRP2 BIGGRP3
```

Repeat this process if more than 225 (15 times 15) users exist within a single netgroup.

To activate and distribute the new NIS map:

```
ellington# cd /var/yp
ellington# make
```

This will generate the three NIS maps netgroup, netgroup.byhost and netgroup.byuser. Use the map key option of ypcat(1) to check if the new NIS maps are available:

```
ellington% ypcat -k netgroup
ellington% ypcat -k netgroup.byhost
ellington% ypcat -k netgroup.byuser
```

The output of the first command should resemble the contents of /var/yp/netgroup . The second command only produces output if host-specific netgroups were created. The third command is used to get the list of netgroups for a user.

To configure a client, use vipw(8) to specify the name of the netgroup. For example, on the server named war, replace this line:

```
+:::::::::
```

with

```
+@IT_EMP:::::::::
```

This specifies that only the users defined in the netgroup IT_EMP will be imported into this system's password database and only those users are allowed to login to this system.

This configuration also applies to the ~ function of the shell and all routines which convert between user names and numerical user IDs. In other words, cd ~*user* will not work, ls -l will show the numerical ID instead of the username, and find . -user joe -print will fail with the message No such user. To fix this, import all user entries without allowing them to login into the servers. This can be achieved by adding an extra line:

528

```
+:::::::::/sbin/nologin
```

This line configures the client to import all entries but to replace the shell in those entries with `/sbin/nologin`.

Make sure that extra line is placed *after* +@IT_EMP:::::::::. Otherwise, all user accounts imported from NIS will have `/sbin/nologin` as their login shell and no one will be able to login to the system.

To configure the less important servers, replace the old +::::::::: on the servers with these lines:

```
+@IT_EMP:::::::::
+@IT_APP:::::::::
+:::::::::/sbin/nologin
```

The corresponding lines for the workstations would be:

```
+@IT_EMP:::::::::
+@USERS:::::::::
+:::::::::/sbin/nologin
```

NIS supports the creation of netgroups from other netgroups which can be useful if the policy regarding user access changes. One possibility is the creation of role-based netgroups. For example, one might create a netgroup called BIGSRV to define the login restrictions for the important servers, another netgroup called SMALLSRV for the less important servers, and a third netgroup called USERBOX for the workstations. Each of these netgroups contains the netgroups that are allowed to login onto these machines. The new entries for the NIS netgroup map would look like this:

```
BIGSRV     IT_EMP  IT_APP
SMALLSRV   IT_EMP  IT_APP   ITINTERN
USERBOX    IT_EMP  ITINTERN USERS
```

This method of defining login restrictions works reasonably well when it is possible to define groups of machines with identical restrictions. Unfortunately, this is the exception and not the rule. Most of the time, the ability to define login restrictions on a per-machine basis is required.

Machine-specific netgroup definitions are another possibility to deal with the policy changes. In this scenario, the `/etc/master.passwd` of each system contains two lines starting with "+". The first line adds a netgroup with the accounts allowed to login onto this machine and the second line adds all other accounts with `/sbin/nologin` as shell. It is recommended to use the "ALL-CAPS" version of the hostname as the name of the netgroup:

```
+@BOXNAME:::::::::
+:::::::::/sbin/nologin
```

Once this task is completed on all the machines, there is no longer a need to modify the local versions of `/etc/master.passwd` ever again. All further changes can be handled by modifying the NIS map. Here is an example of a possible netgroup map for this scenario:

```
# Define groups of users first
IT_EMP   (,alpha,test-domain)    (,beta,test-domain)
IT_APP   (,charlie,test-domain)  (,delta,test-domain)
DEPT1    (,echo,test-domain)     (,foxtrott,test-domain)
DEPT2    (,golf,test-domain)     (,hotel,test-domain)
DEPT3    (,india,test-domain)    (,juliet,test-domain)
ITINTERN (,kilo,test-domain)     (,lima,test-domain)
D_INTERNS (,able,test-domain)    (,baker,test-domain)
#
# Now, define some groups based on roles
USERS    DEPT1   DEPT2      DEPT3
BIGSRV   IT_EMP  IT_APP
SMALLSRV IT_EMP  IT_APP     ITINTERN
USERBOX  IT_EMP  ITINTERN   USERS
#
# And a groups for a special tasks
```

```
# Allow echo and golf to access our anti-virus-machine
SECURITY  IT_EMP  (,echo,test-domain)  (,golf,test-domain)
#
# machine-based netgroups
# Our main servers
WAR       BIGSRV
FAMINE    BIGSRV
# User india needs access to this server
POLLUTION BIGSRV  (,india,test-domain)
#
# This one is really important and needs more access restrictions
DEATH     IT_EMP
#
# The anti-virus-machine mentioned above
ONE       SECURITY
#
# Restrict a machine to a single user
TWO       (,hotel,test-domain)
# [...more groups to follow]
```

It may not always be advisable to use machine-based netgroups. When deploying a couple of dozen or hundreds of systems, role-based netgroups instead of machine-based netgroups may be used to keep the size of the NIS map within reasonable limits.

28.4.9. Password Formats

NIS requires that all hosts within an NIS domain use the same format for encrypting passwords. If users have trouble authenticating on an NIS client, it may be due to a differing password format. In a heterogeneous network, the format must be supported by all operating systems, where DES is the lowest common standard.

To check which format a server or client is using, look at this section of /etc/login.conf:

```
default:\
 :passwd_format=des:\
 :copyright=/etc/COPYRIGHT:\
 [Further entries elided]
```

In this example, the system is using the DES format. Other possible values are blf for Blowfish and md5 for MD5 encrypted passwords.

If the format on a host needs to be edited to match the one being used in the NIS domain, the login capability database must be rebuilt after saving the change:

```
# cap_mkdb /etc/login.conf
```

Note

The format of passwords for existing user accounts will not be updated until each user changes their password *after* the login capability database is rebuilt.

28.5. Lightweight Directory Access Protocol (LDAP)

Written by Tom Rhodes.

The Lightweight Directory Access Protocol (LDAP) is an application layer protocol used to access, modify, and authenticate objects using a distributed directory information service. Think of it as a phone or record book which stores several levels of hierarchical, homogeneous information. It is used in Active Directory and OpenLDAP networks and allows users to access to several levels of internal information utilizing a single account. For example, email authentication, pulling employee contact information, and internal website authentication might all make use of a single user account in the LDAP server's record base.

This section provides a quick start guide for configuring an LDAP server on a FreeBSD system. It assumes that the administrator already has a design plan which includes the type of information to store, what that information will be used for, which users should have access to that information, and how to secure this information from unauthorized access.

28.5.1. LDAP Terminology and Structure

LDAP uses several terms which should be understood before starting the configuration. All directory entries consist of a group of *attributes*. Each of these attribute sets contains a unique identifier known as a *Distinguished Name* (DN) which is normally built from several other attributes such as the common or *Relative Distinguished Name* (RDN). Similar to how directories have absolute and relative paths, consider a DN as an absolute path and the RDN as the relative path.

An example LDAP entry looks like the following. This example searches for the entry for the specified user account (uid), organizational unit (ou), and organization (o):

```
% ldapsearch -xb "uid= trhodes ,ou=users ,o=example.com "
# extended LDIF
#
# LDAPv3
# base <uid=trhodes,ou=users,o=example.com> with scope subtree
# filter: (objectclass=*)
# requesting: ALL
#

# trhodes, users, example.com
dn: uid=trhodes,ou=users,o=example.com
mail: trhodes@example.com
cn: Tom Rhodes
uid: trhodes
telephoneNumber: (123) 456-7890

# search result
search: 2
result: 0 Success

# numResponses: 2
# numEntries: 1
```

This example entry shows the values for the dn, mail, cn, uid, and telephoneNumber attributes. The cn attribute is the RDN.

More information about LDAP and its terminology can be found at http://www.openldap.org/doc/admin24/intro.html.

28.5.2. Configuring an LDAP Server

FreeBSD does not provide a built-in LDAP server. Begin the configuration by installing the net/openldap24-server package or port. Since the port has many configurable options, it is recommended that the default options are reviewed to see if the package is sufficient, and to instead compile the port if any options should be changed. In most cases, the defaults are fine. However, if SQL support is needed, this option must be enabled and the port compiled using the instructions in Section 4.5, "Using the Ports Collection".

Next, create the directories to hold the data and to store the certificates:

```
# mkdir /var/db/openldap-data
# mkdir /usr/local/etc/openldap/private
```

Copy over the database configuration file:

```
# cp /usr/local/etc/openldap/DB_CONFIG.example /var/db/openldap-data/DB_CONFIG
```

The next phase is to configure the certificate authority. The following commands must be executed from /usr/local/etc/openldap/private. This is important as the file permissions need to be restrictive and users should not have access to these files. To create the certificate authority, start with this command and follow the prompts:

```
# openssl req -days 365 -nodes -new -x509 -keyout ca.key -out ../ca.crt
```

The entries for the prompts may be generic *except* for the Common Name. This entry must be *different* than the system hostname. If this will be a self signed certificate, prefix the hostname with CA for certificate authority.

The next task is to create a certificate signing request and a private key. Input this command and follow the prompts:

```
# openssl req -days 365 -nodes -new -keyout server.key -out server.csr
```

During the certificate generation process, be sure to correctly set the Common Name attribute. Once complete, sign the key:

```
# openssl x509 -req -days 365 -in server.csr -out ../server.crt -CA ../ca.crt -CAkey ca.key
  -CAcreateserial
```

The final part of the certificate generation process is to generate and sign the client certificates:

```
# openssl req -days 365 -nodes -new -keyout client.key -out client.csr
# openssl x509 -req -days 3650 -in client.csr -out ../client.crt -CA ../ca.crt -CAkey ca.o
key
```

Remember to use the same Common Name attribute when prompted. When finished, ensure that a total of eight (8) new files have been generated through the proceeding commands. If so, the next step is to edit /usr/local/etc/openldap/slapd.conf and add the following options:

```
TLSCipherSuite HIGH:MEDIUM:+SSLv3
TLSCertificateFile /usr/local/etc/openldap/server.crt
TLSCertificateKeyFile /usr/local/etc/openldap/private/server.key
TLSCACertificateFile /usr/local/etc/openldap/ca.crt
```

Then, edit /usr/local/etc/openldap/ldap.conf and add the following lines:

```
TLS_CACERT /usr/local/etc/openldap/ca.crt
TLS_CIPHER_SUITE HIGH:MEDIUM:+SSLv3
```

While editing this file, uncomment the following entries and set them to the desired values: BASE, URI, SIZELIMIT and TIMELIMIT. Set the URI to contain ldap:// and ldaps://. Then, add two entries pointing to the certificate authority. When finished, the entries should look similar to the following:

```
BASE      dc=example,dc=com
URI       ldap:// ldaps://

SIZELIMIT         12
TIMELIMIT         15

TLS_CACERT /usr/local/etc/openldap/ca.crt
TLS_CIPHER_SUITE HIGH:MEDIUM:+SSLv3
```

The default password for the server should then be changed:

```
# slappasswd -h "{SHA}" >> /usr/local/etc/openldap/slapd.conf
```

This command will prompt for the password and, if the process does not fail, a password hash will be added to the end of slapd.conf. Several hashing formats are supported. Refer to the manual page for slappasswd for more information.

Next, edit /usr/local/etc/openldap/slapd.conf and add the following lines:

```
password-hash {sha}
allow bind_v2
```

The suffix in this file must be updated to match the BASE used in /usr/local/etc/openldap/ldap.conf and rootdn should also be set. A recommended value for rootdn is something like cn=Manager. Before saving this file, place the rootpw in front of the password output from slappasswd and delete the old rootpw. The end result should look similar to this:

```
TLSCipherSuite HIGH:MEDIUM:+SSLv3
TLSCertificateFile /usr/local/etc/openldap/server.crt
TLSCertificateKeyFile /usr/local/etc/openldap/private/server.key
TLSCACertificateFile /usr/local/etc/openldap/ca.crt
rootpw {SHA}W6ph5Mm5Pz8GgiULbPgzG37mj9g=
```

Finally, enable the OpenLDAP service in /etc/rc.conf and set the URI:

```
slapd_enable="YES"
slapd_flags="-4 -h ldaps:///"
```

At this point the server can be started and tested:

```
# service slapd start
```

If everything is configured correctly, a search of the directory should show a successful connection with a single response as in this example:

```
# ldapsearch -Z
# extended LDIF
#
# LDAPv3
# base <dc=example,dc=com> (default) with scope subtree
# filter: (objectclass=*)
# requesting: ALL
#

# search result
search: 3
result: 32 No such object

# numResponses: 1
```

Note

If the command fails and the configuration looks correct, stop the slapd service and restart it with debugging options:

```
# service slapd stop
# /usr/local/libexec/slapd -d -1
```

Once the service is responding, the directory can be populated using ldapadd. In this example, a file containing this list of users is first created. Each user should use the following format:

```
dn: dc=example,dc=com
objectclass: dcObject
objectclass: organization
o: Example
dc: Example

dn: cn=Manager,dc=example,dc=com
```

```
objectclass: organizationalRole
cn: Manager
```

To import this file, specify the file name. The following command will prompt for the password specified earlier and the output should look something like this:

```
# ldapadd -Z -D "cn= Manager ,dc=example ,dc=com" -W -f import.ldif
Enter LDAP Password:
adding new entry "dc=example,dc=com"

adding new entry "cn=Manager,dc=example,dc=com"
```

Verify the data was added by issuing a search on the server using ldapsearch :

```
% ldapsearch -Z
# extended LDIF
#
# LDAPv3
# base <dc=example,dc=com> (default) with scope subtree
# filter: (objectclass=*)
# requesting: ALL
#

# example.com
dn: dc=example,dc=com
objectClass: dcObject
objectClass: organization
o: Example
dc: Example

# Manager, example.com
dn: cn=Manager,dc=example,dc=com
objectClass: organizationalRole
cn: Manager

# search result
search: 3
result: 0 Success

# numResponses: 3
# numEntries: 2
```

At this point, the server should be configured and functioning properly.

28.6. Dynamic Host Configuration Protocol (DHCP)

The Dynamic Host Configuration Protocol (DHCP) allows a system to connect to a network in order to be assigned the necessary addressing information for communication on that network. FreeBSD includes the OpenBSD version of dhclient which is used by the client to obtain the addressing information. FreeBSD does not install a DHCP server, but several servers are available in the FreeBSD Ports Collection. The DHCP protocol is fully described in RFC 2131. Informational resources are also available at isc.org/downloads/dhcp/.

This section describes how to use the built-in DHCP client. It then describes how to install and configure a DHCP server.

Note

In FreeBSD, the bpf(4) device is needed by both the DHCP server and DHCP client. This device is included in the GENERIC kernel that is installed with FreeBSD. Users who prefer to create a custom kernel need to keep this device if DHCP is used.

> It should be noted that bpf also allows privileged users to run network packet sniffers on that system.

28.6.1. Configuring a DHCP Client

DHCP client support is included in the FreeBSD installer, making it easy to configure a newly installed system to automatically receive its networking addressing information from an existing DHCP server. Refer to Section 2.8, "Post-Installation" for examples of network configuration.

When dhclient is executed on the client machine, it begins broadcasting requests for configuration information. By default, these requests use UDP port 68. The server replies on UDP port 67, giving the client an IP address and other relevant network information such as a subnet mask, default gateway, and DNS server addresses. This information is in the form of a DHCP "lease" and is valid for a configurable time. This allows stale IP addresses for clients no longer connected to the network to automatically be reused. DHCP clients can obtain a great deal of information from the server. An exhaustive list may be found in dhcp-options(5).

By default, when a FreeBSD system boots, its DHCP client runs in the background, or *asynchronously*. Other startup scripts continue to run while the DHCP process completes, which speeds up system startup.

Background DHCP works well when the DHCP server responds quickly to the client's requests. However, DHCP may take a long time to complete on some systems. If network services attempt to run before DHCP has assigned the network addressing information, they will fail. Using DHCP in *synchronous* mode prevents this problem as it pauses startup until the DHCP configuration has completed.

This line in /etc/rc.conf is used to configure background or asynchronous mode:

```
ifconfig_fxp0="DHCP"
```

This line may already exist if the system was configured to use DHCP during installation. Replace the *fxp0* shown in these examples with the name of the interface to be dynamically configured, as described in Section 11.5, "Setting Up Network Interface Cards".

To instead configure the system to use synchronous mode, and to pause during startup while DHCP completes, use "SYNCDHCP":

```
ifconfig_fxp0="SYNCDHCP"
```

Additional client options are available. Search for dhclient in rc.conf(5) for details.

The DHCP client uses the following files:

- /etc/dhclient.conf

  The configuration file used by dhclient. Typically, this file contains only comments as the defaults are suitable for most clients. This configuration file is described in dhclient.conf(5).

- /sbin/dhclient

  More information about the command itself can be found in dhclient(8).

- /sbin/dhclient-script

  The FreeBSD-specific DHCP client configuration script. It is described in dhclient-script(8), but should not need any user modification to function properly.

- /var/db/dhclient.leases. *interface*

  The DHCP client keeps a database of valid leases in this file, which is written as a log and is described in dhclient.leases(5).

28.6.2. Installing and Configuring a DHCP Server

This section demonstrates how to configure a FreeBSD system to act as a DHCP server using the Internet Systems Consortium (ISC) implementation of the DHCP server. This implementation and its documentation can be installed using the net/isc-dhcp42-server package or port.

The installation of net/isc-dhcp42-server installs a sample configuration file. Copy /usr/local/etc/dhcpd.conf.example to /usr/local/etc/dhcpd.conf and make any edits to this new file.

The configuration file is comprised of declarations for subnets and hosts which define the information that is provided to DHCP clients. For example, these lines configure the following:

```
option domain-name "example.org";❶
option domain-name-servers ns1.example.org;❷
option subnet-mask 255.255.255.0;❸

default-lease-time 600;❹
max-lease-time 72400;❺
ddns-update-style none;❻

subnet 10.254.239.0 netmask 255.255.255.224 {
  range 10.254.239.10 10.254.239.20;❼
  option routers rtr-239-0-1.example.org, rtr-239-0-2.example.org;❽
}

host fantasia {
  hardware ethernet 08:00:07:26:c0:a5;❾
  fixed-address fantasia.fugue.com;❿
}
```

❶ This option specifies the default search domain that will be provided to clients. Refer to resolv.conf(5) for more information.

❷ This option specifies a comma separated list of DNS servers that the client should use. They can be listed by their Fully Qualified Domain Names (FQDN), as seen in the example, or by their IP addresses.

❸ The subnet mask that will be provided to clients.

❹ The default lease expiry time in seconds. A client can be configured to override this value.

❺ The maximum allowed length of time, in seconds, for a lease. Should a client request a longer lease, a lease will still be issued, but it will only be valid for max-lease-time .

❻ The default of none disables dynamic DNS updates. Changing this to interim configures the DHCP server to update a DNS server whenever it hands out a lease so that the DNS server knows which IP addresses are associated with which computers in the network. Do not change the default setting unless the DNS server has been configured to support dynamic DNS.

❼ This line creates a pool of available IP addresses which are reserved for allocation to DHCP clients. The range of addresses must be valid for the network or subnet specified in the previous line.

❽ Declares the default gateway that is valid for the network or subnet specified before the opening { bracket.

❾ Specifies the hardware MAC address of a client so that the DHCP server can recognize the client when it makes a request.

❿ Specifies that this host should always be given the same IP address. Using the hostname is correct, since the DHCP server will resolve the hostname before returning the lease information.

This configuration file supports many more options. Refer to dhcpd.conf(5), installed with the server, for details and examples.

Once the configuration of dhcpd.conf is complete, enable the DHCP server in /etc/rc.conf :

```
dhcpd_enable="YES"
dhcpd_ifaces="dc0"
```

Replace the dc0 with the interface (or interfaces, separated by whitespace) that the DHCP server should listen on for DHCP client requests.

Start the server by issuing the following command:

```
# service isc-dhcpd start
```

Any future changes to the configuration of the server will require the dhcpd service to be stopped and then started using service(8).

The DHCP server uses the following files. Note that the manual pages are installed with the server software.

- `/usr/local/sbin/dhcpd`

  More information about the dhcpd server can be found in dhcpd(8).

- `/usr/local/etc/dhcpd.conf`

  The server configuration file needs to contain all the information that should be provided to clients, along with information regarding the operation of the server. This configuration file is described in dhcpd.conf(5).

- `/var/db/dhcpd.leases`

  The DHCP server keeps a database of leases it has issued in this file, which is written as a log. Refer to dhcpd.leases(5), which gives a slightly longer description.

- `/usr/local/sbin/dhcrelay`

  This daemon is used in advanced environments where one DHCP server forwards a request from a client to another DHCP server on a separate network. If this functionality is required, install the net/isc-dhcp42-relay package or port. The installation includes dhcrelay(8) which provides more detail.

28.7. Domain Name System (DNS)

Domain Name System (DNS) is the protocol through which domain names are mapped to IP addresses, and vice versa. DNS is coordinated across the Internet through a somewhat complex system of authoritative root, Top Level Domain (TLD), and other smaller-scale name servers, which host and cache individual domain information. It is not necessary to run a name server to perform DNS lookups on a system.

In FreeBSD 10, the Berkeley Internet Name Domain (BIND) has been removed from the base system and replaced with Unbound. Unbound as configured in the FreeBSD Base is a local caching resolver. BIND is still available from The Ports Collection as dns/bind99 or dns/bind98. In FreeBSD 9 and lower, BIND is included in FreeBSD Base. The FreeBSD version provides enhanced security features, a new file system layout, and automated chroot(8) configuration. BIND is maintained by the Internet Systems Consortium.

The following table describes some of the terms associated with DNS:

Table 28.4. DNS Terminology

Term	Definition
Forward DNS	Mapping of hostnames to IP addresses.
Origin	Refers to the domain covered in a particular zone file.
named, BIND	Common names for the BIND name server package within FreeBSD.
Resolver	A system process through which a machine queries a name server for zone information.
Reverse DNS	Mapping of IP addresses to hostnames.
Root zone	The beginning of the Internet zone hierarchy. All zones fall under the root zone, similar to how all files in a file system fall under the root directory.

Term	Definition
Zone	An individual domain, subdomain, or portion of the DNS administered by the same authority.

Examples of zones:

- `.` is how the root zone is usually referred to in documentation.

- `org.` is a Top Level Domain (TLD) under the root zone.

- `example.org.` is a zone under the `org.` TLD.

- `1.168.192.in-addr.arpa` is a zone referencing all IP addresses which fall under the `192.168.1.*` IP address space.

As one can see, the more specific part of a hostname appears to its left. For example, `example.org.` is more specific than `org.`, as `org.` is more specific than the root zone. The layout of each part of a hostname is much like a file system: the `/dev` directory falls within the root, and so on.

28.7.1. Reasons to Run a Name Server

Name servers generally come in two forms: authoritative name servers, and caching (also known as resolving) name servers.

An authoritative name server is needed when:

- One wants to serve DNS information to the world, replying authoritatively to queries.

- A domain, such as `example.org`, is registered and IP addresses need to be assigned to hostnames under it.

- An IP address block requires reverse DNS entries (IP to hostname).

- A backup or second name server, called a slave, will reply to queries.

A caching name server is needed when:

- A local DNS server may cache and respond more quickly than querying an outside name server.

When one queries for `www.FreeBSD.org`, the resolver usually queries the uplink ISP's name server, and retrieves the reply. With a local, caching DNS server, the query only has to be made once to the outside world by the caching DNS server. Additional queries will not have to go outside the local network, since the information is cached locally.

28.7.2. DNS Server Configuration in FreeBSD 10.0 and Later

In FreeBSD 10.0, BIND has been replaced with Unbound. Unbound is a validating caching resolver only. If an authoritative server is needed, many are available from the Ports Collection.

Unbound is provided in the FreeBSD base system. By default, it will provide DNS resolution to the local machine only. While the base system package can be configured to provide resolution services beyond the local machine, it is recommended that such requirements be addressed by installing Unbound from the FreeBSD Ports Collection.

To enable Unbound, add the following to `/etc/rc.conf` :

```
local_unbound_enable="YES"
```

Any existing nameservers in `/etc/resolv.conf` will be configured as forwarders in the new Unbound configuration.

> **Note**
>
> If any of the listed nameservers do not support DNSSEC, local DNS resolution will fail. Be sure to test each nameserver and remove any that fail the test. The following command will show the trust tree or a failure for a nameserver running on `192.168.1.1`:

```
% drill -S FreeBSD.org @ 192.168.1.1
```

Once each nameserver is confirmed to support DNSSEC, start Unbound:

```
# service local_unbound onestart
```

This will take care of updating `/etc/resolv.conf` so that queries for DNSSEC secured domains will now work. For example, run the following to validate the FreeBSD.org DNSSEC trust tree:

```
% drill -S FreeBSD.org
;; Number of trusted keys: 1
;; Chasing: freebsd.org. A

DNSSEC Trust tree:
freebsd.org. (A)
|---freebsd.org. (DNSKEY keytag: 36786 alg: 8 flags: 256)
    |---freebsd.org. (DNSKEY keytag: 32659 alg: 8 flags: 257)
    |---freebsd.org. (DS keytag: 32659 digest type: 2)
        |---org. (DNSKEY keytag: 49587 alg: 7 flags: 256)
            |---org. (DNSKEY keytag: 9795 alg: 7 flags: 257)
            |---org. (DNSKEY keytag: 21366 alg: 7 flags: 257)
            |---org. (DS keytag: 21366 digest type: 1)
            |   |---. (DNSKEY keytag: 40926 alg: 8 flags: 256)
            |       |---. (DNSKEY keytag: 19036 alg: 8 flags: 257)
            |---org. (DS keytag: 21366 digest type: 2)
                |---. (DNSKEY keytag: 40926 alg: 8 flags: 256)
                    |---. (DNSKEY keytag: 19036 alg: 8 flags: 257)
;; Chase successful
```

28.7.3. DNS Server Configuration in FreeBSD 9.X

In FreeBSD, the BIND daemon is called named.

File	Description
named(8)	The BIND daemon.
rndc(8)	Name server control utility.
/etc/namedb	Directory where BIND zone information resides.
/etc/namedb/named.conf	Configuration file of the daemon.

Depending on how a given zone is configured on the server, the files related to that zone can be found in the master, slave, or dynamic subdirectories of the /etc/namedb directory. These files contain the DNS information that will be given out by the name server in response to queries.

28.7.3.1. Starting BIND

Since BIND is installed by default, configuring it is relatively simple.

The default named configuration is that of a basic resolving name server, running in a chroot(8) environment, and restricted to listening on the local IPv4 loopback address (127.0.0.1). To start the server one time with this configuration, use the following command:

```
# service named onestart
```

To ensure the named daemon is started at boot each time, put the following line into the /etc/rc.conf :

```
named_enable="YES"
```

There are many configuration options for /etc/namedb/named.conf that are beyond the scope of this document. Other startup options for named on FreeBSD can be found in the named_* flags in /etc/defaults/rc.conf and in rc.conf(5). The Section 11.4, "Managing Services in FreeBSD" section is also a good read.

28.7.3.2. Configuration Files

Configuration files for named currently reside in /etc/namedb directory and will need modification before use unless all that is needed is a simple resolver. This is where most of the configuration will be performed.

28.7.3.2.1. /etc/namedb/named.conf

```
// $FreeBSD$
//
// Refer to the named.conf(5) and named(8) man pages, and the documentation
// in /usr/share/doc/bind9 for more details.
//
// If you are going to set up an authoritative server, make sure you
// understand the hairy details of how DNS works.  Even with
// simple mistakes, you can break connectivity for affected parties,
// or cause huge amounts of useless Internet traffic.

options {
 // All file and path names are relative to the chroot directory,
 // if any, and should be fully qualified.
 directory "/etc/namedb/working";
 pid-file "/var/run/named/pid";
 dump-file "/var/dump/named_dump.db";
 statistics-file "/var/stats/named.stats";

// If named is being used only as a local resolver, this is a safe default.
// For named to be accessible to the network, comment this option, specify
// the proper IP address, or delete this option.
 listen-on { 127.0.0.1; };

// If you have IPv6 enabled on this system, uncomment this option for
// use as a local resolver.  To give access to the network, specify
// an IPv6 address, or the keyword "any".
// listen-on-v6 { ::1; };

// These zones are already covered by the empty zones listed below.
// If you remove the related empty zones below, comment these lines out.
 disable-empty-zone "255.255.255.255.IN-ADDR.ARPA";
 disable-empty-zone "0.0.0.0.0.0.0.0.0.0.0.0.0.0.0.0.0.0.0.0.0.0.0.0.0.0.0.0.0.0.0.0.↺
IP6.ARPA";
 disable-empty-zone "1.0.0.0.0.0.0.0.0.0.0.0.0.0.0.0.0.0.0.0.0.0.0.0.0.0.0.0.0.0.0.0.↺
IP6.ARPA";

// If you've got a DNS server around at your upstream provider, enter
// its IP address here, and enable the line below.  This will make you
// benefit from its cache, thus reduce overall DNS traffic in the Internet.
/*
 forwarders {
  127.0.0.1;
 };
*/

// If the 'forwarders' clause is not empty the default is to 'forward first'
// which will fall back to sending a query from your local server if the name
// servers in 'forwarders' do not have the answer.  Alternatively you can
// force your name server to never initiate queries of its own by enabling the
```

```
// following line:
// forward only;

// If you wish to have forwarding configured automatically based on
// the entries in /etc/resolv.conf, uncomment the following line and
// set named_auto_forward=yes in /etc/rc.conf.  You can also enable
// named_auto_forward_only (the effect of which is described above).
// include "/etc/namedb/auto_forward.conf";
```

Just as the comment says, to benefit from an uplink's cache, `forwarders` can be enabled here. Under normal circumstances, a name server will recursively query the Internet looking at certain name servers until it finds the answer it is looking for. Having this enabled will have it query the uplink's name server (or name server provided) first, taking advantage of its cache. If the uplink name server in question is a heavily trafficked, fast name server, enabling this may be worthwhile.

Warning

127.0.0.1 will *not* work here. Change this IP address to a name server at the uplink.

```
/*
    Modern versions of BIND use a random UDP port for each outgoing
    query by default in order to dramatically reduce the possibility
    of cache poisoning.  All users are strongly encouraged to utilize
    this feature, and to configure their firewalls to accommodate it.

    AS A LAST RESORT in order to get around a restrictive firewall
    policy you can try enabling the option below.  Use of this option
    will significantly reduce your ability to withstand cache poisoning
    attacks, and should be avoided if at all possible.

    Replace NNNNN in the example with a number between 49160 and 65530.
*/
// query-source address * port NNNNN;
};

// If you enable a local name server, don't forget to enter 127.0.0.1
// first in your /etc/resolv.conf so this server will be queried.
// Also, make sure to enable it in /etc/rc.conf.

// The traditional root hints mechanism. Use this, OR the slave zones below.
zone "." { type hint; file "/etc/namedb/named.root"; };

/* Slaving the following zones from the root name servers has some
significant advantages:
1. Faster local resolution for your users
2. No spurious traffic will be sent from your network to the roots
3. Greater resilience to any potential root server failure/DDoS

On the other hand, this method requires more monitoring than the
hints file to be sure that an unexpected failure mode has not
incapacitated your server.  Name servers that are serving a lot
of clients will benefit more from this approach than individual
hosts.  Use with caution.

To use this mechanism, uncomment the entries below, and comment
the hint zone above.

As documented at http://dns.icann.org/services/axfr/ these zones:
"." (the root), ARPA, IN-ADDR.ARPA, IP6.ARPA, and ROOT-SERVERS.NET
are available for AXFR from these servers on IPv4 and IPv6:
xfr.lax.dns.icann.org, xfr.cjr.dns.icann.org
```

```
*/
/*
zone "." {
 type slave;
 file "/etc/namedb/slave/root.slave";
 masters {
  192.5.5.241; // F.ROOT-SERVERS.NET.
 };
 notify no;
};
zone "arpa" {
 type slave;
 file "/etc/namedb/slave/arpa.slave";
 masters {
  192.5.5.241; // F.ROOT-SERVERS.NET.
 };
 notify no;
};
*/

/* Serving the following zones locally will prevent any queries
 for these zones leaving your network and going to the root
 name servers.  This has two significant advantages:
 1. Faster local resolution for your users
 2. No spurious traffic will be sent from your network to the roots
*/
// RFCs 1912 and 5735 (and BCP 32 for localhost)
zone "localhost" { type master; file "/etc/namedb/master/localhost-forward.db"; };
zone "127.in-addr.arpa" { type master; file "/etc/namedb/master/localhost-reverse.db"; };
zone "255.in-addr.arpa" { type master; file "/etc/namedb/master/empty.db"; };

// RFC 1912-style zone for IPv6 localhost address
zone "0.ip6.arpa" { type master; file "/etc/namedb/master/localhost-reverse.db"; };

// "This" Network (RFCs 1912 and 5735)
zone "0.in-addr.arpa" { type master; file "/etc/namedb/master/empty.db"; };

// Private Use Networks (RFCs 1918 and 5735)
zone "10.in-addr.arpa"    { type master; file "/etc/namedb/master/empty.db"; };
zone "16.172.in-addr.arpa" { type master; file "/etc/namedb/master/empty.db"; };
zone "17.172.in-addr.arpa" { type master; file "/etc/namedb/master/empty.db"; };
zone "18.172.in-addr.arpa" { type master; file "/etc/namedb/master/empty.db"; };
zone "19.172.in-addr.arpa" { type master; file "/etc/namedb/master/empty.db"; };
zone "20.172.in-addr.arpa" { type master; file "/etc/namedb/master/empty.db"; };
zone "21.172.in-addr.arpa" { type master; file "/etc/namedb/master/empty.db"; };
zone "22.172.in-addr.arpa" { type master; file "/etc/namedb/master/empty.db"; };
zone "23.172.in-addr.arpa" { type master; file "/etc/namedb/master/empty.db"; };
zone "24.172.in-addr.arpa" { type master; file "/etc/namedb/master/empty.db"; };
zone "25.172.in-addr.arpa" { type master; file "/etc/namedb/master/empty.db"; };
zone "26.172.in-addr.arpa" { type master; file "/etc/namedb/master/empty.db"; };
zone "27.172.in-addr.arpa" { type master; file "/etc/namedb/master/empty.db"; };
zone "28.172.in-addr.arpa" { type master; file "/etc/namedb/master/empty.db"; };
zone "29.172.in-addr.arpa" { type master; file "/etc/namedb/master/empty.db"; };
zone "30.172.in-addr.arpa" { type master; file "/etc/namedb/master/empty.db"; };
zone "31.172.in-addr.arpa" { type master; file "/etc/namedb/master/empty.db"; };
zone "168.192.in-addr.arpa" { type master; file "/etc/namedb/master/empty.db"; };

// Link-local/APIPA (RFCs 3927 and 5735)
zone "254.169.in-addr.arpa" { type master; file "/etc/namedb/master/empty.db"; };

// IETF protocol assignments (RFCs 5735 and 5736)
zone "0.0.192.in-addr.arpa" { type master; file "/etc/namedb/master/empty.db"; };

// TEST-NET-[1-3] for Documentation (RFCs 5735 and 5737)
zone "2.0.192.in-addr.arpa" { type master; file "/etc/namedb/master/empty.db"; };
zone "100.51.198.in-addr.arpa" { type master; file "/etc/namedb/master/empty.db"; };
```

```
zone "113.0.203.in-addr.arpa" { type master; file "/etc/namedb/master/empty.db"; };

// IPv6 Range for Documentation (RFC 3849)
zone "8.b.d.0.1.0.0.2.ip6.arpa" { type master; file "/etc/namedb/master/empty.db"; };

// Domain Names for Documentation and Testing (BCP 32)
zone "test" { type master; file "/etc/namedb/master/empty.db"; };
zone "example" { type master; file "/etc/namedb/master/empty.db"; };
zone "invalid" { type master; file "/etc/namedb/master/empty.db"; };
zone "example.com" { type master; file "/etc/namedb/master/empty.db"; };
zone "example.net" { type master; file "/etc/namedb/master/empty.db"; };
zone "example.org" { type master; file "/etc/namedb/master/empty.db"; };

// Router Benchmark Testing (RFCs 2544 and 5735)
zone "18.198.in-addr.arpa" { type master; file "/etc/namedb/master/empty.db"; };
zone "19.198.in-addr.arpa" { type master; file "/etc/namedb/master/empty.db"; };

// IANA Reserved - Old Class E Space (RFC 5735)
zone "240.in-addr.arpa" { type master; file "/etc/namedb/master/empty.db"; };
zone "241.in-addr.arpa" { type master; file "/etc/namedb/master/empty.db"; };
zone "242.in-addr.arpa" { type master; file "/etc/namedb/master/empty.db"; };
zone "243.in-addr.arpa" { type master; file "/etc/namedb/master/empty.db"; };
zone "244.in-addr.arpa" { type master; file "/etc/namedb/master/empty.db"; };
zone "245.in-addr.arpa" { type master; file "/etc/namedb/master/empty.db"; };
zone "246.in-addr.arpa" { type master; file "/etc/namedb/master/empty.db"; };
zone "247.in-addr.arpa" { type master; file "/etc/namedb/master/empty.db"; };
zone "248.in-addr.arpa" { type master; file "/etc/namedb/master/empty.db"; };
zone "249.in-addr.arpa" { type master; file "/etc/namedb/master/empty.db"; };
zone "250.in-addr.arpa" { type master; file "/etc/namedb/master/empty.db"; };
zone "251.in-addr.arpa" { type master; file "/etc/namedb/master/empty.db"; };
zone "252.in-addr.arpa" { type master; file "/etc/namedb/master/empty.db"; };
zone "253.in-addr.arpa" { type master; file "/etc/namedb/master/empty.db"; };
zone "254.in-addr.arpa" { type master; file "/etc/namedb/master/empty.db"; };

// IPv6 Unassigned Addresses (RFC 4291)
zone "1.ip6.arpa" { type master; file "/etc/namedb/master/empty.db"; };
zone "3.ip6.arpa" { type master; file "/etc/namedb/master/empty.db"; };
zone "4.ip6.arpa" { type master; file "/etc/namedb/master/empty.db"; };
zone "5.ip6.arpa" { type master; file "/etc/namedb/master/empty.db"; };
zone "6.ip6.arpa" { type master; file "/etc/namedb/master/empty.db"; };
zone "7.ip6.arpa" { type master; file "/etc/namedb/master/empty.db"; };
zone "8.ip6.arpa" { type master; file "/etc/namedb/master/empty.db"; };
zone "9.ip6.arpa" { type master; file "/etc/namedb/master/empty.db"; };
zone "a.ip6.arpa" { type master; file "/etc/namedb/master/empty.db"; };
zone "b.ip6.arpa" { type master; file "/etc/namedb/master/empty.db"; };
zone "c.ip6.arpa" { type master; file "/etc/namedb/master/empty.db"; };
zone "d.ip6.arpa" { type master; file "/etc/namedb/master/empty.db"; };
zone "e.ip6.arpa" { type master; file "/etc/namedb/master/empty.db"; };
zone "0.f.ip6.arpa" { type master; file "/etc/namedb/master/empty.db"; };
zone "1.f.ip6.arpa" { type master; file "/etc/namedb/master/empty.db"; };
zone "2.f.ip6.arpa" { type master; file "/etc/namedb/master/empty.db"; };
zone "3.f.ip6.arpa" { type master; file "/etc/namedb/master/empty.db"; };
zone "4.f.ip6.arpa" { type master; file "/etc/namedb/master/empty.db"; };
zone "5.f.ip6.arpa" { type master; file "/etc/namedb/master/empty.db"; };
zone "6.f.ip6.arpa" { type master; file "/etc/namedb/master/empty.db"; };
zone "7.f.ip6.arpa" { type master; file "/etc/namedb/master/empty.db"; };
zone "8.f.ip6.arpa" { type master; file "/etc/namedb/master/empty.db"; };
zone "9.f.ip6.arpa" { type master; file "/etc/namedb/master/empty.db"; };
zone "a.f.ip6.arpa" { type master; file "/etc/namedb/master/empty.db"; };
zone "b.f.ip6.arpa" { type master; file "/etc/namedb/master/empty.db"; };
zone "0.e.f.ip6.arpa" { type master; file "/etc/namedb/master/empty.db"; };
zone "1.e.f.ip6.arpa" { type master; file "/etc/namedb/master/empty.db"; };
zone "2.e.f.ip6.arpa" { type master; file "/etc/namedb/master/empty.db"; };
zone "3.e.f.ip6.arpa" { type master; file "/etc/namedb/master/empty.db"; };
zone "4.e.f.ip6.arpa" { type master; file "/etc/namedb/master/empty.db"; };
zone "5.e.f.ip6.arpa" { type master; file "/etc/namedb/master/empty.db"; };
```

```
zone "6.e.f.ip6.arpa" { type master; file "/etc/namedb/master/empty.db"; };
zone "7.e.f.ip6.arpa" { type master; file "/etc/namedb/master/empty.db"; };

// IPv6 ULA (RFC 4193)
zone "c.f.ip6.arpa" { type master; file "/etc/namedb/master/empty.db"; };
zone "d.f.ip6.arpa" { type master; file "/etc/namedb/master/empty.db"; };

// IPv6 Link Local (RFC 4291)
zone "8.e.f.ip6.arpa" { type master; file "/etc/namedb/master/empty.db"; };
zone "9.e.f.ip6.arpa" { type master; file "/etc/namedb/master/empty.db"; };
zone "a.e.f.ip6.arpa" { type master; file "/etc/namedb/master/empty.db"; };
zone "b.e.f.ip6.arpa" { type master; file "/etc/namedb/master/empty.db"; };

// IPv6 Deprecated Site-Local Addresses (RFC 3879)
zone "c.e.f.ip6.arpa" { type master; file "/etc/namedb/master/empty.db"; };
zone "d.e.f.ip6.arpa" { type master; file "/etc/namedb/master/empty.db"; };
zone "e.e.f.ip6.arpa" { type master; file "/etc/namedb/master/empty.db"; };
zone "f.e.f.ip6.arpa" { type master; file "/etc/namedb/master/empty.db"; };

// IP6.INT is Deprecated (RFC 4159)
zone "ip6.int"  { type master; file "/etc/namedb/master/empty.db"; };


// NB: Do not use the IP addresses below, they are faked, and only
// serve demonstration/documentation purposes!
//
// Example slave zone config entries.  It can be convenient to become
// a slave at least for the zone your own domain is in.  Ask
// your network administrator for the IP address of the responsible
// master name server.
//
// Do not forget to include the reverse lookup zone!
// This is named after the first bytes of the IP address, in reverse
// order, with ".IN-ADDR.ARPA" appended, or ".IP6.ARPA" for IPv6.
//
// Before starting to set up a master zone, make sure you fully
// understand how DNS and BIND work.  There are sometimes
// non-obvious pitfalls.  Setting up a slave zone is usually simpler.
//
// NB: Don't blindly enable the examples below. :-)  Use actual names
// and addresses instead.

/* An example dynamic zone
key "exampleorgkey" {
 algorithm hmac-md5;
 secret "sf87HJqjkqh8ac87a02lla==";
};
zone "example.org" {
 type master;
 allow-update {
  key "exampleorgkey";
 };
 file "/etc/namedb/dynamic/example.org";
};
*/

/* Example of a slave reverse zone
zone "1.168.192.in-addr.arpa" {
 type slave;
 file "/etc/namedb/slave/1.168.192.in-addr.arpa";
 masters {
  192.168.1.1;
 };
};
*/
```

In `named.conf` , these are examples of slave entries for a forward and reverse zone.

For each new zone served, a new zone entry must be added to `named.conf` .

For example, the simplest zone entry for `example.org` can look like:

```
zone "example.org" {
 type master;
 file "master/example.org";
};
```

The zone is a master, as indicated by the `type` statement, holding its zone information in /etc/namedb/master/example.org indicated by the `file` statement.

```
zone "example.org" {
 type slave;
 file "slave/example.org";
};
```

In the slave case, the zone information is transferred from the master name server for the particular zone, and saved in the file specified. If and when the master server dies or is unreachable, the slave name server will have the transferred zone information and will be able to serve it.

28.7.3.2.2. Zone Files

An example master zone file for `example.org` (existing within /etc/namedb/master/example.org) is as follows:

```
$TTL 3600         -; 1 hour default TTL
example.org.    IN      SOA      ns1.example.org. admin.example.org. (
                                 2006051501      -; Serial
                                 10800           -; Refresh
                                 3600            -; Retry
                                 604800          -; Expire
                                 300             -; Negative Response TTL
                         )

; DNS Servers
                IN      NS      ns1.example.org.
                IN      NS      ns2.example.org.

; MX Records
                IN      MX 10   mx.example.org.
                IN      MX 20   mail.example.org.

                IN      A       192.168.1.1

; Machine Names
localhost       IN      A       127.0.0.1
ns1             IN      A       192.168.1.2
ns2             IN      A       192.168.1.3
mx              IN      A       192.168.1.4
mail            IN      A       192.168.1.5

; Aliases
www             IN      CNAME   example.org.
```

Note that every hostname ending in a ".". is an exact hostname, whereas everything without a trailing "." is relative to the origin. For example, `ns1` is translated into `ns1.example.org.`

The format of a zone file follows:

```
recordname      IN recordtype    value
```

The most commonly used DNS records:

SOA
> start of zone authority

NS
> an authoritative name server

A
> a host address

CNAME
> the canonical name for an alias

MX
> mail exchanger

PTR
> a domain name pointer (used in reverse DNS)

```
example.org. IN SOA ns1.example.org. admin.example.org. (
                2006051501      -; Serial
                10800           -; Refresh after 3 hours
                3600            -; Retry after 1 hour
                604800          -; Expire after 1 week
                300 )           -; Negative Response TTL
```

example.org.
> the domain name, also the origin for this zone file.

ns1.example.org.
> the primary/authoritative name server for this zone.

admin.example.org.
> the responsible person for this zone, email address with "@" replaced. (<admin@example.org> becomes admin.example.org)

2006051501
> the serial number of the file. This must be incremented each time the zone file is modified. Nowadays, many admins prefer a yyyymmddrr format for the serial number. 2006051501 would mean last modified 05/15/2006, the latter 01 being the first time the zone file has been modified this day. The serial number is important as it alerts slave name servers for a zone when it is updated.

```
        IN NS           ns1.example.org.
```

This is an NS entry. Every name server that is going to reply authoritatively for the zone must have one of these entries.

```
localhost       IN      A       127.0.0.1
ns1             IN      A       192.168.1.2
ns2             IN      A       192.168.1.3
mx              IN      A       192.168.1.4
mail            IN      A       192.168.1.5
```

The A record indicates machine names. As seen above, ns1.example.org would resolve to 192.168.1.2.

```
                IN      A       192.168.1.1
```

This line assigns IP address 192.168.1.1 to the current origin, in this case example.org.

```
www             IN CNAME        @
```

The canonical name record is usually used for giving aliases to a machine. In the example, www is aliased to the "master" machine whose name happens to be the same as the domain name example.org (192.168.1.1). CNAMEs can never be used together with another kind of record for the same hostname.

```
            IN MX   10       mail.example.org.
```

The MX record indicates which mail servers are responsible for handling incoming mail for the zone. mail.example.org is the hostname of a mail server, and 10 is the priority of that mail server.

One can have several mail servers, with priorities of 10, 20 and so on. A mail server attempting to deliver to example.org would first try the highest priority MX (the record with the lowest priority number), then the second highest, etc, until the mail can be properly delivered.

For in-addr.arpa zone files (reverse DNS), the same format is used, except with PTR entries instead of A or CNAME.

```
$TTL 3600

1.168.192.in-addr.arpa. IN SOA ns1.example.org. admin.example.org. (
                        2006051501      -; Serial
                        10800           -; Refresh
                        3600            -; Retry
                        604800          -; Expire
                        300 )           -; Negative Response TTL

        IN      NS      ns1.example.org.
        IN      NS      ns2.example.org.

1       IN      PTR     example.org.
2       IN      PTR     ns1.example.org.
3       IN      PTR     ns2.example.org.
4       IN      PTR     mx.example.org.
5       IN      PTR     mail.example.org.
```

This file gives the proper IP address to hostname mappings for the above fictitious domain.

It is worth noting that all names on the right side of a PTR record need to be fully qualified (i.e., end in a "."）.

28.7.3.3. Caching Name Server

A caching name server is a name server whose primary role is to resolve recursive queries. It simply asks queries of its own, and remembers the answers for later use.

28.7.3.4. DNSSEC

Domain Name System Security Extensions, or DNSSEC for short, is a suite of specifications to protect resolving name servers from forged DNS data, such as spoofed DNS records. By using digital signatures, a resolver can verify the integrity of the record. Note that DNSSEC only provides integrity via digitally signing the Resource Records (RRs). It provides neither confidentiality nor protection against false end-user assumptions. This means that it cannot protect against people going to example.net instead of example.com. The only thing DNSSEC does is authenticate that the data has not been compromised in transit. The security of DNS is an important step in securing the Internet in general. For more in-depth details of how DNSSEC works, the relevant RFCs are a good place to start. See the list in Section 28.7.3.6, "Further Reading".

The following sections will demonstrate how to enable DNSSEC for an authoritative DNS server and a recursive (or caching) DNS server running BIND 9. While all versions of BIND 9 support DNSSEC, it is necessary to have at least version 9.6.2 in order to be able to use the signed root zone when validating DNS queries. This is because earlier versions lack the required algorithms to enable validation using the root zone key. It is strongly recommended to use the latest version of BIND 9.7 or later to take advantage of automatic key updating for the root key, as well as other features to automatically keep zones signed and signatures up to date. Where configurations differ between 9.6.2 and 9.7 and later, differences will be pointed out.

28.7.3.4.1. Recursive DNS Server Configuration

Enabling DNSSEC validation of queries performed by a recursive DNS server requires a few changes to `named.conf`. Before making these changes the root zone key, or trust anchor, must be acquired. Currently the root zone key is not available in a file format BIND understands, so it has to be manually converted into the proper format. The key itself can be obtained by querying the root zone for it using dig. By running

```
% dig +multi +noall +answer DNSKEY . > root.dnskey
```

the key will end up in `root.dnskey`. The contents should look something like this:

```
. 93910 IN DNSKEY 257 3 8 (
AwEAAagAIKlVZrpC6Ia7gEzahOR+9W29euxhJhVVLOyQ
bSEWOO8gcCjFFVQUTf6v58fLjwBd0YI0EzrAcQqBGCzh
/RStIoO8g0NfnfL2MTJRkxoXbfDaUeVPQuYEhg37NZWA
JQ9VnMVDxP/VHL496M/QZxkjf5/Efucp2gaDX6RS6CXp
oY68LsvPVjR0ZSwzz1apAzvN9dlzEheX7ICJBBtuA6G3
LQpzW5hOA2hzCTMjJPJ8LbqF6dsV6DoBQzgul0sGIcGO
Yl7OyQdXfZ57relSQageu+ipAdTTJ25AsRTAoub8ONGc
LmqrAmRLKBP1dfwhYB4N7knNnulqQxA+Uk1ihz0=
) -; key id = 19036
. 93910 IN DNSKEY 256 3 8 (
AwEAAcaGQEA+OJmOzfzVfoYN249JId7gx+OZMbxy69Hf
UyuGBbRN0+HuTOpBxxBCkNOL+EJB9qJxt+0FEY6ZUVjE
g58sRr4ZQ6Iu6b1xTBKgc193zUARk4mmQ/PPGxn7Cn5V
EGJ/1h6dNaiXuRHwR+7oWh7DnzkIJChcTqlFrXDW3tjt
) -; key id = 34525
```

Do not be alarmed if the obtained keys differ from this example. They might have changed since these instructions were last updated. This output actually contains two keys. The first key in the listing, with the value 257 after the DNSKEY record type, is the one needed. This value indicates that this is a Secure Entry Point (SEP), commonly known as a Key Signing Key (KSK). The second key, with value 256, is a subordinate key, commonly called a Zone Signing Key (ZSK). More on the different key types later in Section 28.7.3.4.2, "Authoritative DNS Server Configuration".

Now the key must be verified and formatted so that BIND can use it. To verify the key, generate a DS RR set. Create a file containing these RRs with

```
% dnssec-dsfromkey -f root.dnskey . > root.ds
```

These records use SHA-1 and SHA-256 respectively, and should look similar to the following example, where the longer is using SHA-256.

```
.  IN DS 19036 8 1
B256BD09DC8DD59F0E0F0D8541B8328DD986DF6E
. IN DS 19036 8 2 49AAC11D7B6F6446702E54A1607371607A1A41855200FD2CE1CDDE32F24E8FB5
```

The SHA-256 RR can now be compared to the digest in https://data.iana.org/root-anchors/root-anchors.xml. To be absolutely sure that the key has not been tampered with the data in the XML file can be verified using the PGP signature in https://data.iana.org/root-anchors/root-anchors.asc.

Next, the key must be formatted properly. This differs a little between BIND versions 9.6.2 and 9.7 and later. In version 9.7 support was added to automatically track changes to the key and update it as necessary. This is done using `managed-keys` as seen in the example below. When using the older version, the key is added using a `trusted-keys` statement and updates must be done manually. For BIND 9.6.2 the format should look like:

```
trusted-keys {
  "." 257 3 8
  "AwEAAagAIKlVZrpC6Ia7gEzahOR+9W29euxhJhVVLOyQbSEWOO8gcCjF
  FVQUTf6v58fLjwBd0YI0EzrAcQqBGCzh/RStIoO8g0NfnfL2MTJRkxoX
  bfDaUeVPQuYEhg37NZWAJQ9VnMVDxP/VHL496M/QZxkjf5/Efucp2gaD
  X6RS6CXpoY68LsvPVjR0ZSwzz1apAzvN9dlzEheX7ICJBBtuA6G3LQpz
```

```
W5hOA2hzCTMjJPJ8LbqF6dsV6DoBQzgul0sGIcGOYl7OyQdXfZ57relS
Qageu+ipAdTTJ25AsRTAoub8ONGcLmqrAmRLKBP1dfwhYB4N7knNnulq
QxA+Uklihz0=";
};
```

For 9.7 the format will instead be:

```
managed-keys {
  "." initial-key 257 3 8
  "AwEAAagAIKlVZrpC6Ia7gEzahOR+9W29euxhJhVVLOyQbSEWOO8gcCjF
FVQUTf6v58fLjwBd0YI0EzrAcQqBGCzh/RStIoO8g0NfnfL2MTJRkxoX
bfDaUeVPQuYEhg37NZWAJQ9VnMVDxP/VHL496M/QZxkjf5/Efucp2gaD
X6RS6CXpoY68LsvPVjR0ZSwzz1apAzvN9dlzEheX7ICJBBtuA6G3LQpz
W5hOA2hzCTMjJPJ8LbqF6dsV6DoBQzgul0sGIcGOYl7OyQdXfZ57relS
Qageu+ipAdTTJ25AsRTAoub8ONGcLmqrAmRLKBP1dfwhYB4N7knNnulq
QxA+Uklihz0=";
};
```

The root key can now be added to `named.conf` either directly or by including a file containing the key. After these steps, configure BIND to do DNSSEC validation on queries by editing `named.conf` and adding the following to the `options` directive:

```
dnssec-enable yes;
dnssec-validation yes;
```

To verify that it is actually working use dig to make a query for a signed zone using the resolver just configured. A successful reply will contain the `AD` flag to indicate the data was authenticated. Running a query such as

```
% dig @resolver +dnssec se ds
```

should return the DS RR for the `.se` zone. In the `flags:` section the `AD` flag should be set, as seen in:

```
...
;; flags: qr rd ra ad; QUERY: 1, ANSWER: 3, AUTHORITY: 0, ADDITIONAL: 1
...
```

The resolver is now capable of authenticating DNS queries.

28.7.3.4.2. Authoritative DNS Server Configuration

In order to get an authoritative name server to serve a DNSSEC signed zone a little more work is required. A zone is signed using cryptographic keys which must be generated. It is possible to use only one key for this. The preferred method however is to have a strong well-protected Key Signing Key (KSK) that is not rotated very often and a Zone Signing Key (ZSK) that is rotated more frequently. Information on recommended operational practices can be found in RFC 4641: DNSSEC Operational Practices. Practices regarding the root zone can be found in DNSSEC Practice Statement for the Root Zone KSK operator and DNSSEC Practice Statement for the Root Zone ZSK operator. The KSK is used to build a chain of authority to the data in need of validation and as such is also called a Secure Entry Point (SEP) key. A message digest of this key, called a Delegation Signer (DS) record, must be published in the parent zone to establish the trust chain. How this is accomplished depends on the parent zone owner. The ZSK is used to sign the zone, and only needs to be published there.

To enable DNSSEC for the `example.com` zone depicted in previous examples, the first step is to use dnssec-keygen to generate the KSK and ZSK key pair. This key pair can utilize different cryptographic algorithms. It is recommended to use RSA/SHA256 for the keys and 2048 bits key length should be enough. To generate the KSK for `example.com`, run

```
% dnssec-keygen -f KSK -a RSASHA256 -b 2048 -n ZONE example.com
```

and to generate the ZSK, run

```
% dnssec-keygen -a RSASHA256 -b 2048 -n ZONE example.com
```

dnssec-keygen outputs two files, the public and the private keys in files named similar to Kexample.com.+005+nnnnn.key (public) and Kexample.com.+005+nnnnn.private (private). The nnnnn part of the file name is a five digit key ID. Keep track of which key ID belongs to which key. This is especially important when having more than one key in a zone. It is also possible to rename the keys. For each KSK file do:

```
% mv Kexample.com.+005+nnnnn.key Kexample.com.+005+nnnnn.KSK.key
% mv Kexample.com.+005+nnnnn.private Kexample.com.+005+nnnnn.KSK.private
```

For the ZSK files, substitute KSK for ZSK as necessary. The files can now be included in the zone file, using the $include statement. It should look something like this:

```
$include Kexample.com.+005+nnnnn.KSK.key -; KSK
$include Kexample.com.+005+nnnnn.ZSK.key     -; ZSK
```

Finally, sign the zone and tell BIND to use the signed zone file. To sign a zone dnssec-signzone is used. The command to sign the zone example.com, located in example.com.db would look similar to

```
% dnssec-signzone -o
  example.com -k Kexample.com.+005+nnnnn.KSK example.com.db
  Kexample.com.+005+nnnnn.ZSK.key
```

The key supplied to the -k argument is the KSK and the other key file is the ZSK that should be used in the signing. It is possible to supply more than one KSK and ZSK, which will result in the zone being signed with all supplied keys. This can be needed to supply zone data signed using more than one algorithm. The output of dnssec-signzone is a zone file with all RRs signed. This output will end up in a file with the extension .signed, such as example.com.db.signed. The DS records will also be written to a separate file dsset-example.com. To use this signed zone just modify the zone directive in named.conf to use example.com.db.signed. By default, the signatures are only valid 30 days, meaning that the zone needs to be resigned in about 15 days to be sure that resolvers are not caching records with stale signatures. It is possible to make a script and a cron job to do this. See relevant manuals for details.

Be sure to keep private keys confidential, as with all cryptographic keys. When changing a key it is best to include the new key into the zone, while still signing with the old one, and then move over to using the new key to sign. After these steps are done the old key can be removed from the zone. Failure to do this might render the DNS data unavailable for a time, until the new key has propagated through the DNS hierarchy. For more information on key rollovers and other DNSSEC operational issues, see RFC 4641: DNSSEC Operational practices.

28.7.3.4.3. Automation Using BIND 9.7 or Later

Beginning with BIND version 9.7 a new feature called *Smart Signing* was introduced. This feature aims to make the key management and signing process simpler by automating parts of the task. By putting the keys into a directory called a *key repository*, and using the new option auto-dnssec, it is possible to create a dynamic zone which will be resigned as needed. To update this zone use nsupdate with the new option -l. rndc has also grown the ability to sign zones with keys in the key repository, using the option sign. To tell BIND to use this automatic signing and zone updating for example.com, add the following to named.conf:

```
zone example.com {
  type master;
  key-directory "/etc/named/keys";
  update-policy local;
  auto-dnssec maintain;
  file "/etc/named/dynamic/example.com.zone";
};
```

After making these changes, generate keys for the zone as explained in Section 28.7.3.4.2, "Authoritative DNS Server Configuration", put those keys in the key repository given as the argument to the key-directory in the zone configuration and the zone will be signed automatically. Updates to a zone configured this way must be done using nsupdate, which will take care of re-signing the zone with the new data added. For further details, see Section 28.7.3.6, "Further Reading" and the BIND documentation.

28.7.3.5. Security

Although BIND is the most common implementation of DNS, there is always the issue of security. Possible and exploitable security holes are sometimes found.

While FreeBSD automatically drops named into a chroot(8) environment; there are several other security mechanisms in place which could help to lure off possible DNS service attacks.

It is always good idea to read CERT's security advisories and to subscribe to the FreeBSD security notifications mailing list to stay up to date with the current Internet and FreeBSD security issues.

 Tip

If a problem arises, keeping sources up to date and having a fresh build of named may help.

28.7.3.6. Further Reading

BIND/named manual pages: rndc(8) named(8) named.conf(5) nsupdate(1) dnssec-signzone(8) dnssec-keygen(8)

- Official ISC BIND Page

- Official ISC BIND Forum

- O'Reilly DNS and BIND 5th Edition

- Root DNSSEC

- DNSSEC Trust Anchor Publication for the Root Zone

- RFC1034 - Domain Names - Concepts and Facilities

- RFC1035 - Domain Names - Implementation and Specification

- RFC4033 - DNS Security Introduction and Requirements

- RFC4034 - Resource Records for the DNS Security Extensions

- RFC4035 - Protocol Modifications for the DNS Security Extensions

- RFC4641 - DNSSEC Operational Practices

- RFC 5011 - Automated Updates of DNS Security (DNSSEC Trust Anchors

28.8. Apache HTTP Server

Contributed by Murray Stokely.

The open source Apache HTTP Server is the most widely used web server. FreeBSD does not install this web server by default, but it can be installed from the www/apache24 package or port.

This section summarizes how to configure and start version 2.*x* of the Apache HTTP Server on FreeBSD. For more detailed information about Apache 2.X and its configuration directives, refer to httpd.apache.org.

28.8.1. Configuring and Starting Apache

In FreeBSD, the main Apache HTTP Server configuration file is installed as /usr/local/etc/apache2 x/ httpd.conf , where x represents the version number. This ASCII text file begins comment lines with a #. The most frequently modified directives are:

ServerRoot "/usr/local"
> Specifies the default directory hierarchy for the Apache installation. Binaries are stored in the bin and sbin subdirectories of the server root and configuration files are stored in the etc/apache2 x subdirectory.

ServerAdmin you@example.com
> Change this to the email address to receive problems with the server. This address also appears on some server-generated pages, such as error documents.

ServerName www.example.com:80
> Allows an administrator to set a hostname which is sent back to clients for the server. For example, www can be used instead of the actual hostname. If the system does not have a registered DNS name, enter its IP address instead. If the server will listen on an alternate report, change 80 to the alternate port number.

DocumentRoot "/usr/local/www/apache2 x/data"
> The directory where documents will be served from. By default, all requests are taken from this directory, but symbolic links and aliases may be used to point to other locations.

It is always a good idea to make a backup copy of the default Apache configuration file before making changes. When the configuration of Apache is complete, save the file and verify the configuration using apachectl . Running apachectl configtest should return Syntax OK.

To launch Apache at system startup, add the following line to /etc/rc.conf :

```
apache24_enable="YES"
```

If Apache should be started with non-default options, the following line may be added to /etc/rc.conf to specify the needed flags:

```
apache24_flags=""
```

If apachectl does not report configuration errors, start httpd now:

```
# service apache 24 start
```

The httpd service can be tested by entering http:// localhost in a web browser, replacing localhost with the fully-qualified domain name of the machine running httpd. The default web page that is displayed is /usr/local/www/apache 24/data/index.html.

The Apache configuration can be tested for errors after making subsequent configuration changes while httpd is running using the following command:

```
# service apache 24 configtest
```

> **Note**
>
> It is important to note that configtest is not an rc(8) standard, and should not be expected to work for all startup scripts.

28.8.2. Virtual Hosting

Virtual hosting allows multiple websites to run on one Apache server. The virtual hosts can be *IP-based* or *name-based*. IP-based virtual hosting uses a different IP address for each website. Name-based virtual hosting uses the clients HTTP/1.1 headers to figure out the hostname, which allows the websites to share the same IP address.

To setup Apache to use name-based virtual hosting, add a `VirtualHost` block for each website. For example, for the webserver named www.domain.tld with a virtual domain of www.someotherdomain.tld, add the following entries to `httpd.conf`:

```
<VirtualHost *>
ServerName www.domain.tld
DocumentRoot /www/domain.tld
</VirtualHost>

<VirtualHost *>
ServerName www.someotherdomain.tld
DocumentRoot /www/someotherdomain.tld
</VirtualHost>
```

For each virtual host, replace the values for `ServerName` and `DocumentRoot` with the values to be used.

For more information about setting up virtual hosts, consult the official Apache documentation at: `http://httpd.apache.org/docs/vhosts/` .

28.8.3. Apache Modules

Apache uses modules to augment the functionality provided by the basic server. Refer to `http://httpd.apache.org/docs/current/mod/` for a complete listing of and the configuration details for the available modules.

In FreeBSD, some modules can be compiled with the www/apache24 port. Type `make config` within `/usr/ports/www/apache24` to see which modules are available and which are enabled by default. If the module is not compiled with the port, the FreeBSD Ports Collection provides an easy way to install many modules. This section describes three of the most commonly used modules.

28.8.3.1. `mod_ssl`

The `mod_ssl` module uses the OpenSSL library to provide strong cryptography via the Secure Sockets Layer (SSLv3) and Transport Layer Security (TLSv1) protocols. This module provides everything necessary to request a signed certificate from a trusted certificate signing authority to run a secure web server on FreeBSD.

In FreeBSD, `mod_ssl` module is enabled by default in both the package and the port. The available configuration directives are explained at `http://httpd.apache.org/docs/current/mod/mod_ssl.html` .

28.8.3.2. `mod_perl`

The `mod_perl` module makes it possible to write Apache modules in Perl. In addition, the persistent interpreter embedded in the server avoids the overhead of starting an external interpreter and the penalty of Perl start-up time.

The `mod_perl` can be installed using the www/mod_perl2 package or port. Documentation for using this module can be found at `http://perl.apache.org/docs/2.0/index.html` .

28.8.3.3. `mod_php`

Written by Tom Rhodes.

PHP: Hypertext Preprocessor (PHP) is a general-purpose scripting language that is especially suited for web development. Capable of being embedded into HTML, its syntax draws upon C, Java™, and Perl with the intention of allowing web developers to write dynamically generated webpages quickly.

To gain support for PHP5 for the Apache web server, install the www/mod_php56 package or port. This will install and configure the modules required to support dynamic PHP applications. The installation will automatically add this line to `/usr/local/etc/apache2 4/httpd.conf`:

```
LoadModule php5_module        libexec/apache24/libphp5.so
```

553

Then, perform a graceful restart to load the PHP module:

```
# apachectl graceful
```

The PHP support provided by www/mod_php56 is limited. Additional support can be installed using the lang/php56-extensions port which provides a menu driven interface to the available PHP extensions.

Alternatively, individual extensions can be installed using the appropriate port. For instance, to add PHP support for the MySQL database server, install databases/php56-mysql.

After installing an extension, the Apache server must be reloaded to pick up the new configuration changes:

```
# apachectl graceful
```

28.8.4. Dynamic Websites

In addition to mod_perl and mod_php, other languages are available for creating dynamic web content. These include Django and Ruby on Rails.

28.8.4.1. Django

Django is a BSD-licensed framework designed to allow developers to write high performance, elegant web applications quickly. It provides an object-relational mapper so that data types are developed as Python objects. A rich dynamic database-access API is provided for those objects without the developer ever having to write SQL. It also provides an extensible template system so that the logic of the application is separated from the HTML presentation.

Django depends on mod_python , and an SQL database engine. In FreeBSD, the www/py-django port automatically installs mod_python and supports the PostgreSQL, MySQL, or SQLite databases, with the default being SQLite. To change the database engine, type make config within /usr/ports/www/py-django , then install the port.

Once Django is installed, the application will need a project directory along with the Apache configuration in order to use the embedded Python interpreter. This interpreter is used to call the application for specific URLs on the site.

To configure Apache to pass requests for certain URLs to the web application, add the following to httpd.conf , specifying the full path to the project directory:

```
<Location "/">
    SetHandler python-program
    PythonPath "['/dir/to/the/django/packages/ '] + sys.path"
    PythonHandler django.core.handlers.modpython
    SetEnv DJANGO_SETTINGS_MODULE mysite.settings
    PythonAutoReload On
    PythonDebug On
</Location>
```

Refer to https://docs.djangoproject.com/en/1.6/ for more information on how to use Django.

28.8.4.2. Ruby on Rails

Ruby on Rails is another open source web framework that provides a full development stack. It is optimized to make web developers more productive and capable of writing powerful applications quickly. On FreeBSD, it can be installed using the www/rubygem-rails package or port.

Refer to http://rubyonrails.org/documentation for more information on how to use Ruby on Rails.

28.9. File Transfer Protocol (FTP)

The File Transfer Protocol (FTP) provides users with a simple way to transfer files to and from an FTP server. FreeBSD includes FTP server software, ftpd, in the base system.

FreeBSD provides several configuration files for controlling access to the FTP server. This section summarizes these files. Refer to ftpd(8) for more details about the built-in FTP server.

28.9.1. Configuration

The most important configuration step is deciding which accounts will be allowed access to the FTP server. A FreeBSD system has a number of system accounts which should not be allowed FTP access. The list of users disallowed any FTP access can be found in /etc/ftpusers. By default, it includes system accounts. Additional users that should not be allowed access to FTP can be added.

In some cases it may be desirable to restrict the access of some users without preventing them completely from using FTP. This can be accomplished be creating /etc/ftpchroot as described in ftpchroot(5). This file lists users and groups subject to FTP access restrictions.

To enable anonymous FTP access to the server, create a user named `ftp` on the FreeBSD system. Users will then be able to log on to the FTP server with a username of `ftp` or `anonymous`. When prompted for the password, any input will be accepted, but by convention, an email address should be used as the password. The FTP server will call chroot(2) when an anonymous user logs in, to restrict access to only the home directory of the `ftp` user.

There are two text files that can be created to specify welcome messages to be displayed to FTP clients. The contents of /etc/ftpwelcome will be displayed to users before they reach the login prompt. After a successful login, the contents of /etc/ftpmotd will be displayed. Note that the path to this file is relative to the login environment, so the contents of ~ftp/etc/ftpmotd would be displayed for anonymous users.

Once the FTP server has been configured, set the appropriate variable in /etc/rc.conf to start the service during boot:

```
ftpd_enable="YES"
```

To start the service now:

```
# service ftpd start
```

Test the connection to the FTP server by typing:

```
% ftp localhost
```

The ftpd daemon uses syslog(3) to log messages. By default, the system log daemon will write messages related to FTP in /var/log/xferlog. The location of the FTP log can be modified by changing the following line in /etc/syslog.conf:

```
ftp.info        /var/log/xferlog
```

Note

Be aware of the potential problems involved with running an anonymous FTP server. In particular, think twice about allowing anonymous users to upload files. It may turn out that the FTP site becomes a forum for the trade of unlicensed commercial software or worse. If anonymous FTP uploads are required, then verify the permissions so that these files can not be read by other anonymous users until they have been reviewed by an administrator.

28.10. File and Print Services for Microsoft® Windows® Clients (Samba)

Samba is a popular open source software package that provides file and print services using the SMB/CIFS protocol. This protocol is built into Microsoft® Windows® systems. It can be added to non-Microsoft® Windows® systems by installing the Samba client libraries. The protocol allows clients to access shared data and printers. These shares can be mapped as a local disk drive and shared printers can be used as if they were local printers.

On FreeBSD, the Samba client libraries can be installed using the net/samba-smbclient port or package. The client provides the ability for a FreeBSD system to access SMB/CIFS shares in a Microsoft® Windows® network.

A FreeBSD system can also be configured to act as a Samba server. This allows the administrator to create SMB/CIFS shares on the FreeBSD system which can be accessed by clients running Microsoft® Windows® or the Samba client libraries. In order to configure a Samba server on FreeBSD, the net/samba36 port or package must first be installed. The rest of this section provides an overview of how to configure a Samba server on FreeBSD.

28.10.1. Configuration

A default Samba configuration file is installed as /usr/local/share/examples/samba36/smb.conf.default . This file must be copied to /usr/local/etc/smb.conf and customized before Samba can be used.

Runtime configuration information for Samba is found in smb.conf, such as definitions of the printers and "file system shares" that will be shared with Windows® clients. The Samba package includes a web based tool called swat which provides a simple way for configuring smb.conf.

28.10.1.1. Using the Samba Web Administration Tool (SWAT)

The Samba Web Administration Tool (SWAT) runs as a daemon from inetd. Therefore, inetd must be enabled as shown in Section 28.2, "The inetd Super-Server". To enable swat, uncomment the following line in /etc/inetd.conf:

```
swat    stream  tcp     nowait/400      root    /usr/local/sbin/swat    swat
```

As explained in Example 28.1, "Reloading the inetd Configuration File", the inetd configuration must be reloaded after this configuration file is changed.

Once swat has been enabled, use a web browser to connect to http://localhost:901 . At first login, enter the credentials for root.

Once logged in, the main Samba configuration page and the system documentation will be available. Begin configuration by clicking on the Globals tab. The Globals section corresponds to the variables that are set in the [global] section of /usr/local/etc/smb.conf .

28.10.1.2. Global Settings

Whether swat is used or /usr/local/etc/smb.conf is edited directly, the first directives encountered when configuring Samba are:

workgroup
> The domain name or workgroup name for the computers that will be accessing this server.

netbios name
> The NetBIOS name by which a Samba server is known. By default it is the same as the first component of the host's DNS name.

server string
> The string that will be displayed in the output of net view and some other networking tools that seek to display descriptive text about the server.

28.10.1.3. Security Settings

Two of the most important settings in `/usr/local/etc/smb.conf` are the security model and the backend password format for client users. The following directives control these options:

`security`
> The two most common options are `security = share` and `security = user`. If the clients use usernames that are the same as their usernames on the FreeBSD machine, user level security should be used. This is the default security policy and it requires clients to first log on before they can access shared resources.
>
> In share level security, clients do not need to log onto the server with a valid username and password before attempting to connect to a shared resource. This was the default security model for older versions of Samba.

`passdb backend`

> Samba has several different backend authentication models. Clients may be authenticated with LDAP, NIS+, an SQL database, or a modified password file. The default authentication method is `smbpasswd`, and that is all that will be covered here.

Assuming that the default `smbpasswd` backend is used, `/usr/local/etc/samba/smbpasswd` must be created to allow Samba to authenticate clients. To provide UNIX® user accounts access from Windows® clients, use the following command to add each required user to that file:

```
# smbpasswd -a username
```

 Note

The recommended backend is now `tdbsam`. If this backend is selected, use the following command to add user accounts:

```
# pdbedit -a -u username
```

This section has only mentioned the most commonly used settings. Refer to the Official Samba HOWTO for additional information about the available configuration options.

28.10.2. Starting Samba

To enable Samba at boot time, add the following line to `/etc/rc.conf`:

```
samba_enable="YES"
```

Alternately, its services can be started separately:

```
nmbd_enable="YES"
```

```
smbd_enable="YES"
```

To start Samba now:

```
# service samba start
Starting SAMBA: removing stale tdbs :
Starting nmbd.
Starting smbd.
```

Samba consists of three separate daemons. Both the nmbd and smbd daemons are started by `samba_enable`. If winbind name resolution services are enabled in `smb.conf`, the winbindd daemon is started as well.

Samba may be stopped at any time by typing:

```
# service samba stop
```

Samba is a complex software suite with functionality that allows broad integration with Microsoft® Windows® networks. For more information about functionality beyond the basic configuration described here, refer to http://www.samba.org.

28.11. Clock Synchronization with NTP

Over time, a computer's clock is prone to drift. This is problematic as many network services require the computers on a network to share the same accurate time. Accurate time is also needed to ensure that file timestamps stay consistent. The Network Time Protocol (NTP) is one way to provide clock accuracy in a network.

FreeBSD includes ntpd(8) which can be configured to query other NTP servers in order to synchronize the clock on that machine or to provide time services to other computers in the network. The servers which are queried can be local to the network or provided by an ISP. In addition, an online list of publicly accessible NTP servers is available. When choosing a public NTP server, select one that is geographically close and review its usage policy.

Choosing several NTP servers is recommended in case one of the servers becomes unreachable or its clock proves unreliable. As ntpd receives responses, it favors reliable servers over the less reliable ones.

This section describes how to configure ntpd on FreeBSD. Further documentation can be found in /usr/share/doc/ntp/ in HTML format.

28.11.1. NTP Configuration

On FreeBSD, the built-in ntpd can be used to synchronize a system's clock. To enable ntpd at boot time, add ntpd_enable="YES" to /etc/rc.conf. Additional variables can be specified in /etc/rc.conf. Refer to rc.conf(5) and ntpd(8) for details.

This application reads /etc/ntp.conf to determine which NTP servers to query. Here is a simple example of an /etc/ntp.conf:

Example 28.4. Sample **/etc/ntp.conf**

```
server ntplocal.example.com prefer
server timeserver.example.org
server ntp2a.example.net

driftfile /var/db/ntp.drift
```

The format of this file is described in ntp.conf(5). The **server** option specifies which servers to query, with one server listed on each line. If a server entry includes **prefer**, that server is preferred over other servers. A response from a preferred server will be discarded if it differs significantly from other servers' responses; otherwise it will be used. The **prefer** argument should only be used for NTP servers that are known to be highly accurate, such as those with special time monitoring hardware.

The **driftfile** entry specifies which file is used to store the system clock's frequency offset. ntpd uses this to automatically compensate for the clock's natural drift, allowing it to maintain a reasonably correct setting even if it is cut off from all external time sources for a period of time. This file also stores information about previous responses from NTP servers. Since this file contains internal information for NTP, it should not be modified.

By default, an NTP server is accessible to any network host. The **restrict** option in /etc/ntp.conf can be used to control which systems can access the server. For example, to deny all machines from accessing the NTP server, add the following line to /etc/ntp.conf:

```
restrict default ignore
```

Note

This will also prevent access from other NTP servers. If there is a need to synchronize with an external NTP server, allow only that specific server. Refer to ntp.conf(5) for more information.

To allow machines within the network to synchronize their clocks with the server, but ensure they are not allowed to configure the server or be used as peers to synchronize against, instead use:

```
restrict 192.168.1.0 mask 255.255.255.0 nomodify notrap
```

where `192.168.1.0` is the local network address and `255.255.255.0` is the network's subnet mask.

Multiple `restrict` entries are supported. For more details, refer to the `Access Control Support` subsection of ntp.conf(5).

Once `ntpd_enable="YES"` has been added to `/etc/rc.conf`, ntpd can be started now without rebooting the system by typing:

```
# service ntpd start
```

28.11.2. Using NTP with a PPP Connection

ntpd does not need a permanent connection to the Internet to function properly. However, if a PPP connection is configured to dial out on demand, NTP traffic should be prevented from triggering a dial out or keeping the connection alive. This can be configured with `filter` directives in `/etc/ppp/ppp.conf`. For example:

```
set filter dial 0 deny udp src eq 123
# Prevent NTP traffic from initiating dial out
set filter dial 1 permit 0 0
set filter alive 0 deny udp src eq 123
# Prevent incoming NTP traffic from keeping the connection open
set filter alive 1 deny udp dst eq 123
# Prevent outgoing NTP traffic from keeping the connection open
set filter alive 2 permit 0/0 0/0
```

For more details, refer to the `PACKET FILTERING` section in ppp(8) and the examples in `/usr/share/examples/ppp/`.

Note

Some Internet access providers block low-numbered ports, preventing NTP from functioning since replies never reach the machine.

28.12. iSCSI Initiator and Target Configuration

iSCSI is a way to share storage over a network. Unlike NFS, which works at the file system level, iSCSI works at the block device level.

In iSCSI terminology, the system that shares the storage is known as the *target*. The storage can be a physical disk, or an area representing multiple disks or a portion of a physical disk. For example, if the disk(s) are formatted with ZFS, a zvol can be created to use as the iSCSI storage.

The clients which access the iSCSI storage are called *initiators*. To initiators, the storage available through iSCSI appears as a raw, unformatted disk known as a LUN. Device nodes for the disk appear in /dev/ and the device must be separately formatted and mounted.

Beginning with 10.0-RELEASE, FreeBSD provides a native, kernel-based iSCSI target and initiator. This section describes how to configure a FreeBSD system as a target or an initiator.

28.12.1. Configuring an iSCSI Target

> **Note**
>
> The native iSCSI target is supported starting with FreeBSD 10.0-RELEASE. To use iSCSI in older versions of FreeBSD, install a userspace target from the Ports Collection, such as net/istgt. This chapter only describes the native target.

To configure an iSCSI target, create the /etc/ctl.conf configuration file, add a line to /etc/rc.conf to make sure the ctld(8) daemon is automatically started at boot, and then start the daemon.

The following is an example of a simple /etc/ctl.conf configuration file. Refer to ctl.conf(5) for a more complete description of this file's available options.

```
portal-group pg0 {
 discovery-auth-group no-authentication
 listen 0.0.0.0
 listen [::]
}

target iqn.2012-06.com.example:target0 {
 auth-group no-authentication
 portal-group pg0

 lun 0 {
  path /data/target0-0
  size 4G
 }
}
```

The first entry defines the pg0 portal group. Portal groups define which network addresses the ctld(8) daemon will listen on. The discovery-auth-group no-authentication entry indicates that any initiator is allowed to perform iSCSI target discovery without authentication. Lines three and four configure ctld(8) to listen on all IPv4 (listen 0.0.0.0) and IPv6 (listen [::]) addresses on the default port of 3260.

It is not necessary to define a portal group as there is a built-in portal group called default. In this case, the difference between default and pg0 is that with default, target discovery is always denied, while with pg0, it is always allowed.

The second entry defines a single target. Target has two possible meanings: a machine serving iSCSI or a named group of LUNs. This example uses the latter meaning, where iqn.2012-06.com.example:target0 is the target name. This target name is suitable for testing purposes. For actual use, change com.example to the real domain name, reversed. The 2012-06 represents the year and month of acquiring control of that domain name, and target0 can be any value. Any number of targets can be defined in this configuration file.

The auth-group no-authentication line allows all initiators to connect to the specified target and portal-group pg0 makes the target reachable through the pg0 portal group.

The next section defines the LUN. To the initiator, each LUN will be visible as a separate disk device. Multiple LUNs can be defined for each target. Each LUN is identified by a number, where LUN 0 is mandatory. The path /

`data/target0-0` line defines the full path to a file or zvol backing the LUN. That path must exist before starting ctld(8). The second line is optional and specifies the size of the LUN.

Next, to make sure the ctld(8) daemon is started at boot, add this line to `/etc/rc.conf` :

```
ctld_enable="YES"
```

To start ctld(8) now, run this command:

```
# service ctld start
```

As the ctld(8) daemon is started, it reads `/etc/ctl.conf` . If this file is edited after the daemon starts, use this command so that the changes take effect immediately:

```
# service ctld reload
```

28.12.1.1. Authentication

The previous example is inherently insecure as it uses no authentication, granting anyone full access to all targets. To require a username and password to access targets, modify the configuration as follows:

```
auth-group ag0 {
 chap username1 secretsecret
 chap username2 anothersecret
}

portal-group pg0 {
 discovery-auth-group no-authentication
 listen 0.0.0.0
 listen [::]
}

target iqn.2012-06.com.example:target0 {
 auth-group ag0
 portal-group pg0
 lun 0 {
  path /data/target0-0
  size 4G
 }
}
```

The `auth-group` section defines username and password pairs. An initiator trying to connect to `iqn.2012-06.com.example:target0` must first specify a defined username and secret. However, target discovery is still permitted without authentication. To require target discovery authentication, set `discovery-auth-group` to a defined `auth-group` name instead of `no-authentication`.

It is common to define a single exported target for every initiator. As a shorthand for the syntax above, the username and password can be specified directly in the target entry:

```
target iqn.2012-06.com.example:target0 {
 portal-group pg0
 chap username1 secretsecret

 lun 0 {
  path /data/target0-0
  size 4G
 }
}
```

561

28.12.2. Configuring an iSCSI Initiator

 Note

The iSCSI initiator described in this section is supported starting with FreeBSD 10.0-RELEASE. To use the iSCSI initiator available in older versions, refer to iscontrol(8).

The iSCSI initiator requires that the iscsid(8) daemon is running. This daemon does not use a configuration file. To start it automatically at boot, add this line to /etc/rc.conf :

```
iscsid_enable="YES"
```

To start iscsid(8) now, run this command:

```
# service iscsid start
```

Connecting to a target can be done with or without an /etc/iscsi.conf configuration file. This section demonstrates both types of connections.

28.12.2.1. Connecting to a Target Without a Configuration File

To connect an initiator to a single target, specify the IP address of the portal and the name of the target:

```
# iscsictl -A -p 10.10.10.10 -t iqn.2012-06.com.example:target0
```

To verify if the connection succeeded, run `iscsictl` without any arguments. The output should look similar to this:

```
Target name                             Target portal   State
iqn.2012-06.com.example:target0         10.10.10.10     Connected: da0
```

In this example, the iSCSI session was successfully established, with /dev/da0 representing the attached LUN. If the iqn.2012-06.com.example:target0 target exports more than one LUN, multiple device nodes will be shown in that section of the output:

```
Connected: da0 da1 da2.
```

Any errors will be reported in the output, as well as the system logs. For example, this message usually means that the iscsid(8) daemon is not running:

```
Target name                             Target portal   State
iqn.2012-06.com.example:target0         10.10.10.10     Waiting for iscsid(8)
```

The following message suggests a networking problem, such as a wrong IP address or port:

```
Target name                             Target portal   State
iqn.2012-06.com.example:target0         10.10.10.11     Connection refused
```

This message means that the specified target name is wrong:

```
Target name                             Target portal   State
iqn.2012-06.com.example:target0         10.10.10.10     Not found
```

This message means that the target requires authentication:

```
Target name                             Target portal   State
iqn.2012-06.com.example:target0         10.10.10.10     Authentication failed
```

To specify a CHAP username and secret, use this syntax:

```
# iscsictl -A -p 10.10.10.10 -t iqn.2012-06.com.example:target0   -u user -s secretsecret
```

28.12.2.2. Connecting to a Target with a Configuration File

To connect using a configuration file, create `/etc/iscsi.conf` with contents like this:

```
t0 {
  TargetAddress   = 10.10.10.10
  TargetName      = iqn.2012-06.com.example:target0
  AuthMethod      = CHAP
  chapIName       = user
  chapSecret      = secretsecret
}
```

The `t0` specifies a nickname for the configuration file section. It will be used by the initiator to specify which configuration to use. The other lines specify the parameters to use during connection. The `TargetAddress` and `TargetName` are mandatory, whereas the other options are optional. In this example, the CHAP username and secret are shown.

To connect to the defined target, specify the nickname:

```
# iscsictl -An t0
```

Alternately, to connect to all targets defined in the configuration file, use:

```
# iscsictl -Aa
```

To make the initiator automatically connect to all targets in `/etc/iscsi.conf`, add the following to `/etc/rc.conf`:

```
iscsictl_enable="YES"
iscsictl_flags="-Aa"
```

Chapter 29. Firewalls

Contributed by Joseph J. Barbish.
Converted to SGML and updated by Brad Davis.

29.1. Synopsis

Firewalls make it possible to filter the incoming and outgoing traffic that flows through a system. A firewall can use one or more sets of "rules" to inspect network packets as they come in or go out of network connections and either allows the traffic through or blocks it. The rules of a firewall can inspect one or more characteristics of the packets such as the protocol type, source or destination host address, and source or destination port.

Firewalls can enhance the security of a host or a network. They can be used to do one or more of the following:

- Protect and insulate the applications, services, and machines of an internal network from unwanted traffic from the public Internet.

- Limit or disable access from hosts of the internal network to services of the public Internet.

- Support network address translation (NAT), which allows an internal network to use private IP addresses and share a single connection to the public Internet using either a single IP address or a shared pool of automatically assigned public addresses.

FreeBSD has three firewalls built into the base system: PF, IPFW, and IPFILTER, also known as IPF. FreeBSD also provides two traffic shapers for controlling bandwidth usage: altq(4) and dummynet(4). ALTQ has traditionally been closely tied with PF and dummynet with IPFW. Each firewall uses rules to control the access of packets to and from a FreeBSD system, although they go about it in different ways and each has a different rule syntax.

FreeBSD provides multiple firewalls in order to meet the different requirements and preferences for a wide variety of users. Each user should evaluate which firewall best meets their needs.

After reading this chapter, you will know:

- How to define packet filtering rules.

- The differences between the firewalls built into FreeBSD.

- How to use and configure the PF firewall.

- How to use and configure the IPFW firewall.

- How to use and configure the IPFILTER firewall.

Before reading this chapter, you should:

- Understand basic FreeBSD and Internet concepts.

Note

Since all firewalls are based on inspecting the values of selected packet control fields, the creator of the firewall ruleset must have an understanding of how TCP/IP works, what the different values in the packet control fields are, and how these values are used in a normal session conversation. For a good introduction, refer to Daryl's TCP/IP Primer.

29.2. Firewall Concepts

A ruleset contains a group of rules which pass or block packets based on the values contained in the packet. The bi-directional exchange of packets between hosts comprises a session conversation. The firewall ruleset processes both the packets arriving from the public Internet, as well as the packets produced by the system as a response to them. Each TCP/IP service is predefined by its protocol and listening port. Packets destined for a specific service originate from the source address using an unprivileged port and target the specific service port on the destination address. All the above parameters can be used as selection criteria to create rules which will pass or block services.

To lookup unknown port numbers, refer to `/etc/services`. Alternatively, visit `http://en.wikipedia.org/wiki/List_of_TCP_and_UDP_port_numbers` and do a port number lookup to find the purpose of a particular port number.

Check out this link for port numbers used by Trojans `http://www.sans.org/security-resources/idfaq/odd-ports.php`.

FTP has two modes: active mode and passive mode. The difference is in how the data channel is acquired. Passive mode is more secure as the data channel is acquired by the ordinal ftp session requester. For a good explanation of FTP and the different modes, see `http://www.slacksite.com/other/ftp.html`.

A firewall ruleset can be either "exclusive" or "inclusive". An exclusive firewall allows all traffic through except for the traffic matching the ruleset. An inclusive firewall does the reverse as it only allows traffic matching the rules through and blocks everything else.

An inclusive firewall offers better control of the outgoing traffic, making it a better choice for systems that offer services to the public Internet. It also controls the type of traffic originating from the public Internet that can gain access to a private network. All traffic that does not match the rules is blocked and logged. Inclusive firewalls are generally safer than exclusive firewalls because they significantly reduce the risk of allowing unwanted traffic.

Note

Unless noted otherwise, all configuration and example rulesets in this chapter create inclusive firewall rulesets.

Security can be tightened further using a "stateful firewall". This type of firewall keeps track of open connections and only allows traffic which either matches an existing connection or opens a new, allowed connection.

Stateful filtering treats traffic as a bi-directional exchange of packets comprising a session. When state is specified on a matching rule the firewall dynamically generates internal rules for each anticipated packet being exchanged during the session. It has sufficient matching capabilities to determine if a packet is valid for a session. Any packets that do not properly fit the session template are automatically rejected.

When the session completes, it is removed from the dynamic state table.

Stateful filtering allows one to focus on blocking/passing new sessions. If the new session is passed, all its subsequent packets are allowed automatically and any impostor packets are automatically rejected. If a new session is blocked, none of its subsequent packets are allowed. Stateful filtering provides advanced matching abilities capable of defending against the flood of different attack methods employed by attackers.

NAT stands for *Network Address Translation*. NAT function enables the private LAN behind the firewall to share a single ISP-assigned IP address, even if that address is dynamically assigned. NAT allows each computer in the LAN to have Internet access, without having to pay the ISP for multiple Internet accounts or IP addresses.

NAT will automatically translate the private LAN IP address for each system on the LAN to the single public IP address as packets exit the firewall bound for the public Internet. It also performs the reverse translation for returning packets.

According to RFC 1918, the following IP address ranges are reserved for private networks which will never be routed directly to the public Internet, and therefore are available for use with NAT:

- `10.0.0.0/8` .

- `172.16.0.0/12` .

- `192.168.0.0/16` .

Warning

When working with the firewall rules, be *very careful*. Some configurations *can lock the administrator out* of the server. To be on the safe side, consider performing the initial firewall configuration from the local console rather than doing it remotely over ssh.

29.3. PF

Revised and updated by John Ferrell.

Since FreeBSD 5.3, a ported version of OpenBSD's PF firewall has been included as an integrated part of the base system. PF is a complete, full-featured firewall that has optional support for ALTQ (Alternate Queuing), which provides Quality of Service (QoS).

The OpenBSD Project maintains the definitive reference for PF in the PF FAQ. Peter Hansteen maintains a thorough PF tutorial at http://home.nuug.no/~peter/pf/.

Warning

When reading the PF FAQ, keep in mind that FreeBSD uses the same version of PF as OpenBSD 4.5.

The FreeBSD packet filter mailing list is a good place to ask questions about configuring and running the PF firewall. Check the mailing list archives before asking a question as it may have already been answered.

More information about porting PF to FreeBSD can be found at `http://pf4freebsd.love2party.net/` .

This section of the Handbook focuses on PF as it pertains to FreeBSD. It demonstrates how to enable PF and ALTQ. It then provides several examples for creating rulesets on a FreeBSD system.

29.3.1. Enabling PF

In order to use PF, its kernel module must be first loaded. This section describes the entries that can be added to `/etc/rc.conf` in order to enable PF.

Start by adding the following line to `/etc/rc.conf` :

```
pf_enable="YES"
```

Additional options, described in pfctl(8), can be passed to PF when it is started. Add this entry to `/etc/rc.conf` and specify any required flags between the two quotes (`""`):

```
pf_flags=""                      # additional flags for pfctl startup
```

PF will not start if it cannot find its ruleset configuration file. The default ruleset is already created and is named /etc/pf.conf . If a custom ruleset has been saved somewhere else, add a line to /etc/rc.conf which specifies the full path to the file:

```
pf_rules="/path/to/pf.conf "
```

Logging support for PF is provided by pflog(4). To enable logging support, add this line to /etc/rc.conf :

```
pflog_enable="YES"
```

The following lines can also be added in order to change the default location of the log file or to specify any additional flags to pass to pflog(4) when it is started:

```
pflog_logfile="/var/log/pflog"   # where pflogd should store the logfile
pflog_flags=""                   # additional flags for pflogd startup
```

Finally, if there is a LAN behind the firewall and packets need to be forwarded for the computers on the LAN, or NAT is required, add the following option:

```
gateway_enable="YES"             # Enable as LAN gateway
```

After saving the needed edits, PF can be started with logging support by typing:

```
# service pf start
# service pflog start
```

By default, PF reads its configuration rules from /etc/pf.conf and modifies, drops, or passes packets according to the rules or definitions specified in this file. The FreeBSD installation includes several sample files located in /usr/share/examples/pf/ . Refer to the PF FAQ for complete coverage of PF rulesets.

To control PF, use pfctl. Table 29.1, "Useful pfctl Options" summarizes some useful options to this command. Refer to pfctl(8) for a description of all available options:

Table 29.1. Useful pfctl Options

Command	Purpose
pfctl -e	Enable PF.
pfctl -d	Disable PF.
pfctl -F all -f /etc/pf.conf	Flush all NAT, filter, state, and table rules and reload /etc/pf.conf .
pfctl -s [rules | nat state]	Report on the filter rules, NAT rules, or state table.
pfctl -vnf /etc/pf.conf	Check /etc/pf.conf for errors, but do not load ruleset.

Tip

security/sudo is useful for running commands like pfctl that require elevated privileges. It can be installed from the Ports Collection.

To keep an eye on the traffic that passes through the PF firewall, consider installing the sysutils/pftop package or port. Once installed, pftop can be run to view a running snapshot of traffic in a format which is similar to top(1).

29.3.2. Enabling ALTQ

On FreeBSD, ALTQ can be used with PF to provide Quality of Service (QOS). Once ALTQ is enabled, queues can be defined in the ruleset which determine the processing priority of outbound packets.

Before enabling ALTQ, refer to altq(4) to determine if the drivers for the network cards installed on the system support it.

ALTQ is not available as a loadable kernel module. If the system's interfaces support ALTQ, create a custom kernel using the instructions in Chapter 8, *Configuring the FreeBSD Kernel*. The following kernel options are available. The first is needed to enable ALTQ. At least one of the other options is necessary to specify the queueing scheduler algorithm:

```
options        ALTQ
options        ALTQ_CBQ        # Class Based Queuing (CBQ)
options        ALTQ_RED        # Random Early Detection (RED)
options        ALTQ_RIO        # RED In/Out
options        ALTQ_HFSC       # Hierarchical Packet Scheduler (HFSC)
options        ALTQ_PRIQ       # Priority Queuing (PRIQ)
```

The following scheduler algorithms are available:

CBQ

> Class Based Queuing (CBQ) is used to divide a connection's bandwidth into different classes or queues to prioritize traffic based on filter rules.

RED

> Random Early Detection (RED) is used to avoid network congestion by measuring the length of the queue and comparing it to the minimum and maximum thresholds for the queue. When the queue is over the maximum, all new packets are randomly dropped.

RIO

> In Random Early Detection In and Out (RIO) mode, RED maintains multiple average queue lengths and multiple threshold values, one for each QOS level.

HFSC

> Hierarchical Fair Service Curve Packet Scheduler (HFSC) is described in http://www-2.cs.cmu.edu/~hzhang/ HFSC/main.html .

PRIQ

> Priority Queuing (PRIQ) always passes traffic that is in a higher queue first.

More information about the scheduling algorithms and example rulesets are available at http://www.openbsd.org/faq/pf/queueing.html .

29.3.3. PF Rulesets

Contributed by Peter N. M. Hansteen.

This section demonstrates how to create a customized ruleset. It starts with the simplest of rulesets and builds upon its concepts using several examples to demonstrate real-world usage of PF's many features.

The simplest possible ruleset is for a single machine that does not run any services and which needs access to one network, which may be the Internet. To create this minimal ruleset, edit /etc/pf.conf so it looks like this:

```
block in all
pass out all keep state
```

The first rule denies all incoming traffic by default. The second rule allows connections created by this system to pass out, while retaining state information on those connections. This state information allows return traffic for those connections to pass back and should only be used on machines that can be trusted. The ruleset can be loaded with:

```
# pfctl -e -; pfctl -f /etc/pf.conf
```

In addition to keeping state, PF provides *lists* and *macros* which can be defined for use when creating rules. Macros can include lists and need to be defined before use. As an example, insert these lines at the very top of the ruleset:

```
tcp_services = "{ ssh, smtp, domain, www, pop3, auth, pop3s }"
udp_services = "{ domain }"
```

PF understands port names as well as port numbers, as long as the names are listed in /etc/services . This example creates two macros. The first is a list of seven TCP port names and the second is one UDP port name. Once defined, macros can be used in rules. In this example, all traffic is blocked except for the connections initiated by this system for the seven specified TCP services and the one specified UDP service:

```
tcp_services = "{ ssh, smtp, domain, www, pop3, auth, pop3s }"
udp_services = "{ domain }"
block all
pass out proto tcp to any port $tcp_services keep state
pass proto udp to any port $udp_services keep state
```

Even though UDP is considered to be a stateless protocol, PF is able to track some state information. For example, when a UDP request is passed which asks a name server about a domain name, PF will watch for the response in order to pass it back.

Whenever an edit is made to a ruleset, the new rules must be loaded so they can be used:

```
# pfctl -f /etc/pf.conf
```

If there are no syntax errors, pfctl will not output any messages during the rule load. Rules can also be tested before attempting to load them:

```
# pfctl -nf /etc/pf.conf
```

Including -n causes the rules to be interpreted only, but not loaded. This provides an opportunity to correct any errors. At all times, the last valid ruleset loaded will be enforced until either PF is disabled or a new ruleset is loaded.

Tip

Adding -v to a pfctl ruleset verify or load will display the fully parsed rules exactly the way they will be loaded. This is extremely useful when debugging rules.

29.3.3.1. A Simple Gateway with NAT

This section demonstrates how to configure a FreeBSD system running PF to act as a gateway for at least one other machine. The gateway needs at least two network interfaces, each connected to a separate network. In this example, xl1 is connected to the Internet and xl0 is connected to the internal network.

First, enable the gateway in order to let the machine forward the network traffic it receives on one interface to another interface. This sysctl setting will forward IPv4 packets:

```
# sysctl net.inet.ip.forwarding=1
```

To forward IPv6 traffic, use:

```
# sysctl net.inet6.ip6.forwarding=1
```

To enable these settings at system boot, add the following to /etc/rc.conf :

```
gateway_enable="YES"  #for ipv4
ipv6_gateway_enable="YES" #for ipv6
```

Verify with ifconfig that both of the interfaces are up and running.

Next, create the PF rules to allow the gateway to pass traffic. While the following rule allows stateful traffic to pass from the Internet to hosts on the network, the to keyword does not guarantee passage all the way from source to destination:

```
pass in on xl1 from xl1:network to xl0:network port $ports keep state
```

That rule only lets the traffic pass in to the gateway on the internal interface. To let the packets go further, a matching rule is needed:

```
pass out on xl0 from xl1:network to xl0:network port $ports keep state
```

While these two rules will work, rules this specific are rarely needed. For a busy network admin, a readable ruleset is a safer ruleset. The remainder of this section demonstrates how to keep the rules as simple as possible for readability. For example, those two rules could be replaced with one rule:

```
pass from xl1:network to any port $ports keep state
```

The interface:network notation can be replaced with a macro to make the ruleset even more readable. For example, a $localnet macro could be defined as the network directly attached to the internal interface ($xl1:network). Alternatively, the definition of $localnet could be changed to an *IP address/netmask* notation to denote a network, such as 192.168.100.1/24 for a subnet of private addresses.

If required, $localnet could even be defined as a list of networks. Whatever the specific needs, a sensible $localnet definition could be used in a typical pass rule as follows:

```
pass from $localnet to any port $ports keep state
```

The following sample ruleset allows all traffic initiated by machines on the internal network. It first defines two macros to represent the external and internal 3COM interfaces of the gateway.

> ### Note
>
> For dialup users, the external interface will use tun0. For an ADSL connection, specifically those using PPP over Ethernet (PPPoE), the correct external interface is tun0, not the physical Ethernet interface.

```
ext_if = "xl0" # macro for external interface - use tun0 for PPPoE
int_if = "xl1" # macro for internal interface
localnet = $int_if:network
# ext_if IP address could be dynamic, hence ($ext_if)
nat on $ext_if from $localnet to any -> ($ext_if)
block all
pass from { lo0, $localnet } to any keep state
```

This ruleset introduces the nat rule which is used to handle the network address translation from the non-routable addresses inside the internal network to the IP address assigned to the external interface. The parentheses surrounding the last part of the nat rule ($ext_if) is included when the IP address of the external interface is dynamically assigned. It ensures that network traffic runs without serious interruptions even if the external IP address changes.

Note that this ruleset probably allows more traffic to pass out of the network than is needed. One reasonable setup could create this macro:

```
client_out = "{ ftp-data, ftp, ssh, domain, pop3, auth, nntp, http, \
    https, cvspserver, 2628, 5999, 8000, 8080 }"
```

to use in the main pass rule:

```
pass inet proto tcp from $localnet to any port $client_out \
    flags S/SA keep state
```

A few other pass rules may be needed. This one enables SSH on the external interface::

```
pass in inet proto tcp to $ext_if port ssh
```

This macro definition and rule allows DNS and NTP for internal clients:

```
udp_services = "{ domain, ntp }"
pass quick inet proto { tcp, udp } to any port $udp_services keep state
```

Note the `quick` keyword in this rule. Since the ruleset consists of several rules, it is important to understand the relationships between the rules in a ruleset. Rules are evaluated from top to bottom, in the sequence they are written. For each packet or connection evaluated by PF, *the last matching rule* in the ruleset is the one which is applied. However, when a packet matches a rule which contains the `quick` keyword, the rule processing stops and the packet is treated according to that rule. This is very useful when an exception to the general rules is needed.

29.3.3.2. Creating an FTP Proxy

Configuring working FTP rules can be problematic due to the nature of the FTP protocol. FTP pre-dates firewalls by several decades and is insecure in its design. The most common points against using FTP include:

- Passwords are transferred in the clear.

- The protocol demands the use of at least two TCP connections (control and data) on separate ports.

- When a session is established, data is communicated using randomly selected ports.

All of these points present security challenges, even before considering any potential security weaknesses in client or server software. More secure alternatives for file transfer exist, such as sftp(1) or scp(1), which both feature authentication and data transfer over encrypted connections..

For those situations when FTP is required, PF provides redirection of FTP traffic to a small proxy program called ftp-proxy(8), which is included in the base system of FreeBSD. The role of the proxy is to dynamically insert and delete rules in the ruleset, using a set of anchors, in order to correctly handle FTP traffic.

To enable the FTP proxy, add this line to `/etc/rc.conf` :

```
ftpproxy_enable="YES"
```

Then start the proxy by running `service ftp-proxy start` .

For a basic configuration, three elements need to be added to `/etc/pf.conf` . First, the anchors which the proxy will use to insert the rules it generates for the FTP sessions:

```
nat-anchor "ftp-proxy/*"
rdr-anchor "ftp-proxy/*"
```

Second, a pass rule is needed to allow FTP traffic in to the proxy.

Third, redirection and NAT rules need to be defined before the filtering rules. Insert this `rdr` rule immediately after the `nat` rule:

```
rdr pass on $int_if proto tcp from any to any port ftp -> 127.0.0.1 port 8021
```

Finally, allow the redirected traffic to pass:

```
pass out proto tcp from $proxy to any port ftp
```

where `$proxy` expands to the address the proxy daemon is bound to.

Save `/etc/pf.conf` , load the new rules, and verify from a client that FTP connections are working:

```
# pfctl -f /etc/pf.conf
```

This example covers a basic setup where the clients in the local network need to contact FTP servers elsewhere. This basic configuration should work well with most combinations of FTP clients and servers. As shown in ftp-proxy(8), the proxy's behavior can be changed in various ways by adding options to the `ftpproxy_flags=` line. Some clients or servers may have specific quirks that must be compensated for in the configuration, or there may be a need to integrate the proxy in specific ways such as assigning FTP traffic to a specific queue.

For ways to run an FTP server protected by PF and ftp-proxy(8), configure a separate `ftp-proxy` in reverse mode, using -R, on a separate port with its own redirecting pass rule.

29.3.3.3. Managing ICMP

Many of the tools used for debugging or troubleshooting a TCP/IP network rely on the Internet Control Message Protocol (ICMP), which was designed specifically with debugging in mind.

The ICMP protocol sends and receives *control messages* between hosts and gateways, mainly to provide feedback to a sender about any unusual or difficult conditions enroute to the target host. Routers use ICMP to negotiate packet sizes and other transmission parameters in a process often referred to as *path MTU discovery*.

From a firewall perspective, some ICMP control messages are vulnerable to known attack vectors. Also, letting all diagnostic traffic pass unconditionally makes debugging easier, but it also makes it easier for others to extract information about the network. For these reasons, the following rule may not be optimal:

```
pass inet proto icmp from any to any
```

One solution is to let all ICMP traffic from the local network through while stopping all probes from outside the network:

```
pass inet proto icmp from $localnet to any keep state
pass inet proto icmp from any to $ext_if keep state
```

Additional options are available which demonstrate some of PF's flexibility. For example, rather than allowing all ICMP messages, one can specify the messages used by ping(8) and traceroute(8). Start by defining a macro for that type of message:

```
icmp_types = "echoreq"
```

and a rule which uses the macro:

```
pass inet proto icmp all icmp-type $icmp_types keep state
```

If other types of ICMP packets are needed, expand `icmp_types` to a list of those packet types. Type `more /usr/src/contrib/pf/pfctl/pfctl_parser.c` to see the list of ICMP message types supported by PF. Refer to http://www.iana.org/assignments/icmp-parameters/icmp-parameters.xhtml for an explanation of each message type.

Since Unix `traceroute` uses UDP by default, another rule is needed to allow Unix `traceroute`:

```
# allow out the default range for traceroute(8):
pass out on $ext_if inet proto udp from any to any port 33433 >< 33626 keep state
```

Since TRACERT.EXE on Microsoft Windows systems uses ICMP echo request messages, only the first rule is needed to allow network traces from those systems. Unix `traceroute` can be instructed to use other protocols as well, and will use ICMP echo request messages if -I is used. Check the traceroute(8) man page for details.

29.3.3.3.1. Path MTU Discovery

Internet protocols are designed to be device independent, and one consequence of device independence is that the optimal packet size for a given connection cannot always be predicted reliably. The main constraint on packet size is the *Maximum Transmission Unit* (MTU) which sets the upper limit on the packet size for an interface. Type `ifconfig` to view the MTUs for a system's network interfaces.

TCP/IP uses a process known as path MTU discovery to determine the right packet size for a connection. This process sends packets of varying sizes with the "Do not fragment" flag set, expecting an ICMP return packet of "type 3, code 4" when the upper limit has been reached. Type 3 means "destination unreachable", and code 4 is short for "fragmentation needed, but the do-not-fragment flag is set". To allow path MTU discovery in order to support connections to other MTUs, add the `destination unreachable` type to the `icmp_types` macro:

```
icmp_types = "{ echoreq, unreach }"
```

Since the pass rule already uses that macro, it does not need to be modified in order to support the new ICMP type:

```
pass inet proto icmp all icmp-type $icmp_types keep state
```

PF allows filtering on all variations of ICMP types and codes. The list of possible types and codes are documented in icmp(4) and icmp6(4).

29.3.3.4. Using Tables

Some types of data are relevant to filtering and redirection at a given time, but their definition is too long to be included in the ruleset file. PF supports the use of tables, which are defined lists that can be manipulated without needing to reload the entire ruleset, and which can provide fast lookups. Table names are always enclosed within < >, like this:

```
table <clients> { 192.168.2.0/24, !192.168.2.5 }
```

In this example, the `192.168.2.0/24` network is part of the table, except for the address `192.168.2.5` , which is excluded using the ! operator. It is also possible to load tables from files where each item is on a separate line, as seen in this example `/etc/clients` :

```
192.168.2.0/24
!192.168.2.5
```

To refer to the file, define the table like this:

```
table <clients> persist file "/etc/clients"
```

Once the table is defined, it can be referenced by a rule:

```
pass inet proto tcp from <clients> to any port $client_out flags S/SA keep state
```

A table's contents can be manipulated live, using `pfctl`. This example adds another network to the table:

```
# pfctl -t clients -T add 192.168.1.0/16
```

Note that any changes made this way will take affect now, making them ideal for testing, but will not survive a power failure or reboot. To make the changes permanent, modify the definition of the table in the ruleset or edit the file that the table refers to. One can maintain the on-disk copy of the table using a cron(8) job which dumps the table's contents to disk at regular intervals, using a command such as `pfctl -t clients -T show >/etc/clients` . Alternatively, `/etc/clients` can be updated with the in-memory table contents:

```
# pfctl -t clients -T replace -f /etc/clients
```

29.3.3.5. Using Overload Tables to Protect SSH

Those who run SSH on an external interface have probably seen something like this in the authentication logs:

```
Sep 26 03:12:34 skapet sshd[25771]: Failed password for root from 200.72.41.31 port ↩
40992 ssh2
Sep 26 03:12:34 skapet sshd[5279]: Failed password for root from 200.72.41.31 port ↩
40992 ssh2
Sep 26 03:12:35 skapet sshd[5279]: Received disconnect from 200.72.41.31: 11: Bye Bye
Sep 26 03:12:44 skapet sshd[29635]: Invalid user admin from 200.72.41.31
Sep 26 03:12:44 skapet sshd[24703]: input_userauth_request: invalid user admin
Sep 26 03:12:44 skapet sshd[24703]: Failed password for invalid user admin from ↩
200.72.41.31 port 41484 ssh2
```

This is indicative of a brute force attack where somebody or some program is trying to discover the user name and password which will let them into the system.

If external SSH access is needed for legitimate users, changing the default port used by SSH can offer some protection. However, PF provides a more elegant solution. Pass rules can contain limits on what connecting hosts can do and violators can be banished to a table of addresses which are denied some or all access. It is even possible to drop all existing connections from machines which overreach the limits.

To configure this, create this table in the tables section of the ruleset:

```
table <bruteforce> persist
```

Then, somewhere early in the ruleset, add rules to block brute access while allowing legitimate access:

```
block quick from <bruteforce>
pass inet proto tcp from any to $localnet port $tcp_services \
    flags S/SA keep state \
    (max-src-conn 100, max-src-conn-rate 15/5, \
    overload <bruteforce> flush global)
```

The part in parentheses defines the limits and the numbers should be changed to meet local requirements. It can be read as follows:

`max-src-conn` is the number of simultaneous connections allowed from one host.

`max-src-conn-rate` is the rate of new connections allowed from any single host (*15*) per number of seconds (*5*).

`overload <bruteforce>` means that any host which exceeds these limits gets its address added to the `bruteforce` table. The ruleset blocks all traffic from addresses in the `bruteforce` table.

Finally, `flush global` says that when a host reaches the limit, that all (`global`) of that host's connections will be terminated (`flush`).

Note

These rules will *not* block slow bruteforcers, as described in http://home.nuug.no/~peter/hailmary2013/.

This example ruleset is intended mainly as an illustration. For example, if a generous number of connections in general are wanted, but the desire is to be more restrictive when it comes to ssh, supplement the rule above with something like the one below, early on in the rule set:

```
pass quick proto { tcp, udp } from any to any port ssh \
    flags S/SA keep state \
    (max-src-conn 15, max-src-conn-rate 5/3, \
    overload <bruteforce> flush global)
```

It May Not be Necessary to Block All Overloaders

It is worth noting that the overload mechanism is a general technique which does not apply exclusively to SSH, and it is not always optimal to entirely block all traffic from offenders.

For example, an overload rule could be used to protect a mail service or a web service, and the overload table could be used in a rule to assign offenders to a queue with a minimal bandwidth allocation or to redirect to a specific web page.

Over time, tables will be filled by overload rules and their size will grow incrementally, taking up more memory. Sometimes an IP address that is blocked is a dynamically assigned one, which has since been assigned to a host who has a legitimate reason to communicate with hosts in the local network.

For situations like these, pfctl provides the ability to expire table entries. For example, this command will remove <bruteforce> table entries which have not been referenced for 86400 seconds:

```
# pfctl -t bruteforce -T expire 86400
```

Similar functionality is provided by security/expiretable, which removes table entries which have not been accessed for a specified period of time.

Once installed, expiretable can be run to remove <bruteforce> table entries older than a specified age. This example removes all entries older than 24 hours:

```
/usr/local/sbin/expiretable -v -d -t 24h bruteforce
```

29.3.3.6. Protecting Against SPAM

Not to be confused with the spamd daemon which comes bundled with spamassassin, mail/spamd can be configured with PF to provide an outer defense against SPAM. This spamd hooks into the PF configuration using a set of redirections.

Spammers tend to send a large number of messages, and SPAM is mainly sent from a few spammer friendly networks and a large number of hijacked machines, both of which are reported to *blacklists* fairly quickly.

When an SMTP connection from an address in a blacklist is received, spamd presents its banner and immediately switches to a mode where it answers SMTP traffic one byte at a time. This technique, which is intended to waste as much time as possible on the spammer's end, is called *tarpitting*. The specific implementation which uses one byte SMTP replies is often referred to as *stuttering*.

This example demonstrates the basic procedure for setting up spamd with automatically updated blacklists. Refer to the man pages which are installed with mail/spamd for more information.

Procedure 29.1. Configuring spamd

1. Install the mail/spamd package or port. In order to use spamd's greylisting features, fdescfs(5) must be mounted at /dev/fd. Add the following line to /etc/fstab :

    ```
    fdescfs /dev/fd fdescfs rw 0 0
    ```

    Then, mount the filesystem:

    ```
    # mount fdescfs
    ```

2. Next, edit the PF ruleset to include:

    ```
    table <spamd> persist
    table <spamd-white> persist
    rdr pass on $ext_if inet proto tcp from <spamd> to \
        { $ext_if, $localnet } port smtp -> 127.0.0.1 port 8025
    rdr pass on $ext_if inet proto tcp from !<spamd-white> to \
        { $ext_if, $localnet } port smtp -> 127.0.0.1 port 8025
    ```

    The two tables <spamd> and <spamd-white> are essential. SMTP traffic from an address listed in <spamd> but not in <spamd-white> is redirected to the spamd daemon listening at port 8025.

3. The next step is to configure spamd in /usr/local/etc/spamd.conf and to add some rc.conf parameters.

    The installation of mail/spamd includes a sample configuration file (/usr/local/etc/spamd.conf.sample) and a man page for spamd.conf . Refer to these for additional configuration options beyond those shown in this example.

One of the first lines in the configuration file that does not begin with a # comment sign contains the block which defines the all list, which specifies the lists to use:

```
all:\
    :traplist:whitelist:
```

This entry adds the desired blacklists, separated by colons (:). To use a whitelist to subtract addresses from a blacklist, add the name of the whitelist *immediately* after the name of that blacklist. For example: :blacklist:whitelist:.

This is followed by the specified blacklist's definition:

```
traplist:\
    :black:\
    :msg="SPAM. Your address %A has sent spam within the last 24 hours":\
    :method=http:\
    :file=www.openbsd.org/spamd/traplist.gz
```

where the first line is the name of the blacklist and the second line specifies the list type. The msg field contains the message to display to blacklisted senders during the SMTP dialogue. The method field specifies how spamd-setup fetches the list data; supported methods are http, ftp, from a file in a mounted file system, and via exec of an external program. Finally, the file field specifies the name of the file spamd expects to receive.

The definition of the specified whitelist is similar, but omits the msg field since a message is not needed:

```
whitelist:\
    :white:\
    :method=file:\
    :file=/var/mail/whitelist.txt
```

 ## Choose Data Sources with Care

Using all the blacklists in the sample spamd.conf will blacklist large blocks of the Internet. Administrators need to edit the file to create an optimal configuration which uses applicable data sources and, when necessary, uses custom lists.

Next, add this entry to /etc/rc.conf . Additional flags are described in the man page specified by the comment:

```
spamd_flags="-v" # use "" and see spamd-setup(8) for flags
```

When finished, reload the ruleset, start spamd by typing service start obspamd, and complete the configuration using spamd-setup . Finally, create a cron(8) job which calls spamd-setup to update the tables at reasonable intervals.

On a typical gateway in front of a mail server, hosts will soon start getting trapped within a few seconds to several minutes.

PF also supports *greylisting*, which temporarily rejects messages from unknown hosts with 45n codes. Messages from greylisted hosts which try again within a reasonable time are let through. Traffic from senders which are set up to behave within the limits set by RFC 1123 and RFC 2821 are immediately let through.

More information about greylisting as a technique can be found at the greylisting.org web site. The most amazing thing about greylisting, apart from its simplicity, is that it still works. Spammers and malware writers have been very slow to adapt in order to bypass this technique.

The basic procedure for configuring greylisting is as follows:

Procedure 29.2. Configuring Greylisting

1. Make sure that fdescfs(5) is mounted as described in Step 1 of the previous Procedure.

2. To run spamd in greylisting mode, add this line to /etc/rc.conf :

    ```
    spamd_grey="YES"  # use spamd greylisting if YES
    ```

    Refer to the spamd man page for descriptions of additional related parameters.

3. To complete the greylisting setup:

    ```
    # service restart obspamd
    # service start spamlogd
    ```

Behind the scenes, the spamdb database tool and the spamlogd whitelist updater perform essential functions for the greylisting feature. spamdb is the administrator's main interface to managing the black, grey, and white lists via the contents of the /var/db/spamdb database.

29.3.3.7. Network Hygiene

This section describes how block-policy , scrub, and antispoof can be used to make the ruleset behave sanely.

The block-policy is an option which can be set in the options part of the ruleset, which precedes the redirection and filtering rules. This option determines which feedback, if any, PF sends to hosts that are blocked by a rule. The option has two possible values: drop drops blocked packets with no feedback, and return returns a status code such as Connection refused.

If not set, the default policy is drop. To change the block-policy , specify the desired value:

```
set block-policy return
```

In PF, scrub is a keyword which enables network packet normalization. This process reassembles fragmented packets and drops TCP packets that have invalid flag combinations. Enabling scrub provides a measure of protection against certain kinds of attacks based on incorrect handling of packet fragments. A number of options are available, but the simplest form is suitable for most configurations:

```
scrub in all
```

Some services, such as NFS, require specific fragment handling options. Refer to http://www.openbsd.gr/faq/pf/scrub.html for more information.

This example reassembles fragments, clears the "do not fragment" bit, and sets the maximum segment size to 1440 bytes:

```
scrub in all fragment reassemble no-df max-mss 1440
```

The antispoof mechanism protects against activity from spoofed or forged IP addresses, mainly by blocking packets appearing on interfaces and in directions which are logically not possible.

These rules weed out spoofed traffic coming in from the rest of the world as well as any spoofed packets which originate in the local network:

```
antispoof for $ext_if
antispoof for $int_if
```

29.3.3.8. Handling Non-Routable Addresses

Even with a properly configured gateway to handle network address translation, one may have to compensate for other people's misconfigurations. A common misconfiguration is to let traffic with non-routable addresses out to the Internet. Since traffic from non-routeable addresses can play a part in several DoS attack techniques, consider explicitly blocking traffic from non-routeable addresses from entering the network through the external interface.

In this example, a macro containing non-routable addresses is defined, then used in blocking rules. Traffic to and from these addresses is quietly dropped on the gateway's external interface.

```
martians = "{ 127.0.0.0/8, 192.168.0.0/16, 172.16.0.0/12, \
        10.0.0.0/8, 169.254.0.0/16, 192.0.2.0/24, \
        0.0.0.0/8, 240.0.0.0/4 }"

block drop in quick on $ext_if from $martians to any
block drop out quick on $ext_if from any to $martians
```

29.4. IPFW

IPFW is a stateful firewall written for FreeBSD which supports both IPv4 and IPv6. It is comprised of several components: the kernel firewall filter rule processor and its integrated packet accounting facility, the logging facility, NAT, the dummynet(4) traffic shaper, a forward facility, a bridge facility, and an ipstealth facility.

FreeBSD provides a sample ruleset in /etc/rc.firewall which defines several firewall types for common scenarios to assist novice users in generating an appropriate ruleset. IPFW provides a powerful syntax which advanced users can use to craft customized rulesets that meet the security requirements of a given environment.

This section describes how to enable IPFW, provides an overview of its rule syntax, and demonstrates several rulesets for common configuration scenarios.

29.4.1. Enabling IPFW

IPFW is included in the basic FreeBSD install as a kernel loadable module, meaning that a custom kernel is not needed in order to enable IPFW.

For those users who wish to statically compile IPFW support into a custom kernel, refer to the instructions in Chapter 8, *Configuring the FreeBSD Kernel*. The following options are available for the custom kernel configuration file:

```
options    IPFIREWALL    # enables IPFW
options    IPFIREWALL_VERBOSE  # enables logging for rules with log keyword
options    IPFIREWALL_VERBOSE_LIMIT=5 # limits number of logged packets per-entry
options    IPFIREWALL_DEFAULT_TO_ACCEPT # sets default policy to pass what is not ʊ
explicitly denied
options    IPDIVERT    # enables NAT
```

To configure the system to enable IPFW at boot time, add the following entry to /etc/rc.conf :

```
firewall_enable="YES"
```

To use one of the default firewall types provided by FreeBSD, add another line which specifies the type:

```
firewall_type="open"
```

The available types are:

- open: passes all traffic.

- client: protects only this machine.

- simple: protects the whole network.

- closed: entirely disables IP traffic except for the loopback interface.

- workstation: protects only this machine using stateful rules.

- UNKNOWN: disables the loading of firewall rules.

- `filename`: full path of the file containing the firewall ruleset.

If `firewall_type` is set to either `client` or `simple`, modify the default rules found in `/etc/rc.firewall` to fit the configuration of the system.

Note that the `filename` type is used to load a custom ruleset.

An alternate way to load a custom ruleset is to set the `firewall_script` variable to the absolute path of an *executable script* that includes IPFW commands. The examples used in this section assume that the `firewall_script` is set to `/etc/ipfw.rules` :

```
firewall_script="/etc/ipfw.rules"
```

To enable logging, include this line:

```
firewall_logging="YES"
```

There is no `/etc/rc.conf` variable to set logging limits. To limit the number of times a rule is logged per connection attempt, specify the number using this line in `/etc/sysctl.conf` :

```
net.inet.ip.fw.verbose_limit=5
```

After saving the needed edits, start the firewall. To enable logging limits now, also set the `sysctl` value specified above:

```
# service ipfw start
# sysctl net.inet.ip.fw.verbose_limit= 5
```

29.4.2. IPFW Rule Syntax

When a packet enters the IPFW firewall, it is compared against the first rule in the ruleset and progresses one rule at a time, moving from top to bottom in sequence. When the packet matches the selection parameters of a rule, the rule's action is executed and the search of the ruleset terminates for that packet. This is referred to as "first match wins". If the packet does not match any of the rules, it gets caught by the mandatory IPFW default rule number 65535, which denies all packets and silently discards them. However, if the packet matches a rule that contains the `count`, `skipto`, or `tee` keywords, the search continues. Refer to ipfw(8) for details on how these keywords affect rule processing.

When creating an IPFW rule, keywords must be written in the following order. Some keywords are mandatory while other keywords are optional. The words shown in uppercase represent a variable and the words shown in lowercase must precede the variable that follows it. The # symbol is used to mark the start of a comment and may appear at the end of a rule or on its own line. Blank lines are ignored.

CMD RULE_NUMBER set SET_NUMBER ACTION log LOG_AMOUNT PROTO from SRC SRC_PORT to DST DST_PORT OPTIONS

This section provides an overview of these keywords and their options. It is not an exhaustive list of every possible option. Refer to ipfw(8) for a complete description of the rule syntax that can be used when creating IPFW rules.

CMD
: Every rule must start with *ipfw add*.

RULE_NUMBER
: Each rule is associated with a number from 1 to 65534. The number is used to indicate the order of rule processing. Multiple rules can have the same number, in which case they are applied according to the order in which they have been added.

SET_NUMBER
: Each rule is associated with a set number from 0 to 31. Sets can be individually disabled or enabled, making it possible to quickly add or delete a set of rules. If a SET_NUMBER is not specified, the rule will be added to set 0.

ACTION

A rule can be associated with one of the following actions. The specified action will be executed when the packet matches the selection criterion of the rule.

allow | *accept* | *pass* | *permit*: these keywords are equivalent and allow packets that match the rule.

check-state : checks the packet against the dynamic state table. If a match is found, execute the action associated with the rule which generated this dynamic rule, otherwise move to the next rule. A check-state rule does not have selection criterion. If no check-state rule is present in the ruleset, the dynamic rules table is checked at the first keep-state or limit rule.

count: updates counters for all packets that match the rule. The search continues with the next rule.

deny | *drop*: either word silently discards packets that match this rule.

Additional actions are available. Refer to ipfw(8) for details.

LOG_AMOUNT

When a packet matches a rule with the log keyword, a message will be logged to syslogd(8) with a facility name of SECURITY. Logging only occurs if the number of packets logged for that particular rule does not exceed a specified LOG_AMOUNT. If no LOG_AMOUNT is specified, the limit is taken from the value of net.inet.ip.fw.verbose_limit. A value of zero removes the logging limit. Once the limit is reached, logging can be re-enabled by clearing the logging counter or the packet counter for that rule, using ipfw reset log.

> **Note**
>
> Logging is done after all other packet matching conditions have been met, and before performing the final action on the packet. The administrator decides which rules to enable logging on.

PROTO

This optional value can be used to specify any protocol name or number found in /etc/protocols.

SRC

The from keyword must be followed by the source address or a keyword that represents the source address. An address can be represented by any, me (any address configured on an interface on this system), me6, (any IPv6 address configured on an interface on this system), or table followed by the number of a lookup table which contains a list of addresses. When specifying an IP address, it can be optionally followed by its CIDR mask or subnet mask. For example, 1.2.3.4/25 or 1.2.3.4:255.255.255.128 .

SRC_PORT

An optional source port can be specified using the port number or name from /etc/services.

DST

The to keyword must be followed by the destination address or a keyword that represents the destination address. The same keywords and addresses described in the SRC section can be used to describe the destination.

DST_PORT

An optional destination port can be specified using the port number or name from /etc/services.

OPTIONS

Several keywords can follow the source and destination. As the name suggests, OPTIONS are optional. Commonly used options include in or out, which specify the direction of packet flow, icmptypes followed by the type of ICMP message, and keep-state .

When a *keep-state* rule is matched, the firewall will create a dynamic rule which matches bidirectional traffic between the source and destination addresses and ports using the same protocol.

The dynamic rules facility is vulnerable to resource depletion from a SYN-flood attack which would open a huge number of dynamic rules. To counter this type of attack with IPFW, use limit. This option limits the number of simultaneous sessions by checking the open dynamic rules, counting the number of times this rule and IP address combination occurred. If this count is greater than the value specified by limit, the packet is discarded.

Dozens of OPTIONS are available. Refer to ipfw(8) for a description of each available option.

29.4.3. Example Ruleset

This section demonstrates how to create an example stateful firewall ruleset script named /etc/ipfw.rules . In this example, all connection rules use in or out to clarify the direction. They also use via *interface-name* to specify the interface the packet is traveling over.

> Note
>
> When first creating or testing a firewall ruleset, consider temporarily setting this tunable:
>
> ```
> net.inet.ip.fw.default_to_accept="1"
> ```
>
> This sets the default policy of ipfw(8) to be more permissive than the default deny ip from any to any, making it slightly more difficult to get locked out of the system right after a reboot.

The firewall script begins by indicating that it is a Bourne shell script and flushes any existing rules. It then creates the cmd variable so that ipfw add does not have to be typed at the beginning of every rule. It also defines the pif variable which represents the name of the interface that is attached to the Internet.

```
#!/bin/sh
# Flush out the list before we begin.
ipfw -q -f flush

# Set rules command prefix
cmd="ipfw -q add"
pif="dc0"     # interface name of NIC attached to Internet
```

The first two rules allow all traffic on the trusted internal interface and on the loopback interface:

```
# Change xl0 to LAN NIC interface name
$cmd 00005 allow all from any to any via xl0

# No restrictions on Loopback Interface
$cmd 00010 allow all from any to any via lo0
```

The next rule allows the packet through if it matches an existing entry in the dynamic rules table:

```
$cmd 00101 check-state
```

The next set of rules defines which stateful connections internal systems can create to hosts on the Internet:

```
# Allow access to public DNS
# Replace x.x.x.x with the IP address of a public DNS server
# and repeat for each DNS server in /etc/resolv.conf
$cmd 00110 allow tcp from any to x.x.x.x 53 out via $pif setup keep-state
$cmd 00111 allow udp from any to x.x.x.x 53 out via $pif keep-state

# Allow access to ISP's DHCP server for cable/DSL configurations.
# Use the first rule and check log for IP address.
# Then, uncomment the second rule, input the IP address, and delete the first rule
```

```
$cmd 00120 allow log udp from any to any 67 out via $pif keep-state
#$cmd 00120 allow udp from any to x.x.x.x 67 out via $pif keep-state

# Allow outbound HTTP and HTTPS connections
$cmd 00200 allow tcp from any to any 80 out via $pif setup keep-state
$cmd 00220 allow tcp from any to any 443 out via $pif setup keep-state

# Allow outbound email connections
$cmd 00230 allow tcp from any to any 25 out via $pif setup keep-state
$cmd 00231 allow tcp from any to any 110 out via $pif setup keep-state

# Allow outbound ping
$cmd 00250 allow icmp from any to any out via $pif keep-state

# Allow outbound NTP
$cmd 00260 allow tcp from any to any 37 out via $pif setup keep-state

# Allow outbound SSH
$cmd 00280 allow tcp from any to any 22 out via $pif setup keep-state

# deny and log all other outbound connections
$cmd 00299 deny log all from any to any out via $pif
```

The next set of rules controls connections from Internet hosts to the internal network. It starts by denying packets typically associated with attacks and then explicitly allows specific types of connections. All the authorized services that originate from the Internet use limit to prevent flooding.

```
# Deny all inbound traffic from non-routable reserved address spaces
$cmd 00300 deny all from 192.168.0.0/16 to any in via $pif    #RFC 1918 private IP
$cmd 00301 deny all from 172.16.0.0/12 to any in via $pif     #RFC 1918 private IP
$cmd 00302 deny all from 10.0.0.0/8 to any in via $pif        #RFC 1918 private IP
$cmd 00303 deny all from 127.0.0.0/8 to any in via $pif       #loopback
$cmd 00304 deny all from 0.0.0.0/8 to any in via $pif         #loopback
$cmd 00305 deny all from 169.254.0.0/16 to any in via $pif    #DHCP auto-config
$cmd 00306 deny all from 192.0.2.0/24 to any in via $pif      #reserved for docs
$cmd 00307 deny all from 204.152.64.0/23 to any in via $pif   #Sun cluster interconnect
$cmd 00308 deny all from 224.0.0.0/3 to any in via $pif       #Class D & E multicast

# Deny public pings
$cmd 00310 deny icmp from any to any in via $pif

# Deny ident
$cmd 00315 deny tcp from any to any 113 in via $pif

# Deny all Netbios services.
$cmd 00320 deny tcp from any to any 137 in via $pif
$cmd 00321 deny tcp from any to any 138 in via $pif
$cmd 00322 deny tcp from any to any 139 in via $pif
$cmd 00323 deny tcp from any to any 81 in via $pif

# Deny fragments
$cmd 00330 deny all from any to any frag in via $pif

# Deny ACK packets that did not match the dynamic rule table
$cmd 00332 deny tcp from any to any established in via $pif

# Allow traffic from ISP's DHCP server.
# Replace x.x.x.x with the same IP address used in rule 00120.
#$cmd 00360 allow udp from any to x.x.x.x 67 in via $pif keep-state

# Allow HTTP connections to internal web server
$cmd 00400 allow tcp from any to me 80 in via $pif setup limit src-addr 2

# Allow inbound SSH connections
$cmd 00410 allow tcp from any to me 22 in via $pif setup limit src-addr 2
```

```
# Reject and log all other incoming connections
$cmd 00499 deny log all from any to any in via $pif
```

The last rule logs all packets that do not match any of the rules in the ruleset:

```
# Everything else is denied and logged
$cmd 00999 deny log all from any to any
```

29.4.4. Configuring NAT

Contributed by Chern Lee.

FreeBSD's built-in NAT daemon, natd(8), works in conjunction with IPFW to provide network address translation. This can be used to provide an Internet Connection Sharing solution so that several internal computers can connect to the Internet using a single IP address.

To do this, the FreeBSD machine connected to the Internet must act as a gateway. This system must have two NICs, where one is connected to the Internet and the other is connected to the internal LAN. Each machine connected to the LAN should be assigned an IP address in the private network space, as defined by RFC 1918, and have the default gateway set to the natd(8) system's internal IP address.

Some additional configuration is needed in order to activate the NAT function of IPFW. If the system has a custom kernel, the kernel configuration file needs to include **option IPDIVERT** along with the other **IPFIREWALL** options described in Section 29.4.1, "Enabling IPFW".

To enable NAT support at boot time, the following must be in /etc/rc.conf :

```
gateway_enable="YES"  # enables the gateway
natd_enable="YES"  # enables NAT
natd_interface="rl0"  # specify interface name of NIC attached to Internet
natd_flags="-dynamic -m" # -m = preserve port numbers; additional options are listed ↵
in natd(8)
```

> ### Note
>
> It is also possible to specify a configuration file which contains the options to pass to natd(8):
>
> ```
> natd_flags="-f /etc/natd.conf"
> ```
>
> The specified file must contain a list of configuration options, one per line. For example:
>
> ```
> redirect_port tcp 192.168.0.2:6667 6667
> redirect_port tcp 192.168.0.3:80 80
> ```
>
> For more information about this configuration file, consult natd(8).

Next, add the NAT rules to the firewall ruleset. When the rulest contains stateful rules, the positioning of the NAT rules is critical and the **skipto** action is used. The **skipto** action requires a rule number so that it knows which rule to jump to.

The following example builds upon the firewall ruleset shown in the previous section. It adds some additional entries and modifies some existing rules in order to configure the firewall for NAT. It starts by adding some additional variables which represent the rule number to skip to, the **keep-state** option, and a list of TCP ports which will be used to reduce the number of rules:

```
#!/bin/sh
ipfw -q -f flush
cmd="ipfw -q add"
skip="skipto 500"
```

```
pif=dc0
ks="keep-state"
good_tcpo="22,25,37,53,80,443,110"
```

The inbound NAT rule is inserted *after* the two rules which allow all traffic on the trusted internal interface and on the loopback interface and *before* the check-state rule. It is important that the rule number selected for this NAT rule, in this example 100, is higher than the first two rules and lower than the check-state rule:

```
$cmd 005 allow all from any to any via xl0  # exclude LAN traffic
$cmd 010 allow all from any to any via lo0  # exclude loopback traffic
$cmd 100 divert natd ip from any to any in via $pif # NAT any inbound packets
# Allow the packet through if it has an existing entry in the dynamic rules table
$cmd 101 check-state
```

The outbound rules are modified to replace the allow action with the $skip variable, indicating that rule processing will continue at rule 500. The seven tcp rules have been replaced by rule 125 as the $good_tcpo variable contains the seven allowed outbound ports.

```
# Authorized outbound packets
$cmd 120 $skip udp from any to x.x.x.x 53 out via $pif $ks
$cmd 121 $skip udp from any to x.x.x.x 67 out via $pif $ks
$cmd 125 $skip tcp from any to any $good_tcpo out via $pif setup $ks
$cmd 130 $skip icmp from any to any out via $pif $ks
```

The inbound rules remain the same, except for the very last rule which removes the via $pif in order to catch both inbound and outbound rules. The NAT rule must follow this last outbound rule, must have a higher number than that last rule, and the rule number must be referenced by the skipto action. In this ruleset, rule number 500 diverts all packets which match the outbound rules to natd(8) for NAT processing. The next rule allows any packet which has undergone NAT processing to pass.

```
$cmd 499 deny log all from any to any
$cmd 500 divert natd ip from any to any out via $pif # skipto location for outbound ↺
stateful rules
$cmd 510 allow ip from any to any
```

In this example, rules 100, 101, 125, 500, and 510 control the address translation of the outbound and inbound packets so that the entries in the dynamic state table always register the private LAN IP address.

Consider an internal web browser which initializes a new outbound HTTP session over port 80. When the first outbound packet enters the firewall, it does not match rule 100 because it is headed out rather than in. It passes rule 101 because this is the first packet and it has not been posted to the dynamic state table yet. The packet finally matches rule 125 as it is outbound on an allowed port and has a source IP address from the internal LAN. On matching this rule, two actions take place. First, the keep-state action adds an entry to the dynamic state table and the specified action, skipto rule 500, is executed. Next, the packet undergoes NAT and is sent out to the Internet. This packet makes its way to the destination web server, where a response packet is generated and sent back. This new packet enters the top of the ruleset. It matches rule 100 and has its destination IP address mapped back to the original internal address. It then is processed by the check-state rule, is found in the table as an existing session, and is released to the LAN.

On the inbound side, the ruleset has to deny bad packets and allow only authorized services. A packet which matches an inbound rule is posted to the dynamic state table and the packet is released to the LAN. The packet generated as a response is recognized by the check-state rule as belonging to an existing session. It is then sent to rule 500 to undergo NAT before being released to the outbound interface.

29.4.4.1. Port Redirection

The drawback with natd(8) is that the LAN clients are not accessible from the Internet. Clients on the LAN can make outgoing connections to the world but cannot receive incoming ones. This presents a problem if trying to run Internet services on one of the LAN client machines. A simple way around this is to redirect selected Internet ports on the natd(8) machine to a LAN client.

For example, an IRC server runs on client **A** and a web server runs on client **B**. For this to work properly, connections received on ports 6667 (IRC) and 80 (HTTP) must be redirected to the respective machines.

The syntax for -redirect_port is as follows:

```
-redirect_port proto targetIP:targetPORT[-targetPORT]
            [aliasIP:]aliasPORT[-aliasPORT]
            [remoteIP[:remotePORT[-remotePORT]]]
```

In the above example, the argument should be:

```
-redirect_port tcp 192.168.0.2:6667 6667
-redirect_port tcp 192.168.0.3:80 80
```

This redirects the proper TCP ports to the LAN client machines.

Port ranges over individual ports can be indicated with -redirect_port. For example, *tcp 192.168.0.2:2000-3000 2000-3000* would redirect all connections received on ports 2000 to 3000 to ports 2000 to 3000 on client **A**.

These options can be used when directly running natd(8), placed within the natd_flags="" option in /etc/rc.conf, or passed via a configuration file.

For further configuration options, consult natd(8)

29.4.4.2. Address Redirection

Address redirection is useful if more than one IP address is available. Each LAN client can be assigned its own external IP address by natd(8), which will then rewrite outgoing packets from the LAN clients with the proper external IP address and redirects all traffic incoming on that particular IP address back to the specific LAN client. This is also known as static NAT. For example, if IP addresses 128.1.1.1, 128.1.1.2, and 128.1.1.3 are available, 128.1.1.1 can be used as the natd(8) machine's external IP address, while 128.1.1.2 and 128.1.1.3 are forwarded back to LAN clients **A** and **B**.

The -redirect_address syntax is as follows:

```
-redirect_address localIP publicIP
```

localIP	The internal IP address of the LAN client.
publicIP	The external IP address corresponding to the LAN client.

In the example, this argument would read:

```
-redirect_address 192.168.0.2 128.1.1.2
-redirect_address 192.168.0.3 128.1.1.3
```

Like -redirect_port, these arguments are placed within the natd_flags="" option of /etc/rc.conf, or passed via a configuration file. With address redirection, there is no need for port redirection since all data received on a particular IP address is redirected.

The external IP addresses on the natd(8) machine must be active and aliased to the external interface. Refer to rc.conf(5) for details.

29.4.5. The IPFW Command

ipfw can be used to make manual, single rule additions or deletions to the active firewall while it is running. The problem with using this method is that all the changes are lost when the system reboots. It is recommended to instead write all the rules in a file and to use that file to load the rules at boot time and to replace the currently running firewall rules whenever that file changes.

`ipfw` is a useful way to display the running firewall rules to the console screen. The IPFW accounting facility dynamically creates a counter for each rule that counts each packet that matches the rule. During the process of testing a rule, listing the rule with its counter is one way to determine if the rule is functioning as expected.

To list all the running rules in sequence:

```
# ipfw list
```

To list all the running rules with a time stamp of when the last time the rule was matched:

```
# ipfw -t list
```

The next example lists accounting information and the packet count for matched rules along with the rules themselves. The first column is the rule number, followed by the number of matched packets and bytes, followed by the rule itself.

```
# ipfw -a list
```

To list dynamic rules in addition to static rules:

```
# ipfw -d list
```

To also show the expired dynamic rules:

```
# ipfw -d -e list
```

To zero the counters:

```
# ipfw zero
```

To zero the counters for just the rule with number *NUM*:

```
# ipfw zero NUM
```

29.4.5.1. Logging Firewall Messages

Even with the logging facility enabled, IPFW will not generate any rule logging on its own. The firewall administrator decides which rules in the ruleset will be logged, and adds the `log` keyword to those rules. Normally only deny rules are logged. It is customary to duplicate the "ipfw default deny everything" rule with the `log` keyword included as the last rule in the ruleset. This way, it is possible to see all the packets that did not match any of the rules in the ruleset.

Logging is a two edged sword. If one is not careful, an over abundance of log data or a DoS attack can fill the disk with log files. Log messages are not only written to syslogd, but also are displayed on the root console screen and soon become annoying.

The `IPFIREWALL_VERBOSE_LIMIT=5` kernel option limits the number of consecutive messages sent to syslogd(8), concerning the packet matching of a given rule. When this option is enabled in the kernel, the number of consecutive messages concerning a particular rule is capped at the number specified. There is nothing to be gained from 200 identical log messages. With this option set to five, five consecutive messages concerning a particular rule would be logged to syslogd and the remainder identical consecutive messages would be counted and posted to syslogd with a phrase like the following:

```
last message repeated 45 times
```

All logged packets messages are written by default to `/var/log/security` , which is defined in `/etc/syslog.conf` .

29.4.5.2. Building a Rule Script

Most experienced IPFW users create a file containing the rules and code them in a manner compatible with running them as a script. The major benefit of doing this is the firewall rules can be refreshed in mass without the need of rebooting the system to activate them. This method is convenient in testing new rules as the procedure can be executed as many times as needed. Being a script, symbolic substitution can be used for frequently used values to be substituted into multiple rules.

This example script is compatible with the syntax used by the sh(1), csh(1), and tcsh(1) shells. Symbolic substitution fields are prefixed with a dollar sign ($). Symbolic fields do not have the $ prefix. The value to populate the symbolic field must be enclosed in double quotes ("").

Start the rules file like this:

```
############### start of example ipfw rules script #############
#
ipfw -q -f flush        # Delete all rules
# Set defaults
oif="tun0"              # out interface
odns="192.0.2.11"       # ISP's DNS server IP address
cmd="ipfw -q add "      # build rule prefix
ks="keep-state"         # just too lazy to key this each time
$cmd 00500 check-state
$cmd 00502 deny all from any to any frag
$cmd 00501 deny tcp from any to any established
$cmd 00600 allow tcp from any to any 80 out via $oif setup $ks
$cmd 00610 allow tcp from any to $odns 53 out via $oif setup $ks
$cmd 00611 allow udp from any to $odns 53 out via $oif $ks
################## End of example ipfw rules script ###########
```

The rules are not important as the focus of this example is how the symbolic substitution fields are populated.

If the above example was in /etc/ipfw.rules , the rules could be reloaded by the following command:

```
# sh /etc/ipfw.rules
```

/etc/ipfw.rules can be located anywhere and the file can have any name.

The same thing could be accomplished by running these commands by hand:

```
# ipfw -q -f flush
# ipfw -q add check-state
# ipfw -q add deny all from any to any frag
# ipfw -q add deny tcp from any to any established
# ipfw -q add allow tcp from any to any 80 out via tun0 setup keep-state
# ipfw -q add allow tcp from any to 192.0.2.11 53 out via tun0 setup keep-state
# ipfw -q add 00611 allow udp from any to 192.0.2.11 53 out via tun0 keep-state
```

29.5. IPFILTER (IPF)

IPFILTER, also known as IPF, is a cross-platform, open source firewall which has been ported to several operating systems, including FreeBSD, NetBSD, OpenBSD, and Solaris™.

IPFILTER is a kernel-side firewall and NAT mechanism that can be controlled and monitored by userland programs. Firewall rules can be set or deleted using ipf, NAT rules can be set or deleted using ipnat, run-time statistics for the kernel parts of IPFILTER can be printed using ipfstat, and ipmon can be used to log IPFILTER actions to the system log files.

IPF was originally written using a rule processing logic of "the last matching rule wins" and only used stateless rules. Since then, IPF has been enhanced to include the quick and keep state options.

The IPF FAQ is at http://www.phildev.net/ipf/index.html . A searchable archive of the IPFilter mailing list is available at http://marc.info/?l=ipfilter .

This section of the Handbook focuses on IPF as it pertains to FreeBSD. It provides examples of rules that contain the quick and keep state options.

29.5.1. Enabling IPF

IPF is included in the basic FreeBSD install as a kernel loadable module, meaning that a custom kernel is not needed in order to enable IPF.

For users who prefer to statically compile IPF support into a custom kernel, refer to the instructions in Chapter 8, *Configuring the FreeBSD Kernel*. The following kernel options are available:

```
options IPFILTER
options IPFILTER_LOG
options IPFILTER_LOOKUP
options IPFILTER_DEFAULT_BLOCK
```

where `options IPFILTER` enables support for IPFILTER, `options IPFILTER_LOG` enables IPF logging using the `ipl` packet logging pseudo-device for every rule that has the `log` keyword, `IPFILTER_LOOKUP` enables IP pools in order to speed up IP lookups, and `options IPFILTER_DEFAULT_BLOCK` changes the default behavior so that any packet not matching a firewall `pass` rule gets blocked.

To configure the system to enable IPF at boot time, add the following entries to `/etc/rc.conf`. These entries will also enable logging and `default pass all`. To change the default policy to `block all` without compiling a custom kernel, remember to add a `block all` rule at the end of the ruleset.

```
ipfilter_enable="YES"              # Start ipf firewall
ipfilter_rules="/etc/ipf.rules"    # loads rules definition text file
ipmon_enable="YES"                 # Start IP monitor log
ipmon_flags="-Ds"                  # D = start as daemon
                                   # s = log to syslog
                                   # v = log tcp window, ack, seq
                                   # n = map IP & port to names
```

If NAT functionality is needed, also add these lines:

```
gateway_enable="YES"               # Enable as LAN gateway
ipnat_enable="YES"                 # Start ipnat function
ipnat_rules="/etc/ipnat.rules"     # rules definition file for ipnat
```

Then, to start IPF now:

```
# service ipfilter start
```

To load the firewall rules, specify the name of the ruleset file using `ipf`. The following command can be used to replace the currently running firewall rules:

```
# ipf -Fa -f /etc/ipf.rules
```

where `-Fa` flushes all the internal rules tables and `-f` specifies the file containing the rules to load.

This provides the ability to make changes to a custom ruleset and update the running firewall with a fresh copy of the rules without having to reboot the system. This method is convenient for testing new rules as the procedure can be executed as many times as needed.

Refer to ipf(8) for details on the other flags available with this command.

29.5.2. IPF Rule Syntax

This section describes the IPF rule syntax used to create stateful rules. When creating rules, keep in mind that unless the **quick** keyword appears in a rule, every rule is read in order, with the *last matching rule* being the one that is applied. This means that even if the first rule to match a packet is a **pass**, if there is a later matching rule that is a **block**, the packet will be dropped. Sample rulesets can be found in `/usr/share/examples/ipfilter`.

When creating rules, a # character is used to mark the start of a comment and may appear at the end of a rule, to explain that rule's function, or on its own line. Any blank lines are ignored.

The keywords which are used in rules must be written in a specific order, from left to right. Some keywords are mandatory while others are optional. Some keywords have sub-options which may be keywords themselves and also include more sub-options. The keyword order is as follows, where the words shown in uppercase represent a variable and the words shown in lowercase must precede the variable that follows it:

`ACTION DIRECTION OPTIONS proto PROTO_TYPE from SRC_ADDR SRC_PORT to DST_ADDR DST_PORT TCP_FLAG| ICMP_TYPE keep state STATE`

This section describes each of these keywords and their options. It is not an exhaustive list of every possible option. Refer to ipf(5) for a complete description of the rule syntax that can be used when creating IPF rules and examples for using each keyword.

ACTION

The action keyword indicates what to do with the packet if it matches that rule. Every rule *must* have an action. The following actions are recognized:

`block`: drops the packet.

`pass`: allows the packet.

`log`: generates a log record.

`count`: counts the number of packets and bytes which can provide an indication of how often a rule is used.

`auth`: queues the packet for further processing by another program.

`call`: provides access to functions built into IPF that allow more complex actions.

`decapsulate`: removes any headers in order to process the contents of the packet.

DIRECTION

Next, each rule must explicitly state the direction of traffic using one of these keywords:

`in`: the rule is applied against an inbound packet.

`out`: the rule is applied against an outbound packet.

`all`: the rule applies to either direction.

If the system has multiple interfaces, the interface can be specified along with the direction. An example would be `in on fxp0`.

OPTIONS

Options are optional. However, if multiple options are specified, they must be used in the order shown here.

`log`: when performing the specified ACTION, the contents of the packet's headers will be written to the ipl(4) packet log pseudo-device.

`quick`: if a packet matches this rule, the ACTION specified by the rule occurs and no further processing of any following rules will occur for this packet.

`on`: must be followed by the interface name as displayed by ifconfig(8). The rule will only match if the packet is going through the specified interface in the specified direction.

When using the `log` keyword, the following qualifiers may be used in this order:

`body`: indicates that the first 128 bytes of the packet contents will be logged after the headers.

`first`: if the `log` keyword is being used in conjunction with a `keep state` option, this option is recommended so that only the triggering packet is logged and not every packet which matches the stateful connection.

Additional options are available to specify error return messages. Refer to ipf(5) for more details.

PROTO_TYPE

The protocol type is optional. However, it is mandatory if the rule needs to specify a SRC_PORT or a DST_PORT as it defines the type of protocol. When specifying the type of protocol, use the proto keyword followed by either a protocol number or name from /etc/protocols. Example protocol names include tcp, udp, or icmp. If PROTO_TYPE is specified but no SRC_PORT or DST_PORT is specified, all port numbers for that protocol will match that rule.

SRC_ADDR

The from keyword is mandatory and is followed by a keyword which represents the source of the packet. The source can be a hostname, an IP address followed by the CIDR mask, an address pool, or the keyword all. Refer to ipf(5) for examples.

There is no way to match ranges of IP addresses which do not express themselves easily using the dotted numeric form / mask-length notation. The net-mgmt/ipcalc package or port may be used to ease the calculation of the CIDR mask. Additional information is available at the utility's web page: http://jodies.de/ipcalc .

SRC_PORT

The port number of the source is optional. However, if it is used, it requires PROTO_TYPE to be first defined in the rule. The port number must also be preceded by the proto keyword.

A number of different comparison operators are supported: = (equal to), != (not equal to), < (less than), > (greater than), <= (less than or equal to), and >= (greater than or equal to).

To specify port ranges, place the two port numbers between <> (less than and greater than), >< (greater than and less than), or : (greater than or equal to and less than or equal to).

DST_ADDR

The to keyword is mandatory and is followed by a keyword which represents the destination of the packet. Similar to SRC_ADDR, it can be a hostname, an IP address followed by the CIDR mask, an address pool, or the keyword all.

DST_PORT

Similar to SRC_PORT, the port number of the destination is optional. However, if it is used, it requires PROTO_TYPE to be first defined in the rule. The port number must also be preceded by the proto keyword.

TCP_FLAG|ICMP_TYPE

If tcp is specifed as the PROTO_TYPE, flags can be specified as letters, where each letter represents one of the possible TCP flags used to determine the state of a connection. Possible values are: S (SYN), A (ACK), P (PSH), F (FIN), U (URG), R (RST), C (CWN), and E (ECN).

If icmp is specifed as the PROTO_TYPE, the ICMP type to match can be specified. Refer to ipf(5) for the allowable types.

STATE

If a pass rule contains keep state, IPF will add an entry to its dynamic state table and allow subsequent packets that match the connection. IPF can track state for TCP, UDP, and ICMP sessions. Any packet that IPF can be certain is part of an active session, even if it is a different protocol, will be allowed.

In IPF, packets destined to go out through the interface connected to the public Internet are first checked against the dynamic state table. If the packet matches the next expected packet comprising an active session conversation, it exits the firewall and the state of the session conversation flow is updated in the dynamic state table. Packets that do not belong to an already active session are checked against the outbound ruleset. Packets coming in from the interface connected to the public Internet are first checked against the dynamic state table. If the packet matches the next expected packet comprising an active session, it exits the firewall and the state of the session conversation flow is updated in the dynamic state table. Packets that do not belong to an already active session are checked against the inbound ruleset.

Several keywords can be added after `keep state`. If used, these keywords set various options that control stateful filtering, such as setting connection limits or connection age. Refer to ipf(5) for the list of available options and their descriptions.

29.5.3. Example Ruleset

This section demonstrates how to create an example ruleset which only allows services matching `pass` rules and blocks all others.

FreeBSD uses the loopback interface (`lo0`) and the IP address `127.0.0.1` for internal communication. The firewall ruleset must contain rules to allow free movement of these internally used packets:

```
# no restrictions on loopback interface
pass in quick on lo0 all
pass out quick on lo0 all
```

The public interface connected to the Internet is used to authorize and control access of all outbound and inbound connections. If one or more interfaces are cabled to private networks, those internal interfaces may require rules to allow packets originating from the LAN to flow between the internal networks or to the interface attached to the Internet. The ruleset should be organized into three major sections: any trusted internal interfaces, outbound connections through the public interface, and inbound connections through the public interface.

These two rules allow all traffic to pass through a trusted LAN interface named `xl0`:

```
# no restrictions on inside LAN interface for private network
pass out quick on xl0 all
pass in quick on xl0 all
```

The rules for the public interface's outbound and inbound sections should have the most frequently matched rules placed before less commonly matched rules, with the last rule in the section blocking and logging all packets for that interface and direction.

This set of rules defines the outbound section of the public interface named `dc0`. These rules keep state and identify the specific services that internal systems are authorized for public Internet access. All the rules use `quick` and specify the appropriate port numbers and, where applicable, destination addresses.

```
# interface facing Internet (outbound)
# Matches session start requests originating from or behind the
# firewall, destined for the Internet.

# Allow outbound access to public DNS servers.
# Replace x.x.x. with address listed in /etc/resolv.conf.
# Repeat for each DNS server.
pass out quick on dc0 proto tcp from any to x.x.x. port = 53 flags S keep state
pass out quick on dc0 proto udp from any to xxx port = 53 keep state

# Allow access to ISP's specified DHCP server for cable or DSL networks.
# Use the first rule, then check log for the IP address of DHCP server.
# Then, uncomment the second rule, replace z.z.z.z with the IP address,
# and comment out the first rule
pass out log quick on dc0 proto udp from any to any port = 67 keep state
#pass out quick on dc0 proto udp from any to z.z.z.z port = 67 keep state

# Allow HTTP and HTTPS
pass out quick on dc0 proto tcp from any to any port = 80 flags S keep state
pass out quick on dc0 proto tcp from any to any port = 443 flags S keep state

# Allow email
pass out quick on dc0 proto tcp from any to any port = 110 flags S keep state
pass out quick on dc0 proto tcp from any to any port = 25 flags S keep state

# Allow NTP
pass out quick on dc0 proto tcp from any to any port = 37 flags S keep state
```

```
# Allow FTP
pass out quick on dc0 proto tcp from any to any port = 21 flags S keep state

# Allow SSH
pass out quick on dc0 proto tcp from any to any port = 22 flags S keep state

# Allow ping
pass out quick on dc0 proto icmp from any to any icmp-type 8 keep state

# Block and log everything else
block out log first quick on dc0 all
```

This example of the rules in the inbound section of the public interface blocks all undesirable packets first. This reduces the number of packets that are logged by the last rule.

```
# interface facing Internet (inbound)
# Block all inbound traffic from non-routable or reserved address spaces
block in quick on dc0 from 192.168.0.0/16 to any    #RFC 1918 private IP
block in quick on dc0 from 172.16.0.0/12 to any     #RFC 1918 private IP
block in quick on dc0 from 10.0.0.0/8 to any        #RFC 1918 private IP
block in quick on dc0 from 127.0.0.0/8 to any       #loopback
block in quick on dc0 from 0.0.0.0/8 to any         #loopback
block in quick on dc0 from 169.254.0.0/16 to any    #DHCP auto-config
block in quick on dc0 from 192.0.2.0/24 to any      #reserved for docs
block in quick on dc0 from 204.152.64.0/23 to any   #Sun cluster interconnect
block in quick on dc0 from 224.0.0.0/3 to any       #Class D & E multicast

# Block fragments and too short tcp packets
block in quick on dc0 all with frags
block in quick on dc0 proto tcp all with short

# block source routed packets
block in quick on dc0 all with opt lsrr
block in quick on dc0 all with opt ssrr

# Block OS fingerprint attempts and log first occurrence
block in log first quick on dc0 proto tcp from any to any flags FUP

# Block anything with special options
block in quick on dc0 all with ipopts

# Block public pings and ident
block in quick on dc0 proto icmp all icmp-type 8
block in quick on dc0 proto tcp from any to any port = 113

# Block incoming Netbios services
block in log first quick on dc0 proto tcp/udp from any to any port = 137
block in log first quick on dc0 proto tcp/udp from any to any port = 138
block in log first quick on dc0 proto tcp/udp from any to any port = 139
block in log first quick on dc0 proto tcp/udp from any to any port = 81
```

Any time there are logged messages on a rule with the `log first` option, run `ipfstat -hio` to evaluate how many times the rule has been matched. A large number of matches may indicate that the system is under attack.

The rest of the rules in the inbound section define which connections are allowed to be initiated from the Internet. The last rule denies all connections which were not explicitly allowed by previous rules in this section.

```
# Allow traffic in from ISP's DHCP server. Replace z.z.z.z with
# the same IP address used in the outbound section.
pass in quick on dc0 proto udp from z.z.z.z to any port = 68 keep state

# Allow public connections to specified internal web server
pass in quick on dc0 proto tcp from any to x.x.x.x port = 80 flags S keep state

# Block and log only first occurrence of all remaining traffic.
```

```
block in log first quick on dc0 all
```

29.5.4. Configuring NAT

To enable NAT, add these statements to /etc/rc.conf and specify the name of the file containing the NAT rules:

```
gateway_enable="YES"
ipnat_enable="YES"
ipnat_rules="/etc/ipnat.rules"
```

NAT rules are flexible and can accomplish many different things to fit the needs of both commercial and home users. The rule syntax presented here has been simplified to demonstrate common usage. For a complete rule syntax description, refer to ipnat(5).

The basic syntax for a NAT rule is as follows, where map starts the rule and IF should be replaced with the name of the external interface:

```
map IF LAN_IP_RANGE -> PUBLIC_ADDRESS
```

The LAN_IP_RANGE is the range of IP addresses used by internal clients. Usually, it is a private address range such as 192.168.1.0/24 . The PUBLIC_ADDRESS can either be the static external IP address or the keyword 0/32 which represents the IP address assigned to IF.

In IPF, when a packet arrives at the firewall from the LAN with a public destination, it first passes through the outbound rules of the firewall ruleset. Then, the packet is passed to the NAT ruleset which is read from the top down, where the first matching rule wins. IPF tests each NAT rule against the packet's interface name and source IP address. When a packet's interface name matches a NAT rule, the packet's source IP address in the private LAN is checked to see if it falls within the IP address range specified in LAN_IP_RANGE . On a match, the packet has its source IP address rewritten with the public IP address specified by PUBLIC_ADDRESS. IPF posts an entry in its internal NAT table so that when the packet returns from the Internet, it can be mapped back to its original private IP address before being passed to the firewall rules for further processing.

For networks that have large numbers of internal systems or multiple subnets, the process of funneling every private IP address into a single public IP address becomes a resource problem. Two methods are available to relieve this issue.

The first method is to assign a range of ports to use as source ports. By adding the portmap keyword, NAT can be directed to only use source ports in the specified range:

```
map dc0 192.168.1.0/24 -> 0/32 portmap tcp/udp 20000:60000
```

Alternately, use the auto keyword which tells NAT to determine the ports that are available for use:

```
map dc0 192.168.1.0/24 -> 0/32 portmap tcp/udp auto
```

The second method is to use a pool of public addresses. This is useful when there are too many LAN addresses to fit into a single public address and a block of public IP addresses is available. These public addresses can be used as a pool from which NAT selects an IP address as a packet's address is mapped on its way out.

The range of public IP addresses can be specified using a netmask or CIDR notation. These two rules are equivalent:

```
map dc0 192.168.1.0/24 -> 204.134.75.0/255.255.255.0
map dc0 192.168.1.0/24 -> 204.134.75.0/24
```

A common practice is to have a publically accessible web server or mail server segregated to an internal network segment. The traffic from these servers still has to undergo NAT, but port redirection is needed to direct inbound traffic to the correct server. For example, to map a web server using the internal address 10.0.10.25 to its public IP address of 20.20.20.5 , use this rule:

```
rdr dc0 20.20.20.5/32 port 80 -> 10.0.10.25 port 80
```

If it is the only web server, this rule would also work as it redirects all external HTTP requests to `10.0.10.25`:

```
rdr dc0 0.0.0.0/0 port 80 -> 10.0.10.25 port 80
```

IPF has a built in FTP proxy which can be used with NAT. It monitors all outbound traffic for active or passive FTP connection requests and dynamically creates temporary filter rules containing the port number used by the FTP data channel. This eliminates the need to open large ranges of high order ports for FTP connections.

In this example, the first rule calls the proxy for outbound FTP traffic from the internal LAN. The second rule passes the FTP traffic from the firewall to the Internet, and the third rule handles all non-FTP traffic from the internal LAN:

```
map dc0 10.0.10.0/29 -> 0/32 proxy port 21 ftp/tcp
map dc0 0.0.0.0/0 -> 0/32 proxy port 21 ftp/tcp
map dc0 10.0.10.0/29 -> 0/32
```

The FTP `map` rules go before the NAT rule so that when a packet matches an FTP rule, the FTP proxy creates temporary filter rules to let the FTP session packets pass and undergo NAT. All LAN packets that are not FTP will not match the FTP rules but will undergo NAT if they match the third rule.

Without the FTP proxy, the following firewall rules would instead be needed. Note that without the proxy, all ports above `1024` need to be allowed:

```
# Allow out LAN PC client FTP to public Internet
# Active and passive modes
pass out quick on rl0 proto tcp from any to any port = 21 flags S keep state

# Allow out passive mode data channel high order port numbers
pass out quick on rl0 proto tcp from any to any port > 1024 flags S keep state

# Active mode let data channel in from FTP server
pass in quick on rl0 proto tcp from any to any port = 20 flags S keep state
```

Whenever the file containing the NAT rules is edited, run `ipnat` with `-CF` to delete the current NAT rules and flush the contents of the dynamic translation table. Include `-f` and specify the name of the NAT ruleset to load:

```
# ipnat -CF -f /etc/ipnat.rules
```

To display the NAT statistics:

```
# ipnat -s
```

To list the NAT table's current mappings:

```
# ipnat -l
```

To turn verbose mode on and display information relating to rule processing and active rules and table entries:

```
# ipnat -v
```

29.5.5. Viewing IPF Statistics

IPF includes ipfstat(8) which can be used to retrieve and display statistics which are gathered as packets match rules as they go through the firewall. Statistics are accumulated since the firewall was last started or since the last time they were reset to zero using `ipf -Z`.

The default `ipfstat` output looks like this:

```
input packets: blocked 99286 passed 1255609 nomatch 14686 counted 0
 output packets: blocked 4200 passed 1284345 nomatch 14687 counted 0
 input packets logged: blocked 99286 passed 0
 output packets logged: blocked 0 passed 0
 packets logged: input 0 output 0
```

```
log failures: input 3898 output 0
fragment state(in): kept 0 lost 0
fragment state(out): kept 0 lost 0
packet state(in): kept 169364 lost 0
packet state(out): kept 431395 lost 0
ICMP replies: 0 TCP RSTs sent: 0
Result cache hits(in): 1215208 (out): 1098963
IN Pullups succeeded: 2 failed: 0
OUT Pullups succeeded: 0 failed: 0
Fastroute successes: 0 failures: 0
TCP cksum fails(in): 0 (out): 0
Packet log flags set: (0)
```

Several options are available. When supplied with either `-i` for inbound or `-o` for outbound, the command will retrieve and display the appropriate list of filter rules currently installed and in use by the kernel. To also see the rule numbers, include `-n`. For example, `ipfstat -on` displays the outbound rules table with rule numbers:

```
@1 pass out on xl0 from any to any
@2 block out on dc0 from any to any
@3 pass out quick on dc0 proto tcp/udp from any to any keep state
```

Include `-h` to prefix each rule with a count of how many times the rule was matched. For example, `ipfstat -oh` displays the outbound internal rules table, prefixing each rule with its usage count:

```
2451423 pass out on xl0 from any to any
354727 block out on dc0 from any to any
430918 pass out quick on dc0 proto tcp/udp from any to any keep state
```

To display the state table in a format similar to top(1), use `ipfstat -t`. When the firewall is under attack, this option provides the ability to identify and see the attacking packets. The optional sub-flags give the ability to select the destination or source IP, port, or protocol to be monitored in real time. Refer to ipfstat(8) for details.

29.5.6. IPF Logging

IPF provides `ipmon`, which can be used to write the firewall's logging information in a human readable format. It requires that `options IPFILTER_LOG` be first added to a custom kernel using the instructions in Chapter 8, *Configuring the FreeBSD Kernel*.

This command is typically run in daemon mode in order to provide a continuous system log file so that logging of past events may be reviewed. Since FreeBSD has a built in syslogd(8) facility to automatically rotate system logs, the default `rc.conf ipmon_flags` statement uses `-Ds`:

```
ipmon_flags="-Ds" # D = start as daemon
                  # s = log to syslog
                  # v = log tcp window, ack, seq
                  # n = map IP & port to names
```

Logging provides the ability to review, after the fact, information such as which packets were dropped, what addresses they came from, and where they were going. This information is useful in tracking down attackers.

Once the logging facility is enabled in `rc.conf` and started with `service ipmon start`, IPF will only log the rules which contain the `log` keyword. The firewall administrator decides which rules in the ruleset should be logged and normally only deny rules are logged. It is customary to include the `log` keyword in the last rule in the ruleset. This makes it possible to see all the packets that did not match any of the rules in the ruleset.

By default, `ipmon -Ds` mode uses `local0` as the logging facility. The following logging levels can be used to further segregate the logged data:

```
LOG_INFO - packets logged using the "log" keyword as the action rather than pass or ↵
block.
LOG_NOTICE - packets logged which are also passed
LOG_WARNING - packets logged which are also blocked
```

```
LOG_ERR - packets which have been logged and which can be considered short due to an ↺
incomplete header
```

In order to setup IPF to log all data to `/var/log/ipfilter.log` , first create the empty file:

```
# touch /var/log/ipfilter.log
```

Then, to write all logged messages to the specified file, add the following statement to `/etc/syslog.conf` :

```
local0.* /var/log/ipfilter.log
```

To activate the changes and instruct syslogd(8) to read the modified `/etc/syslog.conf` , run `service syslogd reload`.

Do not forget to edit `/etc/newsyslog.conf` to rotate the new log file.

Messages generated by `ipmon` consist of data fields separated by white space. Fields common to all messages are:

1. The date of packet receipt.

2. The time of packet receipt. This is in the form HH:MM:SS.F, for hours, minutes, seconds, and fractions of a second.

3. The name of the interface that processed the packet.

4. The group and rule number of the rule in the format `@0:17`.

5. The action: `p` for passed, `b` for blocked, `S` for a short packet, `n` did not match any rules, and `L` for a log rule.

6. The addresses written as three fields: the source address and port separated by a comma, the -> symbol, and the destination address and port. For example: `209.53.17.22,80 -> 198.73.220.17,1722` .

7. `PR` followed by the protocol name or number: for example, `PR tcp`.

8. `len` followed by the header length and total length of the packet: for example, `len 20 40`.

If the packet is a TCP packet, there will be an additional field starting with a hyphen followed by letters corresponding to any flags that were set. Refer to ipf(5) for a list of letters and their flags.

If the packet is an ICMP packet, there will be two fields at the end: the first always being "icmp" and the next being the ICMP message and sub-message type, separated by a slash. For example: `icmp 3/3` for a port unreachable message.

Chapter 30. Advanced Networking

30.1. Synopsis

This chapter covers a number of advanced networking topics.

After reading this chapter, you will know:

- The basics of gateways and routes.

- How to set up USB tethering.

- How to set up IEEE® 802.11 and Bluetooth® devices.

- How to make FreeBSD act as a bridge.

- How to set up network PXE booting.

- How to set up IPv6 on a FreeBSD machine.

- How to enable and utilize the features of the Common Address Redundancy Protocol (CARP) in FreeBSD.

Before reading this chapter, you should:

- Understand the basics of the /etc/rc scripts.

- Be familiar with basic network terminology.

- Know how to configure and install a new FreeBSD kernel (Chapter 8, *Configuring the FreeBSD Kernel*).

- Know how to install additional third-party software (Chapter 4, *Installing Applications: Packages and Ports*).

30.2. Gateways and Routes

Contributed by Coranth Gryphon.

Routing is the mechanism that allows a system to find the network path to another system. A *route* is a defined pair of addresses which represent the "destination" and a "gateway". The route indicates that when trying to get to the specified destination, send the packets through the specified gateway. There are three types of destinations: individual hosts, subnets, and "default". The "default route" is used if no other routes apply. There are also three types of gateways: individual hosts, interfaces, also called links, and Ethernet hardware (MAC) addresses. Known routes are stored in a routing table.

This section provides an overview of routing basics. It then demonstrates how to configure a FreeBSD system as a router and offers some troubleshooting tips.

30.2.1. Routing Basics

To view the routing table of a FreeBSD system, use netstat(1):

```
% netstat -r
Routing tables

Internet:
Destination      Gateway          Flags   Refs    Use    Netif Expire
default          outside-gw       UGS      37     418     em0
localhost        localhost        UH        0     181     lo0
test0            0:e0:b5:36:cf:4f UHLW      5   63288     re0   77
10.20.30.255     link#1           UHLW      1    2421
```

```
example.com       link#1            UC      0       0
host1             0:e0:a8:37:8:1e   UHLW    3    4601      lo0
host2             0:e0:a8:37:8:1e   UHLW    0       5      lo0 =>
host2.example.com link#1            UC      0       0
224               link#1            UC      0       0
```

The entries in this example are as follows:

default

> The first route in this table specifies the default route. When the local system needs to make a connection to a remote host, it checks the routing table to determine if a known path exists. If the remote host matches an entry in the table, the system checks to see if it can connect using the interface specified in that entry.

> If the destination does not match an entry, or if all known paths fail, the system uses the entry for the default route. For hosts on a local area network, the Gateway field in the default route is set to the system which has a direct connection to the Internet. When reading this entry, verify that the Flags column indicates that the gateway is usable (UG).

> The default route for a machine which itself is functioning as the gateway to the outside world will be the gateway machine at the Internet Service Provider (ISP).

localhost

> The second route is the localhost route. The interface specified in the Netif column for localhost is lo0, also known as the loopback device. This indicates that all traffic for this destination should be internal, rather than sending it out over the network.

MAC address

> The addresses beginning with 0:e0: are MAC addresses. FreeBSD will automatically identify any hosts, test0 in the example, on the local Ethernet and add a route for that host over the Ethernet interface, re0. This type of route has a timeout, seen in the Expire column, which is used if the host does not respond in a specific amount of time. When this happens, the route to this host will be automatically deleted. These hosts are identified using the Routing Information Protocol (RIP), which calculates routes to local hosts based upon a shortest path determination.

subnet

> FreeBSD will automatically add subnet routes for the local subnet. In this example, 10.20.30.255 is the broadcast address for the subnet 10.20.30 and example.com is the domain name associated with that subnet. The designation link#1 refers to the first Ethernet card in the machine.

> Local network hosts and local subnets have their routes automatically configured by a daemon called routed(8). If it is not running, only routes which are statically defined by the administrator will exist.

host

> The host1 line refers to the host by its Ethernet address. Since it is the sending host, FreeBSD knows to use the loopback interface (lo0) rather than the Ethernet interface.

> The two host2 lines represent aliases which were created using ifconfig(8). The => symbol after the lo0 interface says that an alias has been set in addition to the loopback address. Such routes only show up on the host that supports the alias and all other hosts on the local network will have a link#1 line for such routes.

224

> The final line (destination subnet 224) deals with multicasting.

Various attributes of each route can be seen in the Flags column. Table 30.1, "Commonly Seen Routing Table Flags" summarizes some of these flags and their meanings:

Table 30.1. Commonly Seen Routing Table Flags

Command	Purpose
U	The route is active (up).

Command	Purpose
H	The route destination is a single host.
G	Send anything for this destination on to this gateway, which will figure out from there where to send it.
S	This route was statically configured.
C	Clones a new route based upon this route for machines to connect to. This type of route is normally used for local networks.
W	The route was auto-configured based upon a local area network (clone) route.
L	Route involves references to Ethernet (link) hardware.

On a FreeBSD system, the default route can defined in /etc/rc.conf by specifying the IP address of the default gateway:

```
defaultrouter="10.20.30.1"
```

It is also possible to manually add the route using route:

```
# route add default 10.20.30.1
```

Note that manually added routes will not survive a reboot. For more information on manual manipulation of network routing tables, refer to route(8).

30.2.2. Configuring a Router with Static Routes

Contributed by Al Hoang.

A FreeBSD system can be configured as the default gateway, or router, for a network if it is a dual-homed system. A dual-homed system is a host which resides on at least two different networks. Typically, each network is connected to a separate network interface, though IP aliasing can be used to bind multiple addresses, each on a different subnet, to one physical interface.

In order for the system to forward packets between interfaces, FreeBSD must be configured as a router. Internet standards and good engineering practice prevent the FreeBSD Project from enabling this feature by default, but it can be configured to start at boot by adding this line to /etc/rc.conf :

```
gateway_enable="YES"          # Set to YES if this host will be a gateway
```

To enable routing now, set the sysctl(8) variable net.inet.ip.forwarding to 1. To stop routing, reset this variable to 0.

The routing table of a router needs additional routes so it knows how to reach other networks. Routes can be either added manually using static routes or routes can be automatically learned using a routing protocol. Static routes are appropriate for small networks and this section describes how to add a static routing entry for a small network.

Note

For large networks, static routes quickly become unscalable. FreeBSD comes with the standard BSD routing daemon routed(8), which provides the routing protocols RIP, versions 1 and 2, and IRDP. Support for the BGP and OSPF routing protocols can be installed using the net/zebra package or port.

Consider the following network:

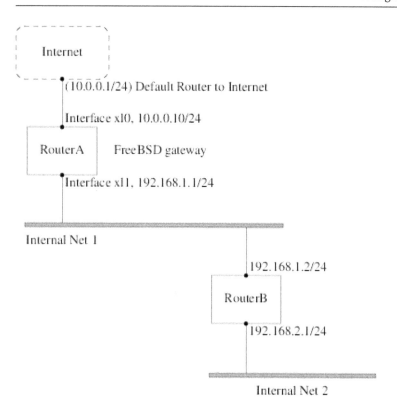

In this scenario, RouterA is a FreeBSD machine that is acting as a router to the rest of the Internet. It has a default route set to 10.0.0.1 which allows it to connect with the outside world. RouterB is already configured to use 192.168.1.1 as its default gateway.

Before adding any static routes, the routing table on RouterA looks like this:

```
% netstat -nr
Routing tables

Internet:
Destination       Gateway        Flags   Refs     Use   Netif  Expire
default           10.0.0.1       UGS        0   49378    xl0
127.0.0.1         127.0.0.1      UH         0       6    lo0
10.0.0.0/24       link#1         UC         0       0    xl0
192.168.1.0/24    link#2         UC         0       0    xl1
```

With the current routing table, RouterA does not have a route to the 192.168.2.0/24 network. The following command adds the Internal Net 2 network to RouterA's routing table using 192.168.1.2 as the next hop:

```
# route add -net 192.168.2.0/24 192.168.1.2
```

Now, RouterA can reach any host on the 192.168.2.0/24 network. However, the routing information will not persist if the FreeBSD system reboots. If a static route needs to be persistent, add it to /etc/rc.conf :

```
# Add Internal Net 2 as a persistent static route
static_routes="internalnet2"
route_internalnet2="-net 192.168.2.0/24 192.168.1.2"
```

The static_routes configuration variable is a list of strings separated by a space, where each string references a route name. The variable route_internalnet2 contains the static route for that route name.

Using more than one string in static_routes creates multiple static routes. The following shows an example of adding static routes for the 192.168.0.0/24 and 192.168.1.0/24 networks:

```
static_routes="net1 net2"
route_net1="-net 192.168.0.0/24 192.168.0.1"
route_net2="-net 192.168.1.0/24 192.168.1.1"
```

30.2.3. Troubleshooting

When an address space is assigned to a network, the service provider configures their routing tables so that all traffic for the network will be sent to the link for the site. But how do external sites know to send their packets to the network's ISP?

There is a system that keeps track of all assigned address spaces and defines their point of connection to the Internet backbone, or the main trunk lines that carry Internet traffic across the country and around the world. Each backbone machine has a copy of a master set of tables, which direct traffic for a particular network to a specific backbone carrier, and from there down the chain of service providers until it reaches a particular network.

It is the task of the service provider to advertise to the backbone sites that they are the point of connection, and thus the path inward, for a site. This is known as route propagation.

Sometimes, there is a problem with route propagation and some sites are unable to connect. Perhaps the most useful command for trying to figure out where routing is breaking down is traceroute. It is useful when ping fails.

When using traceroute, include the address of the remote host to connect to. The output will show the gateway hosts along the path of the attempt, eventually either reaching the target host, or terminating because of a lack of connection. For more information, refer to traceroute(8).

30.2.4. Multicast Considerations

FreeBSD natively supports both multicast applications and multicast routing. Multicast applications do not require any special configuration in order to run on FreeBSD. Support for multicast routing requires that the following option be compiled into a custom kernel:

```
options MROUTING
```

The multicast routing daemon, mrouted can be installed using the net/mrouted package or port. This daemon implements the DVMRP multicast routing protocol and is configured by editing /usr/local/etc/mrouted.conf in order to set up the tunnels and DVMRP. The installation of mrouted also installs map-mbone and mrinfo, as well as their associated man pages. Refer to these for configuration examples.

> **Note**
>
> DVMRP has largely been replaced by the PIM protocol in many multicast installations. Refer to pim(4) for more information.

30.3. Wireless Networking

Loader, Marc Fonvieille and Murray Stokely.

30.3.1. Wireless Networking Basics

Most wireless networks are based on the IEEE® 802.11 standards. A basic wireless network consists of multiple stations communicating with radios that broadcast in either the 2.4GHz or 5GHz band, though this varies according to the locale and is also changing to enable communication in the 2.3GHz and 4.9GHz ranges.

802.11 networks are organized in two ways. In *infrastructure mode*, one station acts as a master with all the other stations associating to it, the network is known as a BSS, and the master station is termed an access point (AP).

In a BSS, all communication passes through the AP; even when one station wants to communicate with another wireless station, messages must go through the AP. In the second form of network, there is no master and stations communicate directly. This form of network is termed an IBSS and is commonly known as an *ad-hoc network*.

802.11 networks were first deployed in the 2.4GHz band using protocols defined by the IEEE® 802.11 and 802.11b standard. These specifications include the operating frequencies and the MAC layer characteristics, including framing and transmission rates, as communication can occur at various rates. Later, the 802.11a standard defined operation in the 5GHz band, including different signaling mechanisms and higher transmission rates. Still later, the 802.11g standard defined the use of 802.11a signaling and transmission mechanisms in the 2.4GHz band in such a way as to be backwards compatible with 802.11b networks.

Separate from the underlying transmission techniques, 802.11 networks have a variety of security mechanisms. The original 802.11 specifications defined a simple security protocol called WEP. This protocol uses a fixed pre-shared key and the RC4 cryptographic cipher to encode data transmitted on a network. Stations must all agree on the fixed key in order to communicate. This scheme was shown to be easily broken and is now rarely used except to discourage transient users from joining networks. Current security practice is given by the IEEE® 802.11i specification that defines new cryptographic ciphers and an additional protocol to authenticate stations to an access point and exchange keys for data communication. Cryptographic keys are periodically refreshed and there are mechanisms for detecting and countering intrusion attempts. Another security protocol specification commonly used in wireless networks is termed WPA, which was a precursor to 802.11i. WPA specifies a subset of the requirements found in 802.11i and is designed for implementation on legacy hardware. Specifically, WPA requires only the TKIP cipher that is derived from the original WEP cipher. 802.11i permits use of TKIP but also requires support for a stronger cipher, AES-CCM, for encrypting data. The AES cipher was not required in WPA because it was deemed too computationally costly to be implemented on legacy hardware.

The other standard to be aware of is 802.11e. It defines protocols for deploying multimedia applications, such as streaming video and voice over IP (VoIP), in an 802.11 network. Like 802.11i, 802.11e also has a precursor specification termed WME (later renamed WMM) that has been defined by an industry group as a subset of 802.11e that can be deployed now to enable multimedia applications while waiting for the final ratification of 802.11e. The most important thing to know about 802.11e and WME/WMM is that it enables prioritized traffic over a wireless network through Quality of Service (QoS) protocols and enhanced media access protocols. Proper implementation of these protocols enables high speed bursting of data and prioritized traffic flow.

FreeBSD supports networks that operate using 802.11a, 802.11b, and 802.11g. The WPA and 802.11i security protocols are likewise supported (in conjunction with any of 11a, 11b, and 11g) and QoS and traffic prioritization required by the WME/WMM protocols are supported for a limited set of wireless devices.

30.3.2. Quick Start

Connecting a computer to an existing wireless network is a very common situation. This procedure shows the steps required.

1. Obtain the SSID (Service Set Identifier) and PSK (Pre-Shared Key) for the wireless network from the network administrator.

2. Identify the wireless adapter. The FreeBSD GENERIC kernel includes drivers for many common wireless adapters. If the wireless adapter is one of those models, it will be shown in the output from ifconfig(8):

```
% ifconfig | grep -B3 -i wireless
```

If a wireless adapter is not listed, an additional kernel module might be required, or it might be a model not supported by FreeBSD.

This example shows the Atheros ath0 wireless adapter.

3. Add an entry for this network to /etc/wpa_supplicant.conf. If the file does not exist, create it. Replace *myssid* and *mypsk* with the SSID and PSK provided by the network administrator.

```
network={
  ssid="myssid"
  psk="mypsk"
}
```

4. Add entries to /etc/rc.conf to configure the network on startup:

```
wlans_ath0="wlan0"
ifconfig_wlan0="WPA SYNCDHCP"
```

5. Restart the computer, or restart the network service to connect to the network:

```
# service netif restart
```

30.3.3. Basic Setup

30.3.3.1. Kernel Configuration

To use wireless networking, a wireless networking card is needed and the kernel needs to be configured with the appropriate wireless networking support. The kernel is separated into multiple modules so that only the required support needs to be configured.

The most commonly used wireless devices are those that use parts made by Atheros. These devices are supported by ath(4) and require the following line to be added to /boot/loader.conf :

```
if_ath_load="YES"
```

The Atheros driver is split up into three separate pieces: the driver (ath(4)), the hardware support layer that handles chip-specific functions (ath_hal(4)), and an algorithm for selecting the rate for transmitting frames. When this support is loaded as kernel modules, any dependencies are automatically handled. To load support for a different type of wireless device, specify the module for that device. This example is for devices based on the Intersil Prism parts (wi(4)) driver:

```
if_wi_load="YES"
```

> Note
>
> The examples in this section use an ath(4) device and the device name in the examples must be changed according to the configuration. A list of available wireless drivers and supported adapters can be found in the FreeBSD Hardware Notes, available on the Release Information page of the FreeBSD website. If a native FreeBSD driver for the wireless device does not exist, it may be possible to use the Windows® driver with the help of the NDIS driver wrapper.

In addition, the modules that implement cryptographic support for the security protocols to use must be loaded. These are intended to be dynamically loaded on demand by the wlan(4) module, but for now they must be manually configured. The following modules are available: wlan_wep(4), wlan_ccmp(4), and wlan_tkip(4). The wlan_ccmp(4) and wlan_tkip(4) drivers are only needed when using the WPA or 802.11i security protocols. If the network does not use encryption, wlan_wep(4) support is not needed. To load these modules at boot time, add the following lines to /boot/loader.conf :

```
wlan_wep_load="YES"
wlan_ccmp_load="YES"
wlan_tkip_load="YES"
```

Once this information has been added to /boot/loader.conf , reboot the FreeBSD box. Alternately, load the modules by hand using kldload(8).

Note

For users who do not want to use modules, it is possible to compile these drivers into the kernel by adding the following lines to a custom kernel configuration file:

```
device wlan              # 802.11 support
device wlan_wep          # 802.11 WEP support
device wlan_ccmp         # 802.11 CCMP support
device wlan_tkip         # 802.11 TKIP support
device wlan_amrr         # AMRR transmit rate control algorithm
device ath               # Atheros pci/cardbus NIC's
device ath_hal           # pci/cardbus chip support
options AH_SUPPORT_AR5416 # enable AR5416 tx/rx descriptors
device ath_rate_sample   # SampleRate tx rate control for ath
```

With this information in the kernel configuration file, recompile the kernel and reboot the FreeBSD machine.

Information about the wireless device should appear in the boot messages, like this:

```
ath0: <Atheros 5212> mem 0x88000000-0x8800ffff irq 11 at device 0.0 on cardbus1
ath0: [ITHREAD]
ath0: AR2413 mac 7.9 RF2413 phy 4.5
```

30.3.4. Infrastructure Mode

Infrastructure (BSS) mode is the mode that is typically used. In this mode, a number of wireless access points are connected to a wired network. Each wireless network has its own name, called the SSID. Wireless clients connect to the wireless access points.

30.3.4.1. FreeBSD Clients

30.3.4.1.1. How to Find Access Points

To scan for available networks, use ifconfig(8). This request may take a few moments to complete as it requires the system to switch to each available wireless frequency and probe for available access points. Only the superuser can initiate a scan:

```
# ifconfig wlan0 create wlandev ath0
# ifconfig wlan0 up scan
SSID/MESH ID    BSSID              CHAN RATE   S:N      INT CAPS
dlinkap         00:13:46:49:41:76  11    54M -90:96    100 EPS  WPA WME
freebsdap       00:11:95:c3:0d:ac  1     54M -83:96    100 EPS  WPA
```

Note

The interface must be up before it can scan. Subsequent scan requests do not require the interface to be marked as up again.

The output of a scan request lists each BSS/IBSS network found. Besides listing the name of the network, the SSID, the output also shows the BSSID, which is the MAC address of the access point. The CAPS field identifies the type of each network and the capabilities of the stations operating there:

Table 30.2. Station Capability Codes

Capability Code	Meaning
E	Extended Service Set (ESS). Indicates that the station is part of an infrastructure network rather than an IBSS/ad-hoc network.
I	IBSS/ad-hoc network. Indicates that the station is part of an ad-hoc network rather than an ESS network.
P	Privacy. Encryption is required for all data frames exchanged within the BSS using cryptographic means such as WEP, TKIP or AES-CCMP.
S	Short Preamble. Indicates that the network is using short preambles, defined in 802.11b High Rate/DSSS PHY, and utilizes a 56 bit sync field rather than the 128 bit field used in long preamble mode.
s	Short slot time. Indicates that the 802.11g network is using a short slot time because there are no legacy (802.11b) stations present.

One can also display the current list of known networks with:

```
# ifconfig wlan0 list scan
```

This information may be updated automatically by the adapter or manually with a scan request. Old data is automatically removed from the cache, so over time this list may shrink unless more scans are done.

30.3.4.1.2. Basic Settings

This section provides a simple example of how to make the wireless network adapter work in FreeBSD without encryption. Once familiar with these concepts, it is strongly recommend to use WPA to set up the wireless network.

There are three basic steps to configure a wireless network: select an access point, authenticate the station, and configure an IP address. The following sections discuss each step.

30.3.4.1.2.1. Selecting an Access Point

Most of the time, it is sufficient to let the system choose an access point using the builtin heuristics. This is the default behaviour when an interface is marked as up or it is listed in /etc/rc.conf :

```
wlans_ath0="wlan0"
ifconfig_wlan0="DHCP"
```

If there are multiple access points, a specific one can be selected by its SSID:

```
wlans_ath0="wlan0"
ifconfig_wlan0="ssid your_ssid_here  DHCP"
```

In an environment where there are multiple access points with the same SSID, which is often done to simplify roaming, it may be necessary to associate to one specific device. In this case, the BSSID of the access point can be specified, with or without the SSID:

```
wlans_ath0="wlan0"
ifconfig_wlan0="ssid your_ssid_here  bssid xx:xx:xx:xx:xx:xx  DHCP"
```

There are other ways to constrain the choice of an access point, such as limiting the set of frequencies the system will scan on. This may be useful for a multi-band wireless card as scanning all the possible channels can be time-consuming. To limit operation to a specific band, use the mode parameter:

```
wlans_ath0="wlan0"
ifconfig_wlan0="mode 11g ssid your_ssid_here  DHCP"
```

This example will force the card to operate in 802.11g, which is defined only for 2.4GHz frequencies so any 5GHz channels will not be considered. This can also be achieved with the `channel` parameter, which locks operation to one specific frequency, and the `chanlist` parameter, to specify a list of channels for scanning. More information about these parameters can be found in ifconfig(8).

30.3.4.1.2.2. Authentication

Once an access point is selected, the station needs to authenticate before it can pass data. Authentication can happen in several ways. The most common scheme, open authentication, allows any station to join the network and communicate. This is the authentication to use for test purposes the first time a wireless network is setup. Other schemes require cryptographic handshakes to be completed before data traffic can flow, either using pre-shared keys or secrets, or more complex schemes that involve backend services such as RADIUS. Open authentication is the default setting. The next most common setup is WPA-PSK, also known as WPA Personal, which is described in Section 30.3.4.1.3.1, "WPA-PSK".

 Note

If using an Apple® AirPort® Extreme base station for an access point, shared-key authentication together with a WEP key needs to be configured. This can be configured in `/etc/rc.conf` or by using wpa_supplicant(8). For a single AirPort® base station, access can be configured with:

```
wlans_ath0="wlan0"
ifconfig_wlan0="authmode shared wepmode on weptxkey 1 wepkey 01234567 ↵
DHCP"
```

In general, shared key authentication should be avoided because it uses the WEP key material in a highly-constrained manner, making it even easier to crack the key. If WEP must be used for compatibility with legacy devices, it is better to use WEP with **open** authentication. More information regarding WEP can be found in Section 30.3.4.1.4, "WEP".

30.3.4.1.2.3. Getting an IP Address with DHCP

Once an access point is selected and the authentication parameters are set, an IP address must be obtained in order to communicate. Most of the time, the IP address is obtained via DHCP. To achieve that, edit `/etc/rc.conf` and add DHCP to the configuration for the device:

```
wlans_ath0="wlan0"
ifconfig_wlan0="DHCP"
```

The wireless interface is now ready to bring up:

```
# service netif start
```

Once the interface is running, use ifconfig(8) to see the status of the interface `ath0`:

```
# ifconfig wlan0
wlan0: flags=8843<UP,BROADCAST,RUNNING,SIMPLEX,MULTICAST> mtu 1500
        ether 00:11:95:d5:43:62
        inet 192.168.1.100 netmask 0xffffff00 broadcast 192.168.1.255
        media: IEEE 802.11 Wireless Ethernet OFDM/54Mbps mode 11g
        status: associated
        ssid dlinkap channel 11 (2462 Mhz 11g) bssid 00:13:46:49:41:76
        country US ecm authmode OPEN privacy OFF txpower 21.5 bmiss 7
        scanvalid 60 bgscan bgscanintvl 300 bgscanidle 250 roam:rssi 7
        roam:rate 5 protmode CTS wme burst
```

The `status: associated` line means that it is connected to the wireless network. The `bssid 00:13:46:49:41:76` is the MAC address of the access point and `authmode OPEN` indicates that the communication is not encrypted.

30.3.4.1.2.4. Static IP Address

In an IP address cannot be obtained from a DHCP server, set a fixed IP address. Replace the DHCP keyword shown above with the address information. Be sure to retain any other parameters for selecting the access point:

```
wlans_ath0="wlan0"
ifconfig_wlan0="inet 192.168.1.100 netmask 255.255.255.0 ssid your_ssid_here "
```

30.3.4.1.3. WPA

Wi-Fi Protected Access (WPA) is a security protocol used together with 802.11 networks to address the lack of proper authentication and the weakness of WEP. WPA leverages the 802.1X authentication protocol and uses one of several ciphers instead of WEP for data integrity. The only cipher required by WPA is the Temporary Key Integrity Protocol (TKIP). TKIP is a cipher that extends the basic RC4 cipher used by WEP by adding integrity checking, tamper detection, and measures for responding to detected intrusions. TKIP is designed to work on legacy hardware with only software modification. It represents a compromise that improves security but is still not entirely immune to attack. WPA also specifies the AES-CCMP cipher as an alternative to TKIP, and that is preferred when possible. For this specification, the term WPA2 or RSN is commonly used.

WPA defines authentication and encryption protocols. Authentication is most commonly done using one of two techniques: by 802.1X and a backend authentication service such as RADIUS, or by a minimal handshake between the station and the access point using a pre-shared secret. The former is commonly termed WPA Enterprise and the latter is known as WPA Personal. Since most people will not set up a RADIUS backend server for their wireless network, WPA-PSK is by far the most commonly encountered configuration for WPA.

The control of the wireless connection and the key negotiation or authentication with a server is done using wpa_supplicant(8). This program requires a configuration file, /etc/wpa_supplicant.conf, to run. More information regarding this file can be found in wpa_supplicant.conf(5).

30.3.4.1.3.1. WPA-PSK

WPA-PSK, also known as WPA Personal, is based on a pre-shared key (PSK) which is generated from a given password and used as the master key in the wireless network. This means every wireless user will share the same key. WPA-PSK is intended for small networks where the use of an authentication server is not possible or desired.

Warning

Always use strong passwords that are sufficiently long and made from a rich alphabet so that they will not be easily guessed or attacked.

The first step is the configuration of /etc/wpa_supplicant.conf with the SSID and the pre-shared key of the network:

```
network={
  ssid="freebsdap"
  psk="freebsdmall"
}
```

Then, in /etc/rc.conf , indicate that the wireless device configuration will be done with WPA and the IP address will be obtained with DHCP:

```
wlans_ath0="wlan0"
ifconfig_wlan0="WPA DHCP"
```

Then, bring up the interface:

```
# service netif start
Starting wpa_supplicant.
```

```
DHCPDISCOVER on wlan0 to 255.255.255.255 port 67 interval 5
DHCPDISCOVER on wlan0 to 255.255.255.255 port 67 interval 6
DHCPOFFER from 192.168.0.1
DHCPREQUEST on wlan0 to 255.255.255.255 port 67
DHCPACK from 192.168.0.1
bound to 192.168.0.254 -- renewal in 300 seconds.
wlan0: flags=8843<UP,BROADCAST,RUNNING,SIMPLEX,MULTICAST> mtu 1500
        ether 00:11:95:d5:43:62
        inet 192.168.0.254 netmask 0xffffff00 broadcast 192.168.0.255
        media: IEEE 802.11 Wireless Ethernet OFDM/36Mbps mode 11g
        status: associated
        ssid freebsdap channel 1 (2412 Mhz 11g) bssid 00:11:95:c3:0d:ac
        country US ecm authmode WPA2/802.11i privacy ON deftxkey UNDEF
        AES-CCM 3:128-bit txpower 21.5 bmiss 7 scanvalid 450 bgscan
        bgscanintvl 300 bgscanidle 250 roam:rssi 7 roam:rate 5 protmode CTS
        wme burst roaming MANUAL
```

Or, try to configure the interface manually using the information in /etc/wpa_supplicant.conf:

```
# wpa_supplicant -i wlan0 -c /etc/wpa_supplicant.conf
Trying to associate with 00:11:95:c3:0d:ac (SSID='freebsdap' freq=2412 MHz)
Associated with 00:11:95:c3:0d:ac
WPA: Key negotiation completed with 00:11:95:c3:0d:ac [PTK=CCMP GTK=CCMP]
CTRL-EVENT-CONNECTED - Connection to 00:11:95:c3:0d:ac completed (auth) [id=0 id_str=]
```

The next operation is to launch dhclient(8) to get the IP address from the DHCP server:

```
# dhclient wlan0
DHCPREQUEST on wlan0 to 255.255.255.255 port 67
DHCPACK from 192.168.0.1
bound to 192.168.0.254 -- renewal in 300 seconds.
# ifconfig wlan0
wlan0: flags=8843<UP,BROADCAST,RUNNING,SIMPLEX,MULTICAST> mtu 1500
        ether 00:11:95:d5:43:62
        inet 192.168.0.254 netmask 0xffffff00 broadcast 192.168.0.255
        media: IEEE 802.11 Wireless Ethernet OFDM/36Mbps mode 11g
        status: associated
        ssid freebsdap channel 1 (2412 Mhz 11g) bssid 00:11:95:c3:0d:ac
        country US ecm authmode WPA2/802.11i privacy ON deftxkey UNDEF
        AES-CCM 3:128-bit txpower 21.5 bmiss 7 scanvalid 450 bgscan
        bgscanintvl 300 bgscanidle 250 roam:rssi 7 roam:rate 5 protmode CTS
        wme burst roaming MANUAL
```

Note

If /etc/rc.conf has an ifconfig_wlan0="DHCP" entry, dhclient(8) will be launched automatically after wpa_supplicant(8) associates with the access point.

If DHCP is not possible or desired, set a static IP address after wpa_supplicant(8) has authenticated the station:

```
# ifconfig wlan0 inet 192.168.0.100 netmask 255.255.255.0
# ifconfig wlan0
wlan0: flags=8843<UP,BROADCAST,RUNNING,SIMPLEX,MULTICAST> mtu 1500
        ether 00:11:95:d5:43:62
        inet 192.168.0.100 netmask 0xffffff00 broadcast 192.168.0.255
        media: IEEE 802.11 Wireless Ethernet OFDM/36Mbps mode 11g
        status: associated
        ssid freebsdap channel 1 (2412 Mhz 11g) bssid 00:11:95:c3:0d:ac
        country US ecm authmode WPA2/802.11i privacy ON deftxkey UNDEF
        AES-CCM 3:128-bit txpower 21.5 bmiss 7 scanvalid 450 bgscan
        bgscanintvl 300 bgscanidle 250 roam:rssi 7 roam:rate 5 protmode CTS
        wme burst roaming MANUAL
```

When DHCP is not used, the default gateway and the nameserver also have to be manually set:

```
# route add default your_default_router
# echo "nameserver  your_DNS_server " >> /etc/resolv.conf
```

30.3.4.1.3.2. WPA with EAP-TLS

The second way to use WPA is with an 802.1X backend authentication server. In this case, WPA is called WPA Enterprise to differentiate it from the less secure WPA Personal. Authentication in WPA Enterprise is based on the Extensible Authentication Protocol (EAP).

EAP does not come with an encryption method. Instead, EAP is embedded inside an encrypted tunnel. There are many EAP authentication methods, but EAP-TLS, EAP-TTLS, and EAP-PEAP are the most common.

EAP with Transport Layer Security (EAP-TLS) is a well-supported wireless authentication protocol since it was the first EAP method to be certified by the Wi-Fi Alliance. EAP-TLS requires three certificates to run: the certificate of the Certificate Authority (CA) installed on all machines, the server certificate for the authentication server, and one client certificate for each wireless client. In this EAP method, both the authentication server and wireless client authenticate each other by presenting their respective certificates, and then verify that these certificates were signed by the organization's CA.

As previously, the configuration is done via /etc/wpa_supplicant.conf:

```
network={
    ssid="freebsdap" ❶
    proto=RSN ❷
    key_mgmt=WPA-EAP ❸
    eap=TLS ❹
    identity="loader" ❺
    ca_cert="/etc/certs/cacert.pem" ❻
    client_cert="/etc/certs/clientcert.pem" ❼
    private_key="/etc/certs/clientkey.pem" ❽
    private_key_passwd="freebsdmallclient" ❾
}
```

❶ This field indicates the network name (SSID).

❷ This example uses the RSN IEEE® 802.11i protocol, also known as WPA2.

❸ The key_mgmt line refers to the key management protocol to use. In this example, it is WPA using EAP authentication.

❹ This field indicates the EAP method for the connection.

❺ The identity field contains the identity string for EAP.

❻ The ca_cert field indicates the pathname of the CA certificate file. This file is needed to verify the server certificate.

❼ The client_cert line gives the pathname to the client certificate file. This certificate is unique to each wireless client of the network.

❽ The private_key field is the pathname to the client certificate private key file.

❾ The private_key_passwd field contains the passphrase for the private key.

Then, add the following lines to /etc/rc.conf :

```
wlans_ath0="wlan0"
ifconfig_wlan0="WPA DHCP"
```

The next step is to bring up the interface:

```
# service netif start
Starting wpa_supplicant.
DHCPREQUEST on wlan0 to 255.255.255.255 port 67 interval 7
DHCPREQUEST on wlan0 to 255.255.255.255 port 67 interval 15
DHCPACK from 192.168.0.20
bound to 192.168.0.254 -- renewal in 300 seconds.
```

```
wlan0: flags=8843<UP,BROADCAST,RUNNING,SIMPLEX,MULTICAST> mtu 1500
        ether 00:11:95:d5:43:62
        inet 192.168.0.254 netmask 0xffffff00 broadcast 192.168.0.255
        media: IEEE 802.11 Wireless Ethernet DS/11Mbps mode 11g
        status: associated
        ssid freebsdap channel 1 (2412 Mhz 11g) bssid 00:11:95:c3:0d:ac
        country US ecm authmode WPA2/802.11i privacy ON deftxkey UNDEF
        AES-CCM 3:128-bit txpower 21.5 bmiss 7 scanvalid 450 bgscan
        bgscanintvl 300 bgscanidle 250 roam:rssi 7 roam:rate 5 protmode CTS
        wme burst roaming MANUAL
```

It is also possible to bring up the interface manually using wpa_supplicant(8) and ifconfig(8).

30.3.4.1.3.3. WPA with EAP-TTLS

With EAP-TTLS, both the authentication server and the client need a certificate. With EAP-TTLS, a client certificate is optional. This method is similar to a web server which creates a secure SSL tunnel even if visitors do not have client-side certificates. EAP-TTLS uses an encrypted TLS tunnel for safe transport of the authentication data.

The required configuration can be added to /etc/wpa_supplicant.conf:

```
network={
  ssid="freebsdap"
  proto=RSN
  key_mgmt=WPA-EAP
  eap=TTLS ❶
  identity="test" ❷
  password="test" ❸
  ca_cert="/etc/certs/cacert.pem" ❹
  phase2="auth=MD5" ❺
}
```

❶   This field specifies the EAP method for the connection.
❷   The identity field contains the identity string for EAP authentication inside the encrypted TLS tunnel.
❸   The password field contains the passphrase for the EAP authentication.
❹   The ca_cert field indicates the pathname of the CA certificate file. This file is needed to verify the server certificate.
❺   This field specifies the authentication method used in the encrypted TLS tunnel. In this example, EAP with MD5-Challenge is used. The "inner authentication" phase is often called "phase2".

Next, add the following lines to /etc/rc.conf :

```
wlans_ath0="wlan0"
ifconfig_wlan0="WPA DHCP"
```

The next step is to bring up the interface:

```
# service netif start
Starting wpa_supplicant.
DHCPREQUEST on wlan0 to 255.255.255.255 port 67 interval 7
DHCPREQUEST on wlan0 to 255.255.255.255 port 67 interval 15
DHCPREQUEST on wlan0 to 255.255.255.255 port 67 interval 21
DHCPACK from 192.168.0.20
bound to 192.168.0.254 -- renewal in 300 seconds.
wlan0: flags=8843<UP,BROADCAST,RUNNING,SIMPLEX,MULTICAST> mtu 1500
        ether 00:11:95:d5:43:62
        inet 192.168.0.254 netmask 0xffffff00 broadcast 192.168.0.255
        media: IEEE 802.11 Wireless Ethernet DS/11Mbps mode 11g
        status: associated
        ssid freebsdap channel 1 (2412 Mhz 11g) bssid 00:11:95:c3:0d:ac
        country US ecm authmode WPA2/802.11i privacy ON deftxkey UNDEF
        AES-CCM 3:128-bit txpower 21.5 bmiss 7 scanvalid 450 bgscan
        bgscanintvl 300 bgscanidle 250 roam:rssi 7 roam:rate 5 protmode CTS
        wme burst roaming MANUAL
```

30.3.4.1.3.4. WPA with EAP-PEAP

 Note

PEAPv0/EAP-MSCHAPv2 is the most common PEAP method. In this chapter, the term PEAP is used to refer to that method.

Protected EAP (PEAP) is designed as an alternative to EAP-TTLS and is the most used EAP standard after EAP-TLS. In a network with mixed operating systems, PEAP should be the most supported standard after EAP-TLS.

PEAP is similar to EAP-TTLS as it uses a server-side certificate to authenticate clients by creating an encrypted TLS tunnel between the client and the authentication server, which protects the ensuing exchange of authentication information. PEAP authentication differs from EAP-TTLS as it broadcasts the username in the clear and only the password is sent in the encrypted TLS tunnel. EAP-TTLS will use the TLS tunnel for both the username and password.

Add the following lines to `/etc/wpa_supplicant.conf` to configure the EAP-PEAP related settings:

```
network={
  ssid="freebsdap"
  proto=RSN
  key_mgmt=WPA-EAP
  eap=PEAP ❶
  identity="test" ❷
  password="test" ❸
  ca_cert="/etc/certs/cacert.pem" ❹
  phase1="peaplabel=0" ❺
  phase2="auth=MSCHAPV2" ❻
}
```

❶ This field specifies the EAP method for the connection.
❷ The `identity` field contains the identity string for EAP authentication inside the encrypted TLS tunnel.
❸ The `password` field contains the passphrase for the EAP authentication.
❹ The `ca_cert` field indicates the pathname of the CA certificate file. This file is needed to verify the server certificate.
❺ This field contains the parameters for the first phase of authentication, the TLS tunnel. According to the authentication server used, specify a specific label for authentication. Most of the time, the label will be "client EAP encryption" which is set by using `peaplabel=0`. More information can be found in wpa_supplicant.conf(5).
❻ This field specifies the authentication protocol used in the encrypted TLS tunnel. In the case of PEAP, it is `auth=MSCHAPV2` .

Add the following to `/etc/rc.conf` :

```
wlans_ath0="wlan0"
ifconfig_wlan0="WPA DHCP"
```

Then, bring up the interface:

```
# service netif start
Starting wpa_supplicant.
DHCPREQUEST on wlan0 to 255.255.255.255 port 67 interval 7
DHCPREQUEST on wlan0 to 255.255.255.255 port 67 interval 15
DHCPREQUEST on wlan0 to 255.255.255.255 port 67 interval 21
DHCPACK from 192.168.0.20
bound to 192.168.0.254 -- renewal in 300 seconds.
wlan0: flags=8843<UP,BROADCAST,RUNNING,SIMPLEX,MULTICAST> mtu 1500
        ether 00:11:95:d5:43:62
        inet 192.168.0.254 netmask 0xffffff00 broadcast 192.168.0.255
```

```
media: IEEE 802.11 Wireless Ethernet DS/11Mbps mode 11g
status: associated
ssid freebsdap channel 1 (2412 Mhz 11g) bssid 00:11:95:c3:0d:ac
country US ecm authmode WPA2/802.11i privacy ON deftxkey UNDEF
AES-CCM 3:128-bit txpower 21.5 bmiss 7 scanvalid 450 bgscan
bgscanintvl 300 bgscanidle 250 roam:rssi 7 roam:rate 5 protmode CTS
wme burst roaming MANUAL
```

30.3.4.1.4. WEP

Wired Equivalent Privacy (WEP) is part of the original 802.11 standard. There is no authentication mechanism, only a weak form of access control which is easily cracked.

WEP can be set up using ifconfig(8):

```
# ifconfig wlan0 create wlandev ath0
# ifconfig wlan0 inet 192.168.1.100 netmask 255.255.255.0 \
    ssid my_net wepmode on weptxkey 3 wepkey 3:0x3456789012
```

- The **weptxkey** specifies which WEP key will be used in the transmission. This example uses the third key. This must match the setting on the access point. When unsure which key is used by the access point, try 1 (the first key) for this value.

- The **wepkey** selects one of the WEP keys. It should be in the format *index:key*. Key 1 is used by default; the index only needs to be set when using a key other than the first key.

Note

Replace the 0x3456789012 with the key configured for use on the access point.

Refer to ifconfig(8) for further information.

The wpa_supplicant(8) facility can be used to configure a wireless interface with WEP. The example above can be set up by adding the following lines to /etc/wpa_supplicant.conf:

```
network={
  ssid="my_net"
  key_mgmt=NONE
  wep_key3=3456789012
  wep_tx_keyidx=3
}
```

Then:

```
# wpa_supplicant -i wlan0 -c /etc/wpa_supplicant.conf
Trying to associate with 00:13:46:49:41:76 (SSID='dlinkap' freq=2437 MHz)
Associated with 00:13:46:49:41:76
```

30.3.5. Ad-hoc Mode

IBSS mode, also called ad-hoc mode, is designed for point to point connections. For example, to establish an ad-hoc network between the machines A and B, choose two IP addresses and a SSID.

On A:

```
# ifconfig wlan0 create wlandev ath0 wlanmode adhoc
# ifconfig wlan0 inet 192.168.0.1 netmask 255.255.255.0 ssid freebsdap
# ifconfig wlan0
  wlan0: flags=8843<UP,BROADCAST,RUNNING,SIMPLEX,MULTICAST> metric 0 mtu 1500
```

```
ether 00:11:95:c3:0d:ac
inet 192.168.0.1 netmask 0xffffff00 broadcast 192.168.0.255
media: IEEE 802.11 Wireless Ethernet autoselect mode 11g <adhoc>
status: running
ssid freebsdap channel 2 (2417 Mhz 11g) bssid 02:11:95:c3:0d:ac
country US ecm authmode OPEN privacy OFF txpower 21.5 scanvalid 60
protmode CTS wme burst
```

The adhoc parameter indicates that the interface is running in IBSS mode.

B should now be able to detect A:

```
# ifconfig wlan0 create wlandev ath0 wlanmode adhoc
# ifconfig wlan0 up scan
  SSID/MESH ID   BSSID             CHAN RATE   S:N     INT CAPS
  freebsdap      02:11:95:c3:0d:ac   2   54M -64:-96  100 IS   WME
```

The I in the output confirms that A is in ad-hoc mode. Now, configure B with a different IP address:

```
# ifconfig wlan0 inet 192.168.0.2 netmask 255.255.255.0 ssid freebsdap
# ifconfig wlan0
  wlan0: flags=8843<UP,BROADCAST,RUNNING,SIMPLEX,MULTICAST> metric 0 mtu 1500
  ether 00:11:95:d5:43:62
  inet 192.168.0.2 netmask 0xffffff00 broadcast 192.168.0.255
  media: IEEE 802.11 Wireless Ethernet autoselect mode 11g <adhoc>
  status: running
  ssid freebsdap channel 2 (2417 Mhz 11g) bssid 02:11:95:c3:0d:ac
  country US ecm authmode OPEN privacy OFF txpower 21.5 scanvalid 60
  protmode CTS wme burst
```

Both A and B are now ready to exchange information.

30.3.6. FreeBSD Host Access Points

FreeBSD can act as an Access Point (AP) which eliminates the need to buy a hardware AP or run an ad-hoc network. This can be particularly useful when a FreeBSD machine is acting as a gateway to another network such as the Internet.

30.3.6.1. Basic Settings

Before configuring a FreeBSD machine as an AP, the kernel must be configured with the appropriate networking support for the wireless card as well as the security protocols being used. For more details, see Section 30.3.3, "Basic Setup".

Note

The NDIS driver wrapper for Windows® drivers does not currently support AP operation. Only native FreeBSD wireless drivers support AP mode.

Once wireless networking support is loaded, check if the wireless device supports the host-based access point mode, also known as hostap mode:

```
# ifconfig wlan0 create wlandev ath0
# ifconfig wlan0 list caps
drivercaps=6f85edc1<STA,FF,TURBOP,IBSS,HOSTAP,AHDEMO,TXPMGT,SHSLOT,SHPREAMBLE,MONITOR,MBSS,WPA1,WPA2,BURST
cryptocaps=1f<WEP,TKIP,AES,AES_CCM,TKIPMIC>
```

This output displays the card's capabilities. The HOSTAP word confirms that this wireless card can act as an AP. Various supported ciphers are also listed: WEP, TKIP, and AES. This information indicates which security protocols can be used on the AP.

The wireless device can only be put into hostap mode during the creation of the network pseudo-device, so a previously created device must be destroyed first:

```
# ifconfig wlan0 destroy
```

then regenerated with the correct option before setting the other parameters:

```
# ifconfig wlan0 create wlandev ath0 wlanmode hostap
# ifconfig wlan0 inet 192.168.0.1 netmask 255.255.255.0 ssid freebsdap mode 11g channel 1
```

Use ifconfig(8) again to see the status of the wlan0 interface:

```
# ifconfig wlan0
  wlan0: flags=8843<UP,BROADCAST,RUNNING,SIMPLEX,MULTICAST> metric 0 mtu 1500
    ether 00:11:95:c3:0d:ac
    inet 192.168.0.1 netmask 0xffffff00 broadcast 192.168.0.255
    media: IEEE 802.11 Wireless Ethernet autoselect mode 11g <hostap>
    status: running
    ssid freebsdap channel 1 (2412 Mhz 11g) bssid 00:11:95:c3:0d:ac
    country US ecm authmode OPEN privacy OFF txpower 21.5 scanvalid 60
    protmode CTS wme burst dtimperiod 1 -dfs
```

The hostap parameter indicates the interface is running in the host-based access point mode.

The interface configuration can be done automatically at boot time by adding the following lines to /etc/rc.conf :

```
wlans_ath0="wlan0"
create_args_wlan0="wlanmode hostap"
ifconfig_wlan0="inet 192.168.0.1 netmask 255.255.255.0 ssid freebsdap mode 11g channel 1"
```

30.3.6.2. Host-based Access Point Without Authentication or Encryption

Although it is not recommended to run an AP without any authentication or encryption, this is a simple way to check if the AP is working. This configuration is also important for debugging client issues.

Once the AP is configured, initiate a scan from another wireless machine to find the AP:

```
# ifconfig wlan0 create wlandev ath0
# ifconfig wlan0 up scan
SSID/MESH ID    BSSID             CHAN RATE   S:N      INT CAPS
freebsdap       00:11:95:c3:0d:ac  1    54M -66:-96  100 ES    WME
```

The client machine found the AP and can be associated with it:

```
# ifconfig wlan0 inet 192.168.0.2 netmask 255.255.255.0 ssid freebsdap
# ifconfig wlan0
  wlan0: flags=8843<UP,BROADCAST,RUNNING,SIMPLEX,MULTICAST> metric 0 mtu 1500
    ether 00:11:95:d5:43:62
    inet 192.168.0.2 netmask 0xffffff00 broadcast 192.168.0.255
    media: IEEE 802.11 Wireless Ethernet OFDM/54Mbps mode 11g
    status: associated
    ssid freebsdap channel 1 (2412 Mhz 11g) bssid 00:11:95:c3:0d:ac
    country US ecm authmode OPEN privacy OFF txpower 21.5 bmiss 7
    scanvalid 60 bgscan bgscanintvl 300 bgscanidle 250 roam:rssi 7
    roam:rate 5 protmode CTS wme burst
```

30.3.6.3. WPA2 Host-based Access Point

This section focuses on setting up a FreeBSD access point using the WPA2 security protocol. More details regarding WPA and the configuration of WPA-based wireless clients can be found in Section 30.3.4.1.3, "WPA".

The hostapd(8) daemon is used to deal with client authentication and key management on the WPA2-enabled AP.

The following configuration operations are performed on the FreeBSD machine acting as the AP. Once the AP is correctly working, hostapd(8) can be automatically started at boot with this line in /etc/rc.conf :

```
hostapd_enable="YES"
```

Before trying to configure hostapd(8), first configure the basic settings introduced in Section 30.3.6.1, "Basic Settings".

30.3.6.3.1. WPA2-PSK

WPA2-PSK is intended for small networks where the use of a backend authentication server is not possible or desired.

The configuration is done in /etc/hostapd.conf :

```
interface=wlan0                       ❶
debug=1                               ❷
ctrl_interface=/var/run/hostapd       ❸
ctrl_interface_group=wheel            ❹
ssid=freebsdap                        ❺
wpa=2                                 ❻
wpa_passphrase=freebsdmall            ❼
wpa_key_mgmt=WPA-PSK                  ❽
wpa_pairwise=CCMP                     ❾
```

❶   Wireless interface used for the access point.
❷   Level of verbosity used during the execution of hostapd(8). A value of 1 represents the minimal level.
❸   Pathname of the directory used by hostapd(8) to store domain socket files for communication with external programs such as hostapd_cli(8). The default value is used in this example.
❹   The group allowed to access the control interface files.
❺   The wireless network name, or SSID, that will appear in wireless scans.
❻   Enable WPA and specify which WPA authentication protocol will be required. A value of 2 configures the AP for WPA2 and is recommended. Set to 1 only if the obsolete WPA is required.
❼   ASCII passphrase for WPA authentication.

Warning

Always use strong passwords that are at least 8 characters long and made from a rich alphabet so that they will not be easily guessed or attacked.

❽   The key management protocol to use. This example sets WPA-PSK.
❾   Encryption algorithms accepted by the access point. In this example, only the CCMP (AES) cipher is accepted. CCMP is an alternative to TKIP and is strongly preferred when possible. TKIP should be allowed only when there are stations incapable of using CCMP.

The next step is to start hostapd(8):

```
# service hostapd forcestart
```

```
# ifconfig wlan0
wlan0: flags=8943<UP,BROADCAST,RUNNING,PROMISC,SIMPLEX,MULTICAST> metric 0 mtu 1500
    ether 04:f0:21:16:8e:10
    inet6 fe80::6f0:21ff:fe16:8e10%wlan0 prefixlen 64 scopeid 0x9
    nd6 options=21<PERFORMNUD,AUTO_LINKLOCAL>
    media: IEEE 802.11 Wireless Ethernet autoselect mode 11na <hostap>
    status: running
    ssid No5ignal channel 36 (5180 MHz 11a ht/40+) bssid 04:f0:21:16:8e:10
    country US ecm authmode WPA2/802.11i privacy MIXED deftxkey 2
    AES-CCM 2:128-bit AES-CCM 3:128-bit txpower 17 mcastrate 6 mgmtrate 6
    scanvalid 60 ampdulimit 64k ampdudensity 8 shortgi wme burst
    dtimperiod 1 -dfs
```

```
groups: wlan
```

Once the AP is running, the clients can associate with it. See Section 30.3.4.1.3, "WPA" for more details. It is possible to see the stations associated with the AP using ifconfig *wlan0* list sta.

30.3.6.4. WEP Host-based Access Point

It is not recommended to use WEP for setting up an AP since there is no authentication mechanism and the encryption is easily cracked. Some legacy wireless cards only support WEP and these cards will only support an AP without authentication or encryption.

The wireless device can now be put into hostap mode and configured with the correct SSID and IP address:

```
# ifconfig wlan0 create wlandev ath0 wlanmode hostap
# ifconfig wlan0 inet 192.168.0.1 netmask 255.255.255.0 \
 ssid freebsdap wepmode on weptxkey 3 wepkey 3:0x3456789012 mode 11g
```

- The weptxkey indicates which WEP key will be used in the transmission. This example uses the third key as key numbering starts with 1. This parameter must be specified in order to encrypt the data.

- The wepkey sets the selected WEP key. It should be in the format *index:key*. If the index is not given, key 1 is set. The index needs to be set when using keys other than the first key.

Use ifconfig(8) to see the status of the wlan0 interface:

```
# ifconfig wlan0
  wlan0: flags=8843<UP,BROADCAST,RUNNING,SIMPLEX,MULTICAST> metric 0 mtu 1500
    ether 00:11:95:c3:0d:ac
    inet 192.168.0.1 netmask 0xffffff00 broadcast 192.168.0.255
    media: IEEE 802.11 Wireless Ethernet autoselect mode 11g <hostap>
    status: running
    ssid freebsdap channel 4 (2427 Mhz 11g) bssid 00:11:95:c3:0d:ac
    country US ecm authmode OPEN privacy ON deftxkey 3 wepkey 3:40-bit
    txpower 21.5 scanvalid 60 protmode CTS wme burst dtimperiod 1 -dfs
```

From another wireless machine, it is now possible to initiate a scan to find the AP:

```
# ifconfig wlan0 create wlandev ath0
# ifconfig wlan0 up scan
SSID              BSSID              CHAN RATE  S:N   INT CAPS
freebsdap         00:11:95:c3:0d:ac   1    54M 22:1   100 EPS
```

In this example, the client machine found the AP and can associate with it using the correct parameters. See Section 30.3.4.1.4, "WEP" for more details.

30.3.7. Using Both Wired and Wireless Connections

A wired connection provides better performance and reliability, while a wireless connection provides flexibility and mobility. Laptop users typically want to roam seamlessly between the two types of connections.

On FreeBSD, it is possible to combine two or even more network interfaces together in a "failover" fashion. This type of configuration uses the most preferred and available connection from a group of network interfaces, and the operating system switches automatically when the link state changes.

Link aggregation and failover is covered in Section 30.7, "Link Aggregation and Failover" and an example for using both wired and wireless connections is provided at Example 30.3, "Failover Mode Between Ethernet and Wireless Interfaces".

30.3.8. Troubleshooting

This section describes a number of steps to help troubleshoot common wireless networking problems.

- If the access point is not listed when scanning, check that the configuration has not limited the wireless device to a limited set of channels.

- If the device cannot associate with an access point, verify that the configuration matches the settings on the access point. This includes the authentication scheme and any security protocols. Simplify the configuration as much as possible. If using a security protocol such as WPA or WEP, configure the access point for open authentication and no security to see if traffic will pass.

  Debugging support is provided by wpa_supplicant(8). Try running this utility manually with **-dd** and look at the system logs.

- Once the system can associate with the access point, diagnose the network configuration using tools like ping(8).

- There are many lower-level debugging tools. Debugging messages can be enabled in the 802.11 protocol support layer using wlandebug(8). For example, to enable console messages related to scanning for access points and the 802.11 protocol handshakes required to arrange communication:

```
# wlandebug -i ath0 +scan+auth+debug+assoc
  net.wlan.0.debug: 0 => 0xc80000<assoc,auth,scan>
```

  Many useful statistics are maintained by the 802.11 layer and `wlanstats`, found in `/usr/src/tools/tools/net80211`, will dump this information. These statistics should display all errors identified by the 802.11 layer. However, some errors are identified in the device drivers that lie below the 802.11 layer so they may not show up. To diagnose device-specific problems, refer to the drivers' documentation.

If the above information does not help to clarify the problem, submit a problem report and include output from the above tools.

30.4. USB Tethering

Many cellphones provide the option to share their data connection over USB (often called "tethering"). This feature uses either the RNDIS, CDC or a custom Apple® iPhone®/iPad® protocol.

- Android™ devices generally use the urndis(4) driver.

- Apple® devices use the ipheth(4) driver.

- Older devices will often use the cdce(4) driver.

Before attaching a device, load the appropriate driver into the kernel:

```
# kldload if_urndis
# kldload ʊ
if_cdce
# kldload if_ipheth
```

Once the device is attached ue0 will be available for use like a normal network device. Be sure that the "USB tethering" option is enabled on the device.

30.5. Bluetooth

Written by Pav Lucistnik.

Bluetooth is a wireless technology for creating personal networks operating in the 2.4 GHz unlicensed band, with a range of 10 meters. Networks are usually formed ad-hoc from portable devices such as cellular phones, handhelds, and laptops. Unlike Wi-Fi wireless technology, Bluetooth offers higher level service profiles, such as FTP-like file servers, file pushing, voice transport, serial line emulation, and more.

This section describes the use of a USB Bluetooth dongle on a FreeBSD system. It then describes the various Bluetooth protocols and utilities.

30.5.1. Loading Bluetooth Support

The Bluetooth stack in FreeBSD is implemented using the netgraph(4) framework. A broad variety of Bluetooth USB dongles is supported by ng_ubt(4). Broadcom BCM2033 based Bluetooth devices are supported by the ubtbcmfw(4) and ng_ubt(4) drivers. The 3Com Bluetooth PC Card 3CRWB60-A is supported by the ng_bt3c(4) driver. Serial and UART based Bluetooth devices are supported by sio(4), ng_h4(4), and hcserialrd(8).

Before attaching a device, determine which of the above drivers it uses, then load the driver. For example, if the device uses the ng_ubt(4) driver:

```
# kldload ng_ubt
```

If the Bluetooth device will be attached to the system during system startup, the system can be configured to load the module at boot time by adding the driver to /boot/loader.conf :

```
ng_ubt_load="YES"
```

Once the driver is loaded, plug in the USB dongle. If the driver load was successful, output similar to the following should appear on the console and in /var/log/messages :

```
ubt0: vendor 0x0a12 product 0x0001, rev 1.10/5.25, addr 2
ubt0: Interface 0 endpoints: interrupt=0x81, bulk-in=0x82, bulk-out=0x2
ubt0: Interface 1 (alt.config 5) endpoints: isoc-in=0x83, isoc-out=0x3,
      wMaxPacketSize=49, nframes=6, buffer size=294
```

To start and stop the Bluetooth stack, use its startup script. It is a good idea to stop the stack before unplugging the device. When starting the stack, the output should be similar to the following:

```
# service bluetooth start ubt0
BD_ADDR: 00:02:72:00:d4:1a
Features: 0xff 0xff 0xf 00 00 00 00 00
<3-Slot> <5-Slot> <Encryption> <Slot offset>
<Timing accuracy> <Switch> <Hold mode> <Sniff mode>
<Park mode> <RSSI> <Channel quality> <SCO link>
<HV2 packets> <HV3 packets> <u-law log> <A-law log> <CVSD>
<Paging scheme> <Power control> <Transparent SCO data>
Max. ACL packet size: 192 bytes
Number of ACL packets: 8
Max. SCO packet size: 64 bytes
Number of SCO packets: 8
```

30.5.2. Finding Other Bluetooth Devices

The Host Controller Interface (HCI) provides a uniform method for accessing Bluetooth baseband capabilities. In FreeBSD, a netgraph HCI node is created for each Bluetooth device. For more details, refer to ng_hci(4).

One of the most common tasks is discovery of Bluetooth devices within RF proximity. This operation is called *inquiry*. Inquiry and other HCI related operations are done using hccontrol(8). The example below shows how to find out which Bluetooth devices are in range. The list of devices should be displayed in a few seconds. Note that a remote device will only answer the inquiry if it is set to *discoverable* mode.

```
% hccontrol -n ubt0hci inquiry
Inquiry result, num_responses=1
Inquiry result #0
       BD_ADDR: 00:80:37:29:19:a4
       Page Scan Rep. Mode: 0x1
       Page Scan Period Mode: 00
       Page Scan Mode: 00
       Class: 52:02:04
```

```
      Clock offset: 0x78ef
Inquiry complete. Status: No error [00]
```

The BD_ADDR is the unique address of a Bluetooth device, similar to the MAC address of a network card. This address is needed for further communication with a device and it is possible to assign a human readable name to a BD_ADDR. Information regarding the known Bluetooth hosts is contained in /etc/bluetooth/hosts . The following example shows how to obtain the human readable name that was assigned to the remote device:

```
% hccontrol -n ubt0hci remote_name_request 00:80:37:29:19:a4
BD_ADDR: 00:80:37:29:19:a4
Name: Pav's T39
```

If an inquiry is performed on a remote Bluetooth device, it will find the computer as "your.host.name (ubt0)". The name assigned to the local device can be changed at any time.

The Bluetooth system provides a point-to-point connection between two Bluetooth units, or a point-to-multipoint connection which is shared among several Bluetooth devices. The following example shows how to obtain the list of active baseband connections for the local device:

```
% hccontrol -n ubt0hci read_connection_list
Remote BD_ADDR    Handle Type Mode Role Encrypt Pending Queue State
00:80:37:29:19:a4    41  ACL    0 MAST    NONE       0     0 OPEN
```

A *connection handle* is useful when termination of the baseband connection is required, though it is normally not required to do this by hand. The stack will automatically terminate inactive baseband connections.

```
# hccontrol -n ubt0hci disconnect 41
Connection handle: 41
Reason: Connection terminated by local host [0x16]
```

Type hccontrol help for a complete listing of available HCI commands. Most of the HCI commands do not require superuser privileges.

30.5.3. Device Pairing

By default, Bluetooth communication is not authenticated, and any device can talk to any other device. A Bluetooth device, such as a cellular phone, may choose to require authentication to provide a particular service. Bluetooth authentication is normally done with a *PIN code*, an ASCII string up to 16 characters in length. The user is required to enter the same PIN code on both devices. Once the user has entered the PIN code, both devices will generate a *link key*. After that, the link key can be stored either in the devices or in a persistent storage. Next time, both devices will use the previously generated link key. This procedure is called *pairing*. Note that if the link key is lost by either device, the pairing must be repeated.

The hcsecd(8) daemon is responsible for handling Bluetooth authentication requests. The default configuration file is /etc/bluetooth/hcsecd.conf . An example section for a cellular phone with the PIN code set to 1234 is shown below:

```
device {
        bdaddr   00:80:37:29:19:a4;
        name     "Pav's T39";
        key      nokey;
        pin      "1234";
    }
```

The only limitation on PIN codes is length. Some devices, such as Bluetooth headsets, may have a fixed PIN code built in. The -d switch forces hcsecd(8) to stay in the foreground, so it is easy to see what is happening. Set the remote device to receive pairing and initiate the Bluetooth connection to the remote device. The remote device should indicate that pairing was accepted and request the PIN code. Enter the same PIN code listed in hcsecd.conf. Now the computer and the remote device are paired. Alternatively, pairing can be initiated on the remote device.

The following line can be added to /etc/rc.conf to configure hcsecd(8) to start automatically on system start:

```
hcsecd_enable="YES"
```

The following is a sample of the hcsecd(8) daemon output:

```
hcsecd[16484]: Got Link_Key_Request event from 'ubt0hci', remote bdaddr 0:80:37:29:19:a4
hcsecd[16484]: Found matching entry, remote bdaddr 0:80:37:29:19:a4, name 'Pav's T39', ↺
link key doesn't exist
hcsecd[16484]: Sending Link_Key_Negative_Reply to 'ubt0hci' for remote bdaddr ↺
0:80:37:29:19:a4
hcsecd[16484]: Got PIN_Code_Request event from 'ubt0hci', remote bdaddr 0:80:37:29:19:a4
hcsecd[16484]: Found matching entry, remote bdaddr 0:80:37:29:19:a4, name 'Pav's T39', ↺
PIN code exists
hcsecd[16484]: Sending PIN_Code_Reply to 'ubt0hci' for remote bdaddr 0:80:37:29:19:a4
```

30.5.4. Network Access with PPP Profiles

A Dial-Up Networking (DUN) profile can be used to configure a cellular phone as a wireless modem for connecting to a dial-up Internet access server. It can also be used to configure a computer to receive data calls from a cellular phone.

Network access with a PPP profile can be used to provide LAN access for a single Bluetooth device or multiple Bluetooth devices. It can also provide PC to PC connection using PPP networking over serial cable emulation.

In FreeBSD, these profiles are implemented with ppp(8) and the rfcomm_pppd(8) wrapper which converts a Bluetooth connection into something PPP can use. Before a profile can be used, a new PPP label must be created in /etc/ppp/ppp.conf . Consult rfcomm_pppd(8) for examples.

In this example, rfcomm_pppd(8) is used to open a connection to a remote device with a **BD_ADDR** of 00:80:37:29:19:a4 on a DUN RFCOMM channel:

```
# rfcomm_pppd -a 00:80:37:29:19:a4 -c -C dun -l rfcomm-dialup
```

The actual channel number will be obtained from the remote device using the SDP protocol. It is possible to specify the RFCOMM channel by hand, and in this case rfcomm_pppd(8) will not perform the SDP query. Use sdpcontrol(8) to find out the RFCOMM channel on the remote device.

In order to provide network access with the PPP LAN service, sdpd(8) must be running and a new entry for LAN clients must be created in /etc/ppp/ppp.conf . Consult rfcomm_pppd(8) for examples. Finally, start the RFCOMM PPP server on a valid RFCOMM channel number. The RFCOMM PPP server will automatically register the Bluetooth LAN service with the local SDP daemon. The example below shows how to start the RFCOMM PPP server.

```
# rfcomm_pppd -s -C 7 -l rfcomm-server
```

30.5.5. Bluetooth Protocols

This section provides an overview of the various Bluetooth protocols, their function, and associated utilities.

30.5.5.1. Logical Link Control and Adaptation Protocol (L2CAP)

The Logical Link Control and Adaptation Protocol (L2CAP) provides connection-oriented and connectionless data services to upper layer protocols. L2CAP permits higher level protocols and applications to transmit and receive L2CAP data packets up to 64 kilobytes in length.

L2CAP is based around the concept of *channels*. A channel is a logical connection on top of a baseband connection, where each channel is bound to a single protocol in a many-to-one fashion. Multiple channels can be bound to the same protocol, but a channel cannot be bound to multiple protocols. Each L2CAP packet received on a channel is directed to the appropriate higher level protocol. Multiple channels can share the same baseband connection.

In FreeBSD, a netgraph L2CAP node is created for each Bluetooth device. This node is normally connected to the downstream Bluetooth HCI node and upstream Bluetooth socket nodes. The default name for the L2CAP node is "devicel2cap". For more details refer to ng_l2cap(4).

622

A useful command is l2ping(8), which can be used to ping other devices. Some Bluetooth implementations might not return all of the data sent to them, so 0 bytes in the following example is normal.

```
# l2ping -a 00:80:37:29:19:a4
0 bytes from 0:80:37:29:19:a4 seq_no=0 time=48.633 ms result=0
0 bytes from 0:80:37:29:19:a4 seq_no=1 time=37.551 ms result=0
0 bytes from 0:80:37:29:19:a4 seq_no=2 time=28.324 ms result=0
0 bytes from 0:80:37:29:19:a4 seq_no=3 time=46.150 ms result=0
```

The l2control(8) utility is used to perform various operations on L2CAP nodes. This example shows how to obtain the list of logical connections (channels) and the list of baseband connections for the local device:

```
% l2control -a 00:02:72:00:d4:1a read_channel_list
L2CAP channels:
Remote BD_ADDR     SCID/ DCID   PSM  IMTU/ OMTU State
00:07:e0:00:0b:ca   66/  64     3    132/  672 OPEN
% l2control -a 00:02:72:00:d4:1a read_connection_list
L2CAP connections:
Remote BD_ADDR    Handle Flags Pending State
00:07:e0:00:0b:ca   41 0           0 OPEN
```

Another diagnostic tool is btsockstat(1). It is similar to netstat(1), but for Bluetooth network-related data structures. The example below shows the same logical connection as l2control(8) above.

```
% btsockstat
Active L2CAP sockets
PCB        Recv-Q Send-Q Local address/PSM       Foreign address    CID    State
c2afe900     0      0 00:02:72:00:d4:1a/3     00:07:e0:00:0b:ca 66    OPEN
Active RFCOMM sessions
L2PCB    PCB      Flag MTU   Out-Q DLCs State
c2afe900 c2b53380 1    127   0     Yes  OPEN
Active RFCOMM sockets
PCB        Recv-Q Send-Q Local address     Foreign address    Chan DLCI State
c2e8bc80     0    250 00:02:72:00:d4:1a 00:07:e0:00:0b:ca 3    6    OPEN
```

30.5.5.2. Radio Frequency Communication (RFCOMM)

The RFCOMM protocol provides emulation of serial ports over the L2CAP protocol. RFCOMM is a simple transport protocol, with additional provisions for emulating the 9 circuits of RS-232 (EIATIA-232-E) serial ports. It supports up to 60 simultaneous connections (RFCOMM channels) between two Bluetooth devices.

For the purposes of RFCOMM, a complete communication path involves two applications running on the communication endpoints with a communication segment between them. RFCOMM is intended to cover applications that make use of the serial ports of the devices in which they reside. The communication segment is a direct connect Bluetooth link from one device to another.

RFCOMM is only concerned with the connection between the devices in the direct connect case, or between the device and a modem in the network case. RFCOMM can support other configurations, such as modules that communicate via Bluetooth wireless technology on one side and provide a wired interface on the other side.

In FreeBSD, RFCOMM is implemented at the Bluetooth sockets layer.

30.5.5.3. Service Discovery Protocol (SDP)

The Service Discovery Protocol (SDP) provides the means for client applications to discover the existence of services provided by server applications as well as the attributes of those services. The attributes of a service include the type or class of service offered and the mechanism or protocol information needed to utilize the service.

SDP involves communication between a SDP server and a SDP client. The server maintains a list of service records that describe the characteristics of services associated with the server. Each service record contains information about a single service. A client may retrieve information from a service record maintained by the SDP server by issuing a SDP request. If the client, or an application associated with the client, decides to use a service, it must open a separate connection to the service provider in order to utilize the service. SDP provides a mechanism for discovering services and their attributes, but it does not provide a mechanism for utilizing those services.

Normally, a SDP client searches for services based on some desired characteristics of the services. However, there are times when it is desirable to discover which types of services are described by an SDP server's service records without any prior information about the services. This process of looking for any offered services is called *browsing*.

The Bluetooth SDP server, sdpd(8), and command line client, sdpcontrol(8), are included in the standard FreeBSD installation. The following example shows how to perform a SDP browse query.

```
% sdpcontrol -a 00:01:03:fc:6e:ec browse
Record Handle: 00000000
Service Class ID List:
        Service Discovery Server (0x1000)
Protocol Descriptor List:
        L2CAP (0x0100)
                Protocol specific parameter #1: u/int/uuid16 1
                Protocol specific parameter #2: u/int/uuid16 1

Record Handle: 0x00000001
Service Class ID List:
        Browse Group Descriptor (0x1001)

Record Handle: 0x00000002
Service Class ID List:
        LAN Access Using PPP (0x1102)
Protocol Descriptor List:
        L2CAP (0x0100)
        RFCOMM (0x0003)
                Protocol specific parameter #1: u/int8/bool 1
Bluetooth Profile Descriptor List:
        LAN Access Using PPP (0x1102) ver. 1.0
```

Note that each service has a list of attributes, such as the RFCOMM channel. Depending on the service, the user might need to make note of some of the attributes. Some Bluetooth implementations do not support service browsing and may return an empty list. In this case, it is possible to search for the specific service. The example below shows how to search for the OBEX Object Push (OPUSH) service:

```
% sdpcontrol -a 00:01:03:fc:6e:ec search OPUSH
```

Offering services on FreeBSD to Bluetooth clients is done with the sdpd(8) server. The following line can be added to /etc/rc.conf :

```
sdpd_enable="YES"
```

Then the sdpd(8) daemon can be started with:

```
# service sdpd start
```

The local server application that wants to provide a Bluetooth service to remote clients will register the service with the local SDP daemon. An example of such an application is rfcomm_pppd(8). Once started, it will register the Bluetooth LAN service with the local SDP daemon.

The list of services registered with the local SDP server can be obtained by issuing a SDP browse query via the local control channel:

```
# sdpcontrol -l browse
```

30.5.5.4. OBEX Object Push (OPUSH)

Object Exchange (OBEX) is a widely used protocol for simple file transfers between mobile devices. Its main use is in infrared communication, where it is used for generic file transfers between notebooks or PDAs, and for sending business cards or calendar entries between cellular phones and other devices with Personal Information Manager (PIM) applications.

The OBEX server and client are implemented by obexapp, which can be installed using the comms/obexapp package or port.

The OBEX client is used to push and/or pull objects from the OBEX server. An example object is a business card or an appointment. The OBEX client can obtain the RFCOMM channel number from the remote device via SDP. This can be done by specifying the service name instead of the RFCOMM channel number. Supported service names are: IrMC, FTRN, and OPUSH. It is also possible to specify the RFCOMM channel as a number. Below is an example of an OBEX session where the device information object is pulled from the cellular phone, and a new object, the business card, is pushed into the phone's directory.

```
% obexapp -a 00:80:37:29:19:a4 -C IrMC
obex> get telecom/devinfo.txt devinfo-t39.txt
Success, response: OK, Success (0x20)
obex> put new.vcf
Success, response: OK, Success (0x20)
obex> di
Success, response: OK, Success (0x20)
```

In order to provide the OPUSH service, sdpd(8) must be running and a root folder, where all incoming objects will be stored, must be created. The default path to the root folder is /var/spool/obex . Finally, start the OBEX server on a valid RFCOMM channel number. The OBEX server will automatically register the OPUSH service with the local SDP daemon. The example below shows how to start the OBEX server.

```
# obexapp -s -C 10
```

30.5.5.5. Serial Port Profile (SPP)

The Serial Port Profile (SPP) allows Bluetooth devices to perform serial cable emulation. This profile allows legacy applications to use Bluetooth as a cable replacement, through a virtual serial port abstraction.

In FreeBSD, rfcomm_sppd(1) implements SPP and a pseudo tty is used as a virtual serial port abstraction. The example below shows how to connect to a remote device's serial port service. A RFCOMM channel does not have to be specified as rfcomm_sppd(1) can obtain it from the remote device via SDP. To override this, specify a RFCOMM channel on the command line.

```
# rfcomm_sppd -a 00:07:E0:00:0B:CA -t
rfcomm_sppd[94692]: Starting on /dev/pts/6...
/dev/pts/6
```

Once connected, the pseudo tty can be used as serial port:

```
# cu -l /dev/pts/6
```

The pseudo tty is printed on stdout and can be read by wrapper scripts:

```
PTS=`rfcomm_sppd -a 00:07:E0:00:0B:CA -t`
cu -l $PTS
```

30.5.6. Troubleshooting

By default, when FreeBSD is accepting a new connection, it tries to perform a role switch and become master. Some older Bluetooth devices which do not support role switching will not be able to connect. Since role switching is performed when a new connection is being established, it is not possible to ask the remote device if it supports role switching. However, there is a HCI option to disable role switching on the local side:

```
# hccontrol -n ubt0hci write_node_role_switch 0
```

To display Bluetooth packets, use the third-party package hcidump, which can be installed using the comms/hcidump package or port. This utility is similar to tcpdump(1) and can be used to display the contents of Bluetooth packets on the terminal and to dump the Bluetooth packets to a file.

30.6. Bridging

Written by Andrew Thompson.

It is sometimes useful to divide a network, such as an Ethernet segment, into network segments without having to create IP subnets and use a router to connect the segments together. A device that connects two networks together in this fashion is called a "bridge".

A bridge works by learning the MAC addresses of the devices on each of its network interfaces. It forwards traffic between networks only when the source and destination MAC addresses are on different networks. In many respects, a bridge is like an Ethernet switch with very few ports. A FreeBSD system with multiple network interfaces can be configured to act as a bridge.

Bridging can be useful in the following situations:

Connecting Networks

The basic operation of a bridge is to join two or more network segments. There are many reasons to use a host-based bridge instead of networking equipment, such as cabling constraints or firewalling. A bridge can also connect a wireless interface running in hostap mode to a wired network and act as an access point.

Filtering/Traffic Shaping Firewall

A bridge can be used when firewall functionality is needed without routing or Network Address Translation (NAT).

An example is a small company that is connected via DSL or ISDN to an ISP. There are thirteen public IP addresses from the ISP and ten computers on the network. In this situation, using a router-based firewall is difficult because of subnetting issues. A bridge-based firewall can be configured without any IP addressing issues.

Network Tap

A bridge can join two network segments in order to inspect all Ethernet frames that pass between them using bpf(4) and tcpdump(1) on the bridge interface or by sending a copy of all frames out an additional interface known as a span port.

Layer 2 VPN

Two Ethernet networks can be joined across an IP link by bridging the networks to an EtherIP tunnel or a tap(4) based solution such as OpenVPN.

Layer 2 Redundancy

A network can be connected together with multiple links and use the Spanning Tree Protocol (STP) to block redundant paths.

This section describes how to configure a FreeBSD system as a bridge using if_bridge(4). A netgraph bridging driver is also available, and is described in ng_bridge(4).

Note

Packet filtering can be used with any firewall package that hooks into the pfil(9) framework. The bridge can be used as a traffic shaper with altq(4) or dummynet(4).

30.6.1. Enabling the Bridge

In FreeBSD, if_bridge(4) is a kernel module which is automatically loaded by ifconfig(8) when creating a bridge interface. It is also possible to compile bridge support into a custom kernel by adding **device if_bridge** to the custom kernel configuration file.

The bridge is created using interface cloning. To create the bridge interface:

```
# ifconfig bridge create
bridge0
# ifconfig bridge0
bridge0: flags=8802<BROADCAST,SIMPLEX,MULTICAST> metric 0 mtu 1500
        ether 96:3d:4b:f1:79:7a
        id 00:00:00:00:00:00 priority 32768 hellotime 2 fwddelay 15
        maxage 20 holdcnt 6 proto rstp maxaddr 100 timeout 1200
        root id 00:00:00:00:00:00 priority 0 ifcost 0 port 0
```

When a bridge interface is created, it is automatically assigned a randomly generated Ethernet address. The `maxaddr` and `timeout` parameters control how many MAC addresses the bridge will keep in its forwarding table and how many seconds before each entry is removed after it is last seen. The other parameters control how STP operates.

Next, specify which network interfaces to add as members of the bridge. For the bridge to forward packets, all member interfaces and the bridge need to be up:

```
# ifconfig bridge0 addm fxp0 addm fxp1 up
# ifconfig fxp0 up
# ifconfig fxp1 up
```

The bridge can now forward Ethernet frames between `fxp0` and `fxp1`. Add the following lines to `/etc/rc.conf` so the bridge is created at startup:

```
cloned_interfaces="bridge0"
ifconfig_bridge0="addm fxp0 addm fxp1 up"
ifconfig_fxp0="up"
ifconfig_fxp1="up"
```

If the bridge host needs an IP address, set it on the bridge interface, not on the member interfaces. The address can be set statically or via DHCP. This example sets a static IP address:

```
# ifconfig bridge0 inet 192.168.0.1/24
```

It is also possible to assign an IPv6 address to a bridge interface. To make the changes permanent, add the addressing information to `/etc/rc.conf` .

 Note

When packet filtering is enabled, bridged packets will pass through the filter inbound on the originating interface on the bridge interface, and outbound on the appropriate interfaces. Either stage can be disabled. When direction of the packet flow is important, it is best to firewall on the member interfaces rather than the bridge itself.

The bridge has several configurable settings for passing non-IP and IP packets, and layer2 firewalling with ipfw(8). See if_bridge(4) for more information.

30.6.2. Enabling Spanning Tree

For an Ethernet network to function properly, only one active path can exist between two devices. The STP protocol detects loops and puts redundant links into a blocked state. Should one of the active links fail, STP calculates a different tree and enables one of the blocked paths to restore connectivity to all points in the network.

The Rapid Spanning Tree Protocol (RSTP or 802.1w) provides backwards compatibility with legacy STP. RSTP provides faster convergence and exchanges information with neighboring switches to quickly transition to forwarding mode without creating loops. FreeBSD supports RSTP and STP as operating modes, with RSTP being the default mode.

STP can be enabled on member interfaces using ifconfig(8). For a bridge with `fxp0` and `fxp1` as the current interfaces, enable STP with:

```
# ifconfig bridge0 stp fxp0 stp fxp1
bridge0: flags=8843<UP,BROADCAST,RUNNING,SIMPLEX,MULTICAST> metric 0 mtu 1500
        ether d6:cf:d5:a0:94:6d
        id 00:01:02:4b:d4:50 priority 32768 hellotime 2 fwddelay 15
        maxage 20 holdcnt 6 proto rstp maxaddr 100 timeout 1200
        root id 00:01:02:4b:d4:50 priority 32768 ifcost 0 port 0
        member: fxp0 flags=1c7<LEARNING,DISCOVER,STP,AUTOEDGE,PTP,AUTOPTP>
                port 3 priority 128 path cost 200000 proto rstp
                role designated state forwarding
        member: fxp1 flags=1c7<LEARNING,DISCOVER,STP,AUTOEDGE,PTP,AUTOPTP>
                port 4 priority 128 path cost 200000 proto rstp
                role designated state forwarding
```

This bridge has a spanning tree ID of 00:01:02:4b:d4:50 and a priority of 32768. As the root id is the same, it indicates that this is the root bridge for the tree.

Another bridge on the network also has STP enabled:

```
bridge0: flags=8843<UP,BROADCAST,RUNNING,SIMPLEX,MULTICAST> metric 0 mtu 1500
        ether 96:3d:4b:f1:79:7a
        id 00:13:d4:9a:06:7a priority 32768 hellotime 2 fwddelay 15
        maxage 20 holdcnt 6 proto rstp maxaddr 100 timeout 1200
        root id 00:01:02:4b:d4:50 priority 32768 ifcost 400000 port 4
        member: fxp0 flags=1c7<LEARNING,DISCOVER,STP,AUTOEDGE,PTP,AUTOPTP>
                port 4 priority 128 path cost 200000 proto rstp
                role root state forwarding
        member: fxp1 flags=1c7<LEARNING,DISCOVER,STP,AUTOEDGE,PTP,AUTOPTP>
                port 5 priority 128 path cost 200000 proto rstp
                role designated state forwarding
```

The line root id 00:01:02:4b:d4:50 priority 32768 ifcost 400000 port 4 shows that the root bridge is 00:01:02:4b:d4:50 and has a path cost of 400000 from this bridge. The path to the root bridge is via port 4 which is fxp0.

30.6.3. Bridge Interface Parameters

Several ifconfig parameters are unique to bridge interfaces. This section summarizes some common uses for these parameters. The complete list of available parameters is described in ifconfig(8).

private

> A private interface does not forward any traffic to any other port that is also designated as a private interface. The traffic is blocked unconditionally so no Ethernet frames will be forwarded, including ARP packets. If traffic needs to be selectively blocked, a firewall should be used instead.

span

> A span port transmits a copy of every Ethernet frame received by the bridge. The number of span ports configured on a bridge is unlimited, but if an interface is designated as a span port, it cannot also be used as a regular bridge port. This is most useful for snooping a bridged network passively on another host connected to one of the span ports of the bridge. For example, to send a copy of all frames out the interface named fxp4:

```
# ifconfig bridge0 span fxp4
```

sticky

> If a bridge member interface is marked as sticky, dynamically learned address entries are treated as static entries in the forwarding cache. Sticky entries are never aged out of the cache or replaced, even if the address is seen on a different interface. This gives the benefit of static address entries without the need to pre-populate the forwarding table. Clients learned on a particular segment of the bridge can not roam to another segment.

> An example of using sticky addresses is to combine the bridge with VLANs in order to isolate customer networks without wasting IP address space. Consider that CustomerA is on vlan100, CustomerB is on vlan101, and the bridge has the address 192.168.0.1 :

```
# ifconfig bridge0 addm vlan100 sticky vlan100 addm vlan101 sticky vlan101
# ifconfig bridge0 inet 192.168.0.1/24
```

In this example, both clients see 192.168.0.1 as their default gateway. Since the bridge cache is sticky, one host can not spoof the MAC address of the other customer in order to intercept their traffic.

Any communication between the VLANs can be blocked using a firewall or, as seen in this example, private interfaces:

```
# ifconfig bridge0 private vlan100 private vlan101
```

The customers are completely isolated from each other and the full /24 address range can be allocated without subnetting.

The number of unique source MAC addresses behind an interface can be limited. Once the limit is reached, packets with unknown source addresses are dropped until an existing host cache entry expires or is removed.

The following example sets the maximum number of Ethernet devices for CustomerA on vlan100 to 10:

```
# ifconfig bridge0 ifmaxaddr vlan100 10
```

Bridge interfaces also support monitor mode, where the packets are discarded after bpf(4) processing and are not processed or forwarded further. This can be used to multiplex the input of two or more interfaces into a single bpf(4) stream. This is useful for reconstructing the traffic for network taps that transmit the RX/TX signals out through two separate interfaces. For example, to read the input from four network interfaces as one stream:

```
# ifconfig bridge0 addm fxp0 addm fxp1 addm fxp2 addm fxp3 monitor up
# tcpdump -i bridge0
```

30.6.4. SNMP Monitoring

The bridge interface and STP parameters can be monitored via bsnmpd(1) which is included in the FreeBSD base system. The exported bridge MIBs conform to IETF standards so any SNMP client or monitoring package can be used to retrieve the data.

To enable monitoring on the bridge, uncomment this line in /etc/snmp.config by removing the beginning # symbol:

```
begemotSnmpdModulePath."bridge" = "/usr/lib/snmp_bridge.so"
```

Other configuration settings, such as community names and access lists, may need to be modified in this file. See bsnmpd(1) and snmp_bridge(3) for more information. Once these edits are saved, add this line to /etc/rc.conf :

```
bsnmpd_enable="YES"
```

Then, start bsnmpd(1):

```
# service bsnmpd start
```

The following examples use the Net-SNMP software (net-mgmt/net-snmp) to query a bridge from a client system. The net-mgmt/bsnmptools port can also be used. From the SNMP client which is running Net-SNMP, add the following lines to $HOME/.snmp/snmp.conf in order to import the bridge MIB definitions:

```
mibdirs +/usr/share/snmp/mibs
mibs +BRIDGE-MIB:RSTP-MIB:BEGEMOT-MIB:BEGEMOT-BRIDGE-MIB
```

To monitor a single bridge using the IETF BRIDGE-MIB (RFC4188):

```
% snmpwalk -v 2c -c public bridge1.example.com mib-2.dot1dBridge
BRIDGE-MIB::dot1dBaseBridgeAddress.0 = STRING: 66:fb:9b:6e:5c:44
BRIDGE-MIB::dot1dBaseNumPorts.0 = INTEGER: 1 ports
BRIDGE-MIB::dot1dStpTimeSinceTopologyChange.0 = Timeticks: (189959) 0:31:39.59 centi-
seconds
```

```
BRIDGE-MIB::dot1dStpTopChanges.0 = Counter32: 2
BRIDGE-MIB::dot1dStpDesignatedRoot.0 = Hex-STRING: 80 00 00 01 02 4B D4 50
...
BRIDGE-MIB::dot1dStpPortState.3 = INTEGER: forwarding(5)
BRIDGE-MIB::dot1dStpPortEnable.3 = INTEGER: enabled(1)
BRIDGE-MIB::dot1dStpPortPathCost.3 = INTEGER: 200000
BRIDGE-MIB::dot1dStpPortDesignatedRoot.3 = Hex-STRING: 80 00 00 01 02 4B D4 50
BRIDGE-MIB::dot1dStpPortDesignatedCost.3 = INTEGER: 0
BRIDGE-MIB::dot1dStpPortDesignatedBridge.3 = Hex-STRING: 80 00 00 01 02 4B D4 50
BRIDGE-MIB::dot1dStpPortDesignatedPort.3 = Hex-STRING: 03 80
BRIDGE-MIB::dot1dStpPortForwardTransitions.3 = Counter32: 1
RSTP-MIB::dot1dStpVersion.0 = INTEGER: rstp(2)
```

The dot1dStpTopChanges.0 value is two, indicating that the STP bridge topology has changed twice. A topology change means that one or more links in the network have changed or failed and a new tree has been calculated. The dot1dStpTimeSinceTopologyChange.0 value will show when this happened.

To monitor multiple bridge interfaces, the private BEGEMOT-BRIDGE-MIB can be used:

```
% snmpwalk -v 2c -c public bridge1.example.com
enterprises.fokus.begemot.begemotBridge
BEGEMOT-BRIDGE-MIB::begemotBridgeBaseName."bridge0" = STRING: bridge0
BEGEMOT-BRIDGE-MIB::begemotBridgeBaseName."bridge2" = STRING: bridge2
BEGEMOT-BRIDGE-MIB::begemotBridgeBaseAddress."bridge0" = STRING: e:ce:3b:5a:9e:13
BEGEMOT-BRIDGE-MIB::begemotBridgeBaseAddress."bridge2" = STRING: 12:5e:4d:74:d:fc
BEGEMOT-BRIDGE-MIB::begemotBridgeBaseNumPorts."bridge0" = INTEGER: 1
BEGEMOT-BRIDGE-MIB::begemotBridgeBaseNumPorts."bridge2" = INTEGER: 1
...
BEGEMOT-BRIDGE-MIB::begemotBridgeStpTimeSinceTopologyChange."bridge0" = Timeticks: ↺
(116927) 0:19:29.27 centi-seconds
BEGEMOT-BRIDGE-MIB::begemotBridgeStpTimeSinceTopologyChange."bridge2" = Timeticks: ↺
(82773) 0:13:47.73 centi-seconds
BEGEMOT-BRIDGE-MIB::begemotBridgeStpTopChanges."bridge0" = Counter32: 1
BEGEMOT-BRIDGE-MIB::begemotBridgeStpTopChanges."bridge2" = Counter32: 1
BEGEMOT-BRIDGE-MIB::begemotBridgeStpDesignatedRoot."bridge0" = Hex-STRING: 80 00 00 40 ↺
95 30 5E 31
BEGEMOT-BRIDGE-MIB::begemotBridgeStpDesignatedRoot."bridge2" = Hex-STRING: 80 00 00 50 ↺
8B B8 C6 A9
```

To change the bridge interface being monitored via the mib-2.dot1dBridge subtree:

```
% snmpset -v 2c -c private bridge1.example.com
BEGEMOT-BRIDGE-MIB::begemotBridgeDefaultBridgeIf.0 s bridge2
```

30.7. Link Aggregation and Failover

Written by Andrew Thompson.

FreeBSD provides the lagg(4) interface which can be used to aggregate multiple network interfaces into one virtual interface in order to provide failover and link aggregation. Failover allows traffic to continue to flow as long as at least one aggregated network interface has an established link. Link aggregation works best on switches which support LACP, as this protocol distributes traffic bi-directionally while responding to the failure of individual links.

The aggregation protocols supported by the lagg interface determine which ports are used for outgoing traffic and whether or not a specific port accepts incoming traffic. The following protocols are supported by lagg(4):

failover

This mode sends and receives traffic only through the master port. If the master port becomes unavailable, the next active port is used. The first interface added to the virtual interface is the master port and all subsequently added interfaces are used as failover devices. If failover to a non-master port occurs, the original port becomes master once it becomes available again.

fec / loadbalance
> Cisco® Fast EtherChannel® (FEC) is found on older Cisco® switches. It provides a static setup and does not negotiate aggregation with the peer or exchange frames to monitor the link. If the switch supports LACP, that should be used instead.

lacp
> The IEEE® 802.3ad Link Aggregation Control Protocol (LACP) negotiates a set of aggregable links with the peer into one or more Link Aggregated Groups (LAGs). Each LAG is composed of ports of the same speed, set to full-duplex operation, and traffic is balanced across the ports in the LAG with the greatest total speed. Typically, there is only one LAG which contains all the ports. In the event of changes in physical connectivity, LACP will quickly converge to a new configuration.
>
> LACP balances outgoing traffic across the active ports based on hashed protocol header information and accepts incoming traffic from any active port. The hash includes the Ethernet source and destination address and, if available, the VLAN tag, and the IPv4 or IPv6 source and destination address.

roundrobin
> This mode distributes outgoing traffic using a round-robin scheduler through all active ports and accepts incoming traffic from any active port. Since this mode violates Ethernet frame ordering, it should be used with caution.

30.7.1. Configuration Examples

This section demonstrates how to configure a Cisco® switch and a FreeBSD system for LACP load balancing. It then shows how to configure two Ethernet interfaces in failover mode as well as how to configure failover mode between an Ethernet and a wireless interface.

Example 30.1. LACP Aggregation with a Cisco® Switch

This example connects two fxp(4) Ethernet interfaces on a FreeBSD machine to the first two Ethernet ports on a Cisco® switch as a single load balanced and fault tolerant link. More interfaces can be added to increase throughput and fault tolerance. Replace the names of the Cisco® ports, Ethernet devices, channel group number, and IP address shown in the example to match the local configuration.

Frame ordering is mandatory on Ethernet links and any traffic between two stations always flows over the same physical link, limiting the maximum speed to that of one interface. The transmit algorithm attempts to use as much information as it can to distinguish different traffic flows and balance the flows across the available interfaces.

On the Cisco® switch, add the *FastEthernet0/1* and *FastEthernet0/2* interfaces to channel group *1*:

```
interface FastEthernet0/1
 channel-group 1 mode active
 channel-protocol lacp
!
interface FastEthernet0/2
 channel-group 1 mode active
 channel-protocol lacp
```

On the FreeBSD system, create the lagg(4) interface using the physical interfaces *fxp0* and *fxp1* and bring the interfaces up with an IP address of *10.0.0.3/24* :

```
# ifconfig fxp0 up
# ifconfig fxp1 up
# ifconfig lagg0 create
# ifconfig lagg0 up laggproto lacp laggport  fxp0 laggport fxp1 10.0.0.3/24
```

Next, verify the status of the virtual interface:

```
# ifconfig lagg0
lagg0: flags=8843<UP,BROADCAST,RUNNING,SIMPLEX,MULTICAST> metric 0 mtu 1500
        options=8<VLAN_MTU>
        ether 00:05:5d:71:8d:b8
        media: Ethernet autoselect
        status: active
        laggproto lacp
        laggport: fxp1 flags=1c<ACTIVE,COLLECTING,DISTRIBUTING>
        laggport: fxp0 flags=1c<ACTIVE,COLLECTING,DISTRIBUTING>
```

Ports marked as ACTIVE are part of the LAG that has been negotiated with the remote switch. Traffic will be transmitted and received through these active ports. Add -v to the above command to view the LAG identifiers.

To see the port status on the Cisco® switch:

```
switch# show lacp neighbor
Flags:  S - Device is requesting Slow LACPDUs
        F - Device is requesting Fast LACPDUs
        A - Device is in Active mode       P - Device is in Passive mode

Channel group 1 neighbors

Partner's information:

                    LACP port                     Oper    Port    Port
Port        Flags   Priority  Dev ID        Age    Key     Number  State
Fa0/1       SA      32768     0005.5d71.8db8  29s    0x146   0x3     0x3D
Fa0/2       SA      32768     0005.5d71.8db8  29s    0x146   0x4     0x3D
```

For more detail, type show lacp neighbor detail.

To retain this configuration across reboots, add the following entries to /etc/rc.conf on the FreeBSD system:

```
ifconfig_fxp0="up"
ifconfig_fxp1="up"
cloned_interfaces="lagg0"
ifconfig_lagg0="laggproto lacp laggport fxp0 laggport fxp1 10.0.0.3/24 "
```

Example 30.2. Failover Mode

Failover mode can be used to switch over to a secondary interface if the link is lost on the master interface. To configure failover, make sure that the underlying physical interfaces are up, then create the lagg(4) interface. In this example, fxp0 is the master interface, fxp1 is the secondary interface, and the virtual interface is assigned an IP address of 10.0.0.15/24 :

```
# ifconfig fxp0 up
# ifconfig fxp1 up
# ifconfig lagg0 create
# ifconfig lagg0 up laggproto failover laggport  fxp0 laggport fxp1 10.0.0.15/24
```

The virtual interface should look something like this:

```
# ifconfig lagg0
lagg0: flags=8843<UP,BROADCAST,RUNNING,SIMPLEX,MULTICAST> metric 0 mtu 1500
        options=8<VLAN_MTU>
        ether 00:05:5d:71:8d:b8
        inet 10.0.0.15 netmask 0xffffff00 broadcast 10.0.0.255
```

```
        media: Ethernet autoselect
        status: active
        laggproto failover
        laggport: fxp1 flags=0<>
        laggport: fxp0 flags=5<MASTER,ACTIVE>
```

Traffic will be transmitted and received on *fxp0*. If the link is lost on *fxp0*, *fxp1* will become the active link. If the link is restored on the master interface, it will once again become the active link.

To retain this configuration across reboots, add the following entries to /etc/rc.conf :

```
ifconfig_fxp0="up"
ifconfig_fxp1="up"
cloned_interfaces="lagg0"
ifconfig_lagg0="laggproto failover laggport fxp0 laggport fxp1 10.0.0.15/24 "
```

Example 30.3. Failover Mode Between Ethernet and Wireless Interfaces

For laptop users, it is usually desirable to configure the wireless device as a secondary which is only used when the Ethernet connection is not available. With lagg(4), it is possible to configure a failover which prefers the Ethernet connection for both performance and security reasons, while maintaining the ability to transfer data over the wireless connection.

This is achieved by overriding the physical wireless interface's MAC address with that of the Ethernet interface.

In this example, the Ethernet interface, *bge0*, is the master and the wireless interface, *wlan0*, is the failover. The *wlan0* device was created from *iwn0* wireless interface, which will be configured with the MAC address of the Ethernet interface. First, determine the MAC address of the Ethernet interface:

```
# ifconfig bge0
bge0: flags=8843<UP,BROADCAST,RUNNING,SIMPLEX,MULTICAST> metric 0 mtu 1500
 options=19b<RXCSUM,TXCSUM,VLAN_MTU,VLAN_HWTAGGING,VLAN_HWCSUM,TSO4>
 ether 00:21:70:da:ae:37
 inet6 fe80::221:70ff:feda:ae37%bge0 prefixlen 64 scopeid 0x2
 nd6 options=29<PERFORMNUD,IFDISABLED,AUTO_LINKLOCAL>
 media: Ethernet autoselect (1000baseT <full-duplex>)
 status: active
```

Replace *bge0* to match the system's Ethernet interface name. The ether line will contain the MAC address of the specified interface. Now, change the MAC address of the underlying wireless interface:

```
# ifconfig iwn0 ether 00:21:70:da:ae:37
```

Bring the wireless interface up, but do not set an IP address:

```
# ifconfig wlan0 create wlandev iwn0 ssid my_router up
```

Make sure the *bge0* interface is up, then create the lagg(4) interface with *bge0* as master with failover to *wlan0*:

```
# ifconfig bge0 up
# ifconfig lagg0 create
# ifconfig lagg0 up laggproto failover laggport  bge0 laggport wlan0
```

The virtual interface should look something like this:

```
# ifconfig lagg0
lagg0: flags=8843<UP,BROADCAST,RUNNING,SIMPLEX,MULTICAST> metric 0 mtu 1500
```

```
        options=8<VLAN_MTU>
        ether 00:21:70:da:ae:37
        media: Ethernet autoselect
        status: active
        laggproto failover
        laggport: wlan0 flags=0<>
        laggport: bge0 flags=5<MASTER,ACTIVE>
```

Then, start the DHCP client to obtain an IP address:

```
# dhclient lagg0
```

To retain this configuration across reboots, add the following entries to /etc/rc.conf :

```
ifconfig_bge0="up"
ifconfig_iwn0="ether 00:21:70:da:ae:37 "
wlans_iwn0="wlan0"
ifconfig_wlan0="WPA"
cloned_interfaces="lagg0"
ifconfig_lagg0="laggproto failover laggport bge0 laggport wlan0 DHCP"
```

30.8. Diskless Operation with PXE

Updated by Jean-François Dockès.
Reorganized and enhanced by Alex Dupre.

The Intel® Preboot eXecution Environment (PXE) allows an operating system to boot over the network. For example, a FreeBSD system can boot over the network and operate without a local disk, using file systems mounted from an NFS server. PXE support is usually available in the BIOS. To use PXE when the machine starts, select the Boot from network option in the BIOS setup or type a function key during system initialization.

In order to provide the files needed for an operating system to boot over the network, a PXE setup also requires properly configured DHCP, TFTP, and NFS servers, where:

- Initial parameters, such as an IP address, executable boot filename and location, server name, and root path are obtained from the DHCP server.

- The operating system loader file is booted using TFTP.

- The file systems are loaded using NFS.

When a computer PXE boots, it receives information over DHCP about where to obtain the initial boot loader file. After the host computer receives this information, it downloads the boot loader via TFTP and then executes the boot loader. In FreeBSD, the boot loader file is /boot/pxeboot . After /boot/pxeboot executes, the FreeBSD kernel is loaded and the rest of the FreeBSD bootup sequence proceeds, as described in Chapter 12, *The FreeBSD Booting Process*.

This section describes how to configure these services on a FreeBSD system so that other systems can PXE boot into FreeBSD. Refer to diskless(8) for more information.

Caution

As described, the system providing these services is insecure. It should live in a protected area of a network and be untrusted by other hosts.

30.8.1. Setting Up the PXE Environment

Written by Craig Rodrigues.

The steps shown in this section configure the built-in NFS and TFTP servers. The next section demonstrates how to install and configure the DHCP server. In this example, the directory which will contain the files used by PXE users is /b/tftpboot/FreeBSD/install . It is important that this directory exists and that the same directory name is set in both /etc/inetd.conf and /usr/local/etc/dhcpd.conf .

1. Create the root directory which will contain a FreeBSD installation to be NFS mounted:

    ```
    # export NFSROOTDIR=/b/tftpboot/FreeBSD/install
    # mkdir -p ${NFSROOTDIR}
    ```

2. Enable the NFS server by adding this line to /etc/rc.conf :

    ```
    nfs_server_enable="YES"
    ```

3. Export the diskless root directory via NFS by adding the following to /etc/exports :

    ```
    /b -ro -alldirs
    ```

4. Start the NFS server:

    ```
    # service nfsd start
    ```

5. Enable inetd(8) by adding the following line to /etc/rc.conf :

    ```
    inetd_enable="YES"
    ```

6. Uncomment the following line in /etc/inetd.conf by making sure it does not start with a # symbol:

    ```
    tftp dgram udp wait root /usr/libexec/tftpd tftpd -l -s /b/tftpboot
    ```

    ### Note

    Some PXE versions require the TCP version of TFTP. In this case, uncomment the second tftp line which contains stream tcp .

    ---

7. Start inetd(8):

    ```
    # service inetd start
    ```

8. Rebuild the FreeBSD kernel and userland (refer to Section 23.6, "Rebuilding World" for more detailed instructions):

    ```
    # cd /usr/src
    # make buildworld
    # make buildkernel
    ```

9. Install FreeBSD into the directory mounted over NFS:

    ```
    # make installworld DESTDIR=${NFSROOTDIR}
    # make installkernel DESTDIR=${NFSROOTDIR}
    # make distribution DESTDIR=${NFSROOTDIR}
    ```

10. Test that the TFTP server works and can download the boot loader which will be obtained via PXE:

    ```
    # tftp localhost
    tftp> get FreeBSD/install/boot/pxeboot
    ```

```
Received 264951 bytes in 0.1 seconds
```

11. Edit ${NFSROOTDIR}/etc/fstab and create an entry to mount the root file system over NFS:

```
# Device                                       Mountpoint   FSType   Options  ↺
Dump Pass
myhost.example.com :/b/tftpboot/FreeBSD/install      /        nfs      ro       0
   0
```

Replace *myhost.example.com* with the hostname or IP address of the NFS server. In this example, the root file system is mounted read-only in order to prevent NFS clients from potentially deleting the contents of the root file system.

12. Set the root password in the PXE environment for client machines which are PXE booting :

```
# chroot ${NFSROOTDIR}
# passwd
```

13. If needed, enable ssh(1) root logins for client machines which are PXE booting by editing ${NFSROOTDIR}/etc/ssh/sshd_config and enabling PermitRootLogin. This option is documented in sshd_config(5).

14. Perform any other needed customizations of the PXE environment in ${NFSROOTDIR}. These customizations could include things like installing packages or editing the password file with vipw(8).

When booting from an NFS root volume, /etc/rc detects the NFS boot and runs /etc/rc.initdiskless. In this case, /etc and /var need to be memory backed file systems so that these directories are writable but the NFS root directory is read-only:

```
# chroot ${NFSROOTDIR}
# mkdir -p conf/base
# tar -c -v -f conf/base/etc.cpio.gz --format cpio --gzip etc
# tar -c -v -f conf/base/var.cpio.gz --format cpio --gzip var
```

When the system boots, memory file systems for /etc and /var will be created and mounted and the contents of the cpio.gz files will be copied into them.

30.8.2. Configuring the DHCP Server

The DHCP server does not need to be the same machine as the TFTP and NFS server, but it needs to be accessible in the network.

DHCP is not part of the FreeBSD base system but can be installed using the net/isc-dhcp42-server port or package.

Once installed, edit the configuration file, /usr/local/etc/dhcpd.conf . Configure the next-server, filename, and root-path settings as seen in this example:

```
subnet 192.168.0.0 netmask 255.255.255.0 {
    range 192.168.0.2 192.168.0.3 -;
    option subnet-mask 255.255.255.0 -;
    option routers 192.168.0.1 -;
    option broadcast-address 192.168.0.255 -;
    option domain-name-servers 192.168.35.35, 192.168.35.36 -;
    option domain-name "example.com";

    # IP address of TFTP server
    next-server 192.168.0.1 -;

    # path of boot loader obtained via tftp
      filename "FreeBSD/install/boot/pxeboot " -;

    # pxeboot boot loader will try to NFS mount this directory for root FS
    option root-path "192.168.0.1:/b/tftpboot/FreeBSD/install/   " -;
```

```
}
```

The `next-server` directive is used to specify the IP address of the TFTP server.

The `filename` directive defines the path to `/boot/pxeboot`. A relative filename is used, meaning that `/b/tftpboot` is not included in the path.

The `root-path` option defines the path to the NFS root file system.

Once the edits are saved, enable DHCP at boot time by adding the following line to `/etc/rc.conf`:

```
dhcpd_enable="YES"
```

Then start the DHCP service:

```
# service isc-dhcpd start
```

30.8.3. Debugging PXE Problems

Once all of the services are configured and started, PXE clients should be able to automatically load FreeBSD over the network. If a particular client is unable to connect, when that client machine boots up, enter the BIOS configuration menu and confirm that it is set to boot from the network.

This section describes some troubleshooting tips for isolating the source of the configuration problem should no clients be able to PXE boot.

1. Use the net/wireshark package or port to debug the network traffic involved during the PXE booting process, which is illustrated in the diagram below.

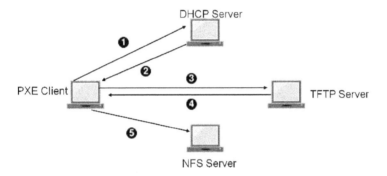

❶ Client broadcasts a `DHCPDISCOVER` message.
❷ The DHCP server responds with the IP address, `next-server`, `filename`, and `root-path` values.
❸ The client sends a TFTP request to `next-server`, asking to retrieve `filename`.
❹ The TFTP server responds and sends `filename` to client.
❺ The client executes `filename`, which is pxeboot(8), which then loads the kernel. When the kernel executes, the root file system specified by `root-path` is mounted over NFS.

Figure 30.1. PXE Booting Process with NFS Root Mount

2. On the TFTP server, read `/var/log/xferlog` to ensure that `pxeboot` is being retrieved from the correct location. To test this example configuration:

```
# tftp 192.168.0.1
tftp> get FreeBSD/install/boot/pxeboot
Received 264951 bytes in 0.1 seconds
```

The `BUGS` sections in tftpd(8) and tftp(1) document some limitations with TFTP.

3. Make sure that the root file system can be mounted via NFS. To test this example configuration:

637

```
# mount -t nfs 192.168.0.1:/b/tftpboot/FreeBSD/install /mnt
```

30.9. IPv6

Originally Written by Aaron Kaplan.
Restructured and Added by Tom Rhodes.
Extended by Brad Davis.

IPv6 is the new version of the well known IP protocol, also known as IPv4. IPv6 provides several advantages over IPv4 as well as many new features:

- Its 128-bit address space allows for 340,282,366,920,938,463,463,374,607,431,768,211,456 addresses. This addresses the IPv4 address shortage and eventual IPv4 address exhaustion.

- Routers only store network aggregation addresses in their routing tables, thus reducing the average space of a routing table to 8192 entries. This addresses the scalability issues associated with IPv4, which required every allocated block of IPv4 addresses to be exchanged between Internet routers, causing their routing tables to become too large to allow efficient routing.

- Address autoconfiguration (RFC2462).

- Mandatory multicast addresses.

- Built-in IPsec (IP security).

- Simplified header structure.

- Support for mobile IP.

- IPv6-to-IPv4 transition mechanisms.

FreeBSD includes the http://www.kame.net/ IPv6 reference implementation and comes with everything needed to use IPv6. This section focuses on getting IPv6 configured and running.

30.9.1. Background on IPv6 Addresses

There are three different types of IPv6 addresses:

Unicast
    A packet sent to a unicast address arrives at the interface belonging to the address.

Anycast
    These addresses are syntactically indistinguishable from unicast addresses but they address a group of interfaces. The packet destined for an anycast address will arrive at the nearest router interface. Anycast addresses are only used by routers.

Multicast
    These addresses identify a group of interfaces. A packet destined for a multicast address will arrive at all interfaces belonging to the multicast group. The IPv4 broadcast address, usually xxx.xxx.xxx.255 , is expressed by multicast addresses in IPv6.

When reading an IPv6 address, the canonical form is represented as x:x:x:x:x:x:x:x , where each x represents a 16 bit hex value. An example is FEBC:A574:382B:23C1:AA49:4592:4EFE:9982 .

Often, an address will have long substrings of all zeros. A :: (double colon) can be used to replace one substring per address. Also, up to three leading 0s per hex value can be omitted. For example, fe80::1 corresponds to the canonical form fe80:0000:0000:0000:0000:0000:0000:0001 .

A third form is to write the last 32 bits using the well known IPv4 notation. For example, `2002::10.0.0.1` corresponds to the hexadecimal canonical representation `2002:0000:0000:0000:0000:0000:0a00:0001`, which in turn is equivalent to `2002::a00:1`.

To view a FreeBSD system's IPv6 address, use ifconfig(8):

```
# ifconfig
```

```
rl0: flags=8943<UP,BROADCAST,RUNNING,PROMISC,SIMPLEX,MULTICAST> mtu 1500
        inet 10.0.0.10 netmask 0xffffff00 broadcast 10.0.0.255
        inet6 fe80::200:21ff:fe03:8e1%rl0 prefixlen 64 scopeid 0x1
        ether 00:00:21:03:08:e1
        media: Ethernet autoselect (100baseTX )
        status: active
```

In this example, the `rl0` interface is using `fe80::200:21ff:fe03:8e1%rl0`, an auto-configured link-local address which was automatically generated from the MAC address.

Some IPv6 addresses are reserved. A summary of these reserved addresses is seen in Table 30.3, "Reserved IPv6 Addresses":

Table 30.3. Reserved IPv6 Addresses

IPv6 address	Prefixlength (Bits)	Description	Notes
::	128 bits	unspecified	Equivalent to 0.0.0.0 in IPv4.
::1	128 bits	loopback address	Equivalent to 127.0.0.1 in IPv4.
::00:xx:xx:xx:xx	96 bits	embedded IPv4	The lower 32 bits are the compatible IPv4 address.
::ff:xx:xx:xx:xx	96 bits	IPv4 mapped IPv6 address	The lower 32 bits are the IPv4 address for hosts which do not support IPv6.
fe80::/10	10 bits	link-local	Equivalent to 169.254.0.0/16 in IPv4.
fc00::/7	7 bits	unique-local	Unique local addresses are intended for local communication and are only routable within a set of co-operating sites.
ff00::	8 bits	multicast	
2000::-3fff::	3 bits	global unicast	All global unicast addresses are assigned from this pool. The first 3 bits are 001.

For further information on the structure of IPv6 addresses, refer to RFC3513.

30.9.2. Configuring IPv6

To configure a FreeBSD system as an IPv6 client, add these two lines to `rc.conf`:

```
ifconfig_rl0_ipv6="inet6 accept_rtadv"
rtsold_enable="YES"
```

The first line enables the specified interface to receive router solicitation messages. The second line enables the router solicitation daemon, rtsol(8).

If the interface needs a statically assigned IPv6 address, add an entry to specify the static address and associated prefix length:

```
ifconfig_rl0_ipv6="inet6 2001:db8:4672:6565:2026:5043:2d42:5344    prefixlen 64"
```

To assign a default router, specify its address:

```
ipv6_defaultrouter="2001:db8:4672:6565::1 "
```

30.9.3. Connecting to a Provider

In order to connect to other IPv6 networks, one must have a provider or a tunnel that supports IPv6:

- Contact an Internet Service Provider to see if they offer IPv6.

- SixXS offers tunnels with end-points all around the globe.

- Hurricane Electric offers tunnels with end-points all around the globe.

 Note

Install the net/freenet6 package or port for a dial-up connection.

This section demonstrates how to take the directions from a tunnel provider and convert them into /etc/rc.conf settings that will persist through reboots.

The first /etc/rc.conf entry creates the generic tunneling interface *gif0*:

```
gif_interfaces="gif0"
```

Next, configure that interface with the IPv4 addresses of the local and remote endpoints. Replace *MY_IPv4_ADDR* and *REMOTE_IPv4_ADDR* with the actual IPv4 addresses:

```
gifconfig_gif0="MY_IPv4_ADDR REMOTE_IPv4_ADDR "
```

To apply the IPv6 address that has been assigned for use as the IPv6 tunnel endpoint, add this line, replacing *MY_ASSIGNED_IPv6_TUNNEL_ENDPOINT_ADDR* with the assigned address:

```
ifconfig_gif0_ipv6="inet6 MY_ASSIGNED_IPv6_TUNNEL_ENDPOINT_ADDR    "
```

Then, set the default route for the other side of the IPv6 tunnel. Replace *MY_IPv6_REMOTE_TUNNEL_ENDPOINT_ADDR* with the default gateway address assigned by the provider:

```
ipv6_defaultrouter="MY_IPv6_REMOTE_TUNNEL_ENDPOINT_ADDR    "
```

If the FreeBSD system will route IPv6 packets between the rest of the network and the world, enable the gateway using this line:

```
ipv6_gateway_enable="YES"
```

30.9.4. Router Advertisement and Host Auto Configuration

This section demonstrates how to setup rtadvd(8) to advertise the IPv6 default route.

To enable rtadvd(8), add the following to /etc/rc.conf :

```
rtadvd_enable="YES"
```

It is important to specify the interface on which to do IPv6 router solicitation. For example, to tell rtadvd(8) to use rl0:

```
rtadvd_interfaces="rl0"
```

Next, create the configuration file, /etc/rtadvd.conf as seen in this example:

```
rl0:\
  :addrs#1:addr="2001:471:1f11:246::":prefixlen#64:tc=ether:
```

Replace rl0 with the interface to be used and 2001:471:1f11:246:: with the prefix of the allocation.

For a dedicated /64 subnet, nothing else needs to be changed. Otherwise, change the prefixlen# to the correct value.

30.9.5. IPv6 and IPv6 Address Mapping

When IPv6 is enabled on a server, there may be a need to enable IPv4 mapped IPv6 address communication. This compatibility option allows for IPv4 addresses to be represented as IPv6 addresses. Permitting IPv6 applications to communicate with IPv4 and vice versa may be a security issue.

This option may not be required in most cases and is available only for compatibility. This option will allow IPv6-only applications to work with IPv4 in a dual stack environment. This is most useful for third party applications which may not support an IPv6-only environment. To enable this feature, add the following to /etc/rc.conf :

```
ipv6_ipv4mapping="YES"
```

Reviewing the information in RFC 3493, section 3.6 and 3.7 as well as RFC 4038 section 4.2 may be useful to some adminstrators.

30.10. Common Address Redundancy Protocol (CARP)

Contributed by Tom Rhodes.
Updated by Allan Jude.

The Common Address Redundancy Protocol (CARP) allows multiple hosts to share the same IP address and Virtual Host ID (VHID) in order to provide *high availability* for one or more services. This means that one or more hosts can fail, and the other hosts will transparently take over so that users do not see a service failure.

In addition to the shared IP address, each host has its own IP address for management and configuration. All of the machines that share an IP address have the same VHID. The VHID for each virtual IP address must be unique across the broadcast domain of the network interface.

High availability using CARP is built into FreeBSD, though the steps to configure it vary slightly depending upon the FreeBSD version. This section provides the same example configuration for versions before and equal to or after FreeBSD 10.

This example configures failover support with three hosts, all with unique IP addresses, but providing the same web content. It has two different masters named hosta.example.org and hostb.example.org, with a shared backup named hostc.example.org.

These machines are load balanced with a Round Robin DNS configuration. The master and backup machines are configured identically except for their hostnames and management IP addresses. These servers must have the same configuration and run the same services. When the failover occurs, requests to the service on the shared IP address can only be answered correctly if the backup server has access to the same content. The backup machine has two additional CARP interfaces, one for each of the master content server's IP addresses. When a failure occurs, the backup server will pick up the failed master machine's IP address.

30.10.1. Using CARP on FreeBSD 10 and Later

Enable boot-time support for CARP by adding an entry for the carp.ko kernel module in /boot/loader.conf :

```
carp_load="YES"
```

To load the module now without rebooting:

```
# kldload carp
```

For users who prefer to use a custom kernel, include the following line in the custom kernel configuration file and compile the kernel as described in Chapter 8, *Configuring the FreeBSD Kernel*:

```
device carp
```

The hostname, management IP address and subnet mask, shared IP address, and VHID are all set by adding entries to /etc/rc.conf . This example is for hosta.example.org:

```
hostname="hosta.example.org "
ifconfig_em0="inet 192.168.1.3  netmask 255.255.255.0 "
ifconfig_em0_alias0="vhid 1 pass testpass alias 192.168.1.50 /32"
```

The next set of entries are for hostb.example.org. Since it represents a second master, it uses a different shared IP address and VHID. However, the passwords specified with **pass** must be identical as CARP will only listen to and accept advertisements from machines with the correct password.

```
hostname="hostb.example.org "
ifconfig_em0="inet 192.168.1.4  netmask 255.255.255.0 "
ifconfig_em0_alias0="vhid 2 pass testpass alias 192.168.1.51 /32"
```

The third machine, hostc.example.org, is configured to handle failover from either master. This machine is configured with two CARP VHIDs, one to handle the virtual IP address for each of the master hosts. The CARP advertising skew, **advskew**, is set to ensure that the backup host advertises later than the master, since **advskew** controls the order of precedence when there are multiple backup servers.

```
hostname="hostc.example.org"
ifconfig_em0="inet 192.168.1.5  netmask 255.255.255.0 "
ifconfig_em0_alias0="vhid 1 advskew 100 pass testpass alias 192.168.1.50 /32"
ifconfig_em0_alias1="vhid 2 advskew 100 pass testpass alias 192.168.1.51 /32"
```

Having two CARP VHIDs configured means that hostc.example.org will notice if either of the master servers becomes unavailable. If a master fails to advertise before the backup server, the backup server will pick up the shared IP address until the master becomes available again.

Note

Preemption is disabled by default. If preemption has been enabled, hostc.example.org might not release the virtual IP address back to the original master server. The administrator can force the backup server to return the IP address to the master with the command:

```
# ifconfig em0 vhid 1 state backup
```

Once the configuration is complete, either restart networking or reboot each system. High availability is now enabled.

CARP functionality can be controlled via several sysctl(8) variables documented in the carp(4) manual pages. Other actions can be triggered from CARP events by using devd(8).

30.10.2. Using CARP on FreeBSD 9 and Earlier

The configuration for these versions of FreeBSD is similar to the one described in the previous section, except that a CARP device must first be created and referred to in the configuration.

Enable boot-time support for CARP by loading the `if_carp.ko` kernel module in `/boot/loader.conf` :

```
if_carp_load="YES"
```

To load the module now without rebooting:

```
# kldload carp
```

For users who prefer to use a custom kernel, include the following line in the custom kernel configuration file and compile the kernel as described in Chapter 8, *Configuring the FreeBSD Kernel*:

```
device carp
```

Next, on each host, create a CARP device:

```
# ifconfig carp0 create
```

Set the hostname, management IP address, the shared IP address, and VHID by adding the required lines to `/etc/rc.conf`. Since a virtual CARP device is used instead of an alias, the actual subnet mask of `/24` is used instead of `/32`. Here are the entries for `hosta.example.org`:

```
hostname="hosta.example.org "
ifconfig_fxp0="inet 192.168.1.3 netmask 255.255.255.0 "
cloned_interfaces="carp0"
ifconfig_carp0="vhid 1 pass testpass 192.168.1.50/24 "
```

On `hostb.example.org`:

```
hostname="hostb.example.org "
ifconfig_fxp0="inet 192.168.1.4 netmask 255.255.255.0 "
cloned_interfaces="carp0"
ifconfig_carp0="vhid 2 pass testpass 192.168.1.51/24 "
```

The third machine, `hostc.example.org`, is configured to handle failover from either of the master hosts:

```
hostname="hostc.example.org "
ifconfig_fxp0="inet 192.168.1.5 netmask 255.255.255.0 "
cloned_interfaces="carp0 carp1"
ifconfig_carp0="vhid 1 advskew 100 pass testpass 192.168.1.50/24 "
ifconfig_carp1="vhid 2 advskew 100 pass testpass 192.168.1.51/24 "
```

Note

Preemption is disabled in the GENERIC FreeBSD kernel. If preemption has been enabled with a custom kernel, `hostc.example.org` may not release the IP address back to the original content server. The administrator can force the backup server to return the IP address to the master with the command:

```
# ifconfig carp0 down && ifconfig carp0 up
```

This should be done on the `carp` interface which corresponds to the correct host.

Once the configuration is complete, either restart networking or reboot each system. High availability is now enabled.

Part V. Appendices

Table of Contents

Appendix A. Obtaining FreeBSD

A.1. CD and DVD Sets

FreeBSD CD and DVD sets are available from several online retailers:

* FreeBSD Mall, Inc.
  2420 Sand Creek Rd C-1 #347
  Brentwood, CA
  94513
  USA
  Phone: +1 925 240-6652
  Fax: +1 925 674-0821
  Email: <info@freebsdmall.com >
  WWW: http://www.freebsdmall.com/

* Getlinux
  78 Rue de la Croix Rochopt
  Épinay-sous-Sénart
  91860
  France
  Email: <contact@getlinux.fr >
  WWW: http://www.getlinux.fr/

* Dr. Hinner EDV
  Kochelseestr. 11
  D-81371 München
  Germany
  Phone: (0177) 428 419 0
  Email: <infow@hinner.de >
  WWW: http://www.hinner.de/linux/freebsd.html

* Linux Center
  Galernaya Street, 55
  Saint-Petersburg
  190000
  Russia
  Phone: +7-812-309-06-86
  Email: <info@linuxcenter.ru >
  WWW: http://linuxcenter.ru/shop/freebsd

A.2. FTP Sites

The official sources for FreeBSD are available via anonymous FTP from a worldwide set of mirror sites. The site `ftp://ftp.FreeBSD.org/pub/FreeBSD/` is available via HTTP and FTP. It is made up of many machines operated by the project cluster administrators and behind GeoDNS to direct users to the closest available mirror.

Additionally, FreeBSD is available via anonymous FTP from the following mirror sites. When obtaining FreeBSD via anonymous FTP, please try to use a nearby site. The mirror sites listed as "Primary Mirror Sites" typically have the entire FreeBSD archive (all the currently available versions for each of the architectures) but faster download speeds are probably available from a site that is in your country or region. The regional sites carry the most recent versions for the most popular architecture(s) but might not carry the entire FreeBSD archive. All sites provide access via anonymous FTP but some sites also provide access via other methods. The access methods available for each site are provided in parentheses after the hostname.

Central Servers, Primary Mirror Sites, Armenia, Australia, Austria, Brazil, Canada, China, Czech Republic, Denmark, Estonia, Finland, France, Germany, Greece, Hong Kong, Ireland, Japan, Korea, Latvia, Lithuania, Netherlands, New Zealand, Norway, Poland, Russia, Saudi Arabia, Slovenia, South Africa, Spain, Sweden, Switzerland, Taiwan, Ukraine, United Kingdom, USA.

(as of UTC)

Central Servers

- ftp://ftp.FreeBSD.org/pub/FreeBSD/ (ftp / ftpv6 / http://ftp.FreeBSD.org/pub/FreeBSD/ / http://ftp.FreeBSD.org/pub/FreeBSD/)

Primary Mirror Sites
In case of problems, please contact the hostmaster <mirror-admin@FreeBSD.org> for this domain.

- ftp://ftp1.FreeBSD.org/pub/FreeBSD/ (ftp)

- ftp://ftp2.FreeBSD.org/pub/FreeBSD/ (ftp)

- ftp://ftp3.FreeBSD.org/pub/FreeBSD/ (ftp)

- ftp://ftp4.FreeBSD.org/pub/FreeBSD/ (ftp / ftpv6 / http://ftp4.FreeBSD.org/pub/FreeBSD/ / http://ftp4.FreeBSD.org/pub/FreeBSD/)

- ftp://ftp5.FreeBSD.org/pub/FreeBSD/ (ftp)

- ftp://ftp6.FreeBSD.org/pub/FreeBSD/ (ftp)

- ftp://ftp7.FreeBSD.org/pub/FreeBSD/ (ftp)

- ftp://ftp10.FreeBSD.org/pub/FreeBSD/ (ftp / ftpv6 / http://ftp10.FreeBSD.org/pub/FreeBSD/ / http://ftp10.FreeBSD.org/pub/FreeBSD/)

- ftp://ftp11.FreeBSD.org/pub/FreeBSD/ (ftp)

- ftp://ftp13.FreeBSD.org/pub/FreeBSD/ (ftp)

- ftp://ftp14.FreeBSD.org/pub/FreeBSD/ (ftp / http://ftp14.FreeBSD.org/pub/FreeBSD/)

Armenia
In case of problems, please contact the hostmaster <hostmaster@am.FreeBSD.org> for this domain.

- ftp://ftp1.am.FreeBSD.org/pub/FreeBSD/ (ftp / http://ftp1.am.FreeBSD.org/pub/FreeBSD/ / rsync)

Australia
In case of problems, please contact the hostmaster <hostmaster@au.FreeBSD.org> for this domain.

- ftp://ftp.au.FreeBSD.org/pub/FreeBSD/ (ftp)

- ftp://ftp2.au.FreeBSD.org/pub/FreeBSD/ (ftp)

- ftp://ftp3.au.FreeBSD.org/pub/FreeBSD/ (ftp)

Austria
In case of problems, please contact the hostmaster <hostmaster@at.FreeBSD.org> for this domain.

- ftp://ftp.at.FreeBSD.org/pub/FreeBSD/ (ftp / ftpv6 / http://ftp.at.FreeBSD.org/pub/FreeBSD/ / http://ftp.at.FreeBSD.org/pub/FreeBSD/)

Brazil
In case of problems, please contact the hostmaster <hostmaster@br.FreeBSD.org> for this domain.

- ftp://ftp2.br.FreeBSD.org/FreeBSD/ (ftp / http://ftp2.br.FreeBSD.org/)

- ftp://ftp3.br.FreeBSD.org/pub/FreeBSD/ (ftp / rsync)

- ftp://ftp4.br.FreeBSD.org/pub/FreeBSD/ (ftp)

Canada
In case of problems, please contact the hostmaster <hostmaster@ca.FreeBSD.org> for this domain.

- ftp://ftp.ca.FreeBSD.org/pub/FreeBSD/ (ftp)

- ftp://ftp2.ca.FreeBSD.org/pub/FreeBSD/ (ftp)

China
In case of problems, please contact the hostmaster <hostmaster@cn.FreeBSD.org> for this domain.

- ftp://ftp.cn.FreeBSD.org/pub/FreeBSD/ (ftp)

Czech Republic
In case of problems, please contact the hostmaster <hostmaster@cz.FreeBSD.org> for this domain.

- ftp://ftp.cz.FreeBSD.org/pub/FreeBSD/ (ftp / ftp://ftp.cz.FreeBSD.org/pub/FreeBSD/ / http://ftp.cz.FreeBSD.org/pub/FreeBSD/ / http://ftp.cz.FreeBSD.org/pub/FreeBSD/ / rsync / rsyncv6)

- ftp://ftp2.cz.FreeBSD.org/pub/FreeBSD/ (ftp / http://ftp2.cz.FreeBSD.org/pub/FreeBSD/)

Denmark
In case of problems, please contact the hostmaster <hostmaster@dk.FreeBSD.org> for this domain.

- ftp://ftp.dk.FreeBSD.org/pub/FreeBSD/ (ftp / ftpv6 / http://ftp.dk.FreeBSD.org/pub/FreeBSD/ / http://ftp.dk.FreeBSD.org/pub/FreeBSD/)

Estonia
In case of problems, please contact the hostmaster <hostmaster@ee.FreeBSD.org> for this domain.

- ftp://ftp.ee.FreeBSD.org/pub/FreeBSD/ (ftp)

Finland
In case of problems, please contact the hostmaster <hostmaster@fi.FreeBSD.org> for this domain.

- ftp://ftp.fi.FreeBSD.org/pub/FreeBSD/ (ftp)

France
In case of problems, please contact the hostmaster <hostmaster@fr.FreeBSD.org> for this domain.

- ftp://ftp.fr.FreeBSD.org/pub/FreeBSD/ (ftp)

- ftp://ftp1.fr.FreeBSD.org/pub/FreeBSD/ (ftp / http://ftp1.fr.FreeBSD.org/pub/FreeBSD/ / rsync)

- ftp://ftp3.fr.FreeBSD.org/pub/FreeBSD/ (ftp)

- ftp://ftp5.fr.FreeBSD.org/pub/FreeBSD/ (ftp)

- ftp://ftp6.fr.FreeBSD.org/pub/FreeBSD/ (ftp / rsync)

- ftp://ftp7.fr.FreeBSD.org/pub/FreeBSD/ (ftp)

- ftp://ftp8.fr.FreeBSD.org/pub/FreeBSD/ (ftp)

Germany
In case of problems, please contact the hostmaster <de-bsd-hubs@de.FreeBSD.org> for this domain.

- ftp://ftp.de.FreeBSD.org/pub/FreeBSD/ (ftp)

- ftp://ftp1.de.FreeBSD.org/freebsd/ (ftp / http://www1.de.FreeBSD.org/freebsd/ / rsync://rsync3.de.Free-BSD.org/freebsd/)

- ftp://ftp2.de.FreeBSD.org/pub/FreeBSD/ (ftp / http://ftp2.de.FreeBSD.org/pub/FreeBSD/ / rsync)

- ftp://ftp4.de.FreeBSD.org/FreeBSD/ (ftp / http://ftp4.de.FreeBSD.org/pub/FreeBSD/)

- ftp://ftp5.de.FreeBSD.org/pub/FreeBSD/ (ftp)

- ftp://ftp7.de.FreeBSD.org/pub/FreeBSD/ (ftp / http://ftp7.de.FreeBSD.org/pub/FreeBSD/)

- ftp://ftp8.de.FreeBSD.org/pub/FreeBSD/ (ftp)

Greece
In case of problems, please contact the hostmaster <hostmaster@gr.FreeBSD.org> for this domain.

- ftp://ftp.gr.FreeBSD.org/pub/FreeBSD/ (ftp)

- ftp://ftp2.gr.FreeBSD.org/pub/FreeBSD/ (ftp)

Hong Kong

- ftp://ftp.hk.FreeBSD.org/pub/FreeBSD/ (ftp)

Ireland
In case of problems, please contact the hostmaster <hostmaster@ie.FreeBSD.org> for this domain.

- ftp://ftp3.ie.FreeBSD.org/pub/FreeBSD/ (ftp / rsync)

Japan
In case of problems, please contact the hostmaster <hostmaster@jp.FreeBSD.org> for this domain.

- ftp://ftp.jp.FreeBSD.org/pub/FreeBSD/ (ftp)

- ftp://ftp2.jp.FreeBSD.org/pub/FreeBSD/ (ftp)

- ftp://ftp3.jp.FreeBSD.org/pub/FreeBSD/ (ftp)

- ftp://ftp4.jp.FreeBSD.org/pub/FreeBSD/ (ftp)

- ftp://ftp5.jp.FreeBSD.org/pub/FreeBSD/ (ftp)

- ftp://ftp6.jp.FreeBSD.org/pub/FreeBSD/ (ftp)

- ftp://ftp7.jp.FreeBSD.org/pub/FreeBSD/ (ftp)

- ftp://ftp8.jp.FreeBSD.org/pub/FreeBSD/ (ftp)

- ftp://ftp9.jp.FreeBSD.org/pub/FreeBSD/ (ftp)

Korea
In case of problems, please contact the hostmaster <hostmaster@kr.FreeBSD.org> for this domain.

- ftp://ftp.kr.FreeBSD.org/pub/FreeBSD/ (ftp / rsync)

- ftp://ftp2.kr.FreeBSD.org/pub/FreeBSD/ (ftp / http://ftp2.kr.FreeBSD.org/pub/FreeBSD/)

Latvia
In case of problems, please contact the hostmaster <hostmaster@lv.FreeBSD.org> for this domain.

- ftp://ftp.lv.FreeBSD.org/pub/FreeBSD/ (ftp / http://ftp.lv.FreeBSD.org/pub/FreeBSD/)

Lithuania
In case of problems, please contact the hostmaster <hostmaster@lt.FreeBSD.org> for this domain.

- ftp://ftp.lt.FreeBSD.org/pub/FreeBSD/ (ftp / http://ftp.lt.FreeBSD.org/pub/FreeBSD/)

Netherlands
In case of problems, please contact the hostmaster <hostmaster@nl.FreeBSD.org> for this domain.

- ftp://ftp.nl.FreeBSD.org/pub/FreeBSD/ (ftp / http://ftp.nl.FreeBSD.org/os/FreeBSD/ / rsync)

- ftp://ftp2.nl.FreeBSD.org/pub/FreeBSD/ (ftp)

New Zealand

- ftp://ftp.nz.FreeBSD.org/pub/FreeBSD/ (ftp / http://ftp.nz.FreeBSD.org/pub/FreeBSD/)

Norway
In case of problems, please contact the hostmaster <hostmaster@no.FreeBSD.org> for this domain.

- ftp://ftp.no.FreeBSD.org/pub/FreeBSD/ (ftp / rsync)

Poland
In case of problems, please contact the hostmaster <hostmaster@pl.FreeBSD.org> for this domain.

- ftp://ftp.pl.FreeBSD.org/pub/FreeBSD/ (ftp)

- ftp2.pl.FreeBSD.org

Russia
In case of problems, please contact the hostmaster <hostmaster@ru.FreeBSD.org> for this domain.

- ftp://ftp.ru.FreeBSD.org/pub/FreeBSD/ (ftp / http://ftp.ru.FreeBSD.org/FreeBSD/ / rsync)

- ftp://ftp2.ru.FreeBSD.org/pub/FreeBSD/ (ftp / http://ftp2.ru.FreeBSD.org/pub/FreeBSD/ / rsync)

- ftp://ftp4.ru.FreeBSD.org/pub/FreeBSD/ (ftp)

- ftp://ftp5.ru.FreeBSD.org/pub/FreeBSD/ (ftp / http://ftp5.ru.FreeBSD.org/pub/FreeBSD/ / rsync)

- ftp://ftp6.ru.FreeBSD.org/pub/FreeBSD/ (ftp)

Saudi Arabia
In case of problems, please contact the hostmaster <ftpadmin@isu.net.sa> for this domain.

- ftp://ftp.isu.net.sa/pub/ftp.freebsd.org/ (ftp)

Slovenia
In case of problems, please contact the hostmaster <hostmaster@si.FreeBSD.org> for this domain.

- ftp://ftp.si.FreeBSD.org/pub/FreeBSD/ (ftp)

South Africa
In case of problems, please contact the hostmaster <hostmaster@za.FreeBSD.org> for this domain.

- ftp://ftp.za.FreeBSD.org/pub/FreeBSD/ **(ftp)**

- ftp://ftp2.za.FreeBSD.org/pub/FreeBSD/ **(ftp)**

- ftp://ftp4.za.FreeBSD.org/pub/FreeBSD/ **(ftp)**

Spain

In case of problems, please contact the hostmaster <hostmaster@es.FreeBSD.org> for this domain.

- ftp://ftp.es.FreeBSD.org/pub/FreeBSD/ **(ftp** / http://ftp.es.FreeBSD.org/pub/FreeBSD/**)**

- ftp://ftp3.es.FreeBSD.org/pub/FreeBSD/ **(ftp)**

Sweden

In case of problems, please contact the hostmaster <hostmaster@se.FreeBSD.org> for this domain.

- ftp://ftp.se.FreeBSD.org/pub/FreeBSD/ **(ftp)**

- ftp://ftp2.se.FreeBSD.org/pub/FreeBSD/ **(ftp** / rsync://ftp2.se.FreeBSD.org/**)**

- ftp://ftp3.se.FreeBSD.org/pub/FreeBSD/ **(ftp)**

- ftp://ftp4.se.FreeBSD.org/pub/FreeBSD/ **(ftp** / ftp://ftp4.se.FreeBSD.org/pub/FreeBSD/ / http://ftp4.se.FreeBSD.org/pub/FreeBSD/ / http://ftp4.se.FreeBSD.org/pub/FreeBSD/ / rsync://ftp4.se.FreeBSD.org/pub/FreeBSD/ / rsync://ftp4.se.FreeBSD.org/pub/FreeBSD/**)**

- ftp://ftp6.se.FreeBSD.org/pub/FreeBSD/ **(ftp** / http://ftp6.se.FreeBSD.org/pub/FreeBSD/**)**

Switzerland

In case of problems, please contact the hostmaster <hostmaster@ch.FreeBSD.org> for this domain.

- ftp://ftp.ch.FreeBSD.org/pub/FreeBSD/ **(ftp** / http://ftp.ch.FreeBSD.org/pub/FreeBSD/**)**

Taiwan

In case of problems, please contact the hostmaster <hostmaster@tw.FreeBSD.org> for this domain.

- ftp://ftp.tw.FreeBSD.org/pub/FreeBSD/ **(ftp** / ftp://ftp.tw.FreeBSD.org/pub/FreeBSD/ / **rsync** / **rsyncv6)**

- ftp://ftp2.tw.FreeBSD.org/pub/FreeBSD/ **(ftp** / ftp://ftp2.tw.FreeBSD.org/pub/FreeBSD/ / http://ftp2.tw.FreeBSD.org/pub/FreeBSD/ / http://ftp2.tw.FreeBSD.org/pub/FreeBSD/ / **rsync** / **rsyncv6)**

- ftp://ftp4.tw.FreeBSD.org/pub/FreeBSD/ **(ftp)**

- ftp://ftp5.tw.FreeBSD.org/pub/FreeBSD/ **(ftp)**

- ftp://ftp6.tw.FreeBSD.org/pub/FreeBSD/ **(ftp** / http://ftp6.tw.FreeBSD.org/ / **rsync)**

- ftp://ftp7.tw.FreeBSD.org/pub/FreeBSD/ **(ftp)**

- ftp://ftp8.tw.FreeBSD.org/pub/FreeBSD/ **(ftp)**

- ftp://ftp11.tw.FreeBSD.org/pub/FreeBSD/ **(ftp** / http://ftp11.tw.FreeBSD.org/FreeBSD/**)**

- ftp://ftp12.tw.FreeBSD.org/pub/FreeBSD/ **(ftp)**

- ftp://ftp13.tw.FreeBSD.org/pub/FreeBSD/ **(ftp)**

- ftp://ftp14.tw.FreeBSD.org/pub/FreeBSD/ **(ftp)**

- ftp://ftp15.tw.FreeBSD.org/pub/FreeBSD/ **(ftp)**

Ukraine

- ftp://ftp.ua.FreeBSD.org/pub/FreeBSD/ (ftp / http://ftp.ua.FreeBSD.org/pub/FreeBSD/)

- ftp://ftp6.ua.FreeBSD.org/pub/FreeBSD/ (ftp / http://ftp6.ua.FreeBSD.org/pub/FreeBSD / rsync://ftp6.ua.FreeBSD.org/FreeBSD/)

- ftp://ftp7.ua.FreeBSD.org/pub/FreeBSD/ (ftp)

United Kingdom
In case of problems, please contact the hostmaster <hostmaster@uk.FreeBSD.org> for this domain.

- ftp://ftp.uk.FreeBSD.org/pub/FreeBSD/ (ftp)

- ftp://ftp2.uk.FreeBSD.org/pub/FreeBSD/ (ftp / rsync://ftp2.uk.FreeBSD.org/ftp.freebsd.org/pub/FreeBSD/)

- ftp://ftp3.uk.FreeBSD.org/pub/FreeBSD/ (ftp)

- ftp://ftp4.uk.FreeBSD.org/pub/FreeBSD/ (ftp)

- ftp://ftp5.uk.FreeBSD.org/pub/FreeBSD/ (ftp)

USA
In case of problems, please contact the hostmaster <hostmaster@us.FreeBSD.org> for this domain.

- ftp://ftp1.us.FreeBSD.org/pub/FreeBSD/ (ftp)

- ftp://ftp2.us.FreeBSD.org/pub/FreeBSD/ (ftp)

- ftp://ftp3.us.FreeBSD.org/pub/FreeBSD/ (ftp)

- ftp://ftp4.us.FreeBSD.org/pub/FreeBSD/ (ftp / ftpv6 / http://ftp4.us.FreeBSD.org/pub/FreeBSD/ / http://ftp4.us.FreeBSD.org/pub/FreeBSD/)

- ftp://ftp5.us.FreeBSD.org/pub/FreeBSD/ (ftp)

- ftp://ftp6.us.FreeBSD.org/pub/FreeBSD/ (ftp)

- ftp://ftp8.us.FreeBSD.org/pub/FreeBSD/ (ftp)

- ftp://ftp10.us.FreeBSD.org/pub/FreeBSD/ (ftp)

- ftp://ftp11.us.FreeBSD.org/pub/FreeBSD/ (ftp)

- ftp://ftp13.us.FreeBSD.org/pub/FreeBSD/ (ftp / http://ftp13.us.FreeBSD.org/pub/FreeBSD/ / rsync)

- ftp://ftp14.us.FreeBSD.org/pub/FreeBSD/ (ftp / http://ftp14.us.FreeBSD.org/pub/FreeBSD/)

- ftp://ftp15.us.FreeBSD.org/pub/FreeBSD/ (ftp)

A.3. Using CTM

CTM is a method for keeping a remote directory tree in sync with a central one. It is built into FreeBSD and can be used to synchronize a system with FreeBSD's source repositories. It supports synchronization of an entire repository or just a specified set of branches.

CTM is specifically designed for use on lousy or non-existent TCP/IP connections and provides the ability for changes to be automatically sent by email. It requires the user to obtain up to three deltas per day for the most active branches. Update sizes are always kept as small as possible and are typically less than 5K. About one in very ten updates is 10-50K in size, and there will occasionally be an update larger than 100K+.

When using CTM to track FreeBSD development, refer to the caveats related to working directly from the development sources rather than a pre-packaged release. These are discussed in Tracking a Development Branch.

Little documentation exists on the process of creating deltas or using CTM for other purposes. Contact the ctm-users mailing list for answers to questions on using CTM.

A.3.1. Getting Deltas

The "deltas" used by CTM can be obtained either through anonymous FTP or email.

FTP deltas can be obtained from the following mirror sites. When using anonymous FTP to obtain CTM deltas, select a mirror that is geographically nearby. In case of problems, contact the ctm-users mailing list.

Global mirror

- `ftp://ftp.FreeBSD.org/pub/FreeBSD/development/CTM/`

South Africa, backup server for old deltas

- `ftp://ftp.za.FreeBSD.org/pub/FreeBSD/CTM/`

Taiwan/R.O.C.

- `ftp://ctm.tw.FreeBSD.org/pub/FreeBSD/development/CTM/`

- `ftp://ctm2.tw.FreeBSD.org/pub/FreeBSD/development/CTM/`

- `ftp://ctm3.tw.FreeBSD.org/pub/FreeBSD/development/CTM/`

To instead receive deltas through email, subscribe to one of the `ctm-src` distribution lists available from `http://lists.freebsd.org/mailman/listinfo`. For example, ctm-src-cur supports the head development branch and ctm-src-9 supports the 9.X release branch.

As CTM updates arrive through email, use `ctm_rmail` to unpack and apply them. This command can be run directly from an entry in `/etc/aliases` in order to automate this process. Refer to ctm_rmail(1) for more details.

> ### Note
>
> Regardless of the method which is used to get deltas, CTM users should subscribe to the ctm-announce mailing list as this is the only mechanism by which CTM announcements are posted.

A.3.2. CTM Usage

Before CTM deltas can be used for the first time, a starting point must be produced.

One method is to apply a "starter" delta to an empty directory. A starter delta can be recognized by the XEmpty in its name, such as `src-cur.3210XEmpty.gz`. The designation following the X corresponds to the origin of the initial "seed", where Empty is an empty directory. As a rule, a base transition from Empty is produced every 100 deltas. Be aware that starter deltas are large and 70 to 80 Megabytes of `gzip`'d data is common for the XEmpty deltas.

Another method is to copy or extract an initial source from a RELEASE media as this can save a significant transfer of data from the Internet.

Once a base delta has been created, apply all deltas with higher numbers. To apply the deltas:

```
# cd /directory/to/store/the/stuff
# ctm -v -v /directory/which/stores/the/deltas/src-xxx.*
```

Multiple deltas can be applied with a single command as they will be processed one at a time and any deltas that are already applied will be ignored. CTM understands `gzip` compressed deltas, which saves disk space.

To verify a delta without applying it, include -c in the command line. CTM will not actually modify the local tree but will instead verify the integrity of the delta to see if it would apply cleanly. Refer to ctm(1) for more information about available options and an overview of the process CTM uses when applying deltas.

To keep the local source tree up-to-date, every time a new delta becomes available, apply it through CTM.

Once applied, it is recommended to not delete the deltas if it is a burden to download them again. This way, a local copy is available in case it is needed for future disaster recovery.

A.3.3. Keeping Local Changes

Developers often experiment with and change files in their local source tree. CTM supports local modifications in a limited way: before checking for the presence of a file, it first looks for a file with the same name and a .ctm extension. If this file exists, CTM will operate on it instead of the original filename.

This behavior provides a simple way to maintain local changes. Before modifying a file, make a copy with a .ctm suffix. Make any changes to the original filename, knowing that CTM will only apply updates to the file with the .ctm suffix.

A.3.4. Other CTM Options

Finding Out Exactly What Would Be Touched by an Update
> To determine the list of changes that CTM will make to the local source repository, use -l. This option is useful for creating logs of the changes or when performing pre- or post-processing on any of the modified files.

Making Backups Before Updating
> To backup all of the files that would be changed by a CTM update, specify -B *backup-file*. This option tells CTM to backup all files touched by the applied CTM delta to `backup-file`.

Restricting the Files Touched by an Update
> To restrict the scope of a given CTM update, or to extract just a few files from a sequence of deltas, filtering regular expressions can be specified using -e, which specifies which files to process, or -x, which specifies which files to ignore.

> For example, to extract an up-to-date copy of `lib/libc/Makefile` from a collection of saved CTM deltas:

```
# cd /directory/to/extract/to/
# ctm -e '^lib/libc/Makefile' /directory/which/stores/the/deltas/src-xxx.*
```

> For every file specified in a CTM delta, -e and -x are applied in the order given on the command line. A file is processed by CTM only if it is marked as eligible after all -e and -x options are applied.

A.4. Using Subversion

A.4.1. Introduction

As of July 2012, FreeBSD uses Subversion as the only version control system for storing all of FreeBSD's source code, documentation, and the Ports Collection.

Note

Subversion is generally a developer tool. Users may prefer to use `freebsd-update` (Section 23.2, "FreeBSD Update") to update the FreeBSD base system, and `portsnap` (Section 4.5, "Using the Ports Collection") to update the FreeBSD Ports Collection.

This section demonstrates how to install Subversion on a FreeBSD system and use it to create a local copy of a FreeBSD repository. Additional information on the use of Subversion is included.

A.4.2. Root SSL Certificates

Installing security/ca_root_nss allows Subversion to verify the identity of HTTPS repository servers. The root SSL certificates can be installed from a port:

```
# cd /usr/ports/security/ca_root_nss
# make install clean
```

or as a package:

```
# pkg install ca_root_nss
```

A.4.3. Svnlite

A lightweight version of Subversion is already installed on FreeBSD as `svnlite`. The port or package version of Subversion is only needed if the Python or Perl API is needed, or if a later version of Subversion is desired.

The only difference from normal Subversion use is that the command name is `svnlite`.

A.4.4. Installation

If `svnlite` is unavailable or the full version of Subversion is needed, then it must be installed.

Subversion can be installed from the Ports Collection:

```
# cd /usr/ports/devel/subversion
# make install clean
```

Subversion can also be installed as a package:

```
# pkg install subversion
```

A.4.5. Running Subversion

To fetch a clean copy of the sources into a local directory, use `svn`. The files in this directory are called a *local working copy*.

Warning

Move or delete an existing destination directory before using `checkout` for the first time.

Checkout over an existing non-`svn` directory can cause conflicts between the existing files and those brought in from the repository.

Subversion uses URLs to designate a repository, taking the form of *protocol://hostname/path*. The first component of the path is the FreeBSD repository to access. There are three different repositories, `base` for the FreeBSD base system source code, `ports` for the Ports Collection, and `doc` for documentation. For example, the URL `https://svn.FreeBSD.org/ports/head/` specifies the main branch of the ports repository, using the `https` protocol.

A checkout from a given repository is performed with a command like this:

```
# svn checkout https://svn.FreeBSD.org/ repository /branch lwcdir
```

where:

- *repository* is one of the Project repositories: `base`, `ports`, or `doc`.

- *branch* depends on the repository used. `ports` and `doc` are mostly updated in the `head` branch, while `base` maintains the latest version of -CURRENT under `head` and the respective latest versions of the -STABLE branches under `stable/9` (9.*x*) and `stable/10` (10.*x*).

- *lwcdir* is the target directory where the contents of the specified branch should be placed. This is usually `/usr/ports` for `ports`, `/usr/src` for `base`, and `/usr/doc` for `doc`.

This example checks out the Ports Collection from the FreeBSD repository using the HTTPS protocol, placing the local working copy in `/usr/ports`. If `/usr/ports` is already present but was not created by `svn`, remember to rename or delete it before the checkout.

```
# svn checkout https://svn.FreeBSD.org/ports/head /usr/ports
```

Because the initial checkout must download the full branch of the remote repository, it can take a while. Please be patient.

After the initial checkout, the local working copy can be updated by running:

```
# svn update lwcdir
```

To update `/usr/ports` created in the example above, use:

```
# svn update /usr/ports
```

The update is much quicker than a checkout, only transferring files that have changed.

An alternate way of updating the local working copy after checkout is provided by the `Makefile` in the `/usr/ports`, `/usr/src`, and `/usr/doc` directories. Set `SVN_UPDATE` and use the `update` target. For example, to update `/usr/src`:

```
# cd /usr/src
# make update SVN_UPDATE=yes
```

A.4.6. Subversion Mirror Sites

The FreeBSD Subversion repository is:

```
svn.FreeBSD.org
```

This is a publicly accessible mirror network that uses GeoDNS to select an appropriate back end server. To view the FreeBSD Subversion repositories through a browser, use http://svnweb.FreeBSD.org/.

Note

The FreeBSD Subversion mirrors previously used self-signed SSL certificates documented in this chapter. As of July 14, 2015, all mirrors now use an official SSL certificate that will be

> recognized by Subversion if the security/ca_root_nss port is installed. The legacy self-signed certificates and server names are still available but are deprecated and no longer supported.

For those without the security/ca_root_nss port installed, the SHA1 and SHA256 fingerprints are:

Hash	Fingerprint
SHA1	E9:37:73:80:B5:32:1B:93:92:94:98:17:59:F0:FA:A2:5F:1E:DE:B9
SHA256	D5:27:1C:B6:55:E6:A8:7D:48:D5:0C:F0:DA:9D:51:60:D7:42:6A:F2:05:F1

HTTPS is the preferred protocol, providing protection against another computer pretending to be the FreeBSD mirror (commonly known as a "man in the middle" attack) or otherwise trying to send bad content to the end user.

If `https` cannot be used due to firewall or other problems, `svn` is the next choice, with slightly faster transfers. When neither can be used, use `http`.

For those still using deprecated server names, the SHA1 and SHA256 fingerprints will be one of:

Hash	Fingerprint
Legacy-SHA1	1C:BD:85:95:11:9F:E- B:75:A5:4B:C8:A3:FE:08:E4:02:73:06:1E:61
Legacy-SHA1	F6:44:AA:B9:03:89:0E:3E:8C:4D:4D:14:F0:27:E6:C7:C1:8B:17:C5
Legacy-SHA256	47:35:A9:09:A3:AB:FA:20:33:36:43:C5:1A:D6:E6:F- B:E- B:C0:C0:83:37:D4:46:9C:A0:AB:89:7F:C2:9C:4C:A3
Legacy-SHA256	48:3C:84:D- B:7C:27:1B:FA:D5:0B:A0:D7:E0:4C:79:AA:A3:8E:A3:FA:84:E6:32:34:7D: B:30:E6:11:01:CF:BE

Seeing one of these legacy certificate fingerprints means it is likely that a deprecated server name is being used.

A.4.7. For More Information

For other information about using Subversion, please see the "Subversion Book", titled Version Control with Subversion, or the Subversion Documentation.

A.5. Using rsync

These sites make FreeBSD available through the rsync protocol. The rsync utility works in much the same way as the rcp(1) command, but has more options and uses the rsync remote-update protocol which transfers only the differences between two sets of files, thus greatly speeding up the synchronization over the network. This is most useful for mirror sites of the FreeBSD FTP server. The rsync suite is available for many operating systems, on FreeBSD, see the net/rsync port or use the package.

Czech Republic
    rsync://ftp.cz.FreeBSD.org/

    Available collections:

    • ftp: A partial mirror of the FreeBSD FTP server.

    • FreeBSD: A full mirror of the FreeBSD FTP server.

Netherlands
    rsync://ftp.nl.FreeBSD.org/

Available collections:

- FreeBSD: A full mirror of the FreeBSD FTP server.

Russia
rsync://ftp.mtu.ru/

Available collections:

- FreeBSD: A full mirror of the FreeBSD FTP server.

- FreeBSD-Archive: The mirror of FreeBSD Archive FTP server.

Sweden
rsync://ftp4.se.freebsd.org/

Available collections:

- FreeBSD: A full mirror of the FreeBSD FTP server.

Taiwan
rsync://ftp.tw.FreeBSD.org/

rsync://ftp2.tw.FreeBSD.org/

rsync://ftp6.tw.FreeBSD.org/

Available collections:

- FreeBSD: A full mirror of the FreeBSD FTP server.

United Kingdom
rsync://rsync.mirrorservice.org/

Available collections:

- ftp.freebsd.org: A full mirror of the FreeBSD FTP server.

United States of America
rsync://ftp-master.FreeBSD.org/

This server may only be used by FreeBSD primary mirror sites.

Available collections:

- FreeBSD: The master archive of the FreeBSD FTP server.

- acl: The FreeBSD master ACL list.

rsync://ftp13.FreeBSD.org/

Available collections:

- FreeBSD: A full mirror of the FreeBSD FTP server.

Appendix B. Bibliography

While manual pages provide a definitive reference for individual pieces of the FreeBSD operating system, they seldom illustrate how to put the pieces together to make the whole operating system run smoothly. For this, there is no substitute for a good book or users' manual on UNIX® system administration.

B.1. Books Specific to FreeBSD

International books:

- Using FreeBSD (in Traditional Chinese), published by Drmaster, 1997. ISBN 9-578-39435-7.

- FreeBSD Unleashed (Simplified Chinese translation), published by China Machine Press. ISBN 7-111-10201-0.

- FreeBSD From Scratch Second Edition (in Simplified Chinese), published by China Machine Press. ISBN 7-111-10286-X.

- FreeBSD Handbook Second Edition (Simplified Chinese translation), published by Posts & Telecom Press. ISBN 7-115-10541-3.

- FreeBSD & Windows (in Simplified Chinese), published by China Railway Publishing House. ISBN 7-113-03845-X

- FreeBSD Internet Services HOWTO (in Simplified Chinese), published by China Railway Publishing House. ISBN 7-113-03423-3

- FreeBSD (in Japanese), published by CUTT. ISBN 4-906391-22-2 C3055 P2400E.

- Complete Introduction to FreeBSD (in Japanese), published by Shoeisha Co., Ltd. ISBN 4-88135-473-6 P3600E.

- Personal UNIX Starter Kit FreeBSD (in Japanese), published by ASCII. ISBN 4-7561-1733-3 P3000E.

- FreeBSD Handbook (Japanese translation), published by ASCII. ISBN 4-7561-1580-2 P3800E.

- FreeBSD mit Methode (in German), published by Computer und Literatur Verlag/Vertrieb Hanser, 1998. ISBN 3-932311-31-0.

- FreeBSD de Luxe (in German), published by Verlag Modere Industrie, 2003. ISBN 3-8266-1343-0.

- FreeBSD Install and Utilization Manual (in Japanese), published by Mainichi Communications Inc., 1998. ISBN 4-8399-0112-0.

- Onno W Purbo, Dodi Maryanto, Syahrial Hubbany, Widjil Widodo *Building Internet Server with FreeBSD* (in Indonesia Language), published by Elex Media Komputindo.

- Absolute BSD: The Ultimate Guide to FreeBSD (Traditional Chinese translation), published by GrandTech Press, 2003. ISBN 986-7944-92-5.

- The FreeBSD 6.0 Book (in Traditional Chinese), published by Drmaster, 2006. ISBN 9-575-27878-X.

English language books:

- Absolute FreeBSD, 2nd Edition: The Complete Guide to FreeBSD, published by No Starch Press, 2007. ISBN: 978-1-59327-151-0

- The Complete FreeBSD, published by O'Reilly, 2003. ISBN: 0596005164

- The FreeBSD Corporate Networker's Guide, published by Addison-Wesley, 2000. ISBN: 0201704811

- FreeBSD: An Open-Source Operating System for Your Personal Computer, published by The Bit Tree Press, 2001. ISBN: 0971204500

- Teach Yourself FreeBSD in 24 Hours, published by Sams, 2002. ISBN: 0672324245

- FreeBSD 6 Unleashed, published by Sams, 2006. ISBN: 0672328755

- FreeBSD: The Complete Reference, published by McGrawHill, 2003. ISBN: 0072224096

B.2. Users' Guides

- Ohio State University has written a UNIX Introductory Course which is available online in HTML and PostScript format.

  An Italian translation of this document is available as part of the FreeBSD Italian Documentation Project.

- Jpman Project, Japan FreeBSD Users Group. FreeBSD User's Reference Manual (Japanese translation). Mainichi Communications Inc., 1998. ISBN4-8399-0088-4 P3800E.

- Edinburgh University has written an Online Guide for newcomers to the UNIX environment.

B.3. Administrators' Guides

- Jpman Project, Japan FreeBSD Users Group. FreeBSD System Administrator's Manual (Japanese translation). Mainichi Communications Inc., 1998. ISBN4-8399-0109-0 P3300E.

- Dreyfus, Emmanuel. Cahiers de l'Admin: BSD 2nd Ed. (in French), Eyrolles, 2004. ISBN 2-212-11463-X

B.4. Programmers' Guides

- Computer Systems Research Group, UC Berkeley. *4.4BSD Programmer's Reference Manual*. O'Reilly & Associates, Inc., 1994. ISBN 1-56592-078-3

- Computer Systems Research Group, UC Berkeley. *4.4BSD Programmer's Supplementary Documents*. O'Reilly & Associates, Inc., 1994. ISBN 1-56592-079-1

- Harbison, Samuel P. and Steele, Guy L. Jr. *C: A Reference Manual*. 4th Ed. Prentice Hall, 1995. ISBN 0-13-326224-3

- Kernighan, Brian and Dennis M. Ritchie. *The C Programming Language*. 2nd Ed. PTR Prentice Hall, 1988. ISBN 0-13-110362-8

- Lehey, Greg. *Porting UNIX Software*. O'Reilly & Associates, Inc., 1995. ISBN 1-56592-126-7

- Plauger, P. J. *The Standard C Library*. Prentice Hall, 1992. ISBN 0-13-131509-9

- Spinellis, Diomidis. *Code Reading: The Open Source Perspective*. Addison-Wesley, 2003. ISBN 0-201-79940-5

- Spinellis, Diomidis. *Code Quality: The Open Source Perspective*. Addison-Wesley, 2006. ISBN 0-321-16607-8

- Stevens, W. Richard and Stephen A. Rago. *Advanced Programming in the UNIX Environment*. 2nd Ed. Reading, Mass. : Addison-Wesley, 2005. ISBN 0-201-43307-9

- Stevens, W. Richard. *UNIX Network Programming*. 2nd Ed, PTR Prentice Hall, 1998. ISBN 0-13-490012-X

B.5. Operating System Internals

- Andleigh, Prabhat K. *UNIX System Architecture*. Prentice-Hall, Inc., 1990. ISBN 0-13-949843-5

- Jolitz, William. "Porting UNIX to the 386". *Dr. Dobb's Journal.* January 1991-July 1992.

- Leffler, Samuel J., Marshall Kirk McKusick, Michael J Karels and John Quarterman *The Design and Implementation of the 4.3BSD UNIX Operating System.* Reading, Mass. : Addison-Wesley, 1989. ISBN 0-201-06196-1

- Leffler, Samuel J., Marshall Kirk McKusick, *The Design and Implementation of the 4.3BSD UNIX Operating System: Answer Book.* Reading, Mass. : Addison-Wesley, 1991. ISBN 0-201-54629-9

- McKusick, Marshall Kirk, Keith Bostic, Michael J Karels, and John Quarterman. *The Design and Implementation of the 4.4BSD Operating System.* Reading, Mass. : Addison-Wesley, 1996. ISBN 0-201-54979-4

  (Chapter 2 of this book is available online as part of the FreeBSD Documentation Project.)

- Marshall Kirk McKusick, George V. Neville-Neil *The Design and Implementation of the FreeBSD Operating System.* Boston, Mass. : Addison-Wesley, 2004. ISBN 0-201-70245-2

- Marshall Kirk McKusick, George V. Neville-Neil, Robert N. M. Watson *The Design and Implementation of the FreeBSD Operating System, 2nd Ed..* Westford, Mass. : Pearson Education, Inc., 2014. ISBN 0-321-96897-2

- Stevens, W. Richard. *TCP/IP Illustrated, Volume 1: The Protocols.* Reading, Mass. : Addison-Wesley, 1996. ISBN 0-201-63346-9

- Schimmel, Curt. *Unix Systems for Modern Architectures.* Reading, Mass. : Addison-Wesley, 1994. ISBN 0-201-63338-8

- Stevens, W. Richard. *TCP/IP Illustrated, Volume 3: TCP for Transactions, HTTP, NNTP and the UNIX Domain Protocols.* Reading, Mass. : Addison-Wesley, 1996. ISBN 0-201-63495-3

- Vahalia, Uresh. *UNIX Internals -- The New Frontiers.* Prentice Hall, 1996. ISBN 0-13-101908-2

- Wright, Gary R. and W. Richard Stevens. *TCP/IP Illustrated, Volume 2: The Implementation.* Reading, Mass. : Addison-Wesley, 1995. ISBN 0-201-63354-X

B.6. Security Reference

- Cheswick, William R. and Steven M. Bellovin. *Firewalls and Internet Security: Repelling the Wily Hacker.* Reading, Mass. : Addison-Wesley, 1995. ISBN 0-201-63357-4

- Garfinkel, Simson. *PGP Pretty Good Privacy* O'Reilly & Associates, Inc., 1995. ISBN 1-56592-098-8

B.7. Hardware Reference

- Anderson, Don and Tom Shanley. *Pentium Processor System Architecture.* 2nd Ed. Reading, Mass. : Addison-Wesley, 1995. ISBN 0-201-40992-5

- Ferraro, Richard F. *Programmer's Guide to the EGA, VGA, and Super VGA Cards.* 3rd ed. Reading, Mass. : Addison-Wesley, 1995. ISBN 0-201-62490-7

- Intel Corporation publishes documentation on their CPUs, chipsets and standards on their developer web site, usually as PDF files.

- Shanley, Tom. *80486 System Architecture.* 3rd Ed. Reading, Mass. : Addison-Wesley, 1995. ISBN 0-201-40994-1

- Shanley, Tom. *ISA System Architecture.* 3rd Ed. Reading, Mass. : Addison-Wesley, 1995. ISBN 0-201-40996-8

- Shanley, Tom. *PCI System Architecture.* 4th Ed. Reading, Mass. : Addison-Wesley, 1999. ISBN 0-201-30974-2

- Van Gilluwe, Frank. *The Undocumented PC,* 2nd Ed. Reading, Mass: Addison-Wesley Pub. Co., 1996. ISBN 0-201-47950-8

- Messmer, Hans-Peter. *The Indispensable PC Hardware Book*, 4th Ed. Reading, Mass : Addison-Wesley Pub. Co., 2002. ISBN 0-201-59616-4

B.8. UNIX® History

- Lion, John *Lion's Commentary on UNIX, 6th Ed. With Source Code*. ITP Media Group, 1996. ISBN 1573980137

- Raymond, Eric S. *The New Hacker's Dictionary, 3rd edition*. MIT Press, 1996. ISBN 0-262-68092-0. Also known as the Jargon File

- Salus, Peter H. *A quarter century of UNIX*. Addison-Wesley Publishing Company, Inc., 1994. ISBN 0-201-54777-5

- Simon Garfinkel, Daniel Weise, Steven Strassmann. *The UNIX-HATERS Handbook*. IDG Books Worldwide, Inc., 1994. ISBN 1-56884-203-1. Out of print, but available online.

- Don Libes, Sandy Ressler *Life with UNIX* — special edition. Prentice-Hall, Inc., 1989. ISBN 0-13-536657-7

- *The BSD family tree.* `https://svnweb.freebsd.org/base/head/share/misc/bsd-family-tree?view=co` or `/usr/share/misc/bsd-family-tree` on a FreeBSD machine.

- *Networked Computer Science Technical Reports Library.* `http://www.ncstrl.org/`

- *Old BSD releases from the Computer Systems Research group (CSRG).* `http://www.mckusick.com/csrg/` : The 4CD set covers all BSD versions from 1BSD to 4.4BSD and 4.4BSD-Lite2 (but not 2.11BSD, unfortunately). The last disk also holds the final sources plus the SCCS files.

B.9. Periodicals, Journals, and Magazines

- Admin Magazin (in German), published by Medialinx AG. ISSN: 2190-1066

- BSD Magazine, published by Software Press Sp. z o.o. SK. ISSN: 1898-9144

- BSD Now — Video Podcast, published by Jupiter Broadcasting LLC

- BSD Talk Podcast, by Will Backman

- FreeBSD Journal, published by S&W Publishing, sponsored by The FreeBSD Foundation. ISBN: 978-0-615-88479-0

Appendix C. Resources on the Internet

The rapid pace of FreeBSD progress makes print media impractical as a means of following the latest developments. Electronic resources are the best, if not often the only, way to stay informed of the latest advances. Since FreeBSD is a volunteer effort, the user community itself also generally serves as a "technical support department" of sorts, with electronic mail, web forums, and USENET news being the most effective way of reaching that community.

The most important points of contact with the FreeBSD user community are outlined below. Please send other resources not mentioned here to the FreeBSD documentation project mailing list so that they may also be included.

C.1. Websites

- The FreeBSD Forums provide a web based discussion forum for FreeBSD questions and technical discussion.

- Planet FreeBSD offers an aggregation feed of dozens of blogs written by FreeBSD developers. Many developers use this to post quick notes about what they are working on, new patches, and other works in progress.

- The BSDConferences YouTube Channel provides a collection of high quality videos from BSD conferences around the world. This is a great way to watch key developers give presentations about new work in FreeBSD.

C.2. Mailing Lists

The mailing lists are the most direct way of addressing questions or opening a technical discussion to a concentrated FreeBSD audience. There are a wide variety of lists on a number of different FreeBSD topics. Sending questions to the most appropriate mailing list will invariably assure a faster and more accurate response.

The charters for the various lists are given at the bottom of this document. *Please read the charter before joining or sending mail to any list.* Most list subscribers receive many hundreds of FreeBSD related messages every day, and the charters and rules for use are meant to keep the signal-to-noise ratio of the lists high. To do less would see the mailing lists ultimately fail as an effective communications medium for the Project.

>
> ### Note
> *To test the ability to send email to FreeBSD lists, send a test message to freebsd-test.* Please do not send test messages to any other list.

When in doubt about what list to post a question to, see How to get best results from the FreeBSD-questions mailing list.

Before posting to any list, please learn about how to best use the mailing lists, such as how to help avoid frequently-repeated discussions, by reading the Mailing List Frequently Asked Questions (FAQ) document.

Archives are kept for all of the mailing lists and can be searched using the FreeBSD World Wide Web server. The keyword searchable archive offers an excellent way of finding answers to frequently asked questions and should be consulted before posting a question. Note that this also means that messages sent to FreeBSD mailing lists are archived in perpetuity. When protecting privacy is a concern, consider using a disposable secondary email address and posting only public information.

C.2.1. List Summary

General lists: The following are general lists which anyone is free (and encouraged) to join:

List	Purpose
freebsd-advocacy	FreeBSD Evangelism
freebsd-announce	Important events and Project milestones (moderated)
freebsd-arch	Architecture and design discussions
freebsd-bugbusters	Discussions pertaining to the maintenance of the Free-BSD problem report database and related tools
freebsd-bugs	Bug reports
freebsd-chat	Non-technical items related to the FreeBSD community
freebsd-chromium	FreeBSD-specific Chromium issues
freebsd-current	Discussion concerning the use of FreeBSD-CURRENT
freebsd-isp	Issues for Internet Service Providers using FreeBSD
freebsd-jobs	FreeBSD employment and consulting opportunities
freebsd-questions	User questions and technical support
freebsd-security-notifications	Security notifications (moderated)
freebsd-stable	Discussion concerning the use of FreeBSD-STABLE
freebsd-test	Where to send test messages instead of to one of the actual lists

Technical lists: The following lists are for technical discussion. Read the charter for each list carefully before joining or sending mail to one as there are firm guidelines for their use and content.

List	Purpose
freebsd-acpi	ACPI and power management development
freebsd-afs	Porting AFS to FreeBSD
freebsd-aic7xxx	Developing drivers for the Adaptec® AIC 7xxx
freebsd-amd64	Porting FreeBSD to AMD64 systems (moderated)
freebsd-apache	Discussion about Apache related ports
freebsd-arm	Porting FreeBSD to ARM® processors
freebsd-atm	Using ATM networking with FreeBSD
freebsd-bluetooth	Using Bluetooth® technology in FreeBSD
freebsd-cloud	FreeBSD on cloud platforms (EC2, GCE, Azure, etc.)
freebsd-cluster	Using FreeBSD in a clustered environment
freebsd-database	Discussing database use and development under Free-BSD
freebsd-desktop	Using and improving FreeBSD on the desktop
freebsd-doc	Creating FreeBSD related documents
freebsd-drivers	Writing device drivers for FreeBSD
freebsd-dtrace	Using and working on DTrace in FreeBSD
freebsd-eclipse	FreeBSD users of Eclipse IDE, tools, rich client applications and ports.
freebsd-embedded	Using FreeBSD in embedded applications

List	Purpose
freebsd-eol	Peer support of FreeBSD-related software that is no longer supported by the FreeBSD Project.
freebsd-emulation	Emulation of other systems such as Linux/MS-DOS®/Windows®
freebsd-enlightenment	Porting Enlightenment and Enlightenment applications
freebsd-firewire	FreeBSD FireWire® (iLink, IEEE 1394) technical discussion
freebsd-fortran	Fortran on FreeBSD
freebsd-fs	File systems
freebsd-games	Support for Games on FreeBSD
freebsd-gecko	Gecko Rendering Engine issues
freebsd-geom	GEOM-specific discussions and implementations
freebsd-git	Discussion of git use in the FreeBSD project
freebsd-gnome	Porting GNOME and GNOME applications
freebsd-hackers	General technical discussion
freebsd-hardware	General discussion of hardware for running FreeBSD
freebsd-i18n	FreeBSD Internationalization
freebsd-ia32	FreeBSD on the IA-32 (Intel® x86) platform
freebsd-ia64	Porting FreeBSD to Intel®'s upcoming IA64 systems
freebsd-infiniband	Infiniband on FreeBSD
freebsd-ipfw	Technical discussion concerning the redesign of the IP firewall code
freebsd-isdn	ISDN developers
freebsd-jail	Discussion about the jail(8) facility
freebsd-java	Java™ developers and people porting JDK™s to FreeBSD
freebsd-lfs	Porting LFS to FreeBSD
freebsd-mips	Porting FreeBSD to MIPS®
freebsd-mobile	Discussions about mobile computing
freebsd-mono	Mono and C# applications on FreeBSD
freebsd-multimedia	Multimedia applications
freebsd-new-bus	Technical discussions about bus architecture
freebsd-net	Networking discussion and TCP/IP source code
freebsd-numerics	Discussions of high quality implementation of libm functions
freebsd-office	Office applications on FreeBSD
freebsd-performance	Performance tuning questions for high performance/load installations
freebsd-perl	Maintenance of a number of Perl-related ports
freebsd-pf	Discussion and questions about the packet filter firewall system

List	Purpose
freebsd-pkg	Binary package management and package tools discussion
freebsd-pkg-fallout	Fallout logs from package building
freebsd-platforms	Concerning ports to non Intel® architecture platforms
freebsd-ports	Discussion of the Ports Collection
freebsd-ports-announce	Important news and instructions about the Ports Collection (moderated)
freebsd-ports-bugs	Discussion of the ports bugs/PRs
freebsd-ppc	Porting FreeBSD to the PowerPC®
freebsd-proliant	Technical discussion of FreeBSD on HP ProLiant server platforms
freebsd-python	FreeBSD-specific Python issues
freebsd-rc	Discussion related to the rc.d system and its development
freebsd-realtime	Development of realtime extensions to FreeBSD
freebsd-ruby	FreeBSD-specific Ruby discussions
freebsd-scsi	The SCSI subsystem
freebsd-security	Security issues affecting FreeBSD
freebsd-small	Using FreeBSD in embedded applications (obsolete; use freebsd-embedded instead)
freebsd-snapshots	FreeBSD Development Snapshot Announcements
freebsd-sparc64	Porting FreeBSD to SPARC® based systems
freebsd-standards	FreeBSD's conformance to the C99 and the POSIX® standards
freebsd-sysinstall	sysinstall(8) development
freebsd-tcltk	FreeBSD-specific Tcl/Tk discussions
freebsd-testing	Testing on FreeBSD
freebsd-tex	Porting TeX and its applications to FreeBSD
freebsd-threads	Threading in FreeBSD
freebsd-tilera	Porting FreeBSD to the Tilera family of CPUs
freebsd-tokenring	Support Token Ring in FreeBSD
freebsd-toolchain	Maintenance of FreeBSD's integrated toolchain
freebsd-translators	Translating FreeBSD documents and programs
freebsd-transport	Discussions of transport level network protocols in FreeBSD
freebsd-usb	Discussing FreeBSD support for USB
freebsd-virtualization	Discussion of various virtualization techniques supported by FreeBSD
freebsd-vuxml	Discussion on VuXML infrastructure
freebsd-x11	Maintenance and support of X11 on FreeBSD

List	Purpose
freebsd-xen	Discussion of the FreeBSD port to Xen™ — implementation and usage
freebsd-xfce	XFCE for FreeBSD — porting and maintaining
freebsd-zope	Zope for FreeBSD — porting and maintaining

Limited lists: The following lists are for more specialized (and demanding) audiences and are probably not of interest to the general public. It is also a good idea to establish a presence in the technical lists before joining one of these limited lists in order to understand the communications etiquette involved.

List	Purpose
freebsd-hubs	People running mirror sites (infrastructural support)
freebsd-user-groups	User group coordination
freebsd-wip-status	FreeBSD Work-In-Progress Status
freebsd-wireless	Discussions of 802.11 stack, tools, device driver development

Digest lists: All of the above lists are available in a digest format. Once subscribed to a list, the digest options can be changed in the account options section.

SVN lists: The following lists are for people interested in seeing the log messages for changes to various areas of the source tree. They are *Read-Only* lists and should not have mail sent to them.

List	Source area	Area Description (source for)
svn-doc-all	/usr/doc	All changes to the doc Subversion repository (except for user, projects and translations)
svn-doc-head	/usr/doc	All changes to the "head" branch of the doc Subversion repository
svn-doc-projects	/usr/doc/projects	All changes to the projects area of the doc Subversion repository
svn-doc-svnadmin	/usr/doc	All changes to the administrative scripts, hooks, and other configuration data of the doc Subversion repository
svn-ports-all	/usr/ports	All changes to the ports Subversion repository
svn-ports-head	/usr/ports	All changes to the "head" branch of the ports Subversion repository
svn-ports-svnadmin	/usr/ports	All changes to the administrative scripts, hooks, and other configuration data of the ports Subversion repository
svn-src-all	/usr/src	All changes to the src Subversion repository (except for user and projects)
svn-src-head	/usr/src	All changes to the "head" branch of the src Subversion repository (the FreeBSD-CURRENT branch)

List	Source area	Area Description (source for)
svn-src-projects	/usr/projects	All changes to the projects area of the src Subversion repository
svn-src-release	/usr/src	All changes to the releases area of the src Subversion repository
svn-src-releng	/usr/src	All changes to the releng branches of the src Subversion repository (the security / release engineering branches)
svn-src-stable	/usr/src	All changes to the all stable branches of the src Subversion repository
svn-src-stable-6	/usr/src	All changes to the stable/6 branch of the src Subversion repository
svn-src-stable-7	/usr/src	All changes to the stable/7 branch of the src Subversion repository
svn-src-stable-8	/usr/src	All changes to the stable/8 branch of the src Subversion repository
svn-src-stable-9	/usr/src	All changes to the stable/9 branch of the src Subversion repository
svn-src-stable-10	/usr/src	All changes to the stable/10 branch of the src Subversion repository
svn-src-stable-other	/usr/src	All changes to the older stable branches of the src Subversion repository
svn-src-svnadmin	/usr/src	All changes to the administrative scripts, hooks, and other configuration data of the src Subversion repository
svn-src-user	/usr/src	All changes to the experimental user area of the src Subversion repository
svn-src-vendor	/usr/src	All changes to the vendor work area of the src Subversion repository

C.2.2. How to Subscribe

To subscribe to a list, click the list name at http://lists.FreeBSD.org/mailman/listinfo. The page that is displayed should contain all of the necessary subscription instructions for that list.

To actually post to a given list, send mail to <listname@FreeBSD.org>. It will then be redistributed to mailing list members world-wide.

To unsubscribe from a list, click on the URL found at the bottom of every email received from the list. It is also possible to send an email to <listname-unsubscribe@FreeBSD.org> to unsubscribe.

It is important to keep discussion in the technical mailing lists on a technical track. To only receive important announcements, instead join the FreeBSD announcements mailing list, which is intended for infrequent traffic.

C.2.3. List Charters

All FreeBSD mailing lists have certain basic rules which must be adhered to by anyone using them. Failure to comply with these guidelines will result in two (2) written warnings from the FreeBSD Postmaster <postmaster@Free-BSD.org>, after which, on a third offense, the poster will removed from all FreeBSD mailing lists and filtered from further posting to them. We regret that such rules and measures are necessary at all, but today's Internet is a pretty harsh environment, it would seem, and many fail to appreciate just how fragile some of its mechanisms are.

Rules of the road:

- The topic of any posting should adhere to the basic charter of the list it is posted to. If the list is about technical issues, the posting should contain technical discussion. Ongoing irrelevant chatter or flaming only detracts from the value of the mailing list for everyone on it and will not be tolerated. For free-form discussion on no particular topic, the FreeBSD chat mailing list is freely available and should be used instead.

- No posting should be made to more than 2 mailing lists, and only to 2 when a clear and obvious need to post to both lists exists. For most lists, there is already a great deal of subscriber overlap and except for the most esoteric mixes (say "-stable & -scsi"), there really is no reason to post to more than one list at a time. If a message is received with multiple mailing lists on the Cc line, trim the Cc line before replying. *The person who replies is still responsible for cross-posting, no matter who the originator might have been.*

- Personal attacks and profanity (in the context of an argument) are not allowed, and that includes users and developers alike. Gross breaches of netiquette, like excerpting or reposting private mail when permission to do so was not and would not be forthcoming, are frowned upon but not specifically enforced. *However,* there are also very few cases where such content would fit within the charter of a list and it would therefore probably rate a warning (or ban) on that basis alone.

- Advertising of non-FreeBSD related products or services is strictly prohibited and will result in an immediate ban if it is clear that the offender is advertising by spam.

Individual list charters:

freebsd-acpi
: *ACPI and power management development*

freebsd-afs
: *Andrew File System*

This list is for discussion on porting and using AFS from CMU/Transarc

freebsd-announce
: *Important events / milestones*

This is the mailing list for people interested only in occasional announcements of significant FreeBSD events. This includes announcements about snapshots and other releases. It contains announcements of new FreeBSD capabilities. It may contain calls for volunteers etc. This is a low volume, strictly moderated mailing list.

freebsd-arch
: *Architecture and design discussions*

This list is for discussion of the FreeBSD architecture. Messages will mostly be kept strictly technical in nature. Examples of suitable topics are:

- How to re-vamp the build system to have several customized builds running at the same time.

- What needs to be fixed with VFS to make Heidemann layers work.

- How do we change the device driver interface to be able to use the same drivers cleanly on many buses and architectures.

- How to write a network driver.

freebsd-bluetooth
: *Bluetooth® in FreeBSD*

This is the forum where FreeBSD's Bluetooth® users congregate. Design issues, implementation details, patches, bug reports, status reports, feature requests, and all matters related to Bluetooth® are fair game.

freebsd-bugbusters

Coordination of the Problem Report handling effort

The purpose of this list is to serve as a coordination and discussion forum for the Bugmeister, his Bugbusters, and any other parties who have a genuine interest in the PR database. This list is not for discussions about specific bugs, patches or PRs.

freebsd-bugs

Bug reports

This is the mailing list for reporting bugs in FreeBSD. Whenever possible, bugs should be submitted using the web interface to it.

freebsd-chat

Non technical items related to the FreeBSD community

This list contains the overflow from the other lists about non-technical, social information. It includes discussion about whether Jordan looks like a toon ferret or not, whether or not to type in capitals, who is drinking too much coffee, where the best beer is brewed, who is brewing beer in their basement, and so on. Occasional announcements of important events (such as upcoming parties, weddings, births, new jobs, etc) can be made to the technical lists, but the follow ups should be directed to this -chat list.

freebsd-chromium

FreeBSD-specific Chromium issues

This is a list for the discussion of Chromium support for FreeBSD. This is a technical list to discuss development and installation of Chromium.

freebsd-cloud

Running FreeBSD on various cloud platforms

This list discusses running FreeBSD on Amazon EC2, Google Compute Engine, Microsoft Azure, and other cloud computing platforms.

freebsd-core

FreeBSD core team

This is an internal mailing list for use by the core members. Messages can be sent to it when a serious FreeBSD-related matter requires arbitration or high-level scrutiny.

freebsd-current

Discussions about the use of FreeBSD-CURRENT

This is the mailing list for users of FreeBSD-CURRENT. It includes warnings about new features coming out in -CURRENT that will affect the users, and instructions on steps that must be taken to remain -CURRENT. Anyone running "CURRENT" must subscribe to this list. This is a technical mailing list for which strictly technical content is expected.

freebsd-desktop

Using and improving FreeBSD on the desktop

This is a forum for discussion of FreeBSD on the desktop. It is primarily a place for desktop porters and users to discuss issues and improve FreeBSD's desktop support.

freebsd-doc

Documentation Project

This mailing list is for the discussion of issues and projects related to the creation of documentation for Free-BSD. The members of this mailing list are collectively referred to as "The FreeBSD Documentation Project". It is an open list; feel free to join and contribute!

freebsd-drivers

Writing device drivers for FreeBSD

This is a forum for technical discussions related to device drivers on FreeBSD. It is primarily a place for device driver writers to ask questions about how to write device drivers using the APIs in the FreeBSD kernel.

freebsd-dtrace

Using and working on DTrace in FreeBSD

DTrace is an integrated component of FreeBSD that provides a framework for understanding the kernel as well as user space programs at run time. The mailing list is an archived discussion for developers of the code as well as those using it.

freebsd-eclipse

FreeBSD users of Eclipse IDE, tools, rich client applications and ports.

The intention of this list is to provide mutual support for everything to do with choosing, installing, using, developing and maintaining the Eclipse IDE, tools, rich client applications on the FreeBSD platform and assisting with the porting of Eclipse IDE and plugins to the FreeBSD environment.

The intention is also to facilitate exchange of information between the Eclipse community and the FreeBSD community to the mutual benefit of both.

Although this list is focused primarily on the needs of Eclipse users it will also provide a forum for those who would like to develop FreeBSD specific applications using the Eclipse framework.

freebsd-embedded

Using FreeBSD in embedded applications

This list discusses topics related to using FreeBSD in embedded systems. This is a technical mailing list for which strictly technical content is expected. For the purpose of this list, embedded systems are those computing devices which are not desktops and which usually serve a single purpose as opposed to being general computing environments. Examples include, but are not limited to, all kinds of phone handsets, network equipment such as routers, switches and PBXs, remote measuring equipment, PDAs, Point Of Sale systems, and so on.

freebsd-emulation

Emulation of other systems such as Linux/MS-DOS®/Windows®

This is a forum for technical discussions related to running programs written for other operating systems on FreeBSD.

freebsd-enlightenment

Enlightenment

Discussions concerning the Enlightenment Desktop Environment for FreeBSD systems. This is a technical mailing list for which strictly technical content is expected.

freebsd-eol

Peer support of FreeBSD-related software that is no longer supported by the FreeBSD Project.

This list is for those interested in providing or making use of peer support of FreeBSD-related software for which the FreeBSD Project no longer provides official support in the form of security advisories and patches.

freebsd-firewire

FireWire® (iLink, IEEE 1394)

This is a mailing list for discussion of the design and implementation of a FireWire® (aka IEEE 1394 aka iLink) subsystem for FreeBSD. Relevant topics specifically include the standards, bus devices and their protocols, adapter boards/cards/chips sets, and the architecture and implementation of code for their proper support.

freebsd-fortran

Fortran on FreeBSD

This is the mailing list for discussion of Fortran related ports on FreeBSD: compilers, libraries, scientific and engineering applications from laptops to HPC clusters.

freebsd-fs

File systems

Discussions concerning FreeBSD filesystems. This is a technical mailing list for which strictly technical content is expected.

freebsd-games

Games on FreeBSD

This is a technical list for discussions related to bringing games to FreeBSD. It is for individuals actively working on porting games to FreeBSD, to bring up problems or discuss alternative solutions. Individuals interested in following the technical discussion are also welcome.

freebsd-gecko

Gecko Rendering Engine

This is a forum about Gecko applications using FreeBSD.

Discussion centers around Gecko Ports applications, their installation, their development and their support within FreeBSD.

freebsd-geom

GEOM

Discussions specific to GEOM and related implementations. This is a technical mailing list for which strictly technical content is expected.

freebsd-git

Use of git in the FreeBSD project

Discussions of how to use git in FreeBSD infrastructure including the github mirror and other uses of git for project collaboration. Discussion area for people using git against the FreeBSD github mirror. People wanting to get started with the mirror or git in general on FreeBSD can ask here.

freebsd-gnome

GNOME

Discussions concerning The GNOME Desktop Environment for FreeBSD systems. This is a technical mailing list for which strictly technical content is expected.

freebsd-infiniband

Infiniband on FreeBSD

Technical mailing list discussing Infiniband, OFED, and OpenSM on FreeBSD.

freebsd-ipfw

IP Firewall

This is the forum for technical discussions concerning the redesign of the IP firewall code in FreeBSD. This is a technical mailing list for which strictly technical content is expected.

freebsd-ia64

Porting FreeBSD to IA64

This is a technical mailing list for individuals actively working on porting FreeBSD to the IA-64 platform from Intel®, to bring up problems or discuss alternative solutions. Individuals interested in following the technical discussion are also welcome.

freebsd-isdn

ISDN Communications

This is the mailing list for people discussing the development of ISDN support for FreeBSD.

freebsd-java

Java™ Development

This is the mailing list for people discussing the development of significant Java™ applications for FreeBSD and the porting and maintenance of JDK™s.

freebsd-jobs

Jobs offered and sought

This is a forum for posting employment notices specifically related to FreeBSD and resumes from those seeking FreeBSD-related employment. This is *not* a mailing list for general employment issues since adequate forums for that already exist elsewhere.

Note that this list, like other `FreeBSD.org` mailing lists, is distributed worldwide. Be clear about the geographic location and the extent to which telecommuting or assistance with relocation is available.

Email should use open formats only — preferably plain text, but basic Portable Document Format (PDF), HTML, and a few others are acceptable to many readers. Closed formats such as Microsoft® Word (`.doc`) will be rejected by the mailing list server.

freebsd-kde

KDE

Discussions concerning KDE on FreeBSD systems. This is a technical mailing list for which strictly technical content is expected.

freebsd-hackers

Technical discussions

This is a forum for technical discussions related to FreeBSD. This is the primary technical mailing list. It is for individuals actively working on FreeBSD, to bring up problems or discuss alternative solutions. Individuals interested in following the technical discussion are also welcome. This is a technical mailing list for which strictly technical content is expected.

freebsd-hardware

General discussion of FreeBSD hardware

General discussion about the types of hardware that FreeBSD runs on, various problems and suggestions concerning what to buy or avoid.

freebsd-hubs

Mirror sites

Announcements and discussion for people who run FreeBSD mirror sites.

freebsd-isp

Issues for Internet Service Providers

This mailing list is for discussing topics relevant to Internet Service Providers (ISPs) using FreeBSD. This is a technical mailing list for which strictly technical content is expected.

freebsd-mono

Mono and C# applications on FreeBSD

This is a list for discussions related to the Mono development framework on FreeBSD. This is a technical mailing list. It is for individuals actively working on porting Mono or C# applications to FreeBSD, to bring up problems or discuss alternative solutions. Individuals interested in following the technical discussion are also welcome.

freebsd-office

Office applications on FreeBSD

Discussion centers around office applications, their installation, their development and their support within FreeBSD.

freebsd-ops-announce

Project Infrastructure Announcements

This is the mailing list for people interested in changes and issues related to the FreeBSD.org Project infrastructure.

This moderated list is strictly for announcements: no replies, requests, discussions, or opinions.

freebsd-performance

Discussions about tuning or speeding up FreeBSD

This mailing list exists to provide a place for hackers, administrators, and/or concerned parties to discuss performance related topics pertaining to FreeBSD. Acceptable topics includes talking about FreeBSD installations that are either under high load, are experiencing performance problems, or are pushing the limits of FreeBSD. Concerned parties that are willing to work toward improving the performance of FreeBSD are highly encouraged to subscribe to this list. This is a highly technical list ideally suited for experienced FreeBSD users, hackers, or administrators interested in keeping FreeBSD fast, robust, and scalable. This list is not a question-and-answer list that replaces reading through documentation, but it is a place to make contributions or inquire about unanswered performance related topics.

freebsd-pf

Discussion and questions about the packet filter firewall system

Discussion concerning the packet filter (pf) firewall system in terms of FreeBSD. Technical discussion and user questions are both welcome. This list is also a place to discuss the ALTQ QoS framework.

freebsd-pkg

Binary package management and package tools discussion

Discussion of all aspects of managing FreeBSD systems by using binary packages to install software, including binary package toolkits and formats, their development and support within FreeBSD, package repository management, and third party packages.

Note that discussion of ports which fail to generate packages correctly should generally be considered as ports problems, and so inappropriate for this list.

freebsd-pkg-fallout

Fallout logs from package building

All packages building failures logs from the package building clusters

freebsd-platforms

Porting to Non Intel® platforms

Cross-platform FreeBSD issues, general discussion and proposals for non Intel® FreeBSD ports. This is a technical mailing list for which strictly technical content is expected.

freebsd-ports

Discussion of "ports"

Discussions concerning FreeBSD's "ports collection" (`/usr/ports`), ports infrastructure, and general ports coordination efforts. This is a technical mailing list for which strictly technical content is expected.

freebsd-ports-announce

Important news and instructions about the FreeBSD "Ports Collection"

Important news for developers, porters, and users of the "Ports Collection" (`/usr/ports`), including architecture/infrastructure changes, new capabilities, critical upgrade instructions, and release engineering information. This is a low-volume mailing list, intended for announcements.

freebsd-ports-bugs

Discussion of "ports" bugs

Discussions concerning problem reports for FreeBSD's "ports collection" (`/usr/ports`), proposed ports, or modifications to ports. This is a technical mailing list for which strictly technical content is expected.

freebsd-proliant

Technical discussion of FreeBSD on HP ProLiant server platforms

This mailing list is to be used for the technical discussion of the usage of FreeBSD on HP ProLiant servers, including the discussion of ProLiant-specific drivers, management software, configuration tools, and BIOS updates. As such, this is the primary place to discuss the hpasmd, hpasmcli, and hpacucli modules.

freebsd-python

Python on FreeBSD

This is a list for discussions related to improving Python-support on FreeBSD. This is a technical mailing list. It is for individuals working on porting Python, its third party modules and Zope stuff to FreeBSD. Individuals interested in following the technical discussion are also welcome.

freebsd-questions

User questions

This is the mailing list for questions about FreeBSD. Do not send "how to" questions to the technical lists unless the question is quite technical.

freebsd-ruby

FreeBSD-specific Ruby discussions

This is a list for discussions related to the Ruby support on FreeBSD. This is a technical mailing list. It is for individuals working on Ruby ports, third party libraries and frameworks.

Individuals interested in the technical discussion are also welcome.

freebsd-scsi

SCSI subsystem

This is the mailing list for people working on the SCSI subsystem for FreeBSD. This is a technical mailing list for which strictly technical content is expected.

freebsd-security

Security issues

FreeBSD computer security issues (DES, Kerberos, known security holes and fixes, etc). This is a technical mailing list for which strictly technical discussion is expected. Note that this is not a question-and-answer list, but that contributions (BOTH question AND answer) to the FAQ are welcome.

freebsd-security-notifications

Security Notifications

Notifications of FreeBSD security problems and fixes. This is not a discussion list. The discussion list is Free-BSD-security.

freebsd-small

Using FreeBSD in embedded applications

This list discusses topics related to unusually small and embedded FreeBSD installations. This is a technical mailing list for which strictly technical content is expected.

Note

This list has been obsoleted by freebsd-embedded.

freebsd-snapshots

FreeBSD Development Snapshot Announcements

This list provides notifications about the availability of new FreeBSD development snapshots for the head/ and stable/ branches.

freebsd-stable

Discussions about the use of FreeBSD-STABLE

This is the mailing list for users of FreeBSD-STABLE. "STABLE" is the branch where development continues after a RELEASE, including bug fixes and new features. The ABI is kept stable for binary compatibility. It includes warnings about new features coming out in -STABLE that will affect the users, and instructions on steps that must be taken to remain -STABLE. Anyone running "STABLE" should subscribe to this list. This is a technical mailing list for which strictly technical content is expected.

freebsd-standards

C99 & POSIX Conformance

This is a forum for technical discussions related to FreeBSD Conformance to the C99 and the POSIX standards.

freebsd-testing

Testing on FreeBSD

Technical mailing list discussing testing on FreeBSD, including ATF/Kyua, test build infrastructure, port tests to FreeBSD from other operating systems (NetBSD, ...), etc.

freebsd-tex

Porting TeX and its applications to FreeBSD

This is a technical mailing list for discussions related to TeX and its applications on FreeBSD. It is for individuals actively working on porting TeX to FreeBSD, to bring up problems or discuss alternative solutions. Individuals interested in following the technical discussion are also welcome.

freebsd-toolchain

Maintenance of FreeBSD's integrated toolchain

This is the mailing list for discussions related to the maintenance of the toolchain shipped with FreeBSD. This could include the state of Clang and GCC, but also pieces of software such as assemblers, linkers and debuggers.

freebsd-transport

Discussions of transport level network protocols in FreeBSD

The transport mailing list exists for the discussion of issues and designs around the transport level protocols in the FreeBSD network stack, including TCP, SCTP and UDP. Other networking topics, including driver specific and network protocol issues should be discussed on the FreeBSD networking mailing list.

freebsd-translators

Translating FreeBSD documents and programs

A discussion list where translators of FreeBSD documents from English into other languages can talk about translation methods and tools. New members are asked to introduce themselves and mention the languages they are interested in translating.

freebsd-usb

Discussing FreeBSD support for USB

This is a mailing list for technical discussions related to FreeBSD support for USB.

freebsd-user-groups

User Group Coordination List

This is the mailing list for the coordinators from each of the local area Users Groups to discuss matters with each other and a designated individual from the Core Team. This mail list should be limited to meeting synopsis and coordination of projects that span User Groups.

freebsd-virtualization

Discussion of various virtualization techniques supported by FreeBSD

A list to discuss the various virtualization techniques supported by FreeBSD. On one hand the focus will be on the implementation of the basic functionality as well as adding new features. On the other hand users will have a forum to ask for help in case of problems or to discuss their use cases.

freebsd-wip-status

FreeBSD Work-In-Progress Status

This mailing list can be used by developers to announce the creation and progress of FreeBSD related work. Messages will be moderated. It is suggested to send the message "To:" a more topical FreeBSD list and only "BCC:" this list. This way the WIP can also be discussed on the topical list, as no discussion is allowed on this list.

Look inside the archives for examples of suitable messages.

An editorial digest of the messages to this list might be posted to the FreeBSD website every few months as part of the Status Reports [1]. Past reports are archived.

freebsd-wireless

Discussions of 802.11 stack, tools device driver development

The FreeBSD-wireless list focuses on 802.11 stack (sys/net80211), device driver and tools development. This includes bugs, new features and maintenance.

freebsd-xen

Discussion of the FreeBSD port to Xen™ — implementation and usage

---

[1]`http://www.freebsd.org/news/status/`

A list that focuses on the FreeBSD Xen™ port. The anticipated traffic level is small enough that it is intended as a forum for both technical discussions of the implementation and design details as well as administrative deployment issues.

freebsd-xfce

> *XFCE*

This is a forum for discussions related to bring the XFCE environment to FreeBSD. This is a technical mailing list. It is for individuals actively working on porting XFCE to FreeBSD, to bring up problems or discuss alternative solutions. Individuals interested in following the technical discussion are also welcome.

freebsd-zope

> *Zope*

This is a forum for discussions related to bring the Zope environment to FreeBSD. This is a technical mailing list. It is for individuals actively working on porting Zope to FreeBSD, to bring up problems or discuss alternative solutions. Individuals interested in following the technical discussion are also welcome.

C.2.4. Filtering on the Mailing Lists

The FreeBSD mailing lists are filtered in multiple ways to avoid the distribution of spam, viruses, and other unwanted emails. The filtering actions described in this section do not include all those used to protect the mailing lists.

Only certain types of attachments are allowed on the mailing lists. All attachments with a MIME content type not found in the list below will be stripped before an email is distributed on the mailing lists.

- application/octet-stream
- application/pdf
- application/pgp-signature
- application/x-pkcs7-signature
- message/rfc822
- multipart/alternative
- multipart/related
- multipart/signed
- text/html
- text/plain
- text/x-diff
- text/x-patch

Note

Some of the mailing lists might allow attachments of other MIME content types, but the above list should be applicable for most of the mailing lists.

If an email contains both an HTML and a plain text version, the HTML version will be removed. If an email contains only an HTML version, it will be converted to plain text.

C.3. Usenet Newsgroups

In addition to two FreeBSD specific newsgroups, there are many others in which FreeBSD is discussed or are otherwise relevant to FreeBSD users.

C.3.1. BSD Specific Newsgroups

- comp.unix.bsd.freebsd.announce

- comp.unix.bsd.freebsd.misc

- de.comp.os.unix.bsd (German)

- fr.comp.os.bsd (French)

- it.comp.os.freebsd (Italian)

C.3.2. Other UNIX® Newsgroups of Interest

- comp.unix

- comp.unix.questions

- comp.unix.admin

- comp.unix.programmer

- comp.unix.shell

- comp.unix.misc

- comp.unix.bsd

C.3.3. X Window System

- comp.windows.x

- comp.windows.x.apps

- comp.windows.x.announce

- comp.emulators.ms-windows.wine

C.4. Official Mirrors

Central Servers, Armenia, Australia, Austria, Canada, Czech Republic, Denmark, Finland, France, Germany, Hong Kong, Ireland, Japan, Latvia, Lithuania, Netherlands, Norway, Russia, Slovenia, South Africa, Spain, Sweden, Switzerland, Taiwan, United Kingdom, USA.

(as of UTC)

-
  Central Servers

  - http://www.FreeBSD.org/

-
  Armenia

  - http://www1.am.FreeBSD.org/ (IPv6)

- Australia

  - http://www.au.FreeBSD.org/

  - http://www2.au.FreeBSD.org/

- Austria

  - http://www.at.FreeBSD.org/ (IPv6)

- Canada

  - http://www.ca.FreeBSD.org/

  - http://www2.ca.FreeBSD.org/

- Czech Republic

  - http://www.cz.FreeBSD.org/ (IPv6)

- Denmark

  - http://www.dk.FreeBSD.org/ (IPv6)

- Finland

  - http://www.fi.FreeBSD.org/

- France

  - http://www1.fr.FreeBSD.org/

- Germany

  - http://www.de.FreeBSD.org/

- Hong Kong

  - http://www.hk.FreeBSD.org/

- Ireland

  - http://www.ie.FreeBSD.org/

- Japan

  - http://www.jp.FreeBSD.org/www.FreeBSD.org/ (IPv6)

- Latvia

  - http://www.lv.FreeBSD.org/

- Lithuania

  - http://www.lt.FreeBSD.org/

- Netherlands

  - http://www.nl.FreeBSD.org/

- Norway

  - http://www.no.FreeBSD.org/

- Russia

  - http://www.ru.FreeBSD.org/ (IPv6)

- Slovenia

  - http://www.si.FreeBSD.org/

- South Africa

  - http://www.za.FreeBSD.org/

- Spain

  - http://www.es.FreeBSD.org/
  - http://www2.es.FreeBSD.org/

- Sweden

  - http://www.se.FreeBSD.org/

- Switzerland

  - http://www.ch.FreeBSD.org/ (IPv6)
  - http://www2.ch.FreeBSD.org/ (IPv6)

- Taiwan

  - http://www.tw.FreeBSD.org/
  - http://www2.tw.FreeBSD.org/
  - http://www4.tw.FreeBSD.org/
  - http://www5.tw.FreeBSD.org/ (IPv6)

- United Kingdom

  - http://www1.uk.FreeBSD.org/

- http://www3.uk.FreeBSD.org/

-

USA

- http://www5.us.FreeBSD.org/ (IPv6)

Appendix D. OpenPGP Keys

The OpenPGP keys of the `FreeBSD.org` officers are shown here. These keys can be used to verify a signature or send encrypted email to one of the officers. A full list of FreeBSD OpenPGP keys is available in the PGP Keys article. The complete keyring can be downloaded at https://www.FreeBSD.org/doc/pgpkeyring.txt.

D.1. Officers

D.1.1. Security Officer Team `<security-officer@FreeBSD.org>`

```
pub   rsa4096/ED67ECD65DCF6AE7 2013-09-24 [expires: 2018-01-01]
      Key fingerprint = 1CF7 FF6F ADF5 CA9F BE1B  8CB2 ED67 ECD6 5DCF 6AE7
uid                     FreeBSD Security Officer <security-officer@FreeBSD.org>
sub   rsa4096/B64357A343D9CBAE 2013-09-24 [expires: 2018-01-01]
```

```
-----BEGIN PGP PUBLIC KEY BLOCK-----

mQINBFJBjOYBEADuKnefrbTVFTZf9mITVx1lFAqwDHPRHZeWBr2Vq1B/Y1eKKsen
BKbK/O/CXaLuGFRn/6Ptvi9eLuWnho88qzaPU1Aa7BFRRiZlN+WrTmaDwdONJnJQ
p1LTPjqHmLVAkD7mFZe/H8Glxot62zEqY7LrEs+ZuxQ8oI51YKjhGaACvkrFMinO
09+TDey1fupVH1+yskVKQZo1zp//Hl/IrPbZKfGCxIGePQowZF7YLvl8DKPo4jI5
KO4tZ1kOPcPL2CqwhuCDy0fpUhrQZBswp6tsGx5mRJxDxfgePRBYDK4tMK+BSVsR
putIKOZ4zoBf12hYFiJ8Yd7e9cqxTiPa7AhxPbAjppiH7qJ3NJKCXOOp9DcSvrfb
ymu9cbDIPNwh/LQ1wt3T+U8QkD6a1a2kJL5+mdg03Ny+8Ej8hUyuJOEx+sxLs+JX
4TS1KRreLzxN7Ak21dNMr8361lB+Uprgi9lOBNLO31TWPABtJhIzwBOhohSqstB9
w6I2ZsPpLqUp/p9BrWlw6+UfOqNDFILZ0CqL1CyFIyrkjutXrUshqniSc/u1VbTU
RlIcufZhN3FtW1P6ktUq5ss4dqEh/QZfR1WxBYRMbKXXAN61XO8M2t44I+44DHi7
jOs1q6jrbfAli1ZGYam/5wjOJkvQ3xemP6SaDKnCKOnPHC45EAt2SEVGywARAQAB
tDdGcmVlQlNEIFNlY3VyaXR5IE9mZmljZXIgPHNlY3VyaXR5LW9mZmljZXJARnJl
ZUJTRC5vcmc+iQI9BBMBCgAnBQJSQYzmAhsDBQkIB+1BBQsJCAcDBRUKCQgLBRYC
AwEAAh4BAheAAAoJEO1n7NZdz2rnKEkQAJWJ2ctNY7vg2pqrabavfRZ4UOWrLi4A
gOMnKrsm4ozZ1mc7NVMRj0Ve8jLLHrySW5QaSmp8TcaI6twxKD8FfTOFYjBU35DU
liyRlcbZmsBk7aG561TPwaK0XnF47RyPZWKbHrO7WgiDveGx52AmBdm2VRyMBwnu
e3b5RlKnNVMMSm4RLmrolkL0SAZNAWZGG4FqFtaxPRZo7LR9fEv/NydQN91b2cR8
SnLc2F2yiVc5mq/1f/t8dMBEbNx2+NoFaqP1O+1JeGYgmA/vE9fk1oDnn1pHej8O
hoJJ9SsQEuaITvzKP9bU+5/o/UqYzAX+y8QbTthjhzpkRwjqwjuMVmp6/f/o8ivl
nzD5K1lQOP/OJAki63h5LDUC/JHYkT/XN/bbgoSNveFSGV7cdocdSpCoBaZUJ9pf
zZpqRxypRB57f7bKBCI36E42KJKJ3wo873MJeElAeo31tXi2pBvTN/Idmrl6sDCN
PWwgsIOmu4Xd2FG5lanbTsXHKebCDPh/KK51mWra5judWWFVxChsNSwRHJACBXVa
2fPsahfz4GAEVp0/VbC1l4m8CHrgm3nh/ZAyNjgJQN5jJ37gQjx2LFsAhW5WKK8U
0Es5YXffjLEiNOnmJ+q8IZj6Mj5lWXkbCvrqjfNTOKnzzZGws+6y4gRQkgkSY3BP
p+mpCQPjORc/iEYEEBEKAAYFAlJBjuoACgkQFdaIBMps37Jv6QCeJjxijseWZzn/
z7Cv3zSwSFMAWPwAnig7ZgzoqKKqwpvnwAXsQpGSnE8K5iQIcBBABCgAGBQJSQZHe
AAoJEJLIQ0VtpqZu8r8P/jHm+xi5yMz3DVj6emMazJdXLtnnGrKTNw5xLlX10a1R
vmo+sj4J1gmL+Cy2hM6fl6r054E/BYt9GVGaIC4eYiF6DUzlcPWkwniDKfillNJz
NIja4qhanuGrK7EJtZXACRhUuNr2EzEm4dd3nXNaBQZv9FlIn79tk4vVho7wK7ui
IT7nseUMWDh7T0h4IVSs2LWdvP71WDx8acoyfspI35C2pKXB5GRWxnzN+wOl+V0k
Dn2fGd+nL7ZEb/c/01h6AfyYJGetCXY1omkXSSzgD9KKu/RqZuxL8TMMjNN6z4SAy
MTthOHW0lTK/5h55dJYSquBQwuEAX0Z8RT8S4Nva5LKGr25IpIJuP/TxaHIgdncr
in4D0FtuG0JMOxjuzNdo2lOiMZ/lqZ75l6lC68GuKAhU2Rn1toqc/NReLlyLhHoM
1o3EvovAfZmzX3sOugU2N8L+oiTnFFXezpY5Huup5KUkrX+C5EErBIVfvKjNyhhK
Fru6Jwy9z3qiGhxNUFAAzftVYhNT1lDkMNqa4jPjOrcWS6+gwVfQAo9k0p5uwPNb
Iw59RA2q/wwhZuRoai4nqN9WkgnwmWn0sS9XO87jwN3uvK0IF97MGPSXNcmAGX1x
zF3GBFHYf/bpagrvT4v+DE+gLpgfplo86oZbjDPsXGhVNu1iffC64R+vecw7r3Di
iQEcBBABCAAGBQJSRqY/AAoJEFF75hSlwe7HvwsIAJUnlLFMOBLvlBrRuxVeAO6X
8DhytdD5YlRzt866cXq6A/dw57O9qwyyDy3upJIGRy6hYlL18ngGZXv5djcw7Rch
QmvBJ9ROkmkCHLe3+fYn668nkxtgQJHWADd90MGFHkLDWa4Pbu5yJKqkTy3tqx2N
mBDEz317F6mMtyTP56QI8PVnh1p6w0McQIVctS3LOC3u4Wjbw7l3Hwof9Pl3u4BZ
L/gJz5KAozUa5TqNV4SLwtUqXBg7kipwfshXVuQekG9XfMC84GaFMqEKTExscHoF
VdSzrBKHn6VlEl1sdhcdS9aKSOsqMXB25xhBe0hOl4Ddw63j7b47XCqcyqAE5eiJ
```

AhwEEAEIAAYFAlJHAsIACgkQ8cUWs8g1l1OXkhAAvXUR237vXF/sZCZgG0748Dp0
eOhish/c4ODgW3JRehVWAyAlTAit/+xK6oI5xkQA+z3KO6+/bAtnDQgikAkykgpt
VeVW/6v4GGBarUTc/CTcofEpC3rsrEm1ZwPLyva3YuFFnYHATq/2Qi1a5PnSfj5C
O3fZrOgJTXsm6eNt21bH7RYF4DYi4kDNQHxtBOaEcUhcIkS1MsMz5F+/YeqOd12/
FrcIPDq8c0G3Ol+QsHFx+Y6b5Fp/HgkQem9Pzu7XkNcf7nj5UFJw+qx+BivaVYhJ
8Ugq3pXYkNkhYSy/AP/YYp7moOgpo2tY5e+fqho4pVlrHoPqWTNKJJrfYg2Mg/vP
e0nPxiCU3anmFXhfeZy87QLrA2Br00I45StbU3uBhzTldfNW2BIgxg+LqUZyTrZ2
qHq8TOPsnplu5Xn/UjEDQ5soTq1zDpslEjCX36R8wL3eai74HUTjstF4xq+kiXmK
bX7HhGKD9TILRjU+toOPXY0ffbS7FOUijLqOJqWEW1nBpoYoHbGfMHn2g2rNFGzz
wiLZgbL2HZsC+kDoog33s60b//A9E3yFIIiPtk668kQmiobs9Iel3RC+eOdHP8lD
gcMN/Rc/5B1S9a+wYC8VTf6KInUTq5YwC0veKbg1s+Ow7tB9ejqgxtHT7iFjR5NB
oOpVkI4UtHDpewRAW9SJAhwEEAEIAAYFAlJIEEoACgkQi+h5sChzHhzyGQ//e6o3
y+pnFTS4UWjUxFTKCtqJeqtS84jvcbXhXFGKfnXX15atLYkVoD2LcO5yvrFRNvY6
PjRkxJmLo2Lb/MpoDupRMfR1PxotFYuNYodmoHxVUun+1eIFQ5XUSiQSsIsjcUYd
EcOoZFzMfWIHZUOA1cGAtb8WL/Ql6cLcZT3fhPjEO25308XcxKmU7sJ1sCCh3tyL
CY0dvLffA0jgxEXUYmf3DpC6p+MNkPU3EDk600Uzy4/C2HT26Lt4NR6TNcEZg6O/
lPvmD1/ATO9fAHCb4uEIkqR3VLdeg31EHND32gO/2HXc4Xp2dbV8qs+ts13w5L26
D+94PSsTwYF+85mfgu8nBhPOOn7lqWxIO/1MnOrEIVNu+K/fwh4lu8v/6PJYEYIn
LtYkDH3/LcKTsK6N/2KLbtROlHXeNKXyt0UliINteDlV9xYkn6TtzUcTrZ4Xa3HM
yN5mi+a0vptJFBPxyonMMHDAXRkLR8BexxUJqdk2aupIs0Y0Cet6Vk+8Q9bn04gl
pKjTjnnarJJsTlhrdmVobkDhbEGYB3KyrjZp2JmdYYzAbHXbdp3T7yJ4R3/7aQRg
XJIQgEHjmgFf0Wwzxs1JIN2URDZS8k2pyuI6M8ndPtJiYbwqy1Wcflz57aWYAOVf
b/G4IEsicSd1mHjYjsaMV/kp1kGrWihB/Dt79nWJAhwEEwECAAYFAlJJfnUACgkQ
cTWO1j93QHkxbA//SKb0a0wo5dTJpMp7pUL4pkCx1gR3YCZMyiJHAGnC0vHoTmxI
+6+YAU9DBFWjQk2uqqn+GW+3AxLEN08s2xYvNoxJHUB1bF43HI9lXscGmzfjDR62
cIptcWtggeMw6M66UStdFWUudwDM6WV8BTxg2LYD3upeY69GnN92HinMj90D6PMc
iQjfUdZxZAYLKEhic12dKHpWRC0PH9NIAS0EchARkZQmjyPc4trWevAyhmpqdw+H
gxh9EBH2I194SvIXVuU5Gyl/l3a/6ntEUZnitBijU3uUjRnkS5XkJfqy1MjdrJ0o
ymo8mlxOVFKV879ez10KBnE1BLe9ioylOeGQRNcyYehFE7GmzkZHbOk+Pqd1Meaf
AjNIgQxrqgh8pJ2F8Zd8pGDrYspjICGbbdR0WRNcoN4kckJruTWFQ1xr//Kfwp1b
kCQWRwYcRL/RNVVZuHGgvTiTa2wZNbWfZk3tF9cXaYHIqhYU8l7Lc1zK0Fhv2E1t
Phw4pu495RbGRAFOE14S+QmknIy+DgIkTzQls36vnI4SVw9zs0D4Np6d1mF1p4gi
VVrgTQnlF3poZNppCUK9Rih8s5kMnyuRruGm/Lod4jL3wcbBz4sxBkCgrc2pyU1M
SNAjM2V8c7cGLgPOqX0eVqgXJoTnlNItF07aIZyFEA6e7YeiTeXxPfU10Q2ISgQQ
EQoACgUCUk3NEAMFAXgACgkQOfuToMruuMAgxQCfScnmgUcnT0J07KNsLKLMGW/6
ffAAn2J50o8KV/wu8auCY1o6EkjpiJt/iEYEEBECAAYFAlJKlYkACgkQ20zMSyow
1ymmfwCeLqsUDHBH8JnuaJjEUYqACGWZo88An0wcNy95yGdSJtgBFXNPZQJL2gSu
iF4EEBEIAAYFAlJNSA0ACgkQUYUJaGx+XoKvBAD/bUBqzL0oZtaF7WUDXchb4yki
f0ko+zh832R2Ad0KfygBAKNEUUKOnZFLJ8GZqAXmIWktgMiWFOMSxAXDLsyionoh
iQIcBBABCAAGBQJSTYUGAAoJECC3DeE/HR5PCH4P/ic8LWEp8aJLLlOR+DSB9H3I
cES36ulQLHKmmWMc/ysR/bLhGhBqF8TM3hzvdTqj6p7zMZKThhKKVLLBxjlV2MLc
OVwhCzQow/D8EpUqQw3ufpWDYzCI7SF4nohremXjjv9FZVV80QhxLSqDfeopIBGs
ZD6v5mZn0CtT0hBXD1rowcZVo2Zdgx7/HgL4BRH19ZMiKMVdp365ZQzGlRVNTbww
fs13UTINcchA4ggbJXX5h5oUo8pbp3yXso6cMnuuawFRDu15JjQctkpaDyB0QohS
z3i5LqA912kRR1rEQjgXH8GcudfQ671FKZ+SJ7lwd+s7vdUMIfAXf1CUCKMLAaFP
QB/J/ZT7FEwlO3ZeFKrWcYmkx0Af9/ieKO/ptdiOf2OX7VvE6AkReRBiqAeK9M4a
dgS1hnvs+QdPB40dTXEFRuk7+hcEqqan+ZuMhWohJlAhTHxTF8Vxl0oyNyXiXiJi
mJMTsGmvF2x+uQ/S4+7Mg8+A0oGYjwvnFC+0jWO92Ix9M3y+upxkc8KOM1/U9nq5
p7wje5MNdcCHyVTpSxvg/bDaQYopKTD6aVu94u4OlbhUXki4JnTQlwqFVkGHnpW+
BPbpQyqhY+t1QoaUWgRL+n8+WBVCqlFQF8vIoqbYGP4WxeVfylZTfSVWDoJUPKKv
bEsyhpVFj5XT70vJ866EiQIcBBABAgAGBQJSRaaeAAoJECZJ5ijF000F4jIP+weC
FBeCkY7sprDa61kp10GNF4YujiZ1QKQDgrQA9ipgv3pN+5ovC/ClzZm5baVGi+j5
zWD/blG9YZAApM/kkpAIvCPYIuQ9b+/crOUjuxyywuE2HSbaFuh66lW7Eox3NT8N
NMEl6Zry6m8RDHqTZIpwJPBiCgEcNqr/dcbtE0XgzJj94NOWSuq1URpP4wIT9aAV
Bqdj+0KQDkDk6Sqvmf59Cjt8hihvXAhOqcguKo8y262ABEO8kxwfqvRYECCE+eDE
APUEyOi/6uI0dQjQMytTWKogPIYg4wQjpG+Pa7wl7AnxOTBp4WvoS0BuCgjSYaxn
wVKHBMvxSCuDHBurLN0wqOaKSg9ib6m/Vy2vfi9ak8crXJFZ6eLrIxt73gyiozfK
Efvd6LBOJ9AeXstnubEs7ltNq9qKyW4+vR9eABmn/wABxCsHNjW+mmi8xAVhhc1K
qZC/D4vm6r8ZwrVAsmTADqcTr6A48J15FmIwcaQRWQ4oytxTGA7rHRFVjrt3YIj
/WP62byp8s59HOKJE+mA9q7ksAvnToLfrMiNA8/18Zm4CADKUny6GLzpuKgcYwTu
cqE/zBWUszI2NrJNtaKWafdXyEAwgBxNIl1FiYF9+ntoMWlqDQROPZLYChRThJvR
nNNsT+WwcuSHSFexLl14yrPJ3MBEe7e+2Vpj9HR2iQIcBBABAgAGBQJSSFmrAAoJ
EDpFFvNRg85IHx8P/3exX3fATzNwqfININlvYjxMzuGIHdVO3w2pHrOllmPX28/U
UHSQL9yRRNhzimm/9v3dvu5XHzjUzCEozoAa74DnICe8wUfju8sGmN5FKolbvSz7
VvcW4mAC5RY85zk+7luTg2wHZIIdgirTDrgPSirtYkm+qpuX/k5LAkwmYtH6gghq
v7rnYNKUChh+Ga+4yNbsdD7blWYr52UwnfT3evbgI5GqBMZEbghmqNiR2fcII6tr

NnuawH646UcucwogxPtLxLuZnslEpWiHQlAVvHlrCMoEkYqS+NRXOwZF04zTwRpL
CUlj0PxlRInvTrEpBd1KVejbkNWKK7wfyL/bF3rR9pMGWuDC32/9BfjtGgNDXJhQ
MDGntyAeQfiI3Ml5b5SA8bT5DsR/FIQDg0UDe5jjeVIEGZKunmRT/IqOLFMpZoMH
qNqWW8YrHlpN2o2c0/VqWSLzPKmocgqLwlkx5oqvn/F12xUzazGhFTFp6IXpqQVT
lkSPdDsVJuidj9ZJLMRoKfFD9tISqTocGw3suLqp8u5KZf43THWspBi4tD4IoN5r
lrLWtPnkteffyO62NZOOyg7rPUGJYlpgAMIDkXmsp58CyXqrL1/art0Ymcy5z8ea
1eUCnq/ZJJxrj+HrXuwko4fXTewf+nzSbJ2GEL/fMBkzAOKl9j5bOPAKwiD9iQIc
BBABAgAGBQJSTTdGAAoJEE2hFOXEouV/uSQP/i/yJbvVkxXlWZhk2JFhDpZaewdL
TUCkgsDeS9M7fde1Y/NbnVwSm/TtzysI6XPa5lIeXUTTlbwGiI/ZqFPDaDptUmL5
1b3cgMReW2o5zfLtnDZZHYPn8wosMFMhj2wk0XpQv7DOJBQf5MNnPHublBwY05o4
dfDBKi0GKVWl8ZkHInGvREJw7wF6ukYtnWQOIaW//qmVwokv36I2EJoooFdl7oFh
a+Pq1n3DhQAgiln6/Mz/96fn7NvYvdbQlMGluPRANVuKjfP9zQroF8BmhWQbEHZG
aLT+FsD06A/CjWlKkb3Ys/N0wDi9kQ2ez/DZhjXgBMXhJrdPmeTEHrnX701Am+2D
CSpz7bbkOayILC5gx8DWq4hjGu5JtGcpJE4AsN69dXn4r/w8IUecoGZG/CjVQyAc
RxsIc9nOJmzbJkQGrP8A26Io0/xrwOjU2gGkYR+EaR3o9Qa8tY/uZpYb3t3yh+b0
Pqn8pLOMnpo16uJni3/tIY/kiqBnGF53yVLjlekwfORXBRFZ3GNroe21OXrfbHQ7
9BytMjTBsQahfaMdFZF1QINvENdJ+PQhhx7R2g80yxj67oa0F/W0zdqYDbYnM2bt
Mw89mv/q1f0xmdtaTJXz6ZpLPY3MtDWCJ/LcKDKUQqnyS7XilD95HdFnck9GPKQe
F/mgs5YlQeQZg8cSiQEcBBABAgAGBQJTMetBAAoJEEE5xLeoRUEkcGgIAL9ZRsk/
BMWQf4tK9RTY82bihv5T5XL5ybqnXuuPMC+E2IHDR1hGE9WcFr237nyfVxdnlBKn
IUbPrghdeGAWg6ki2IWOjgy1Q46M+P69yroc6KCa3V6LdM5L/CCk5Sr7L1LbvZ9g
Mj4AkN0xGhy3NNZGsomiXZWmBOiOQ4EJwlIwtFgMCKc4KmRD/h+f+/opMW9782bN
L6txp3tk5MOUXa+Xk1gy8MzGtowL2Q+P4zxa94NSVYQ6picYFvjWGtzUJ5izdyb/
se9wLIT8p0iyPrADP+P93EjkUrH4Im4OuY9ieKc3hFsnLhnI5VLpPSy29xXCi3C5
t72Nl5dU+/JJrtyJAZwEEwECAAYFAlQUczoACgkQjw7rxHtHFslqFAwAka5jXdrV
IGHT/n2YWzGTfgy5+bJfMZXUa6fuo+zzvB4hS3MH3YMpHRjwUrpkAjTh3dFkziVU
Ns7j4+7x5uEOE9Y1Baj6DTzEAxZNwtSeCYzCA0FZ/ufuUxGfZElcrU7AN6/ep/lm
gsE3+5tak8VYJxDjgu56uEIz449Lscj4G3FO6eXhCiiWIb7+y0a9m6cZ3yE7k8fo
TVObr8xdhGzw4+YEx3/4usD89GIKwLN3LZFjndqdPnYidneJ9NCrGH9g4+DRlOkw
8LGlSFxcNLqeVBDBS2bw1GlZSsd0NH+8deeAf9rEsmOT4CQKOWdgTnkK809erwvi
dUvsANlOypecGbHMo+NoS6kjR/CwPF8vDnwhEpy3N+VRZGhSD77D4LUWKBLQDisv
6HuyALmE02Lq9v5cK8fWy5cehS8hvAdn/FU0GOvPg6JowBZkyvqbOQDHIO3buAr6
NtnPdhhOd/eCOOkCPgcTAdwqWrX+l7D4SImMYjFAe9GWONAkkcRVMo6jiQIcBBAB
AgAGBQJUdXNxAAoJECZwmtY/E3EPJ80P/1AuTYo48UmvVkLd443cvaUpItzLUfrW
4q24KjiCTT63ETf1+V8RZCRreqt3mFJnZIOn8X+hSLAIPdJrJ1xtIKDoEWbQ1U8j
ClFq4FtUaqSHkQIWvW2VzGgVz2MvPTWK0EbWHdD9vhtotnYrq4H+T5cBuSyrW9Zu
Gct6zsZbC/O/iyiKQg3Kz6PtCiSPP3AHNH3ok1Nh0QsSQl1ggGp1J4gr9A0/Kcf7
lQ+/X0G7kHVxQnKzzuYI7XsV25Mp3oBsioQB/9aHt/JVfjrKpH0FtdTUEUcMfJqe
TMxW6xXHvslOIj3iXj8frSMYuJaQXVjTwu2yhY2oZfnI+JG0Gc9TA20lijhfyOW7
2wE/qdFW3I7CY/3hBYa63IwNGUK/t0520mOZmhrzKADvWc6lCGG02M7fY/Q+IgOT
PS4+5A1fs708Ds7qHj/TkltVmJftaCkBZCTWqvQ2XxStzYnHVojNxsTCqhIOZLM8
+/SSUMzox4G2d+z4WTlok+HLwcf4h5iAOQg2HAzGO84bamwOE/r+hB19YV07dGND
h/7TI25Slhk46CbuLajnAiIfg4UnbMpUZt+ZC+tdCuKsFQcRl7cUXqkJ3gKAiFOl
8Dly72t5gYwYUEZDkuKisAztRMCvdI1bg8j8ALFjbtd5cYbrtyLYVbg5Nm+mawXh
/U5lqcrjWdbFiQIcBBABAgAGBQJUdg4iAAoJEGJ6sNnqQ9eZRyIP/1geWFuerAtS
jO9ew9bhqC6oCVBi7R/DNT9WLNXvV5h3DYzGXnlhoEHdBzF3G4RmC6RaxZcjTQaI
lYF0qGtvZXWsQG4W6UIT58E6vyNyOj1Ugl4Siqvo1L7IxCt0Bdti0sQ082P44B2K
bSWqN8zMww3lMjnnmrRIb+PcC8PQgLZU5twosEOl/MuuDXRTAgPa4jXuKY17V/6K
NPND4d/rnsENr3+YXlG7/pdAgT9CAdNfFBKSRAUHQ454QzGaJln54FAs5INXf6iv
phfbRQp5on7MyShFNQr5AIeF5SNg/ktBlvrHItCdwM/FnOk5fg8EM3eqZHNC8HE2
SxGKa95o8QcbI2E/0iPJqzLWlmLAxaaV53Ei4RzVkGzPfS0hWFuP/NVg2FYqUTZK
Ie5Btsqd9rPvCTqywjGMKcQUIVK/aiqcDV1J7SewjxuIG4+4eaTNiQgVZspqGCbH
FHdssU/oedCIURRV2vMCCWaFEKR94vIK4IbXF07AVAZPsOlitZj6PWaFZ1zwLbWt
+VmgkM8Pj5L7xy+vX/bGQRO75JYrLYP1a9h/iG/Am0ezZQrtjTPtV07hLBQDOmpt
s3BhEsl9VCH2GkqBhsHjxhYM9cnQqMCMSp5fERRqphxyCoNcBdLHurikt34XMuql
otgC2RQoYGsIdQlYX2dxIQhDbij70GrRiQIcBBMBAgAGBQJUFHNAAAoJEDk/yxUg
Q+mJ4NwP/1gH4LefqQu+pbXAD6zezvM7r4dLca2TeFMCWSIRpRdtMqiavsrBtubp
kInXup616EcEY1nKi+mNiHYZx7TiUxdlLljrkr0HVtp3MD/AgBoal+J1muESe5Yb
0frp+NwJOLikUBG1v2cY2mZgIAkFvbfwVFCtJmwGL8nLyZrG1QRy242I179lNFCA
1xZu+9vKbakwnn4rqwT8ihft8o2POY2cq/MHs0XNmalUhF9Emc6sNR0vXkDeBKAA
gk+3lcbabqSni6IOpruX1XWtfnlIEqZVU49unNYbvylh4NTl2vjawsXAec+tbVQp
aFWvwru+07kC8BwOKb83IiBHDLQC+oE6c1CdkbyfmQ+aH/OJs0cyGqJGeh4Q0Pfk
RSd44Ew3l/rzuHWjw++/JpfznK5mhVObpmWd3HH77gwm+FNeo5C60tkPtMfVfPqK
PbBTrzzdN1l26VloqFcRzXAnIKMqEP4J1Jd4l5awopqeBfRwVx4+XVV0y2qfvP/6
DyKWk6D97p7jrB6yuMoYbKvJKoxx75SxiGMv4gubj22iqIp8tJarrbBONdnhZCcx
LfDMcVJDSzI2LmDk5SXvNycNyxLCVvda6upMDB9O4wDE1EJJnsvkhudbwAdYEYCW

```
8CnF3toHcP1bGRiJGJ6Qrl11NPCdCjOmbq9KSxfkadBQ93uXo56QiQIiBBMBCgAM
BQJTd5xqBYMHhh+AAAoJEGwc0Sh9sBEAfBgP/ieZTSvyMwnOZOPNlQYnhkhaZRHP
i5fzOMzbwd+hC/3mi2U8mZOYXvTeN6+JiWJ7s+4UB0+JoOwwMkkNGYWygMF0OUl+
03FJB9cDIxFW5n3rjjbwX2RLcbx2ATQnNHRSsZdXWg1jTbzoRpOAL9ZhoyWJtRYz
fCd+r5JZrd59zGgc70aDAjF77PVA5L6lZXzTH4U4hlQzF8ugAmtNqTEfEhKRo5pt
ecu6Slf360Lc1L6Coc4amU3fMCPXP6IK5aMBPwzfXahAylITvxjbujIkh/y3KifL
cgsgc6a5y24+0Bo02RzCnB1QB+alr6312b3FMrixsev2RfyPzWxfN8eE8JElobbz
4sPd5SgQ3P+iF+g9E4fTnXhk5f4u+wU5PtiWXxzWy6EYz0hGgE4Dz/uQ2fcRBASO
xMJQvPAeFM59SVTJGiFRzeNY6H/zWeC8DTE9jKbzhZ8kIzxyr9iTd7XJhp5pCVez
zkG7R9xDALq3ySMO0s7cWNB1V8Ne0YwNPZlStCpW6kW8nfC4qmNorukPcVk8tRYf
Gy+ebrWdXphdhLRZB5NpQ4ECG8kOIP/1bSRNvMs4WHU1C+hkOn8vcfOZDMO8zPro
SCNnHB0MUbXENfv4+ZXM6I39fAHohQlHw2LlqibeJHr5lbIukGQ6v8qdo5xdaoel
JnXUSVN4XvroE+uZiQJFBBABCgAvBQJTd6AZKBpodHRwczovL3BhZXBzLmN4L3Bn
cC9zaWduYW5nLXBvbGljeS5hc2MACgkQu14sRioPqLA7cQ/+NvSnh6fW7Gf89uy9
l4+/8hjGm0REFQf0LlYdiqf1pJ9N6Vf4MdhEFZs/2bvOgitSZzyScvxkAuv0LXE4
xPxOnwVYQ/VuxLSOBdTjU2srdnHrHaQxos16WLq85C2NsCSZNLOCXalMZk3XD0FH
HrcyWGfyiX4vr0tn+4G70FWbsfrK1Epmx3v+nCpCPmgBjdLRy9iU6uUjWB0w/ZVE
eD5MNAWyWumLJz32gpEQFSpELcviBoYxec8pIzlfV0db5ydJGZlsWM5W/KOy1ZFm
dpCfsl/hPGbBEtEeEf0mszchZDGtwaSpo0oiZj0LX6kSUTsp5GhjeTtntu2Hk9oq
b+u4TtAJbKHaYovJn2cySmWyE7Hqvvh2Lo+uxwm9RjKRNbtYBylZnV6QFaeMejen
RFwLdtdiil1UmXhV6MUHNIIZ0oJZ1zo+GkZKWQdoFpzayrWpfkAC+x2ovV106RYM
BAEcGg12ZZ1RcCytM/67efGG9KxjukARycsv1pU6Cf6l0yjqOikM3pnxWfdLvybU
9E4U7THfJ0sfXfs2U7d7LAX8WfWru1I90ZmFBLO5Fm3WMAOplJmdaSoNJ22IJrZb
StCDb7GynBD9x/qUGrRfIxKtzxGZghor5xHWxTtn6hLgxvoF5cDmN8g6dI0snbXK
DljubF4feV9MBwiGwpjeG/71PcKJARwEEAEIAAYFAlWTlaIACgkQogW5MOpw+irQ
+gf/TRWhT+XFhokH4E3v+J9lTqhQ+IBjVfYVZm1nzBxTkvrEt48i3VBuJjp2Q5H+
cnRr2VE76IVNsvt8liUe9GF+1tylVA7qDGDMOlqkGjPVfD1viGRgtrGBJFg3oVr6
uyjKUyhzELQPkGU+lfbhXLVE3oMyhLxf3xUd/TvGXEeaqMoPgNFGiwfjtSX6oxas
HEu3HFDO2EqM45dtjbHoj98gvDSb4ReA2ZknD/gYnNt8cMdHnv/VieeCpSDxiD6D
qljpYSPUXjz0kh/LwcVZaMm+nD5BzKcXu2lD8A0fy6hVKSm2tGyKzfWr0oZw47e2
eVMBPG/l4YB2H1Im8PPsuSAeQbkCDQRSQYzmARAAtqDVVjJvadVMDJipe7K1POK4
QtcFswiKYAwc0JOkOeM0tDirorP869gdHtkuKr3fEuW0rtId5OeAjSCI9NIihX0r
0A2iJ1PrdhhleoV7CF0u0DxTVAo/Z9HSmuQWoTz3zr01XXyb7pSzJb8oGMLGFuQ4
X1yNRZw/0daGN3jYmxRWLJj+/vlUazvzt8L24JdJJ4PEZ3TNTOOophZDjnzxGMR2
6d9Fb3MV9kCcBIpIv3e1I8IKJyigmlOUqGRCmuv6CMADM0NWEGRBkAUg+YjP7C25
QR7DtFLSyorpJ2QXUax2Bwg8F2b1+54pfXbQO28nYRszy0/ySirYjahrT+LiKOgK
N5HLTn6vIb/KZgmaPR4F1cVJYPjlxDibu26kRIlHBIZuYJ9diZSpm/ump4ZXy5R8
41NjoGZBpIFsfm4or02nLuxEof6khy2K1l9WO8U9AjG05azNQhDGijv4GB4KXfnL
xDW51q8PZWmPxwBEi7mQbh/d2DyqzVLnIQiUWMk4OOCB3VEHWzS0sMOf9NBHWOC8
jhlHak9zzB3qNsJ6x1DXIHC3f4D8owFAqy6z2BVkKQys7mxXzciTvyYIqrb5ynRt
sLL2GMdn1NeMFziB51yMak9BDMGGymXObY3Gmg22gFwnb+ZBx+rNAGt4R3ngk+/C
0jeXHyGQNns6wwoCyuMAEQEAAYkCJQQYAQoADwUCUkGM5gIbDAUJCAftQQAKCRDt
Z+zWXc9q5+HLD/94Jdl4HSb2bA6N1k+Snajvy7C2xCS6GpOMIkDaIo+Aowe85ixc
JeqiNM4lBr80GMqAe2z0cMs4BvPHudNmN/4ceBsxwUnmcCr1hJiEaQr4eAR/lDC/
pz6gvkCndDKSeOvg5FiiXIqf6sTXpMu4euabQO4485obSBaF7/3z0Uf03Rtadw0h
zEcv/XaiCToA8fwGFNjGhAml/O7uaPmAI3rel4HMEHNxIgqARMiYNmFP8nVgJi7O
qz6rv65/E9shtNVQiHBgEXGZf/lsrxBsQJsgG2Vj+ggkDZPX5AfT7KCV4UrHtM+d
X3yKbwiWwosPwKmgzYxR5qX6JZyAr+72Zs5/eb56NGEGUJYKLmWJd85zCQHTZirF
sDIuZs87oYdrDYmFrwoWmoxZqSLeBCNbURu/BbO4nnJWzr3fwlqWO6LPO7rCafUK
6/mdYPJt4CpmDe3oGntdP/UVA10ZQ7qWYHTzNK2heBm4NHY0QMBXYoAE5bHMCDnN
YVN4QRVxUyjsXKfgjOyi0jZHX+9/CHihIXaCqOI4MdLwRx7dUwhoKOt519/Wlh71
w0qvg9kVt63A7Etyr7xj/IPpEGURDfD/EhXXn0offWL8+BKcLYp1Tbp9gJe3Ab/F
3VOWuafMlpON+Ii4YEem56Al/Ei8sDA+BN7cpw7o5Xf+HAG70CdcRDn7Vg==
=mLLk
-----END PGP PUBLIC KEY BLOCK-----
```

D.1.2. Security Team Secretary <secteam-secretary@FreeBSD.org>

```
pub   4096R/3CB2EAFCC3D6C666 2013-09-24 [expires: 2018-01-01]
      Key fingerprint = FA97 AA04 4DF9 0969 D5EF  4ADA 3CB2 EAFC C3D6 C666
uid                          FreeBSD Security Team Secretary <secteam-secretary@FreeBSD.ʊ
org>
sub   4096R/509B26612335EB65 2013-09-24 [expires: 2018-01-01]
```

-----BEGIN PGP PUBLIC KEY BLOCK-----

mQINBFJBjIIBEADadvvpXSkdnBOGV2xcsFwBBcSwAdryWuLk6v2VxjwsPcY6Lwqz
NAZr20x1BaSgX7106Psa6v9si8nxoOtMc5BCM/ps/fmedFU48YtqOTGF+utxvACg
Ou6SKintEMUaleoPcwwljzDZ3mxx49bQaNAJLjVxeiAZoYHe9loTe1fxsprCONnx
EralhrI+YA2KjMWDORcwa0sSXRCI3V+b4PUnbMUOQa3fFVUriM4QjjUBU6hW0Ub0
GDPcZq45nd7PoPPtb3/EauaYfk/zdx8Xt0OmuKTi9/vMkvB09AEUyShbyzoebaKH
dKtXlzyAPCZoH9dihFM67rhUg4umckFLc8vc5P2tNblwYrnhgL8ymUaOIjZB/fOi
Z2OZLVCiDeHNjjK3VZ6jLAiPyiYTG1Hrk9E8NaZDeUgIb9X/K06JXVBQIKNSGfX5
LLp/j2wr+Kbg3QtEBkcStlUGBOzfcbhKpE2nySnuIyspfDb/6JbhD/qYqMJerX0T
d5ekkJ1tXtM6aX2iTXgZ8cqv+5gyouEF5akrkLilySgZetQfjm+zhy/lx/NjGd0u
35QbUye7sTbfSimwzCXKIIpy06zIO4iNA0P/vgG4v7ydjMvXsW8FRULSecDT19Gq
xOZGfSPVrSRSAhgNxHzwUivxJbr05NNdwhJSbx9m57naXouLfvVPAMeJYwARAQAB
tD9GcmVlQlNEIFNlY3VyaXR5IFRlYW0gU2VjcmV0YXJ5IDxzZWN0ZWFtLXNlY3Jl
dGFyeUBGcmVlQlNELm9yZz6JAj0EEwEKACcFAlJBjIICGwMFCQgH7b8FCwkIBwMF
FQoJCAsFFgIDAQACHgECF4AACgkQPLLq/MPWxmYt8Q/+IfFhPIbqglh4rwFzgR58
8YonMZcq+5Op3qiUBh6tE6yRz6VEqBqTahyCQGIk4xGzrHSIOIj2e6gEk5a4zYtf
0jNJprk3pxu2Og05USJmd8lPSbyBF20FVm5W0dhWMKHagL5dGS8zInlwRYxr6mMi
UuJjj+2Hm3PoUNGAwLlSH2BVOeAeudtzu80vAlbRlujYVmjIDn/dWVjqnWgEBNHT
SD+WpA3yW4mBJyxWil0sAJQbTlt5EM/XPORVZ2tvETxJIrXea/Sda9mFwvJ02pJn
gHi6TGyOYydmbu0ob9Ma9AvUrRlxv8V9eN7eZUtvNa6n+IT8WEJj2+snJlO4SpHL
D3Z+l7zwfYeM8FOdzGZdVFgxeyBU7t3AnPjYfHmoneqgLcCO0nJDKq/98ohz5T9i
FbNR/vtLaEiYFBeX3C9Ee96pP6BU26BXhw+dRSnFeyIhD+4g+/AZ0XJ1CPF19D+5
z0ojanJkh7lZn4JL+V6+mF1eOExiGrydIiiSXDA/p5FhavMMu8Om4S0sn5iaQ2aX
wRUv2SUKhbHDqhIILLeQKlB3X26obx1Vg0nRhy47qNQn/xc9oSWLAQSVOgsShQeC
6DSzrKIBdKB3V8uWOmuM7lWAoCP53bDRW+XIOu9wfpSaXN2VTyqzU7zpTq5BHX1a
+XRw8KNHZGnCSAOCofZWnKyJAhwEEAEKAAYFAlJBjYgACgkQ7Wfsl3PaudFcQ//
UiM7EXsIHLwHxez32TzA/0uNMPWFHQN4Ezzg4PKB6Cc4amva5qbgbhoeCPuP+XPI
2ELfRviAHbmyZ/zIgqplDC4nmyisMoKlpK0Yo1w4qbix9EVVZr2ztL8F43qN3Xe/
NUSMTBgt/Jio7l5lYyhuVS3JQCfDlYGbq6NPk0xfYoYOMOZASoPhEquCxM5D4D0Z
3J3CBeAjyVzdF37HUw9rVQe2IRlxGn1YAyMb5EpR2Ij612GFad8c/5ikzDh5q6JD
tB9ApdvLkr0czTBucDljChSpFJ7ENPjAgZuH9N5Dmx2rRUj2mdBmi7HKqxAN9Kdm
+pg/6vZ3vM18rBlXmw1poQdc3srAL+6MHmIfHHrq49oksLyHwyeL8T6B04d4nTZU
xObP7PLAeWrdrd1Sb3EWlZJ9HB/m2UL9w9Om1c6cb6X2DoCzQAStVypAE6SQCMBK
pxkWRj90L41BS62snja+BlZTELuuLTHULRkWqS3fFkUxlDSMUn96QksWlwZLcxCv
hKxJXOX+pHAiUuMIImaPQ0TBDBWWf5d8zOQlNPsyhSGFR5Skwzlg+m9ErQ+jy7Uz
UmNCNztlYgRKeckXuvr73seoKoNXHrn7vWQ6qB1IRURj2bfphsqlmYuITmcBhfFS
Dw0fdYXSDXrmG9wad98g49g4HwCJhPAl0j55f93gHLGIRgQQEQoABgUCUkGO5gAK
CRAVlogEymzfsol4AKCI7rOnptuoXgwYx2Z9HkUKuugSRwCgkyW9pxa5EovDijEF
j1jG/cdxTOaJAhwEEAEKAAYFAlJBkdUACgkQkshDRW2mpm6aLxAAzpWNHMZVFt7e
wQnCJnf/FMLTjduGTEhVFnVCkEtI+YKarveE6pclqKJfSRFDxruZ6PHGG2CDfMig
J6mdDdmXCkN//TbIlRGowVgsxpIRg4jQVh4S3D0Nz50h+Zb7CHbjp6WAPVoWZz7b
Myp+pN7qx/miJJwEiw22Eet4Hjj1QymKwjWyY146V928BV/wDBS/xiwfg3xIVPZr
RqtiOGN/AGpMGeGQKKpleITY7AXiAd+mL4H/eNf8b+o0Ce2Z9oSxSsGPF3DzMTL
kIX7sWD3rjy3Xe2BM20stIDrJS2a1fbnIwFvqszS3Z3sF5bLc6W0iyPJdtbQ0pt6
nekRl9nboAdUs0R+n/6QNYBkj4AcSh3jpZKe82NwnD/6WyzHWtC0SDRTVkcQWXPW
EaWLmv8VqfzdBiw6aLcxlmXQSAr0cUA6zo6/bMQZosKwiCfGl3tR4Pbwgvbyjoii
pF+ZXfz7rWWUqZ2C79hy3YTytwIlVMOnp3MyOV+9ubOsFhLuRDxAksIMaRTsO7ii
5J4z1d+jzWMW4g1B50CoQ8W+FyAfVp/8qGwzvGN7wxN8P1iR+DZjtpCt7J+Xb9Pt
L+lRKSO/aOgOfDksyt2fEKY4yEWdzq9A3VkRo1HCdUQY6SJ/qt7IyQHumxvL90F6
vbB3edrR/fVGeJsz4vE10hzy7kI1QT65Ag0EUkGMggEQAMTsvyKEdUsgEehymKz9
MRn9wiwfHEX5CLmpJAvnX9MITgcsTX8MKiPyrTBnyY/QzA0rh+yyhzkY/y55yxMP
INdplL5xgJCS1SHyJK85HOdN77uKDCkwHfphlWYGlBPuaXyxkiWYXJTVUggSju04b
jeKwDqFl/4Xc0XeZNgWVjqHtKF91wwgdXXgAzUL1/nwN3IglxiIR31y10GQdOQEG
4T3ufx6gv73+qbFc0RzgZUQiJykQ3tZK1+Gw6aDirgjQYOc90o2Je0RJHjdObyZQ
aQc4PTZ2DC7CElFEt2EHJCXLyP/taeLq+IdpKe6sLPckwakqtbqwunWVoPTbgkxo
Q1eCMzgrkRu23B2TJaY9zbZAFP3cpL65vQAVJVQISqJvDL8K5hvAWJ3vi92qfBcz
jqydAcbhjkzJUI9t44v63cIXTI0+QyqTQhqkvEJhHZkbb8MYoimebDVxFVtQ3I1p
Eyn0YPfn4IMvaItLFbkgZpR/zjHYau5snErR9NC4AOIfNFpxM+fFFJQ7W88JP3cG
JLl9dcRGERq28PDU/CTDH9rlk1kZ0xzpRDkJijKDnFIxT2ajijVOZx7l2jPL1njx
s4xa1jK0/39kh6XnrCgK49WQsJM5IflVR2JAi8BLi2q/e0NQG2pgn0QL695Sqbbp
NbrrJGRcRJD9sUkQTpMsLlQTABEBAAGJAiUEGAEKAA8FAlJBjIICGwwFCQgH7b8A
CgkQPLLq/MPWxmZAew//et/LToMVR3q6/qP/pf9ob/QwQ3MgejkC0DY3Md7JBRl/
6GWfySYnO0Vm5IoJofcv1hbhc/y30eZTvK4s+BOQsNokYe34mCxZG4dypNaepkQi
x0mLujeU/n4Y0p0LTLjhGLVdKina2dM9HmllgYr4KumT58g6eGjxs2oZD6z5ty0L
viU5tx3lz3o0c3I9soH2RN2zNHVjXNW0EvWJwFLxFeLJbk/Y3UY1/kXCtcyMzLua

```
S5L5012eU0EvaZr5iYDKjy+wOxY4SUCNYf0GPmSej8CBbwHOF2XCwXytSzm6hNb3
5TRgCGbOSFTIy9MxfV5lpddQcdzijmuFSl8LySkL2yuJxjlI7uKNDN+NlfODIPMg
rdH0hBSyKci6Uz7Nz/Up3qdE+aISq68k+Hk1fiKJG1UcBRJidheds29FCzj3hoyZ
VDmf6OL60hL0YI1/4GjIkJyetlPzjMp8J7K3GweOUkfHcFihYZlbiMe7z+oIWEc7
0fNScrAGF/+JN3L6mjXKB6Pv+ER5ztzpfuhBJ/j7AV5BaNMmDXAVO4aTphWl7Dje
iecENuGTpkK8Ugv5cMJc4QJaWDkj/9sACc0EFgigPo68KjegvKg5R8jUPwb8E7T6
lIjBtlclVhaUrE2uLx/yTz2Apbm+GAmD8M0dQ7IYsOFlZNBW9zjgLLCtWDW+p1A=
=5gJ7
-----END PGP PUBLIC KEY BLOCK-----
```

D.1.3. Core Team Secretary <core-secretary@FreeBSD.org>

```
pub   rsa4096/36A7C05FE1ECF9BB 2014-07-09 [expires: 2016-07-08]
      Key fingerprint = C07B F5E3 10AE 64BF 6120  B0F6 36A7 C05F E1EC F9BB
uid                          Core Secretary <core-secretary@freebsd.org>
uid                          FreeBSD Core Team Secretary <core-secretary@freebsd.org>
sub   rsa4096/7B5150C8D7CE5D02 2014-07-09 [expires: 2016-07-08]
```

```
-----BEGIN PGP PUBLIC KEY BLOCK-----

mQINBFO9HvEBEADRfuWeoNUwib7ZjNmhg0Kt1kjiGEEosf3O2yMDfYuAXt4De6qK
S4KECe5+vZH2T8g+zmNLl/7JxdqHiWj9cnoZ6T3bqKh7w7pW7QzC/Q2k4mZsQkGl
xzhStHvaHSPKw5808TME0d3ewAfs0dQkDuA0eari0HipCbOVzqHUMTIROr/syPXs
jHxb2bj0KVzzq7wgy+vF4Cv25VzaAPBVgPv3HAoO/gLOr4SnXqBCw2vgprWx335t
QX1JslWlsUDmwwq40q4+eMnSFPZ0ing1DgfhMb+Dnrl6Rbxhb0pwPhbwubppUKfe
W6owOrTuUbATVoAhsfNySmUWQKc2p9w/8uFV/jJj9HOSgIMKrNONvqekPrjWOQn9
/lcQtGhldWmtPbMogOfaQisBEn1XjMZ3VEOagQxIe/6LDjU7GGoYvSdwf8Z0wXUY
/qDntPwudjJA4wQid1Tzf53gpUjr0tYq7aclpiBGs3F5EOs4HMXq5/xlwRGtBDHY
i9RNAlbRSfSD2s1nGsfsImPowlpjtLa+3PqYs/cRLGDu51DsgV/p/CqtAyebG+9O
WsF0Ydt4Q62jEuU8HY7SOj+AuKJVdUkyAZGk5vkPvsKzjdZUqRslurme7d3LqKai
FjBGj8UyId/IomDCjth3baGc/Y4e+JKyx1XDXgFY2HoQ2KzEoANrizjy5QARAQAB
tDhGcmVlQlNEIENvcmUgVGVhbSBTZWNyZXRhcnkgPGNvcmUtc2VjcmV0YXJ5QGZy
ZWVic2Qub3JnPokCPQQTAQoAJwUCU70sxwIbAwUJAeEzgAULCQgHAwUVCgkICwUW
AwIBAAIeAQIXgAAKCRA2p8Bf4ez5u2R4D/4o7Qb/hFz3XFRiBLtcsr+v5CS1fYgk
VN2Xp40dOTtt+Xo257+1oQDsS6McNXT7XSAFOTrFW+XID8GBnY6+ZpRYzontMCJd
25qGHzGBs2aFA/ROfhdvpOkhngxsYG89+IOUjS6SRNqG85Iro6eI7ZLi8sznEhZd
lH1jEWHiJhEubOvcedWS1zSHpOZwNIpyQV5d2O3/EhAOJRWgy8VmegeQLGg0zqdL
r9MKfg8/OwNQlysjrsA5MRnZMZAm6kEO381zYg8+Rwe+HtspzL/1cu4M7k5aBw0m
a8nShgXTqfgX+pwW2zBBL8c42p5D3Jh4Oe7KQ1KEvysZJGWO5ZjR9p4KLu49X2Yl
9cuD3Ii6+Nz9/cUlEGaMm4I8N3jpSNH+GCj7k1Wa9KWMh2ZxmVO5AML8h4g+A7aT
qNasKpG4XLXpcZ38sOw2/h6G2kwnrCel1ViCeOZ4pxeW95bxREqs6pkkym7Wz4sy
F5Mkba0uwFhWg5zBANBteXfOS/WU3fLEWeHXvZu9t44vyvP84qqZfNzBhz9puDVi
kPAY4uiZK4BTDkYZZr3YNKIIwEQ/rjcJSDKZKGJ6dsHKBSi0oGxFZpCE+YMH/Zqq
hTQHgXbMKWLgJ7xxRYJS/apvgnTd1Dc7zc5J7IT7XCdML0+Qj8eD48DwyMu+uAAq
/048iyhu/R8RP4kCHAQQAQoABgUCU70tAgAKCRADb2ye5/Oevxk0D/4wEJarg3nO
/B8ks+s7DadvpmNZrNSGeeR4qSEeZlH1ye30xD1HDE+ekJXC97Td4mKWKTrbRVEX
Fly1aBCe8tL5BbsRDmwzKwpv30qQ1rhowlAKZD8hdBEyEn15ciaoRisFKpWAv+mm
mZeTnG5sYOo9BFlv36WrX+9AOvy7yduVcZE3kLNoivS+8bXe5ULj6uMoyo/eC5uk
q35flp1qBzrplMc+vs7z8Npc7YFP2ORhR/mVg0rYFLkPVdPV3uFkrkb/Z2SVuo2B
IFWEeJojEBEbFNfziHUaQ8Z7ZdtkZ90IS1Z0Wuy64xjgORWVcTlRe4AwZKVC8DJs
Fs9Gk9gnsPmfLgM46pcKaac445w9uUQzKLxdCBKLPxMV/JHBRrMghyahevwnpsuB
Ok+ldsCNqjFaeAnVAmv3YtTbZ1JdorupeFa65JyjQon7l1JwWD67P7N0xrn1gxJ+
9uGUeHwGAvDF3IRr5ECISKAW92NfLYuNpyv6re/bt6A+FxaSA+E8P7Z+I4Gl5l37
czz+9ciYipiusweDuxectOlEnh13/WKXuUb68v6ZzbwGjkW8wunavhAN9fWxqqgF
WOtKtmpAOHFzmNOw5WGPfGdKOzc+g5ZqRt3CREVHj/uizNJsHzfadkTqYum+kQTa
y4tSgGH0S3EAiHGsEy4YZ4M/nxdIyakmsIkBHAQQAQIABgUCU701xQAKCRBNWP3N
LKSXdmOGCADEySzz4Q6wKsx/gLiAyhYNbEJbiv1Mirxhj IYGP9MqNpxxI1+Q3kuj
01K6ELIMuAhehoQOgU4AssJQxu7q78+hz207s+V0Syl+pvEOl2zUCgAmOYfle+BQ
75ZEEiINBuh6SOXBVLhfNp90FZ55KUSW4EeyoT+A4nRGHRgCTEfZ5WHi3lGlaLQd
Z9viLfNKA/DxrLWww+joTPIEhc3eUlmgDrcmfxo/L95EmTyUa5BtE0WuLwQEaY8H
J3eBgA9Y130ubuzzY4jGl4SCNedMzeIroHw2Bogd3V+E5aFtGd8gZUjXXr8rM6yX
PpttP2Hc8Bie2YXI2NffqwVqpL0dxo3uiQIcBBABAgAGBQJTvTYRAAoJEMATMJ1t
fkRccM4P/Rbg0W6l4KPFUvyKcUE6odRwoXExRGHdG9qW8Vf6xtW5eXUX/AZoCnXD
```

f3yWWttxgzN1e8iNRh0aYfuNSFTuHcHut/xw6GZ1yqASbuDmGWQ6uTb0yHYQcwQ5
ioaRaZZo5cpnSs0qZUpnrSzdUzyVmlKsD+1ut0/Z8yM8WGRyhplWX0dfXKnUUxJG
yh4GQc2dQon1vrsiuDTD2hr3EVues7le4WU+csegZTGPgPjhTSH6ZNFdDs4Y5KPi
unjXx+X6avPKPSJCnC9YlPMkI0RcokVLJW+K3+4QnbqU8m2MpZWVaaOo5s9PCx1I
208EHQ77A7EAFYNFrPZmtSV5X3BhU2rYNoRu0fpsNqJC340i7JdZdplPoO7FHRAC
AyQJyv8KUG8VVzK7m6Kt/0kq7LBc8RuvLQpUHSv1Z19fQvFgTegM5Pcpp3/ful/H
QIIc7XRElM57e+t8kbsoRpOlaKa3Okl3KisXdksWB4Fu6XdVArY/jIIQGs6dCpYa
jhRZcjkjHUAPvY/OqD2mBSwj0YwP0RoMVvFHMP1cgB3gjaB37A+DJeiKEXTWzGe1
fKC1TxCcOUZsrcqXnUyy23lKV9CXC7za3eB23dPIfWzJnD9BsVgYsemRVJx8r3Sv
QIL5zjKVDRAuV3M/HbCtSOgO68MExC0TFEl/8LPIMW8oVCY4+iqliQIcBBABCgAG
BQJTvUdSAAoJEO1n7NZdz2rnXxsP/R8WHku1nxjELqdM9M72JLD8UBlaAIwLStDy
hnTvLa0GO6eN0r2eJ1+tG8mKB+PZKOvNt8eZcSO/kjUvTIBILt7fAtN1BhsWpjQz
n+tuVWs4GVoPQssM4N09AYUzx8ni4byADY6n9l4zof2HsPsjXvuw/bzYXctKTQxg
gD3nswtLGY3q6unYewIChyaG8DStihFLcXIhXbwc6EOqdPN3VWwNInG/602UTO2L
eXoEM+tTaXkE51P5otACVH37AW0Vqqh1GxklYlMYLrKKn/YIBRvLVS5G+95iKs3g
MJhnaeFND2s9dmOTXyKyfTUffr/XTL/PVJSCbdqwiuXZQp8J77MtYyJn1262H8ko
590lPtqvpBNuywco0/F8BOFvSTw5sS8CmU0EHvyunKaofS3mxCFd2B0DzX89+AoY
ZY7CKU8OYt/VqhsfsL0C+DL4+XschBOUoTg6HrqG4F69+gerkK4Ps2984vOeTXe3
IqlYN/Bn92m9rGy9PKkpqG5C6w5X58BgvfeWTAkM4X32rZHKOmyYSCdRJQw7MGSR
240aWKPmgKvMaH8MQaJx9oSaAgF1y1892+ykVI9ntCVwywkmxNg1lfMuVFM4Vh9j
+C7OngnbQbhYtbFG90z9zfoMln39z8KT2yDP4A7Hklw0xmmT6t8KduGD2tfmaW4+
oz9attTyiQIcBBABCgAGBQJTvUdkAAoJEJLIQ0VtpqZuLNQP/RazXTtk1mixmLfu
nrScgh/1Gtb6XPVDTP5SGb/8HVdY1a+dDBClUIAFbEAUBIcB04/NVlW9un4IHyri
xdD/ijE/Cr/BMLnSFU5EmHKn8yOc3Bv6eTTRbJ8EYru0Cj5MdSIAoq8JKF8Lbxba
hBFw9ZSIpREPGlxnKI3TEuHJQreSZR07/GPk50suTK2CXxzEsk4VZesSTnwt/1m+
hrdtyNke3+wy8R0Use+KKgmTzpQ9phc8wq3uhHFzLJ5HbE21VRHgFd5+osZuSDuH
jw5o/zU5o0Bq9DDY3TWXPD9lgqKQ2PgH5DG6od9gjpjJdvXpXpck08HJDu2V+u7M
zW5lsnthDsW39YVLRD4ZwZJQaw+0wBuGDDxV+8x4fYhYJnXD8ZtUHCQ56FlcMyzL
m00WRLNxBSJjRvH12geg5xK3JWZ8V6Ce+XhvIAduDkajuUKQoWvTMzYaviqQhfV1
zXNNt5rxDNT+jMiwnAtDeCTZPMfGvzOPw9sYBz5RUa4liVPrGiEW/snAhcMB9JDK
jMAsKHvJwIvB9QrRC9sz6JIgEqv+jlsdkslEVU2AALlcJ3QuXlW0j9Z26q0sNGt8
5FVqhc4DOyXtZhKR5Ru8Lyc3swYRi2ofu9Roycq3L0swcMoGnOikRbj2PuuRdQiU
ozJ7mT6JmNF8ynlx/1+uzniVneEliQIcBBIBCAAGBQJUGDc+AAoJEOqwPFi/3EeP
EpUP/i2p7BLtyrujFmwr6wxru8G2HBWySFeRZ7YC5iH1ZIiGPPi7nuinWEv6FaW6
dW8fzrwmJy0iUpstKM8CUdR10PZ66Un6A9yfj9MuYSWBDQwzkd3wSJ2+HPLeaTsc
hb545CYnIJBaUAWyfufyoeB2+u3DNQd4oHv5ceI781D6J0h9MUz1bNgV2w3prubD
9o8ycaUvXqHrADqDZiUA1zblm19AmbJIJbgeUaXD8iwkyk2hRHScVe9aLzd2J4TX
PIQt9Dj/VnW3TLvTtMPEls1SM+pQ9xYF3IBz5BWbrMuk3o3mpsIijs+vfjJdv77Q
UeyT0Ur0fJ5xa7zWxCs5AMpCFDdLGRW1jzFYipJBBhDVkylIjpr3eoIIU/RxVC6f
5dTaW8GeaspllyJT8BKe54R9u/uf7QPgIkuXdIdaZ4qbbftLxvyBJk6A2gSM/sLY
qeoo+zRxKi+lMZ/Zw8MUZ/ON+yE1ccQJAk1GDqAhUs5f7zCPU6xBLFeXhz9d6bFP
BGWZ3dy7mZaHgALDGqSd240hIoknwzqHaWZK5lWTmzIVUUQPV1Vn68stcaVsuaFd
tnGHv/JMvAj1F9ZlDDRwaPx0ATTXQbBI6JlvDQ8u2tTKIYEswtez/enkjX1dALFl
tV5FNartIWGiHWYxkGVRlh/QtAb0NsBU4/5uZkWpWzG0GtOniQI9BBMBCgAnAhsD
BQsJCAcDBRUKCQgLBRYDAgEAAh4BAheABQJVntrCBQkDwu9RAAoJEDanwF/h7Pm7
aw8QAIJadQ8+oJgvc9yMS+kW+EzkdmGQUDk/7Ozkkj8gk3Fyh2gTI6AenQaDm3QD
/qvShJts/JX9+zVREwGU7WAvXm2EGIB2OB6pVQOGhNc0V8BihykQ27BtetvMivgp
KTYCwdh/CWdF3hAGaPFcc/GkrQThTBZARISUC5zce/FvCSugvRsMdGYjhaCA/LYp
YBGRzXZIrfCaT19tvfW89WdFamT5dVcMVs0uVHw1qYzz9EyH8cj3KwVanZ/KF7zA
pENdsmx2/+EPmVL/oGqctcx5vXtzMYTdr54aRay67oDbtWZNqYoIksShaw5rsNkI
OnqMXCqQkDd0lf46CmqAqqwH0bNlnxTpm8cEcfGIee1yNUc0BGs7qgmtm/7+96My
WPKHixQR48OPiTAdT6/n8msm/+MeL8aRWvhLUkhi3zDWoilScPW121JbE0QytpWP
v+2QCRtvnJritKrzyfjO2CRHOoe5zOY/yRd91CVBde7Tpd0UdQP3vw3B0MznahYQ
+qdt1bMD6NLgADNDP0B2yWMnUS6xku6iBANwZcdLSav4gE7gVFbePKNJnGW6rOIp
ljl0Ivm//KVufLPNX0DAokfvHIvDNNuVuk82UpvVSVxrIaig4HhbWDOnYiDhtE0Q
CDNP7v5e9u/iC3VwBVI73iOsDpPGqEFp1E6UZF6Uvfcxmsp5tCtDb3JlIFNlY3Jl
dGFyeSA8Y29yZS1zZWNyZXRhcnlAZnJlZWJzZC5vcmc+iQIcBBABCgAGBQJTvR9B
AAoJEANvbJ7n856/QGAQANf7Qn3AvTB1Co9oCtKobbtLxOx/FFw6/jnfurJxQ2Y1
8N9zTNJ1KCzI8pYbanicWQFqUfC1wu6FrnSlNGQvW464NqcERElbFE41pvqX+Tb6
/dOX07mMBZYK8wgLDcHEjl4i7NHurx1AKA2ro/5utRvfIqmhPxcHwhNiP1He4MD1
NgkyrxmRWtO4VM99mhXdm+pl/8XwuFJrdg4v36pEws6tYJgPwDc86/XrmeJT6GOC
RFREdwXn6osSvvVYnx4Pyto/xTG5Fm4sa7S4bxgvvSzp2/L+eO4JpOGXuhiIGhfE
wIStalyf14GKTa4a0Qd+gquml4yd1DBybNoa0zcz/sJOBULe/CLKzSs5IuGkfdH0
os1WEjdqQ7JPct3Yizb7Iw/j1YfvDmnM+tt3EMU1DJ1ttY9+XB6pZvtjSHNApaDP
fSeizstpolle3kvECBJyEIr5u/hL72dYEZtFiYFlHcvWIq6KqWJlIJr0a7vG7r58
6qstiG270tCeaVOfZT5grKNcDf4vYEoxL+2NKcHVA0rogRWPMwSWZbWEAaIilK/6

AVzc8xmefZJEHHxH7PprcPsH3MPpOwmWjfheHBKfIfEu1UqWAD+cRQmE+jEz1vc6
DzVUfA4c27j9/GXT9/NQsBTamC6rT3YUZKWlFulCC3ncRwf9ZTGSsiT5qCuV1ECn
iQIcBBABCgAGBQJTvUdSAAoJEO1n7NZdz2rnVCcP/3zh4y7MrLnV536rB0tDOM+l
sP3UYDmclWZmTENZ+r0ESM4YJzDjKO6ltXhh+MdYQDddY3vqLnsKTNYuMjKiu6jd
0ETy4ThzHxVhcyrgl1yWxyaSsdi5gMOnwNVClHfOD5gaOF0jdRJnLTLMueAEM3fy
NzSUjBOHJpk+RcIV3r/u8LvPFV2qwLWa937vYwfLRJ9jaQur5MnEVOWBz7CB0g1F
06JAcLv16FyWiLCOBxXZJd974lKXHd2yEMkSlF3Of1qX5FI6FK3HQU+c6eJcrWc5
4++zvgWHZTM3SwY9g5r157Wz9Vpi13Ev6ArIIIEQ9P1ViwK4zyW78rFoM09juqHk
N4uUCWuk0f57XCFkrDA/n6YCSfAxSYXc1I+MKpAm/6yBYiBNpyS3Jz5HGO2S0QGs
PsBcUHGEmO6k/Z6boJLwaCAGx2dSQ84R4DQeFAd3NjBPab2xTNlitcOi+xnidCJZ
oDWQqx5dSLwLeORsw25ikOWroUS1hqfta2HDnnou4zuyppov0Q+50JGFJIril8sv
oUmLfuSk3XUrlxPHgL57Wp5K8NOIU4u/DStX4UaRuHQ+Uu9GV+c6rr3F46+MooqX
ISAw5cm/kDMwu0fQ4GOo8J/ADUfLQa6a/JnWFg3hb/rgt/lHJxjZliOZy8GO8HyB
ddNfKCTBauqEyPYWTHzgiQIcBBABCgAGBQJTvUdkAAoJEJLIQ9VtpqZu/g0QAMXE
q8sNraENb3z08wisdE0UZXOGuQduXDSrwpe26L9mCR/usjeWeGqbG9b6mP+fAwXx
m/BovdkF3bWguolGCzztEHy+aTB4voxI6lEnyDKB8GG3mlkVjNAbDjVi/jCZfe6T
bJ6xDhX7633ees1An8tvizMHRr+z8zQ3xF4MNjlxLzawPE7/As5uHaT6Q3NhGTGy
G1oGsVl08pYp97p2E/d44m6IlY5XEzO2A2fIq+0N4dcy8omTX8P4eUZFlUezRbbZ
tNP8Av77hESXO79gpmQir9fC5/qMBgJN+3iB9O+VcB0SeLm0TvUWtSFULqEdDkKA
rLOgZf0HNnsu7/rb1tR9zqSYN8gsF3MvF0RNHUdbyEh189LZTmapwSxcaoUYPcoO
Bfwo0MqMuEuyCkMWSD53BvsaSbcs20WKYAp+oluM0TrnLup3702G/EbxmMRHZVVy
uX60pIQDXO4DjLo9tqbM6OUNCG+1tKEX7Bs9GIzUL2mxZ072qE8x1A+eidSzy5Tx
2nE7DOurziiuv8G3JPFDtLkUVtPx9gqyyG3wmfThkMCl1jnutYDjetpeC8LcI5S9
mFE8BXBka7qEEY19GI/1LJcfMI8lMn16OITYv4/cwqWPMbjSMg6JpWBCFdsxRmIW
iggKodt6LfnuEciChejk8ewTf6/47z7aVhdBkYaOiQIcBBIBCAAGBQJUGDc+AAoJ
EOqwPFi/3EePCM0QAKFrkt0wW+am/O8ZzIejSCY+htWilGAIa6REk5gv00k2dKPC
Wf5rNPAXeQRAX4qItmd35hz7czElm2EVbrylDD+F9uN8wbkCMLdIe88caWfoj12l
JACAd0NiBSwJPgrajvER92fr173I31cKT6hwXP6bgjU3J4HICc1h7h5j7g+/YSeH
UacPSiY4MuXAQao6e2BtFI77LOwFvIFFdCEMdZDwoH+7lIF9I+Krm7ojMF5fauaS
K4e3kL029QugIFYlgb7HeDGLlonBSn40YXPenafAin0lNGWMWVv3SKN7tweNkKEh
MVoVReropjYpRg+khKaMumwJ9bdGkYP8jq7DwCKXy/J2rfCUzsyVX5Ga7keT8Ztn
y4RO6YqFtTryraiSPrxDZQ0Gt6kc1m3u+4vh93qJk+foUDRSLWfWjmX9aRf+7+4z
dsYBOrpt3tab6FqXrW7IcI+p8PCyBW4c/WHkU3YWreEba21BXGiMDoxfhQ90yvSH
t6G8kg09+k8sRY/78oGYxR4Aait8/Y54DmHkyZKSewu96So0+TDmcbkeatatDhra
sbjfQLWx8363tnQvmhWpw/bpWGmDQDLVTHn90cXlckGU1fiUM7721g4s2UdijTMp
yYWfsLTaxOujHyxkwkBBtGV3DCas5Ep2KPMfSOgf3YVtPQH9IaotJSw/A6FdiQI9
BBMBCgAnBQJTvR7xAhsDBQkB4T0ABQsJCAcDBRUKCQgLBRYDAgEAAh4BAheAAAoJ
EDanwF/h7Pm7QvMQAKE3pM3e7LrDH6+xsdafxb/RxnVwUI6FaoN3dIZRjIIh7Dyd
6WypD43+f4c4AeIX+b78RuCuu+oZMMkHk4/Y4PIRv6jw1wuGa67iHopFXy9KPYjE
QOtLptZUAorqC62CzoVJxwbpIPw1AkKBag7FFKtiymQKbxSAkEkCOTa64RF+FFDJ
zUqbRQPJMMhKR35lJ/W3TfNQQViF/nydDdNmSY+gYAPU8kqhx4K7K9al9DUwVa/P
dL0l549BLOHzmFcEtw4FQOGMYt4Gkma5+6OIMJOuoM/ADAUz7qdcWYYdsFl42HzC
73u7MGLcfGkElcZKkH8sn2zuKsTTtTKD5rhLfIiu132vK7vqoONdJLd7U1X2Bwif
/ub1we7x4eGonZjhKajENpD3o/1Y072gLy8rlZ1r6/J+GQ9TEwUBNV8NNOfDPv0p
xTP6OCFPHEFA4toG0rRBm7OIxmQXFWmfxMT3NnwBqPCufWl0m20JhaU/pefPCqHJ
Vc8Ap+k6/bct3iNuAg1buggFVDWg89uBqF9vfdELiCDF3nRYm4bQ6S1cWxvnu5aq
9MZdt4Dc1WnTSNfY9/zjKJWmG3miv1D1eo3fSyVJNYVfVzQ23KMOPwR/jdr47Gle
8/5OM38zPhZ+vC+XD//Lq0/c8iMO39B4pwQ0Bb8FAhk/6Ug0cYbap+lPWkY+iQI9
BBMBCgAnAhsDBQsJCAcDBRUKCQgLBRYDAgEAAh4BAheABQJVntr0BQkDwu9RAAoJ
EDanwF/h7Pm77qQQALNcLFh7Eqc6gztkIySQtqDgieH1Frj2YGMrTxdzP7fnl4sT
wWQF2H0rsLgvOTZszACwLm9Rg2GaRi/bFZ9S8AIM1klQEQmu5LoQDSPrfX0pNxDl
1WhESECgEAF7++HDk3kHUxr5bCr+AN6kG3mY2nuKtw33G5ZbPtM5Nwgk/GT8dB0w
EazZVAN103RpdDmqGgWhYP/dYjGZJjLQCjGyM4VoQcEu+dPrUlAxhFbm13wRyfgi
fBkOug9pB0lpblEXAbB3slDw+4A1++lUjTLzGHayRZIys3d4uM4l1C1b8Z5SeU4r
mpDcqvRbDkhxwVh6e7YdEbf1VTWjQ2WgvEDQXG74N/nN3npbjPfnyFF79udHTZvb
qW+uqyozxXdtLvIbcEHWVDdQGqqTeeRinRu7sK8PRuJxbI7YaECGFw/1QrXdIUzi
1jxRWgtfWihCArXiEuo1LBwdto8CaSxkKV+QTsaH/t5mUiA+fHzsMlexWe55K/7i
OZ5wViUcffNYwbQ7DgcRxwuzc+IYaGg0GYGzJfWeKnrpwm8uZSccH1LLXdIyf5vp
Q9UojD0qz1+byBPt15/DBwFi5st248YMnXCItIYkjTfLeXQp4oSi3AHH0TEAxhUt
MLoI7CRnIiuCLmssfGI3sNH55wJQQeD7h8c/DaBI8yDuJ28dNY6H5zjPc82suQIN
BFO9HvEBEACynbl7EgcRIGWP706h1O6mrYXNZ2JpJBgYosqizdDHyru2nQSrNfgi
wAM1feB2NLJC0coQzRO1sDK2JP770+eK3ZhbWSP5BWN2toSFVEGlVpGWLBGoefae
ZnZA22IDzpOIjIi7iC92JBsTXESSsBoV8iG1rylQl5pcE03IQEuuDu9r7H8RJ3vTf
X1c+a+B8MUHn56kn3QkdG2blV0/3gjFqqavZeOxZpAmyn9n9Vc3yCCPkagtNQwle
NyZOSOLjjVpBjncE6dATdLOj85phfOU6eO/0bMXAgTr7mY41EIqYqdPQYrY93ySG
gBvBkyNaH5AlDNZZwJ4ddtDMFoP8nUhBoRrf5ApYyHcEmSXahLfW3a2qrPm/w5VL

694

```
EGLt53/6GZvEetpP+TtBLAxX6XaC2SXAOrzfSZENdYt/Ew6F/dTCZ622m0eW65iV
wSi1sNZD2hNFPs/12a2tem7DAWqD2bi8BltKRbO+8T7BARwIl5hXGq5+YnO+DgTI
f4SYkSt8aiPYwDAF3YSkzpiUmZoBSRt6Sb9sZ3zIxpfnrtLFmSeujzinyCVNzFdn
+HKxZvI9Mc3Tv/LqPruVuWHtlAj+eygH5bRZw4PTsMNX1FxM/K8hRY91A6Fyp3GC
kb5RzqdEGuSONBseaZirC0d+EYZ4smyljydpzwT1O8VjY4wi5BdgwQARAQABiQIl
BBgBCgAPBQJTvR7xAhsMBQkB4TOAAAoJEDanwF/h7Pm7gzUP/Auq4I876RUqAP2D
gPNArjuc7jqvIIsgqBvwS2Vdvxg0pFQmsL13nvlmFHR1dp+yOhiz1WmXIVGa9UoB
rVdmDrzqCifHUVlFct99DLJlM+hNmQnHgTABTsClR4idkekOvyEgAW/gsgddYfqm
N8nRKSrokFZvwoR7HlCcSXEuATbqgHjJC8IuJuIgDWjshy3yVLIo5v/g/Yuio4bx
tRTJm72DtUIdDH3tDejc37wd945Rzk4hKzet64inF6XfRhqBsRob1m6/wtP62xPc
Gbb1GlzxYg9WllRJ/ZOTktB4BemVjRn4/0KU93YyxFxHOtXsoZpRGDlovQBUhRkd
b2JEyHaLnFVKa7w7JFKW9d+OdGjV93l//6139QEQlcuocV4QciXZOXTZkWsaKQOb
6WkrSwkQwvNFS2yeUd0x6HD0xebztmSGoXL3uCKyeIxP/8MJjJUkWHh/+DLue4kh
lHwva7Wym0cvYoS3RzfYd26t9OgM7rflE0tOeJovaoaKP6Aant/EkQj2Wb1MssO/
Ia44NyMTrLARAPlAEGW/HI5JL9DZDnmUtByf29yqaHDuJCZS3nvR3T/4q+pblTVd
xQgwopUWjiKkg72yCXMhr/6FcOr9Xgqn++GuMZzh/TFdEoFoJn9stUaScYsoMoih
ym2NFbd1l2Pw/ifTQk5/KpQD/HkwiQIlBBgBCgAPAhsMBQJVnts0BQkDwu/DAAoJ
EDanwF/h7Pm7fV4P/Rb4aYTZmpajgk26vnXIJ2L/Xorx1lV7+a1bDxct71qWSLv3
aCDGDXe1ZLYMnyaNCJHNn4SP2biF7QrRhRmGdETA2VXXCFYLDS7s40QKltF3p1DS
1UPozfIyXkCFGbOasbaDtJ9SOSv04q1E6nXfCcF8xgjxMHbbrCsGiiHSNet+5A9f
AeZPWKWeUDgc3U7tho0FWyHZWgCjt5x1pYlCsUPgV3vlyo8HqRiWxLYF1WQ7SwV/
1536r5DD5vFbzhdxQ03mPDqLh0VZwPlQ6nb+bKwDX/75Q6tBNBkUQGM7XqI5tZ07
CjjIl/sTYMJz+GNnkIgrSiBr3vihtJgUzbJFfJqoIPkSdpayCP17k2Mdk9eCW6mc
tmtfhU91lzJUvAl30glTQP/wiyPQhTrQOlonwkrzY/Bve9Ilh2ZDt/9Q+XzEtSdG
59phFT4s7Yt5f9gVGx2hUhE5mmLN27rQJ2JnyIkA9IyNiycFPRo4ZURXI0yzCwXH
bwLEmA2FVnnyotURN7Z1k2PzUOL6lb7j2fMJZBbaFDR1G7J2pKNihJO3IY80z7Le
tpRpWKSdHTpSW1UXJFQBFT4W7fja03aEXP3bK+RV1MkAp/TCWlVCsqnyJae7BnEu
g9NgaY6PRozzy5ZAdWM36ylnwFyz48fgUWHFhDc7fMCHjwqDtP62K1TbRvFM
=cQn3
-----END PGP PUBLIC KEY BLOCK-----
```

D.1.4. Ports Management Team Secretary <portmgr-secretary@FreeBSD.org>

```
pub    2048R/D8294EC3BBC4D7D5 2012-07-24
       Key fingerprint = FB37 45C8 6F15 E8ED AC81  32FC D829 4EC3 BBC4 D7D5
uid                          FreeBSD Ports Management Team Secretary <portmgr-
secretary@FreeBSD.org>
sub    2048R/5CC117965F65CFE7 2012-07-24
sub    4096R/CA20328577064EB7 2013-10-05
sub    4096R/8B114B3613867E00 2013-10-05
```

```
-----BEGIN PGP PUBLIC KEY BLOCK-----

mQENBFAOzqYBCACYd+KGv0/DduIRpSEKWZG2yfDILStzWfdaQMD+8zdWihB0x7dd
JDBUpV0o0Ixzt9mvu5CHybx+9lOHeFRhZshFXc+bIJOPyi+JrSs100o7Lo6jg6+c
Si2vME0ixG4x9YjCi8DisXIGJ1kZiDXhmVWwCvL+vLInpeXrtJnK8yFkmszCOr4Y
Q3GXuvdU0BF2tL/Wo/eCbSf+3U9syopVS2L2wKcP76bbYU0io035Y503rJEK6R5G
TchwYvYjSXuhv4ec7N1/j3thrMC9GNpoqjVninTynOk2kn+YZuMpO3c6b/pfoNcq
MxoizGlTu8VT40O/SF1y52OkKjpAsENbFaNTABEBAAG0R0ZyWVCU0QgUG9ydHMg
TWFuYWdlbWVudCBUZWFtIFNlY3JldGFyeSA8cG9ydG1nci1zZWNyZXRhcnlARnJl
ZUJTRC5vcmc+iQE4BBMBAgAiBQJQDs6mAhsDBgsJCAcDAgYVCAIJCgsEFgIDAQIe
AQIXgAAKCRDYKU7Du8TX1QW2B/0coHe8utbTfGKpeM4BY9IyC+PFgkE58Hq50o8d
shoB9gfommcUaK9PNwJPxTEJNlwiKPZy+VoKs/+dO8gahovchbRdSyP1ejn3CFy+
H8pol0hDDU4n7Ldc50q54GLuZijdcJZqlgOloZqWOYtXFklKPZjdUvYN8KHAntgf
u361rwM4DZ40HngYY9fdGc4SbXurGA5m+vLAURLzPv+QRQqHfaI1DZF6gzMgY49x
qS1JBF4kPoicpgvs3o6CuX8MD9ewGFSAMM3EdzV6ZdC8pnpXC8+8Q+p6FjNqmtjk
GpW39Zq/p8SJVg1RortCH6qWLe7dW7TaFYov7gF1V/DYwDN5iQEcBBABAgAGBQJQ
DuVrAAoJENk3EJekc8mQ3KwIAImNDMXAF8ajPwCZFpM6KDi3F/jpwyBPISGY1oWu
YPEi1zN94k5jS90aZb3W8Y8x4JTh35Ewb6XODi3uGLSLCmnlqu2a80yPfXf5IuWm
IQdFNQxvosj9UHrg+icZGFmm+f0hPJxMTsZREv3AvivQfnb/N3xIICxW4SjKSYXQ
cq4hr4ObhUx7GKnjayq+ofU2cRlujr87uOH0fO3xhOJG4+cX5mI1HGK38k0Csc1z
qYa/66Qe5dnIZz+sNXpEPMLAHIt1a45UB967igJdZSDFN33bPl1QWmf3aUXU3d1V
ttiSyHkpm4kb9KgsDkUk1IJ5nUe9OXydWtoqNW5afDa5N0aIRgQQEQIABgUCUA7l
```

wwAKCRB59uBxdBRinNh2AJ41+zfsaQSRHWvSkqOXGcP/fgOduwCfUJDT+M1eXe2u
dmKof/9yzGYMirKJASIEEAECAAwFAlAaIT8FAwASdQAACgkQlxC4m8pXrXwCHAf+
J7l+L7AvRpqlQcezjnjFS/zG1098qkDflThHZlpVnrBMJZaXdvL6LzVgiIYVWZC5
CSSazW9EWFjp9VjM7FBHdWFZNMV7GAuUt0jzx6gGXOWwi+/v/hs1P11RyDZN5hIC
HdPNmyZVupciDxe+sIEP9aEbVxcaiccqzM/pFzIVIMMP5tCiA42q6Mz3h0hy6hnt
UKptS8Uon6sje5cDVcVlKAUj1wO2cphCqkYlwMQfZV5J9f/hcW5ODriD3cBwK8So
cA2Cq5JYF8kYDL1+pXnUutGnvAHUYt87RWvQdKmfXjzBcMFJ2LlPUB1+IFvwQ13V
9R8j9B/EdLmSWQYT9qRA2rkBDQRQDs6mAQgAzNxJYpf5PrqV8pdRXkn36Fe45q67
1YtbZ2WrT7D0CVZ8Z+AZsxnP/tiY1SrM2MepCeA2xBAhKGsWBWolaRk5mfZOksKs
iXsi2XeBVhdZlCkrOMKBTVian7I1lH59ZnNIMX0Nl0tlj3L1IjeWWNvfej43URV8
1S9EmSwpjaWboatr2A+1oJku5m7nPD9JIOckE1TzBsyhx7zIUN9w6MKr7gFw8DCz
ypwUKyYgKYToVm8QlkT/L3B0fuQHWhT6ROGk4o8SC71ia5tc1TzUzGEZ1AQO8bbn
bmJLBDKveWHCoaeAkRzINzoD9wAn9z4pnilze59QtKC1cOqUksTvBSDh6wARAQAB
iQEfBBgBAgAJBQJQDs6mAhsMAAoJENgpTsO7xNfVOHoH/i5VyggVdwpqPX8YBmN5
mXQziYZNQoiON8IhOsxpX4W2nXCj5m6MACV6nJDVV6wyUH8/VvDQC9nHarCe1oaN
sHXJz0HamYt5gHJ0G1bYuBcuJp/FEjLa48XFI7nXQjJHn8rlwZMjK/PWj1lw2WZi
ekviuzTEDH8c3YStGJSa+gYe8Eyq3XJVAe2VQOhImoWgGDR3tWfgrya/IdEFb/jm
jHSG5XUfbI0vNwqlf832BqSQKPG/Zix4MmBJgvAz4R71PH8WBmbmNFjDelxVyfz8
0+iMgEb9aL91MfeBNC2KB1pFmg91mQTsiq7ajwVLVJK8NplHAkdLmkBCO8MgMjzG
hlG5Ag0EUk+ViAEQALKCj95Jmvmfgyt0xnR1w8xnQBuUxtYxf+BWwqU0IfOMBxAm
XDRfbfe9Bc3DDZygmjrZ0RCDcVJ40mDNRc/vvoTst870so49dM1h2i6aWUhhD4Hy
cNjkx0wAIyZ9jXidT3LyAhCTSf/GjtpcORCvmAsXcJHzhhbJ5eM2SBkXmNdn4MeC
/hCbfUfzN64fmsGR4tKKIlPPayyQaQv/dOP3ofEh4SWRc8KtjEA6uIyHztWMWEJQ
KN/7nSeVuwDpVJL9l4yUGB0TqlK0p/necoQkOolnHUX5oK7Emin9TjPYCGqYAEWu
M1BbWXiYIdivlEm3ZU+vqq6CbSw/SKDZ2ZuK4UzDGQnW7WycsbXqZ18aewh1mdf+
5+YBxeXazRJvfFapB/WvtVqi84LOWior1IBMMg3PCyBiCjhHwXvoV5V6M3lthrnV
gyiCTreLXvTLNgIKQQFUvwW2Jscuwa3HhBgkhkJBSCPmpWAIZ9eA1RugvFQ893Xh
t8vy+z33WqxgUzhD8ZonKCBEZa29Zj7SeIYXcZmVmxCbRt4PYkgFoq6VC+93qtXu
OaOvC+0b9qkmNj5EqvozRt6SNv0sDe844T0LacR6QS9Pq/YMjAs8ao3gw0iwOAlV
vpiZfoEb6purf0Tz0h/URRHUZngEBsFmhciZxuCg9g/GaD8o/+PX0nzOWH4PABEB
AAGJAz4EGAECAAkFAlJPlYgCGwICKCKQkQ2ClOw7vE19XBXSAEGQECAAYFAlJPlYgA
CgkQyiAyhXcGTrfF9g/8C6JhufyxnYO0DmPURCFV0em3WjXcxQkhQa03u/sU8OFN
yp2UOB8jxI3XAsGe4RnclPF273K5G50fUAJ2hjWFGrMqXGNLlsuJvDJCUmdHnI6c
sw1RvOn2myMzUSTqxPQynkvntughqiyXbGQaoxQJVWjruhogcIkVYvOT4nMGXCyk
9Q+uooLNw8xpzsZBw83znWhjjzemu/BbOfjXbf3qdK9NWMkBfcaR9sDhRA+YY4bc
o7oTKXFfh3gMN1pqTuAM8dbGc0/bS558yNQuFaJ+cX3lbSLXz5oibJi6kudyL9E/
CkVvMFWTLcQQWCPS5rK0dctodW1x8JnwVnaG80trFIxmQ+wk4S156CdYwTv/1LbW
GKcVz90g1e9wIL2LsVaLD90IRnx4G8dLqZJz4pmGEES7CX6rrJuSpXxNOg4PthiP
s0z/q9deohKJkUgj6tln0OCgI8203GSSLq3FTAFer2VS+m1XMkA2mqk1Wv6tZeyY
MnYAZCBzc16F2zMg5dVKmV114bHmRTX0b5QQNB7JU3C34kdTagjLr4dz/5BhXgof
zjP9HgVQKCp7JvTdUT7N0y/k+mRMmnK8vnWdbOZH48IOELDhMkU5QIiKHoJaXsw7
wVo68LtSQItfIoA/m6E0RGZxUWCi/8G+kBK6NEExR1dlAW+M+fRhzNgqvqoLrcfR
4wgAkQGq3M2/hGdU/Z1j6CDKEvA1/iSRpnBnfVM8KUR661QrEctmIo1YwSU7x5+g
H5lfDUjU2cIlD+HgfxERKwl+hb2KY9OyLq2AUhhf8rAvG2dU9djDp7TWIvF3wexL
liu4C6EWcwlnEecCpkPUYv7/PKb0h0xAx32Umb6dzkfd24miWZTI/Gg7R1Qyl1DC
wBM9kgPRgEhnV3ummsD3KPXf5UwzHPslhqWT01p2iML4exnXlknL7mJKjj4d3gyi
5LxVVSzt2xi5MyCkFhiHFkSfItihcRpHdzxsBW+7YWw1ELlcKMeOkZQcyBm3VpE/
ZD4DQK6zwGfk4y8WS7A5SJEjJrkCDQRST5W/ARAAwbT4loEoK7ZY8fzt8hyhdBgS
bpXFWAB6yeyGDYp9ucG4ySjlfZIAew/EOzIR/68pKiGzIE0+kxKjlvVDcJoqWfrr
gomondGK2oyK35qOsYOlae6tsZm73InJuGSC+fZ1Vv0HBIn8JZpJXFV7z4FotaG5
iaKDdZCjxawVEWDl7z0zDSLKgPLtK4uSsEVsQIhPo5YLSqT7mCnleCqdNu3S4cun
tXaZmmSZnfv3qnkiPNNNSagZrMUK349fVCdvnJ4hKDbMAEgbxZVwEeB4HFicjwAN
UQTO1qSc+h8bwkrN/RgaT0Zz3nak+DJOOrKRV5VWWemx40y2oT08SqMRbhip/veI
LvrV+rKH+lb9uxp0vYWnRvWodOlEla0NeBzfz6Sv8ZI2D+xLJ260mIB4f4BUYCBi
SDu8UKTDffYba+50I9RgV9+umJ2WTcp/PA5/5M9e6R2F3dcM0Qey8hVDcf+rPY2
thXymS85IHcPauDjvjpHpx1xvhoEu2iX0yJwBDUX/xVWwH/lei7DT0cd1dB1pKiP
zNvWSoPp6zhqcB6tUvE69CLRzotmb20iAkFOReEVkcATL+bG9PBN0zWtSXJuCSL5
WAb+syRzBGwLA7+iQOY0yXCZ+Etl6BG8rsyQkBRwpTG5jXzDKUTl2hmKGFmU72xc
cPeNxhbq1tGMGfDVVmkAEQEAAYkBHwQYAQAQIACQUCUk+VvwIbDAAKCRDYKU7Du8TX
1cEOB/0WwX3yF/MC8upI0YAbjht+KG4cLgU6qo1ydZgQyHpAf8cttzq/uCDu4wLE
g0CDmreTXoiNR9W0ULhkn1LFkZQI6Z2uSH/wqQUJrE4P90o61TXClIzvjBoEufkS
3bg3wuAKiQ4cD1XxyThUG3qa4nbGVvKi4eWYuubpzJof7QD75LudHmLneY4mtCNA
ZgmgEWA2Utn0GWN1QNfoy1NGeLt0kza0VFjm6l6KeMc28ULZZztg0KbuFmQIreN9
JHQbJrrqX8ev57SqEtanoPyX4IjxVJFEmTn4xVSlRXY2uFZZtlB1SuyEPYmrdnjb
pDN9ZUgVOk/c+0+5u+G3JBRYu6P1
=fyj0

```
-----END PGP PUBLIC KEY BLOCK-----
```

FreeBSD Glossary

This glossary contains terms and acronyms used within the FreeBSD community and documentation.

A

ACL   See Access Control List.

ACPI   See Advanced Configuration and Power Interface.

AMD   See Automatic Mount Daemon.

AML   See ACPI Machine Language.

API   See Application Programming Interface.

APIC   See Advanced Programmable Interrupt Controller.

APM   See Advanced Power Management.

APOP   See Authenticated Post Office Protocol.

ASL   See ACPI Source Language.

ATA   See Advanced Technology Attachment.

ATM   See Asynchronous Transfer Mode.

ACPI Machine Language   Pseudocode, interpreted by a virtual machine within an ACPI-compliant operating system, providing a layer between the underlying hardware and the documented interface presented to the OS.

ACPI Source Language   The programming language AML is written in.

Access Control List   A list of permissions attached to an object, usually either a file or a network device.

Advanced Configuration and Power Interface   A specification which provides an abstraction of the interface the hardware presents to the operating system, so that the operating system should need to know nothing about the underlying hardware to make the most of it. ACPI evolves and supersedes the functionality provided previously by APM, PNPBIOS and other technologies, and provides facilities for controlling power consumption, machine suspension, device enabling and disabling, etc.

Application Programming Interface   A set of procedures, protocols and tools that specify the canonical interaction of one or more program parts; how, when and why they do work together, and what data they share or operate on.

Advanced Power Management   An API enabling the operating system to work in conjunction with the BIOS in order to achieve power management. APM has been superseded by the much more generic and powerful ACPI specification for most applications.

Advanced Programmable Interrupt Controller

Advanced Technology Attachment

Asynchronous Transfer Mode

Authenticated Post Office Protocol	
Automatic Mount Daemon	A daemon that automatically mounts a filesystem when a file or directory within that filesystem is accessed.

B

BAR	See Base Address Register.
BIND	See Berkeley Internet Name Domain.
BIOS	See Basic Input/Output System.
BSD	See Berkeley Software Distribution.
Base Address Register	The registers that determine which address range a PCI device will respond to.
Basic Input/Output System	The definition of BIOS depends a bit on the context. Some people refer to it as the ROM chip with a basic set of routines to provide an interface between software and hardware. Others refer to it as the set of routines contained in the chip that help in bootstrapping the system. Some might also refer to it as the screen used to configure the boostrapping process. The BIOS is PC-specific but other systems have something similar.
Berkeley Internet Name Domain	An implementation of the DNS protocols.
Berkeley Software Distribution	This is the name that the Computer Systems Research Group (CSRG) at The University of California at Berkeley gave to their improvements and modifications to AT&T's 32V UNIX®. FreeBSD is a descendant of the CSRG work.
Bikeshed Building	A phenomenon whereby many people will give an opinion on an uncomplicated topic, whilst a complex topic receives little or no discussion. See the FAQ for the origin of the term.

C

CD	See Carrier Detect.
CHAP	See Challenge Handshake Authentication Protocol.
CLIP	See Classical IP over ATM.
COFF	See Common Object File Format.
CPU	See Central Processing Unit.
CTS	See Clear To Send.
CVS	See Concurrent Versions System.
Carrier Detect	An RS232C signal indicating that a carrier has been detected.
Central Processing Unit	Also known as the processor. This is the brain of the computer where all calculations take place. There are a number of different architectures with different instruction sets. Among the more well-known are the Intel-x86 and derivatives, Sun SPARC, PowerPC, and Alpha.

Challenge Handshake Authentication Protocol	A method of authenticating a user, based on a secret shared between client and server.
Classical IP over ATM	
Clear To Send	An RS232C signal giving the remote system permission to send data. See Also Request To Send.
Common Object File Format	
Concurrent Versions System	A version control system, providing a method of working with and keeping track of many different revisions of files. CVS provides the ability to extract, merge and revert individual changes or sets of changes, and offers the ability to keep track of which changes were made, by who and for what reason.

D

DAC	See Discretionary Access Control.
DDB	See Debugger.
DES	See Data Encryption Standard.
DHCP	See Dynamic Host Configuration Protocol.
DNS	See Domain Name System.
DSDT	See Differentiated System Description Table.
DSR	See Data Set Ready.
DTR	See Data Terminal Ready.
DVMRP	See Distance-Vector Multicast Routing Protocol.
Discretionary Access Control	
Data Encryption Standard	A method of encrypting information, traditionally used as the method of encryption for UNIX® passwords and the crypt(3) function.
Data Set Ready	An RS232C signal sent from the modem to the computer or terminal indicating a readiness to send and receive data. See Also Data Terminal Ready.
Data Terminal Ready	An RS232C signal sent from the computer or terminal to the modem indicating a readiness to send and receive data.
Debugger	An interactive in-kernel facility for examining the status of a system, often used after a system has crashed to establish the events surrounding the failure.
Differentiated System Description Table	An ACPI table, supplying basic configuration information about the base system.
Distance-Vector Multicast Routing Protocol	
Domain Name System	The system that converts humanly readable hostnames (i.e., mail.example.net) to Internet addresses and vice versa.
Dynamic Host Configuration Protocol	A protocol that dynamically assigns IP addresses to a computer (host) when it requests one from the server. The address assignment is called a "lease".

701

E

ECOFF	See Extended COFF.
ELF	See Executable and Linking Format.
ESP	See Encapsulated Security Payload.
Encapsulated Security Payload	
Executable and Linking Format	
Extended COFF	

F

FADT	See Fixed ACPI Description Table.
FAT	See File Allocation Table.
FAT16	See File Allocation Table (16-bit).
FTP	See File Transfer Protocol.
File Allocation Table	
File Allocation Table (16-bit)	
File Transfer Protocol	A member of the family of high-level protocols implemented on top of TCP which can be used to transfer files over a TCP/IP network.
Fixed ACPI Description Table	

G

GUI	See Graphical User Interface.
Giant	The name of a mutual exclusion mechanism (a `sleep mutex`) that protects a large set of kernel resources. Although a simple locking mechanism was adequate in the days where a machine might have only a few dozen processes, one networking card, and certainly only one processor, in current times it is an unacceptable performance bottleneck. FreeBSD developers are actively working to replace it with locks that protect individual resources, which will allow a much greater degree of parallelism for both single-processor and multi-processor machines.
Graphical User Interface	A system where the user and computer interact with graphics.

H

HTML	See HyperText Markup Language.
HUP	See HangUp.
HangUp	
HyperText Markup Language	The markup language used to create web pages.

I

I/O	See Input/Output.
IASL	See Intel's ASL compiler.
IMAP	See Internet Message Access Protocol.
IP	See Internet Protocol.
IPFW	See IP Firewall.
IPP	See Internet Printing Protocol.
IPv4	See IP Version 4.
IPv6	See IP Version 6.
ISP	See Internet Service Provider.
IP Firewall	
IP Version 4	The IP protocol version 4, which uses 32 bits for addressing. This version is still the most widely used, but it is slowly being replaced with IPv6. See Also IP Version 6.
IP Version 6	The new IP protocol. Invented because the address space in IPv4 is running out. Uses 128 bits for addressing.
Input/Output	
Intel's ASL compiler	Intel's compiler for converting ASL into AML.
Internet Message Access Protocol	A protocol for accessing email messages on a mail server, characterised by the messages usually being kept on the server as opposed to being downloaded to the mail reader client. See Also Post Office Protocol Version 3.
Internet Printing Protocol	
Internet Protocol	The packet transmitting protocol that is the basic protocol on the Internet. Originally developed at the U.S. Department of Defense and an extremely important part of the TCP/IP stack. Without the Internet Protocol, the Internet would not have become what it is today. For more information, see RFC 791.
Internet Service Provider	A company that provides access to the Internet.

K

KAME	Japanese for "turtle", the term KAME is used in computing circles to refer to the KAME Project, who work on an implementation of IPv6.
KDC	See Key Distribution Center.
KLD	See Kernel ld(1).
KSE	See Kernel Scheduler Entities.
KVA	See Kernel Virtual Address.
Kbps	See Kilo Bits Per Second.

Kernel ld(1)	A method of dynamically loading functionality into a FreeBSD kernel without rebooting the system.
Kernel Scheduler Entities	A kernel-supported threading system. See the project home page for further details.
Kernel Virtual Address	
Key Distribution Center	
Kilo Bits Per Second	Used to measure bandwidth (how much data can pass a given point at a specified amount of time). Alternates to the Kilo prefix include Mega, Giga, Tera, and so forth.

L

LAN	See Local Area Network.
LOR	See Lock Order Reversal.
LPD	See Line Printer Daemon.
Line Printer Daemon	
Local Area Network	A network used on a local area, e.g. office, home, or so forth.
Lock Order Reversal	The FreeBSD kernel uses a number of resource locks to arbitrate contention for those resources. A run-time lock diagnostic system found in FreeBSD-CURRENT kernels (but removed for releases), called witness(4), detects the potential for deadlocks due to locking errors. (witness(4) is actually slightly conservative, so it is possible to get false positives.) A true positive report indicates that "if you were unlucky, a deadlock would have happened here".

True positive LORs tend to get fixed quickly, so check http://lists.Free-BSD.org/mailman/listinfo/freebsd-current and the LORs Seen page before posting to the mailing lists. |

M

MAC	See Mandatory Access Control.
MADT	See Multiple APIC Description Table.
MFC	See Merge From Current.
MFP4	See Merge From Perforce.
MFS	See Merge From Stable.
MIT	See Massachusetts Institute of Technology.
MLS	See Multi-Level Security.
MOTD	See Message Of The Day.
MTA	See Mail Transfer Agent.
MUA	See Mail User Agent.

Mail Transfer Agent	An application used to transfer email. An MTA has traditionally been part of the BSD base system. Today Sendmail is included in the base system, but there are many other MTAs, such as postfix, qmail and Exim.
Mail User Agent	An application used by users to display and write email.
Mandatory Access Control	
Massachusetts Institute of Technology	
Merge From Current	To merge functionality or a patch from the -CURRENT branch to another, most often -STABLE.
Merge From Perforce	To merge functionality or a patch from the Perforce repository to the -CURRENT branch. See Also Perforce.
Merge From Stable	In the normal course of FreeBSD development, a change will be committed to the -CURRENT branch for testing before being merged to -STABLE. On rare occasions, a change will go into -STABLE first and then be merged to -CURRENT. This term is also used when a patch is merged from -STABLE to a security branch. See Also Merge From Current.
Message Of The Day	A message, usually shown on login, often used to distribute information to users of the system.
Multi-Level Security	
Multiple APIC Description Table	

N

NAT	See Network Address Translation.
NDISulator	See Project Evil.
NFS	See Network File System.
NTFS	See New Technology File System.
NTP	See Network Time Protocol.
Network Address Translation	A technique where IP packets are rewritten on the way through a gateway, enabling many machines behind the gateway to effectively share a single IP address.
Network File System	
New Technology File System	A filesystem developed by Microsoft and available in its "New Technology" operating systems, such as Windows® 2000, Windows NT® and Windows® XP.
Network Time Protocol	A means of synchronizing clocks over a network.

O

OBE	See Overtaken By Events.

ODMR   See On-Demand Mail Relay.

OS   See Operating System.

On-Demand Mail Relay

Operating System   A set of programs, libraries and tools that provide access to the hardware resources of a computer. Operating systems range today from simplistic designs that support only one program running at a time, accessing only one device to fully multi-user, multi-tasking and multi-process systems that can serve thousands of users simultaneously, each of them running dozens of different applications.

Overtaken By Events   Indicates a suggested change (such as a Problem Report or a feature request) which is no longer relevant or applicable due to such things as later changes to FreeBSD, changes in networking standards, the affected hardware having since become obsolete, and so forth.

P

p4   See Perforce.

PAE   See Physical Address Extensions.

PAM   See Pluggable Authentication Modules.

PAP   See Password Authentication Protocol.

PC   See Personal Computer.

PCNSFD   See Personal Computer Network File System Daemon.

PDF   See Portable Document Format.

PID   See Process ID.

POLA   See Principle Of Least Astonishment.

POP   See Post Office Protocol.

POP3   See Post Office Protocol Version 3.

PPD   See PostScript Printer Description.

PPP   See Point-to-Point Protocol.

PPPoA   See PPP over ATM.

PPPoE   See PPP over Ethernet.

PPP over ATM

PPP over Ethernet

PR   See Problem Report.

PXE   See Preboot eXecution Environment.

Password Authentication Protocol

Perforce	A source code control product made by Perforce Software which is more advanced than CVS. Although not open source, its use is free of charge to open-source projects such as FreeBSD.
	Some FreeBSD developers use a Perforce repository as a staging area for code that is considered too experimental for the -CURRENT branch.
Personal Computer	
Personal Computer Network File System Daemon	
Physical Address Extensions	A method of enabling access to up to 64 GB of RAM on systems which only physically have a 32-bit wide address space (and would therefore be limited to 4 GB without PAE).
Pluggable Authentication Modules	
Point-to-Point Protocol	
Pointy Hat	A mythical piece of headgear, much like a dunce cap, awarded to any FreeBSD committer who breaks the build, makes revision numbers go backwards, or creates any other kind of havoc in the source base. Any committer worth his or her salt will soon accumulate a large collection. The usage is (almost always?) humorous.
Portable Document Format	
Post Office Protocol	See Also Post Office Protocol Version 3.
Post Office Protocol Version 3	A protocol for accessing email messages on a mail server, characterised by the messages usually being downloaded from the server to the client, as opposed to remaining on the server. See Also Internet Message Access Protocol.
PostScript Printer Description	
Preboot eXecution Environment	
Principle Of Least Astonishment	As FreeBSD evolves, changes visible to the user should be kept as unsurprising as possible. For example, arbitrarily rearranging system startup variables in /etc/defaults/rc.conf violates POLA. Developers consider POLA when contemplating user-visible system changes.
Problem Report	A description of some kind of problem that has been found in either the FreeBSD source or documentation. See Writing FreeBSD Problem Reports.
Process ID	A number, unique to a particular process on a system, which identifies it and allows actions to be taken against it.
Project Evil	The working title for the NDISulator, written by Bill Paul, who named it referring to how awful it is (from a philosophical standpoint) to need to have something like this in the first place. The NDISulator is a special compatibility module to allow Microsoft Windows™ NDIS miniport network drivers to be used with FreeBSD/i386. This is usually the only way to use cards where the driver is closed-source. See src/sys/compat/ndis/subr_ndis.c .

R

RA	See Router Advertisement.

RAID	See Redundant Array of Inexpensive Disks.
RAM	See Random Access Memory.
RD	See Received Data.
RFC	See Request For Comments.
RISC	See Reduced Instruction Set Computer.
RPC	See Remote Procedure Call.
RS232C	See Recommended Standard 232C.
RTS	See Request To Send.
Random Access Memory	
Revision Control System	The *Revision Control System* (RCS) is one of the oldest software suites that implement "revision control" for plain files. It allows the storage, retrieval, archival, logging, identification and merging of multiple revisions for each file. RCS consists of many small tools that work together. It lacks some of the features found in more modern revision control systems, like CVS or Subversion, but it is very simple to install, configure, and start using for a small set of files. Implementations of RCS can be found on every major UNIX-like OS. See Also Concurrent Versions System, Subversion.
Received Data	An RS232C pin or wire that data is received on. See Also Transmitted Data.
Recommended Standard 232C	A standard for communications between serial devices.
Reduced Instruction Set Computer	An approach to processor design where the operations the hardware can perform are simplified but made as general purpose as possible. This can lead to lower power consumption, fewer transistors and in some cases, better performance and increased code density. Examples of RISC processors include the Alpha, SPARC®, ARM® and PowerPC®.
Redundant Array of Inexpensive Disks	
Remote Procedure Call	
repocopy	See Repository Copy.
Repository Copy	A direct copying of files within the CVS repository.
	Without a repocopy, if a file needed to be copied or moved to another place in the repository, the committer would run **cvs add** to put the file in its new location, and then **cvs rm** on the old file if the old copy was being removed.
	The disadvantage of this method is that the history (i.e. the entries in the CVS logs) of the file would not be copied to the new location. As the FreeBSD Project considers this history very useful, a repository copy is often used instead. This is a process where one of the repository meisters will copy the files directly within the repository, rather than using the cvs(1) program.
Request For Comments	A set of documents defining Internet standards, protocols, and so forth. See www.rfc-editor.org.
	Also used as a general term when someone has a suggested change and wants feedback.

Request To Send	An RS232C signal requesting that the remote system commences transmission of data. See Also Clear To Send.
Router Advertisement	

S

SCI	See System Control Interrupt.
SCSI	See Small Computer System Interface.
SG	See Signal Ground.
SMB	See Server Message Block.
SMP	See Symmetric MultiProcessor.
SMTP	See Simple Mail Transfer Protocol.
SMTP AUTH	See SMTP Authentication.
SSH	See Secure Shell.
STR	See Suspend To RAM.
SVN	See Subversion.
SMTP Authentication	
Server Message Block	
Signal Ground	An RS232 pin or wire that is the ground reference for the signal.
Simple Mail Transfer Protocol	
Secure Shell	
Small Computer System Interface	
Subversion	Subversion is a version control system, similar to CVS, but with an expanded feature list. See Also Concurrent Versions System.
Suspend To RAM	
Symmetric MultiProcessor	
System Control Interrupt	

T

TCP	See Transmission Control Protocol.
TCP/IP	See Transmission Control Protocol/Internet Protocol.
TD	See Transmitted Data.
TFTP	See Trivial FTP.

TGT	See Ticket-Granting Ticket.
TSC	See Time Stamp Counter.
Ticket-Granting Ticket	
Time Stamp Counter	A profiling counter internal to modern Pentium® processors that counts core frequency clock ticks.
Transmission Control Protocol	A protocol that sits on top of (e.g.) the IP protocol and guarantees that packets are delivered in a reliable, ordered, fashion.
Transmission Control Protocol/Internet Protocol	The term for the combination of the TCP protocol running over the IP protocol. Much of the Internet runs over TCP/IP.
Transmitted Data	An RS232C pin or wire that data is transmitted on. See Also Received Data.
Trivial FTP	

U

UDP	See User Datagram Protocol.
UFS1	See Unix File System Version 1.
UFS2	See Unix File System Version 2.
UID	See User ID.
URL	See Uniform Resource Locator.
USB	See Universal Serial Bus.
Uniform Resource Locator	A method of locating a resource, such as a document on the Internet and a means to identify that resource.
Unix File System Version 1	The original UNIX® file system, sometimes called the Berkeley Fast File System.
Unix File System Version 2	An extension to UFS1, introduced in FreeBSD 5-CURRENT. UFS2 adds 64 bit block pointers (breaking the 1T barrier), support for extended file storage and other features.
Universal Serial Bus	A hardware standard used to connect a wide variety of computer peripherals to a universal interface.
User ID	A unique number assigned to each user of a computer, by which the resources and permissions assigned to that user can be identified.
User Datagram Protocol	A simple, unreliable datagram protocol which is used for exchanging data on a TCP/IP network. UDP does not provide error checking and correction like TCP.

V

VPN	See Virtual Private Network.
Virtual Private Network	A method of using a public telecommunication such as the Internet, to provide remote access to a localized network, such as a corporate LAN.

Index

Symbols

-CURRENT, 445
  compiling, 446
  using, 446
-STABLE, 445
  compiling, 447
  using, 447
.k5login, 233
.k5users, 233
.rhosts, 312
/boot/kernel.old, 155
/etc, 26
/etc/groups, 59
/etc/login.conf, 253
/etc/mail/access, 495
/etc/mail/aliases, 495
/etc/mail/local-host-names, 495
/etc/mail/mailer.conf, 495
/etc/mail/mailertable, 495
/etc/mail/sendmail.cf, 495
/etc/mail/virtusertable, 495
/etc/remote, 474
/etc/ttys, 473
/usr, 26
/usr/bin/login, 472
/usr/share/skel, 56
/var, 26
386BSD, 9, 9
386BSD Patchkit, 9
4.3BSD-Lite, 9
4.4BSD-Lite, 5, 6
802.11 (see wireless networking)

A

AbiWord, 129
accounting
  disk space, 317
accounts
  adding, 56
  changing password, 58
  daemon, 54
  groups, 59
  limiting, 253
  modifying, 55
  nobody, 54
  operator, 54
  removing, 57
  superuser (root), 55
  system, 54
  user, 54
ACL, 246
ACPI, 204, 205
  ASL, 206, 207
  debugging, 207

problems, 205, 207, 208
address redirection, 586
adduser, 56, 431
AIX, 520
amd, 518
anti-aliased fonts, 109
Apache, 7, 551
  configuration file, 551
  modules, 553
  starting or stopping, 552
Apache OpenOffice , 129
APIC
  disabling, 206
APM, 204
Apple, 7
ASCII, 430
AT&T, 10
AUDIT, 289
autofs, 519
automatic mounter daemon, 518
automounter subsystem, 519
AutoPPP, 486

B

backup software, 314
  cpio, 313
  dump / restore, 312
  pax, 313
  tar, 313
Basic Input/Output System (see BIOS)
BGP, 601
binary compatibility
  BSD/OS, 5
  Linux, 5, 169
  NetBSD, 5
  SCO, 5
  SVR4, 5
BIND, 498, 537
  caching name server, 547
  configuration files, 540
  DNS security extensions, 547
  starting, 539
  zone files, 545
BIOS, 211
bits-per-second, 465
Bluetooth, 619
Boot Loader, 212
Boot Manager, 212, 212
boot-loader, 213
booting, 211
bootstrap, 211
Bourne shells, 78
bridge, 626
browsers
  web, 125
BSD Copyright, 10
BSD Router, 8
bsdlabel, 314

Colophon

This book is the combined work of hundreds of contributors to "The FreeBSD Documentation Project". The text is authored in XML according to the DocBook DTD and is formatted from XML into many different presentation formats using XSLT. The printed version of this document would not be possible without Donald Knuth's TeX typesetting language, Leslie Lamport's LaTeX, or Sebastian Rahtz's JadeTeX macro package.